PRAGUE AND BOH

Medieval Art, Architecture and Cultural Exchange in Central Europe

General Editor   Sarah Brown

PRAGUE AND BOHEMIA
Medieval Art, Architecture and Cultural Exchange in Central Europe

Edited by
Zoë Opačić

The British Archaeological Association
Conference Transactions XXXII

Cover illustration: Emperor Charles IV: bust in the choir triforium of Prague Cathedral
Martin Frouz

ISBN Hardback 978 1 906540 59 3
Paperback 978 1 906540 58 6

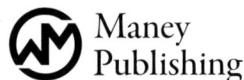

Maney
Publishing

PUBLISHED BY THE BRITISH ARCHAEOLOGICAL ASSOCIATION AND MANEY PUBLISHING
JOSEPH'S WELL, HANOVER WALK, LEEDS LS3 1AB, UK

Contents

List of Contributors

MILENA BARTLOVÁ
Masarykova univerzita, Brno

KLÁRA BENEŠOVSKÁ
Ústav dějin umění, Akademie věd České republiky, Prague

PAUL CROSSLEY
Courtauld Institute of Art, London

ZDENĚK DRAGOUN
Národní památkový ústav, Prague

ERIC FERNIE
Courtauld Institute of Art, London

JAN CHLÍBEC
Ústav dějin umění, Akademie věd České republiky, Prague

TIM JUCKES
Universität Wien

ZOË OPAČIĆ
Birkbeck College, London

TAŤÁNA PETRASOVÁ
Ústav dějin umění, Akademie věd České republiky, Prague

ANDREAS PUTH
Courtauld Institute of Art, London

AGNIESZKA ROŻNOWSKA-SADRAEI
CgMs Consulting, Birmingham

MARC CAREL SCHURR
Université de Fribourg, Suisse

MILADA STUDNIČKOVÁ
Ústav dějin umění, Akademie věd České republiky, Prague

MAREK SUCHÝ
Archiv Pražského hradu, Prague

ACHIM TIMMERMANN
University of Michigan, Ann Arbor

EVELIN WETTER
Abegg-Stiftung, Riggisberg

Acknowledgements

ON behalf of the British Archaeological Association, I would like to express my deep gratitude to Dr Klára Benešovská of the Ústav dějin umění, Akademie věd České republiky (Institute for the History of Art of the Czech Academy of Sciences). My collaboration with Dr Benešovská as co-convenor of the BAA Prague conference was a truly rewarding experience, and there is no doubt that her tireless efforts made the whole event possible. The Czech Academy proved a most generous host, and we were given a warm welcome by Prof. Lubomír Konečný, director of the Institute for the History of Art. The organisation and the running of the conference were made infinitely easier thanks to the professionalism and experience of Karen Impey, the conference organiser, and Dr Kate Heard, the conference secretary. The steadfast support of the former president of the BAA, Dr Nicola Coldstream, and of the Association's treasurer, John Dunlop, was essential and much appreciated. Jana Juzová helped resolve considerable logistical problems. Memorable visits to sites in Prague, Křivoklát, Karlstein, Kolín and Kutná Hora were made possible and greatly assisted by Prof. Milena Bartlová, Dr Zdeněk Dragoun, Prof. Eric Fernie, L. Frencl, Dr Hana Hlavačková, Dr Jan Chlíbec, Jaromír Kubů, Dr Hana Logan, Dr Aleš Pospíšil, Dr Marc Schurr, Dr Milada Studničková, Jan Škoda, and Dr Vít Vlnas. Prof. Paul Crossley's extemporary site presentations, enlightening interventions, and customary good humour contributed in no small measure to the success of the conference. Dr Dušan Buran and Dr Jiří Fajt delivered stimulating papers at the conference but were sadly unable to submit them for this volume.

In working on the transactions Dr Joseph Spooner's editorial assistance was indispensable: he ensured that high standards were maintained throughout a linguistically complex volume and advised on the translation of German and Latin citations into English. I am also grateful to the current president of the BAA, Peter Draper, and to the general editor Sarah Brown for their knowledgeable advice, as well as to Linda Fisher and Maney Publishing for their hard work on producing the book.

Finally, I would like to thank my family for the support and inspiration they have given me, especially Christopher, and Emilia, whose first year of life coincided almost exactly with the preparation of this volume.

Zoë Opačić

COLOUR PLATE I

PLATE Ia (BARTLOVÁ FIG. 1). Prague Cathedral: choir triforium, looking north-west
Martin Frouz

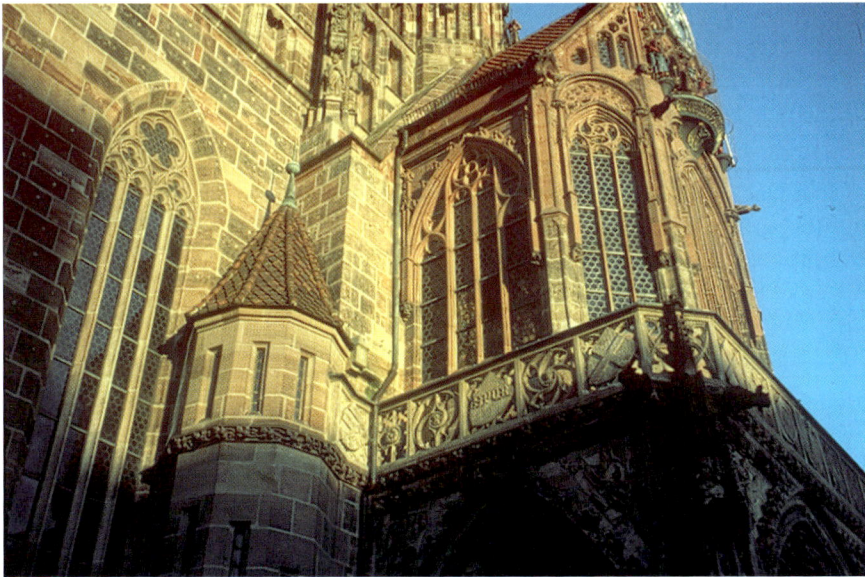

PLATE Ib (CROSSLEY FIG. 4). Nuremberg: the Frauenkirche, St Michael's chapel
Andreas Puth

COLOUR PLATE II

PLATE IIA (CHLÍBEC FIG. 7). Kadaň, monastery of the Franciscan Observants: presbytery wall relief of Jan Hasištejnský of Lobkowicz, 1516

Jan Chlíbec

PLATE IIB (BENEŠOVSKÁ FIG. 5A). Museum hlavního města Prahy: statue of a man-at-arms from the façade of the House at the Stone Bell

Vlado Bohdan

Plate IIIa (Dragoun Fig. 8). Prague, Malá Strana Square: the round nave of the St Wenceslas rotunda

Libor Smutka

Plate IIIb (Dragoun Fig. 9). Prague, Malá Strana Square: a Romanesque relief of terracotta tiles preserved in the north-eastern part of the nave in the St Wenceslas rotunda

Martin Pavala

PLATE IV (PUTH FIG. 6). Vienna,
Wien Museum: first Habsburg
window, photomontage (edges of
panels cropped)
Bundesdenkmalamt, Wien

COLOUR PLATE V

PLATE VA (PUTH FIG. 7). Vienna, Wien Museum: second Habsburg window, without bottom-left panel of Friedrich II

Bundesdenkmalamt, Wien

PLATE VB (ROŻNOWSKA-SADRAEI FIG. 8). Missal KP3: St Wenceslas, fol. 202v

Cracow, Archiwa Katedry krakowskiej

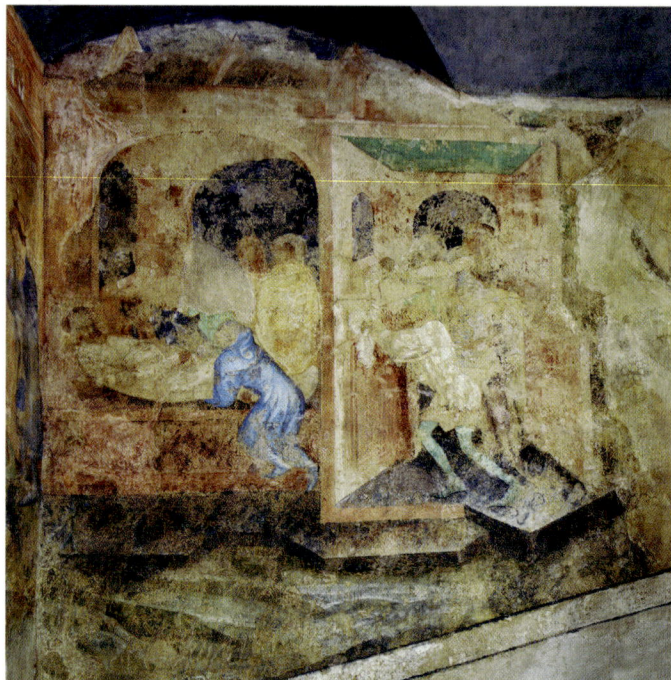

PLATE VIa (STUDNIČKOVÁ FIG. 12). Karlstein Castle, Great Tower staircase: burying the body of St Wenceslas in a grave; wiping of the martyr's blood from the door of the church in Stará Boleslav
Vlado Bohdan

PLATE VIb (TIMMERMANN FIG. 5). Execution of Fürwittig, with poor sinners' cross in the middle ground on the right, 1517 (*Abenteuer des Ritters Theuerdank* (as in n. 17))

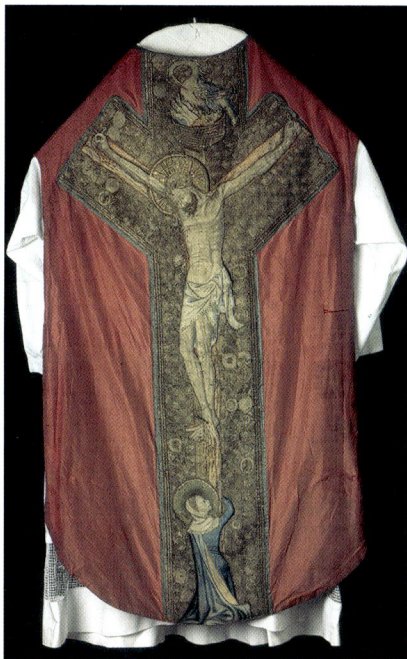

PLATE VIIA (*top left*) (WETTER FIG. 5). Chasuble from St Peter's Church in Görlitz: the orphrey Prague, *c.* 1380 (Görlitz, Kunst- und Kulturhistorisches Museum)

Friedemann Raatz, Leipzig

PLATE VIIB (*bottom left*) (WETTER FIG. 2). Chasuble in St. Marienstern (Upper Lusatia): the orphrey Bohemia(?), end of the 14th century, with later changes (St. Marienstern, Zisterzienserinnenabtei)

János Steckovics, Halle

PLATE VIIC (*bottom right*) (WETTER FIG. 4). Orphrey, eastern Central Europe, second quarter of the 15th century (Riggisberg, Abegg-Stiftung)

Abegg-Stiftung, CH 3132 Riggisberg (Christoph von Viràg)

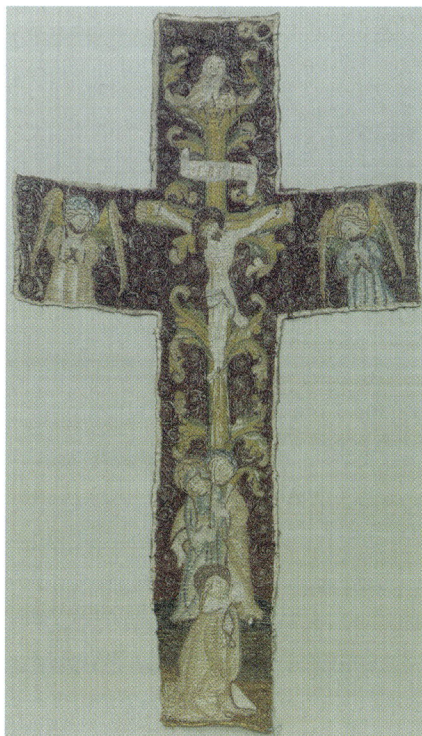

PLATE VIII (JUCKES FIG. 1). Košice, St Elizabeth's: aerial view from south, with charnel chapel of St Michael (Buran ed., *Gotika* (as in n. 13), 207)

Introduction. Medieval Prague, Bohemia and their Neighbours: New Perspectives and Connections

ZOË OPAČIĆ

ON 12 June 1493, the Nuremberg physician, *magister artium* and avid bibliophile Hartmann Schedel (1440–1514) saw the publication of his life's work. The *Liber cronicarum*, his history of the world, soon to be followed by its German version, *Buch der Chroniken und Geschichten* ('Book of Chronicles and Histories', or simply *Weltchronik*, 'World Chronicle'), was not only unique in its ambitious scope, but also provided the first recognisable glimpse of medieval Europe. A few years prior to the book's publication, Michael Wolgemut, a painter and printmaker from Nuremberg who counted Albrecht Dürer among his pupils, was commissioned, together with his talented stepson Wilhelm Pleydenwurff, to produce almost 2,000 woodcuts for the volume.[1] What resulted are the extraordinary and often-copied panoramas of European cities, from the Mediterranean to the Baltic Sea. And it is here, on page 230, that we encounter the first known view of Prague (Fig. 1), its architectural landmarks instantly apparent: the cathedral and the royal palace with its own 'Sainte-Chapelle' on the distant castle hill of Hradčany; the New Town Slavonic monastery known as the Emmaus (Emauzy or Na Slovanech), with its distinctive saddleback roof (foreground, right); and just to the left of it — in the engraving's compressed perspective — the aqueduct-like form of the Charles Bridge (Karlův most). The Old Town and its Jewish quarter (Josefov) — the commercial hub of the city — remain obscured by the Emmaus and its elevated site, the rocky promontory of Skalka. On the River Vltava's left bank and immediately below the castle is Malá Strana (the Lesser Town), founded in 1257 by Přemysl Otakar II as a settlement for Prague's German merchants, but much enlarged and refortified by Charles IV with an impressive circuit of walls whose battlements and towers can be seen disappearing over the horizon on the far left.

Schedel's evocative and remarkably accurate image of Prague is a record of the city's transformation under the Luxembourg dynasty, which acceded to the Bohemian throne in 1310, when John of Luxembourg married Elizabeth Přemyslovna. Their son Charles IV's rise to the imperial throne in 1346/47 initiated a large-scale rebuilding of the city as it assumed the role of an imperial seat. On closer inspection of the print, however, we find the signs that the city's fortunes had changed yet again. Their dramatic reversal was brought about by the religious wars (following the execution of Jan Hus at the Council of Constance in 1415), and the sudden end to Luxembourg rule, first with the death of Wenceslas IV (in 1419) and then of his half-brother Sigismund (in 1437). Prague — the place its contemporaries once saw as an heir to Rome and Constantinople[2] — appears forlorn. The New Town, Charles IV's colossal new district that doubled the size of the city, lies mostly empty of buildings. On

FIG. 1.   View of Prague from Hartmann Schedel's *Liber cronicarum*
Collection of the author

the opposite bank, the cathedral's tower and nave are left incomplete, while the extravagant tracery crest of its transept, like a rhetorical flourish, seems abandoned mid-sentence. Only the rectangular shapes of the palace's windows, inserted by the architect Benedikt Reid at the time of the chronicle's publication, betray the presence of a new owner — the Polish-born king of Bohemia, Vladislav Jagiełło (1456–1516).

It seems fitting that Prague, one of the most cosmopolitan and culturally sophisticated cities of the later Middle Ages, with a townscape as evocative today as it was in Schedel's time, was the host to the British Archaeological Association's first conference in Central Europe. The conference was held 7–12 July 2006 under the generous auspices of the Ústav dějin umění, Akademie věd České republiky (Institute for the History of Art of the Czech Academy of Sciences), at the Academy's elegant premises at Národní třída 3. Formal papers delivered in the conference hall were complemented by convivial discussions and presentations on sites around the city, and also on visits to Křivoklát, Karlstein, Kolín and Kutná Hora. For those of us present, this was in many respects a uniquely memorable event. It brought together 102 participants, including sixteen speakers, who came not only from Great Britain and the Czech Republic, but also from the wider region, including Poland, Slovakia, Austria, Switzerland and Germany, and from as far afield as the USA. Only twenty years ago, an international gathering on this scale and from the different sides of the political divide would have been thwarted by countless bureaucratic obstacles. Equally, the sight of a sizeable, mainly foreign contingent traversing Prague's streets, undeterred by the relentless July sun, on a trail of another Romanesque cellar, Gothic church or a synagogue, would have provoked suspicion rather than the bemused bafflement of onlookers. But beyond the now largely forgotten irrationalities of Cold War politics, the conference amply demonstrated a significant scholarly shift in the way architecture and art of this region are understood and discussed. From a western perspective, Bohemia no longer occupies an exotic and largely unknown periphery of Europe, but is rightly seen as one of its leading centres, particularly in the 14th century. In the same vein, scholarly discourse in the Czech Republic has now moved on from inward-looking and sometimes nationalistically coloured debates. Complex cultural and political connections in the region produced monuments that are both idiosyncratic and cosmopolitan, and in recent years these have attracted the interest of a growing number of international students and researchers, who made an important contribution to the conference, as they do in this volume.

2

The opening two essays, by a Czech and an English scholar respectively, demonstrate the benefits of this mutual intellectual engagement. Marek Suchý's study of cultural contacts between England and Bohemia at the time of the marriage of Charles IV's daughter Anne to Richard II fills many gaps with a plethora of fascinating detail preserved in the Czech archives. This dynastic marriage, although by all accounts affectionate, never brought about the hoped-for cordiality between the two realms; it did however determine the fate of those Bohemians who followed Anne to England, where they remained as spouses, priests and soldiers, all the while maintaining contact with their homeland through letters and gifts dispatched and received across the Channel.

More enigmatic and almost certainly coincidental overlaps between England and Central Europe are noted by Eric Fernie in his study of the small Romanesque church of St Bartholomew in Kyje on the outskirts of Prague. Fernie reminds us of the significance of nomenclature, for what links the churches in Kyje, North Elmham in Norfolk and Indensen in Saxony are not conventional patronal links or itinerant masons, but their status as bishops' chapels. Kyje's unusual architectural solutions, in the shape of a powerful western tower and a gallery, stand out because they were intended to. The level of sophistication expressed in this relatively modest building draws our attention to an important period of Bohemian architecture, often overlooked even by the most dedicated students of Bohemian history.

Although much of the surviving medieval fabric of Prague is the legacy of Charles IV's reign, the city had been a place of architectural distinction since the early Middle Ages. Zdeněk Dragoun's essay unveils the extent of Romanesque Prague, a thriving fortified town of three districts that boasted, by the beginning of the 13th century, over fifty religious institutions, a large number of stone houses, some two or three storeys high, and the Judith Bridge (Juditin most), the predecessor to the more famous Charles Bridge, which copies many of its features.

Recent finds, such as those made during construction works on Náměstí Republiky (Square of the Republic), continue to shed new light on the city's fertile architectural past, but few can match the rediscovery of the magnificent residence on the Old Town Square, known as the House at the Stone Bell. In the 1960s, crumbling stucco brought back to life a house with a significant history. Klára Benešovská's painstaking research shows that this house and its eponymous attribute — the stone bell — may have played a crucial role in the coup that brought the brief and unhappy reign of Henry of Carinthia (1306–10) to an abrupt end and installed John of Luxembourg and his Přemyslid wife on the Bohemian throne. The house was not only the couple's temporary town residence, but it provided a powerful backdrop to the royal court of law and the assembly of allegiance that inaugurated the new regime. The façade's tiered structure and its four fragmented statues suggest an iconography of rulership closely analogous with that of the Old Town Bridge Tower (Staroměstská mostecká věž) built decades later. The unmistakably French flair of the sculpture points to the increasingly international and especially Francophile outlook of the Prague court at the beginning of the 14th century. John's decision to send Charles, his heir, to be educated at the Valois court in Paris had a lasting effect on the young prince, nurturing his artistic tastes, acquisitive piety, and a particularly exalted view of rulership. Charles seems to have been impressed above all by the fashionable new French architecture, its theatricality and regal decorum. On returning to Prague in 1333 with his first wife, Blanche of Valois, Charles set about remodelling the old castle district into a French-inspired acropolis. The royal palace was rebuilt in the

French manner ('modo Gallico'),[3] and the Romanesque palace chapel of All Saints was transformed into a luminous glass cage, in open homage to the Sainte-Chapelle. For his most famous project, the rebuilding of Prague Cathedral as the Gothic masterpiece we know today, Charles chose architects with impeccable Rayonnant credentials. Unlike the first *magister operis*, Matthias of Arras, the second, Peter Parler, was not French, but did use the most advanced forms of the Rhenish-Rayonnant style to create architecture so original that it was instantly and almost universally copied. Few buildings can be credited with determining the course of Gothic architecture in Central Europe as much as Prague Cathedral. In his analysis of Parler's creative virtuosity, Paul Crossley detects striking similarities in approach between the cathedral choir and two other buildings founded by Emperor Charles IV and quite probably designed by Parler himself: the western porch with the oriel chapel of St Michael of the Frauenkirche in Nuremberg, and the chapel of All Saints in Prague Castle. The west end of the Nuremberg's church (constructed in the mid-1350s) in particular seems to anticipate the distinctive aesthetic contrasts between the upper and the lower parts of the Prague choir and the unconventional, dynamic handling of its wall-planes. But, as Crossley points out, the formal concept is not the only aspect that binds the two projects: both buildings were occupied by similar, special colleges of priests, known as mansionaries, devoted to the cult of the Virgin Mary. As Peter Parler occupied himself with the construction of the choir in the early 1370s, issues of decorum would have turned his mind to Nuremberg, and he may have used it as a starting point for a far grander design befitting the cathedral.

This is not the only instance in which Parler looked to his own work for inspiration while calibrating his designs to fit specific commissions. When he was called to design the choir of St Bartholomew's in the royal city of Kolín, Parler applied 'reduced' forms of the Prague choir and modified its details to suit the rank of a parish church. Marc Schurr argues that these skilful 'articulations', subtle nuancing of the same stylistic idiom, gave architects the formal means by which to express a range of hier-archical, liturgical and institutional distinctions. Those distinctions were becoming increasingly important at the time, when burghers were using their newly acquired wealth to emulate traditional patrons of architecture, the clergy and aristocracy. Wealthy towns such as Kolín, and notably Košice in Hungary (now Slovakia), embarked on ambitious and costly expansions of their parish churches, engaging the most advanced workshops familiar with the up-to-date work of the cathedral lodges in Vienna and Prague. One of the most enduring legacies of Peter Parler and his followers in the region is the autonomy and expressiveness they accorded to vaults; their complex net, star and pendant forms could override or accentuate interior bay divisions, or highlight significant discrete sections of the building, such as a chapel, a sacristy or a porch. In focusing on this particular aspect of St Elizabeth's in Košice, Tim Juckes finds that the mason in charge was able to express his creativity in a series of vault designs of astonishing complexity, unhindered by his otherwise controlling patrons. Juckes's essay urges us to re-examine our notions of centre and periphery and cautions against a discourse that favours metropolitan projects as an exclusive source of new ideas. To ignore towns like Košice would be to leave out an important piece of evidence for a generation of masons who shaped the Central European architectural landscape in the decades following the disintegration of the Prague Cathedral lodge.

Nevertheless, only Habsburg Vienna could seriously challenge the pre-eminence of Luxembourg Prague by the quality and scale of its commissions. The Habsburgs also understood that art and architecture can be used to great effect to articulate power, whether real or aspirational, and in particular that dynastic propaganda — so skilfully manipulated by Charles IV — is a powerful political tool. Andreas Puth shows how in the 1380s, at the time of acute crisis in the Bohemian kingdom, Albrecht III (1365–95) challenged visually as well as politically his brother-in-law Wenceslas IV's claim to the imperial crown. Albrecht's lavishly set yet selective genealogy of the Habsburgs, commissioned for the windows of his chapel in the south-west gallery of St Stephen's, projects an image of a 'youthful' dynasty of noble princes destined for the highest office. But in doing so Albrecht and his craftsmen borrowed extensively from the visual and conceptual vocabulary of sacred kingship cultivated by Charles IV and displayed on the walls of his palaces at Karlstein, Prague and Tangermünde.

Jiří Fajt and Robert Suckale's observation that imitation can 'be an expression of grudging dependency as well as of admiration'[4] sums up not only the creative competition between Prague and Vienna but also Prague's relationship with other neighbours. Agnieszka Rożnowska-Sadraei, for example, challenges the notion that Cracow, the capital of medieval Poland and the city of St Stanislas, remained immune to Prague's cultural advances. During the brief period of Bohemian rule over Poland at the beginning of the 14th century, St Wenceslas, Bohemia's most venerated patron saint, was actively promoted by Cracow's religious and secular elites. Bishop Jan Muskata planned a Bohemian-influenced chevet for the cathedral's new choir, where Wenceslas's relics would have occupied the pride of place at the crossing, while the town councillors and jurists demoted St Stanislas on their seals in favour of St Wenceslas. Many of these initiatives were quickly reversed by the Piast-led regime, and yet this Bohemian interlude in Cracow is also evidence of the growing international popularity of Wenceslas's cult. Nationally, Wenceslas was honoured with the rebuilding of Prague Cathedral, for centuries the main focus for the saint's veneration. The design of the Gothic choir, devised by Charles IV and his architects, revolves architecturally and symbolically around Wenceslas's shrine and its dazzling new chapel in recognition of his unique standing in the pantheon of Bohemian saints.

A less public statement of Charles IV's devotion to Wenceslas is detected by Milada Studničková in the pictorial programme of Karlstein Castle. Wenceslas's exemplary life and martyrdom (and that of his grandmother Ludmila), painted on the walls of the staircase of the castle's Great Tower, offer spiritual guidance on a gradual ascent towards the Heavenly Jerusalem memorably evoked by the Holy Cross Chapel. On the landing before the chapel's entrance, we move from ancient past to the eternal present as we join the emperor's family in prayer to witness Charles IV depositing an ampoule of the saint's blood into a reliquary cross. St Wenceslas's sacrifice thus becomes the key that unlocks the gates of Paradise. The Great Tower's 'heavenly ladder' is just one of the many theological metaphors discerned by Studničková in the conceptual fabric of the 'relic castle'. At Karlstein, architectural forms, and visual and written exegesis converge to transform the secular setting of a castle, albeit one treasuring the precious relics of Christ's Passion, into a profound religious experience.

The notion that architecture — and urban landscape — can act as a vehicle for personal salvation was the guiding principle of many projects devised by Charles IV and his circle. Although the monuments created in this process are unique, some of the strategies employed are already familiar: they derive from the moralising, allegorical approach developed by the church since the 13th century, in its effort to define the fundamental mysteries of the faith. For theologians such as William Durandus the apparatus of the altar, including the vestments worn by the officiating priests, were active ingredients of the multi-sensory experience of those participating in the mystical body of Christ. That body, notes Evelin Wetter, became a focus of a distinctive Crucifixion iconography on Central European orphreys developed in the 14th century (and still faithfully copied by workshops into the 17th century). Influenced by the contemporary pietistic writing such as that by Bridget of Sweden and by Prague's archbishop Jan of Jenstein, this iconography centred on Christ's Eucharistic body (*Corpus Christi*), whose triumph over death is symbolised by the living cross (*Arbor vitae*), sometimes with the empathetic presence of Mary Magdalene at the foot of the cross. However, as Wetter points out, this imagery should not be seen as a visual gloss of the textual sources, but as a part of a complex semiotic system where true meaning is activated through ritual: a priest clad in the chasuble thus becomes Christ's living image; or, as in a rare recorded case from Brandenburg, a crimson-red chasuble used in the veiling and unveiling of the cross on Good Friday is part of the *mise-en-scène* of salvation.

At the other extreme of sensory experiences, discussed in this volume by Achim Timmermann, the image of Christ's sacrifice provided spiritual consolation in the highly charged theatre of death. Through the perspective of an overlooked 15th-century 'poor sinners' cross' in Brno, known as the Zderad Column, our attention is drawn to an extended family of monuments whose presence shaped the quotidian landscape of the late Middle Ages. Constructed as a plain stele or as a riot of microarchitectural forms, usually with an image of Crucifixion or a martyrdom at its core, poor sinners' crosses were not only ominous markers of the places of executions at judicial boundaries of towns, they were also the stations of last hope, where condemned men and women were given their final glimpse of redemption. Extraordinary in its concept, this is but one example of many such public monuments that inhabited the cities, roadsides, boundaries and fields of medieval Europe, structuring the experience of everyday life and giving it a moral focus. In this optically crowded environment people did not look for salvation only in churches — they lived and died in the company of the Virgin, Christ, and His Saints.

Death, even by medieval standards, seemed omnipresent in 15th-century Bohemia. Wenceslas IV's apoplectic rage at the news of the civil unrest may have hastened him to his grave, but many of his subjects suffered a grimmer fate in the ensuing conflict (and plague) that depopulated Prague, filled the graveyards, and turned Bohemia's countryside into battlefields. In these violent times, the need to preserve one's identity — through institutional allegiances and personal commemoration — acquired a new sense of urgency. For the Bohemian and Moravian Catholic minority the rallying point was provided by the charismatic Italian preacher John Capistran, whose order of Franciscan Observants found a receptive audience among the kingdom's rural aristocracy. Jan Chlíbec shows how the order's ostentatious monasteries in Bechyně and Kadaň created a setting for a distinctive type of a sculpted funerary monument that captured the pervasive horror and the inevitability of the physical act of dying, known · as the transi tomb. The macabre detail of the decaying human form on these tombs was in stark contrast to the startlingly 'realistic' death-defying portraits of the deceased commissioned as effigies and for commemorative epitaphs.

Although part of a different cultural and artistic milieu, these works share the self-commemorative discourse of the older 'royal' monuments discussed in this volume, such as the statuary of the House at the Stone Bell, the Old Town Bridge Tower, and the triforium of Prague Cathedral. The famous gallery of busts on the cathedral triforium is often hailed as an early instance of portraiture, of a kind characterised by idealism rather than the unflinching realism of the 15th century, but its precise role in the conceptual programme of the choir has been the subject of different interpretations. Milena Bartlová considers the importance of the choir as the site of *memoria* of Charles IV and his family, who were buried before the altar. The emperor's bust and those of his family and court, chosen (argues Bartlová) principally for their role as benefactors of the cathedral, are all part of the same commemorative circle whose place in the building's collective memory was 'fixed' not only by the recognisable features of their sculpted portraits and by heraldry, but also by the biographical inscriptions painted above them. But are these unique, frequently cited vignettes good enough to be true? In focusing on many apparent flaws found in the copied texts, Bartlová exposes the inscriptions as being — at least in part — the product of later restorations. Her argument may force us to reconsider our evidence for the lives and careers of the leading members of Prague court and chapter, including those of the cathedral's two principal architects.

Bartlová's salutary scepticism reminds us that the prism of history can distort as well as sharpen our perspective. Nowhere is this more true than in the pioneering work of the Czech 19th-century neo-Gothic movement and its most famous exponent Josef Mocker. In an article written specially for this volume, Taťána Petrasová outlines the remarkably prolific career of this architect, whose restoration projects touched on almost every major medieval monument, from Prague Cathedral and Karlstein Castle to the numerous secular and religious buildings in Prague — in some tragic cases providing our only record before their demolition; in other cases Mocker seems to have colluded with city authorities over new grandiose schemes, such as the clearing (*asanace* in Czech) of the ancient Jewish quarter, Josefov. Mocker's unquestioned dedication earned him lasting admiration, but his methods provoked criticism and praise in equal measure, even among his contemporaries. Although at times misguided in their approach, Mocker and his historically minded colleagues turned public attention to the material past, and ignited a debate among experts that shaped the conservation movement of the following century. Like Pugin in England and Viollet-le-Duc in France, Mocker may have over-romanticised Gothic architecture, but his visionary drive to revitalise ruined monuments defines our view of medieval Prague today, just as Schedel did in 1493. Looking through the eyes of a 15th-century engraver or a 19th-century restorer, we are confronted in each case with an image — vivid and enduring, if not always strictly accurate — of a city whose extraordinary history is written in its buildings.

NOTES

1. A. Wilson, *The Making of the Nuremberg Chronicle* (Amsterdam 1978), 50–52 (for the translation of Wolgemut and Pleydenwurff's contract of 1491); E. Rücker, *Hartmann Schedels Weltchronik, das größte Buchunternehmen der Dürer-Zeit* (Munich 1988), 185 (for Schedel's description of Prague); *Praha na nejstarších grafických listech 1493–1757*, exhibition catalogue (Prague 1996), 6–20.

2. Notably by Heinrich Truchsess of Diessenhofen and by Umberto Decembrio: *Fontes rerum Germanicarum, IV: Henricus de Diessenhofen und andere Geschichtsquellen Deutschlands im späteren Mittelalter*, ed. J. F. Böhmer and A. Huber (Stuttgart 1868), 116; K. Kubínová, *Imitatio Romae: Karel IV. a Řím* (Prague 2006), 275, n. 328.

3. 'Chronicon Aulae Regiae', *Fontes rerum Bohemicarum*, ed. J. Emler, 8 vols (Prague 1873–1932), IV (1884), 1–337, here 331.

4. J. Fajt and R. Suckale, 'The example of Prague in Europe', in *Prague: The Crown of Bohemia 1347–1437*, ed. B. D. Boehm and J. Fajt, exhibition catalogue (New York 2005), 47–57, here 52.

England and Bohemia in the Time of Anne of Luxembourg: Dynastic Marriage as a Precondition for Cultural Contact in the Late Middle Ages

MAREK SUCHÝ

The political circumstances of the late 1370s and early 1380s that had brought England and Bohemia closer together diplomatically culminated in the marriage of Anne of Luxembourg, daughter of Emperor Charles IV, to the English King Richard II in 1382. The divisions in Europe caused by the Great Schism of 1378 did not lead the Luxembourgs to abandon their neutral stance in favour of England. The English marriage did, however, counterbalance the Luxembourgs' dynastic allegiance to the French Valois court. The Bohemian princess was accompanied to her new land by a large entourage, recruited from the younger members of the circle of families involved in negotiating the Anglo-imperial treaty. Marriages between members of the entourage and English spouses were not uncommon, and some of the entourage remained in the country even after Richard's dethronement in 1399. In particular, evidence for contacts between the Luxembourg and Plantagenet royal families and the duchy of Těšín can be found in written sources. People, news, gifts and ideas travelled in both directions. Although English–Bohemian relations lost their dynastic dimension after the premature death of Queen Anne in 1394, travellers between Bohemia and England continued to avail themselves of the Main-Rhine route; for its part, Bohemia continued to be one of the possible transit countries for English pilgrims travelling to the Holy Land.

IT is common knowledge that Anne, daughter of Emperor Charles IV, was married to the English King Richard II. The question remains, however, to what extent this dynastic alliance influenced contact between the two countries. The aim of this paper is not to seek traces of English influence in Bohemia and vice versa, but rather to examine the circumstances for the interaction of the two cultures in the second half of the 14th century.[1] Firstly, it is necessary to understand that travelling the distance between the two countries was not as arduous as it may seem. Although it took Anne several months to cover the route between Prague and London, it was nevertheless not expected that a future queen would travel with unseemly haste.[2] Messengers or diplomats, on the other hand, who had to deliver messages as quickly as possible, managed to cover the same route in the course of six weeks (Fig. 1).[3]

Traditionally, mutual contacts were maintained by monastic orders in particular; this seems to be confirmed by the fact that the death of Thomas Becket in 1171 was also recorded by the contemporary chronicler Jarloch, abbot of the Premonstratensian

FIG. 1. Map of Europe. ■ The journey from Prague to Brussels according to the
contemporary itinerary (*c.* 1400). ● Henry of Derby's expedition to the Holy Land
(between the Baltic and Mediterranean seas) according to his journey accounts (1392).
Broken lines indicate modern international borders

Marek Suchý

monastery in Milevsko in South Bohemia.[4] Later, the Přemyslid King Wenceslas II
(1278–1305) had his chaplain Gottfried sent to the court of Edward I in 1302 with a
request for relics of the martyred archbishop of Canterbury.[5] An altar consecrated 'in
honore S. Thome Canthuriensis episcopi' appears in sources dating from 1337 in
connection with the Romanesque basilica[6] and later also with the newly built Gothic
cathedral at Prague Castle.[7] Wenceslas's father Přemysl Otakar II (1253–78), however,
had already maintained relations with Richard of Cornwall (younger brother of the
English King Henry III), who as king of the Romans confirmed Otakar in the holding of
Austria and Styria in 1262 and possibly also appointed him as the guardian of imperial
lands on the eastern side of the Rhine.[8]

The Přemyslids were not successful in their policy of expansion, but in the first half of
the 14th century the Luxembourgs broadened the political ambitions of the Bohemian
kings further west through their well-established dynastic contacts with the French royal

9

family. King John of Luxembourg fought (and died) on the French side in the Battle of Crecy in 1346, but with the election of his son as king of the Romans in the same year, the interests of the Valois and the Luxembourgs came into conflict on the western border of the empire. Charles IV's response to this new situation was to endeavour not to be drawn into the Anglo-French conflict, and he prevented the French kings from penetrating the western parts of the empire. This policy is particularly in evidence in 1347–48 and 1356–57, when he concluded or renewed treaties of friendship with both England and France. During his last great diplomatic visit to France, in 1377–78, Charles clearly also adopted a position of neutrality in the west with the aim of expanding his influence in the east.[9]

The political tension escalated again in the autumn of 1378 with the outbreak of the Great Schism. The subsequent ecclesiastical and political division of Europe worsened the discrepancy in the interests of the Luxembourgs and the Valois, and diverted Charles's long-standing neutrality in western Europe to a stance favourable to England. Without hesitation, the Roman Pope Urban VI used the situation to form an Anglo-imperial alliance against pro-Avignon France in particular, with the aim of resolving the Great Schism on his terms. The papal nuncio Pileo da Prato was even entrusted with re-opening the talks on the marriage of Anne of Bohemia to the English King Richard II, a proposal that had already been presented by Emperor Charles before his last diplomatic journey to France.[10]

After the death of Charles in November 1378, the negotiations were taken over by his son and successor Wenceslas IV, who also finally confirmed the alliance with Richard II in 1381.[11] The agreement was directed 'contra omnes schismaticos', but nevertheless did not compel either side to take action against the supporters of the Avignon pope.[12] Throughout the negotiations, Wenceslas maintained good relations with the Valois, which culminated in a friendship agreement in July 1380.[13] Despite Wenceslas's offer, arising from the alliance with England, to act as intermediary in Anglo-French peace talks,[14] even the schism did not much alter the political neutrality of the Luxembourgs in the west of Europe. The English coronation of Wenceslas's sister Anne, which took place as part of the alliance agreements in January 1382, nevertheless created a significant counterbalance to the traditional dynastic orientation towards the French royal family.[15]

In English history Queen Anne has been seen first and foremost as a conciliator during great political crises.[16] Although it may seem to be a conventional role for a queen, it is not without interest that the pardons 'at the supplication of the queen' issued throughout her reign often have no clear connection with politics.[17] One of the contemporary sources that praises her skill in settling conflicts ('jurgia sedavit') is the inscription on the tomb of the royal couple.[18] It is certainly no coincidence that Anne is described in almost the same terms ('rixas sedavit, discordes pacificavit, mansuetis favit') in the necrology preserved in a manuscript (Prague, Archiv Pražského Hradu, Knihovna metropolitní kapituly, H.15) that also contains a description of London in which the tomb in Westminster Abbey features (Figs 2, 3).[19]

The administrative positions in the queen's household may have been in the hands of the English;[20] nevertheless, Anne did disembark in England with *moderata familia*.[21] It is true that some members of her entourage returned home directly from Calais, where they handed Anne over to the English ambassadors in December 1381.[22] Others may have joined Johanna of Brabant (*Domina Lantegravissa de Lucembergh*), who sailed back to the Continent at the beginning of February 1382 after escorting her niece to her new homeland;[23] still others left the country in August of the same year, in the entourage of the chief Bohemian negotiator Přemysl, duke of Těšín (a region and town now divided

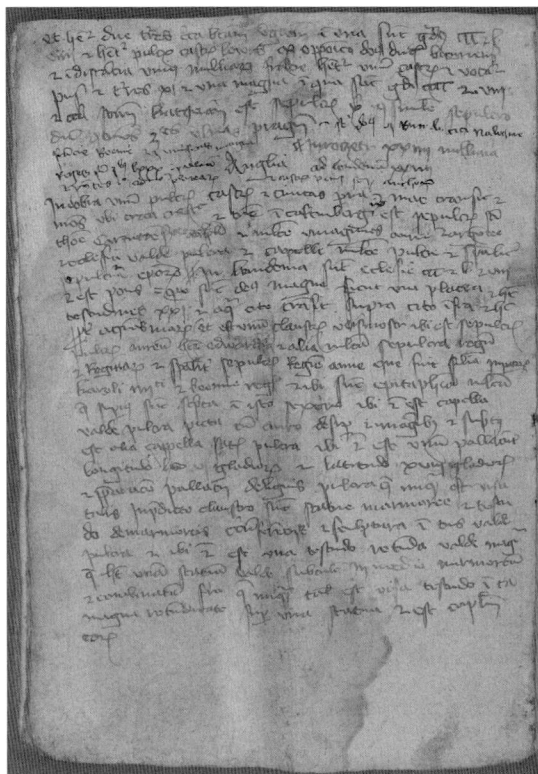

FIG. 2. Manuscript description of Queen Anne's tomb (Prague, Archiv Pražského Hradu, Knihovna metropolitní kapituly, H.15, fol. 92v)

Marek Suchý

between the Czech Republic and Poland, where the name is Cieszyn).[24] Many, however, remained and appear in the sources, even after 1388, when the Merciless Parliament required them to leave the kingdom;[25] at the very least Richard's knight Roger Siglem of Bohemia was in the country in 1399, when he switched his allegiance to Henry IV after Richard's deposition.[26]

It is understandable that one might find the queen's Bohemians among her confessors,[27] but in a letter to her brother Wenceslas Anne also mentions a *dominus Nicholaus*, a Bohemian knight in the service of her husband, who can be identified as Nikolaus Reibnitz.[28] A further two knights from Bohemia can also be found among the 142 paid leaders of military contingents for the Scottish campaign of 1385: Henry Hask, who joined the army with two knights and nine squires, and Henry Burzebo, who led another thirty squires. If all the men-at-arms from their contingents were fellow-countrymen, then more than forty Bohemians set off for Scotland.[29] Another knight from Bohemia, who appears in sources five years later in connection with a foul at the tournament in Saint-Inglevert (near Calais) in 1390, perhaps also took part in the military campaign in Scotland.[30]

Although the queen's Bohemians did not hold senior posts in the household and their precise number is difficult to estimate, their influence was so intense that a contemporary chronicler described them as the 'queen's compatriots who fed off the fat of the land, forgetful of their own country, and though only guests, they were shamelessly and grimly unwilling to return home'.[31] Thomas Walshingham explicitly mentions the tour that

FIG. 3.   Westminster Abbey, tomb effigy of Anne of Bohemia, 1396–99
Marek Suchý

Richard made with Anne and her numerous Bohemian entourage round the English monasteries in the summer of 1383, though his negative observations should be understood in the context of a general dislike of foreigners not exclusive to medieval England. The problem was that Anne spent most of her time with Richard and until 1388 contributed nothing to Richard's wardrobe, in spite of the fact that soon after her arrival she was endowed with landed property that was intended to make her independent of the exchequer.[32] This was all the more problematic, as the Bohemian princess had arrived in England without a dowry, and Richard had provided Wenceslas with a considerable loan that was never repaid.[33]

The criticism of contemporary chroniclers was also aimed at the king's alleged excessive generosity to foreigners and especially at the queen's ladies-in-waiting when they married into local nobility (*viri nobiles*).[34] Best known is the scandalous case of Robert de Vere, earl of Oxford, who repudiated his noble wife in favour of Agnes Lancecrona in 1387.[35] In addition, Margaret, daughter of Přemysl, duke of Těšín, died in Norfolk in 1416 as the first wife of the king's standard-bearer Simon Felbrigge.[36] It is therefore unsurprising that the Anglo-imperial negotiations were also attended by Robert's uncle Aubrey de Vere and Simon's father George, or that Přemysl spent almost nine months in England in 1381–82.[37] Moreover, according to one theory, Agnes came from Landštejn Castle,[38] which belonged to Konrád Krajíř (Conrad Crayer),[39] who participated with his son Leopold in the mission to England in the spring of 1381.[40]

Another of the queen's ladies-in-waiting, Eliška, figures later in sources as the spouse of the Bohemian knight Here Mistilburg.[41] The marriages of the Bohemian court ladies were evidently not, then, exclusively concentrated on English admirers, although Roger Siglem of Bohemia, mentioned above, married an English Katherine, and Nikolaus Reibnitz married Anne Gomenys.[42] Many others, however, remain anonymous or unrecorded;[43] probably not all of them had 'criminal' fates, received exclusive gifts, or married the king's favourites. Nevertheless it seems evident that in the course of the negotiations in Frankfurt, Bruges, Calais, London and Prague, diplomats on both sides made personal contacts, which in some cases at least were confirmed by dynastic marriages.

It is true that of the former negotiators only Bořivoj of Svinaře, who rose through the ranks during the negotiations to the position of Wenceslas's representative in the empire, is documented later in England.[44] Contacts with the duchy of Těšín, however, can be traced in sources relatively clearly. For example, the king's knight of the chamber John Harleston made a pilgrimage to Loreta under the safe conduct of the duke of Těšín (*dux Tessinensis*), and when he was imprisoned on the way through Germany Richard II intervened on his behalf, not only with Přemysl, but also with King Wenceslas.[45] It is also known that Bernard Lobdewe, a clerk and servitor of the 'king's kinsman' the duke of Těšín (*Theslyn*), received revenues at the request of Queen Anne (1383),[46] and that one of her chaplains, Henry de Reybutz, was explicitly from the diocese of Wrocław (*Wartizlanen*), to which the duchy of Těšín belonged.[47] Moreover, Ofka (Eufemia),[48] one of the queen's maidens, bore a name that had a certain tradition in the families of the Silesian nobility.[49]

Naturally the easiest contacts to map out are those between the two royal families, for with Anne's arrival in England regular correspondence also began.[50] This did not revolve exclusively around international political events such as the Hungarian coronation of the queen's brother Sigismund in 1387,[51] or the Anglo-French peace negotiations in 1389.[52] In many cases these missives were simply *littere de statu*, and one of them may even indicate that Agnes Lancecrona's Bohemian origin influenced Robert de Vere's choice of exile after he was on the losing side at the Battle of Radcot Bridge in 1387.[53] It is also not without interest that the confessors of Queen Anne and Robert de Vere were brothers (Thomas and Richard Roughton, both exempted from the general pardon of the Merciless Parliament),[54] and that one of Robert's servants was a Bohemian Martin Medritz.[55]

Richard's expressed desire to be kept informed whenever it so happened that somebody was passing through Wenceslas's court (in Bohemia or elsewhere) suggests that such encounters were not uncommon;[56] furthermore, the missives did not simply convey information, they also accompanied goods or gifts. Simon de Burely, the king's former tutor, and Robert Braybrook, later bishop of London, bought horses for Richard during a mission to Germany in 1381, and those entrusted with a similar task in 1387 included John de Roches (John de Roos) and Sithilus de Bohemia, who could be identified with above mentioned Roger Siglem.[57] The popularity of warhorses from Central Europe was clearly legendary, as one was also handed over in 1383 to John of Gaunt, duke of Lancaster, by Wenceslas's knight Henry Poto.[58] Almost immediately after her arrival in England, Queen Anne bought and sent 'home' 'Res, Cameras, et Ornamenta ad usum, Serenissimae Dominae, Imperatricis, Matris sue carissimae' ('objects, valuables and jewels . . . for her dearest mother's use')[59] and later, in the summer of 1389, we hear of a consignment of various types of cloth for her mother Empress Elizabeth.[60]

Although the two monarchs never met,[61] Wenceslas had the opportunity to meet the son of the duke of Lancaster in Bohemia. Henry of Derby, Richard's cousin and future successor to the English throne, decided during his second expedition to Prussia[62] to make a pilgrimage to the Holy Land, so he travelled firstly through Pomerania, Brandenburg and Lusatia by the Zittau road to Prague.[63] He visited Prague Cathedral, and on his way to see Wenceslas at the castle of Žebrák[64] he also saw Karlstein and the relics deposited there. After eleven days spent in central Bohemia, he and his retinue continued on their way to Moravia and evidently visited Anne's cousin Margrave Jošt in Brno.[65] The subsequent detour on his way to Vienna can be explained by his meeting with Sigismund of Luxembourg in Holíč.[66] On the way to Venice Henry also spent an evening with the patriarch of Aquileia, Jan Soběslav, another of Queen Anne's cousins.[67] It may be assumed that these high-level dynastic visits included the exchange of gifts,[68] and it is not without interest that Henry had his coat of arms painted or hung up in his rooms in Prague, Brno and Vienna (Figs 1, 4).[69]

It is interesting to find that 'in partibus Bohemie' (between Görlitz and Vienna) clearly only Prague, the centre of the Holy Roman Empire, afforded ample opportunity for making purchases. Apart from the normal travel requisites (bread, beer and wine, candles, horseshoes and fodder, etc.),[70] a relatively rich range of meats, seasonings and sweetmeats appears in the travel accounts, but also flour, purchased for stores 'per manus diuersorum'

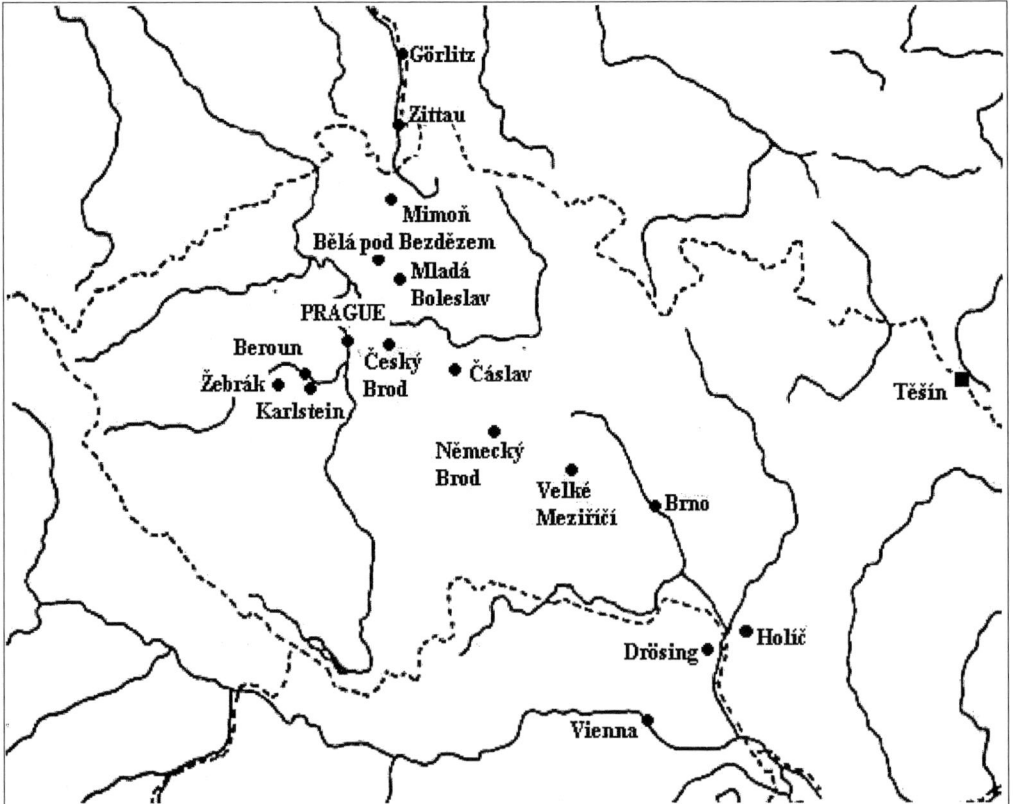

FIG. 4. Henry of Derby's expedition to the Holy Land 'in partibus Bohemie', according to his journey accounts (1392). Broken lines indicate modern international borders

Marek Suchý

('through the agency of various people').[71] Longer stopovers were also used to purchase two horses,[72] effect repairs to saddles,[73] and buy part of the armour of the earl of Derby.[74] The approaching winter clearly prompted the acquisition of fur clothing and satin material,[75] and new clothing was also acquired by Henry's two henksmen.[76] The Prague purchases, however, also included a costly belt ('sinctura argentea et deaurata'),[77] which Mowbray le Heraud bought in the same workshop in which Henry's chaplain and confessor Hugo Herlee acquired altarpieces, later consecrated by the archbishop of Prague, Jan of Jenstein.[78] One can also connect the acquisition of the altarpieces with the purchase of a bookmark for a breviary,[79] and it is not improbable that this took place in the workshop of Hanz Goldsmyth, who is explicitly mentioned in relation to the purchase of fourteen gold or gilded collars.[80]

The purpose of Henry's visit was clearly to visit his noble Luxembourg relatives, yet, although there was certainly an exchange of information as well as gifts, his journey was not primarily a diplomatic mission. Professional diplomats who were sent to the empire were often accompanied by people with local experience who knew not only the situation, but also the language. One of these was Bernard van Zetles, who had established his career in the time of Richard's father the Black Prince; he took part in the agreement with Charles IV in 1348, as well as in the Anglo-imperial negotiations at the beginning of the 1380s.[81] His successors were then clearly recruited from the ranks of the Bohemians who came to the country with Princess Anne. Knight of the Chamber Nikolaus Reibnitz accompanied Richard Abberbury on two missions during the negotiations with Rupert of Bavaria in 1394–95,[82] and Roger Siglem was repeatedly sent to the empire, even after the death of Queen Anne.[83] The Bohemians' missions were not necessarily restricted to Central Europe, however: two knights, Lupuldus and Lecze de Cockericz, were sent with the squire Erchardus de Euczembergh to the court of the king of Portugal,[84] and Johannes Lantgraf evidently led a diplomatic mission to Norway.[85]

Thus those who travelled between England and Central Europe not only bore messages and probably also gifts, but also brought with them experience, knowledge of languages, ideas, and fashion.[86] The extent to which this vibrant exchange included manuscripts is unclear, although books were widely used in both courts.[87] The king's tutor Simon de Burley clearly also owned a travel dictionary,[88] and a Bohemian pilgrim left records of his visit to England.[89] The queen herself allegedly not only read the Bible in Latin, German and Czech, but may also have owned an English translation.[90] The presence of so-called Lollard knights at the court even led to speculation as to whether she or her court participated directly in the transfer of Wycliffism to Bohemia.[91] There is no direct evidence, but it is a fact that explicit mention is made of Bohemian students and scholars who came to England to obtain and copy Wycliffe's texts in sources as late as 1399–1401 (Jeroným of Prague) and 1406–07 (Mikuláš Faulfiš and Jiří of Kněhnice).[92] Anne Hudson aptly commented that their horses could hardly have carried all the books that must have made the journey between Oxford and Prague.[93]

It seems evident nevertheless that in the time of Queen Anne the roads following the Rhine and Main route between London and Prague experienced relatively heavy traffic. Dynastic contacts at the top level were indeed disrupted by the premature death of the childless Anne in 1394, but it is certainly not without significance that some of her courtiers remained in England, even after the deposition of her husband five years later. Indeed, for English travellers Central Europe continued to offer an attractive alternative route to Jerusalem.[94] The fact that in 1397 Richard considered accepting the Roman crown against his former brother-in-law Wenceslas[95] proves only that with Anne's death Anglo-Bohemian relations lost their dynastic dimension, and that the imperial crown began to be used again as an instrument of political pressure in western Europe.

ACKNOWLEDGEMENTS

Special thanks are due to the Open Society Fund - Prague, which enabled the author to make his first short study visit to London, in 1996.

NOTES

1. In the text that follows, the term Bohemian denotes (if not otherwise specified) any person who came to England from the crown lands of Bohemia, regardless of his/her other possible origin, i.e., Moravia, Silesia, Lusatia, etc.

2. Wenceslas confirmed the London treaty on 1 September 1381, and Anne arrived in Calais in mid-December to spend Christmas at Leeds Castle; E. Perroy, *L'Angleterre et le Grand Schisme d'Occident* (London 1933), 154–55. See also M. V. Labarge, *Medieval Travellers: The Rich and Restless* (London 1982, repr. 2005), 136–39.

3. See *Acta imperii inedita seculi XIII et XIV*, ed. E. Winkelmann, 2 vols (Innsbruck 1880, 1885), II, 643–44, no. 984, and Perroy, *Grand Schisme* (as in n. 2), 164, n. 1. Reitemeier even states that Nikolaus Reibnitz got from Nuremberg to London within twenty-four days in 1397; A. Reitemeier, *Aussenpolitik im Spätmittelalter: Die diplomatischen Beziehungen zwischen dem Reich und England 1377–1422* (Paderborn/Munich/Vienna/Zurich 1999), 372.

4. J. Emler ed., *Fontes rerum bohemicarum* (Prague 1873–84, repr. Olms 2004), II (1874), 464. The existence of this report was noted in O. Odložilík, *Wyclif and Bohemia* (Prague 1936), 3–4.

5. CCR (*Calendar of Close Rolls*) (London 1892–1927), Edward I (IV, 611); CPR (*Calendar of Patent Rolls*) (London 1894–1916), Edward I (IV, 72). Wenceslas was buried in 'medio sanctuario' of the Cistercian abbey that he founded in Zbraslav near Prague; see, for example, J. Kuthan, 'Cisterciácké kláštery jako pohřební místa vladařských rodů střední Evropy', in *Historická inspirace*, ed. M. Kubelík, M. Pavlík and J. Štulc (Prague 2001), 212–13.

6. Archiv Pražského hradu (APH), Archiv metropolitní kapituly (AMK), 143-VI-26. See also *Regesta diplomatica nec non epistolaria Bohemiae et Moraviae*, 4 vols (Prague 1855–92), IV (1333–46), ed. J. Emler (1892), 197, no. 493.

7. The altar is listed in church inventories from the second half of the 14th century; APH, AMK (as in n. 6), cod. IX, fol. 43r; and APH, AMK, cod. XIX/1, fol. 5v. The altar is mentioned in W. W. Tomek, *Základy starého místopisu Pražského*, 4 vols with index (Prague 1866–75), IV (1872), 109, 245. The inventory from cod. XIX/1, fols 1r–20r was published by J. Pelikán, 'Inventář oltářů kostela sv. Víta v Praze z r. 1397', *Památky archaeologické (skupina historická)*, 42 (1939–46), 123–31.

8. B. Weiler, 'Image and Reality in Richard of Cornwall's German Career', *English Historical Review*, 113 (1998), 1111–42. It is interesting that Sir William de Moravia and Adam de Moravia are mentioned in sources in connection with Scotland and Anglia in the 1290s and 1300s; CPR (as in n. 5), Edward I (II, 355; III, 444, 611, 616), Edward II (I, 198, 375; III, 78).

9. For discussion and primary sources, see V. Hrubý, 'Studie k dílu "Archivum coronae regni Bohemiae"', *Časopis archivní školy*, 2 (1924–25), 112–27; B. Mendl and F. Quicke, 'Les relations entre l'empereur et le roi de France de 1355 à 1356', *Revue Belge de philologie et d'histoire*, 8 (1929), 469–510; B. Mendl, 'Vyjednávání o českofrancouzský spolek 1355', in *Českou minulostí* (Prague 1929), 111–23; F. Quicke, 'Karel IV. a Francie v letech 1355 a 1356', *Časopis archivní školy*, 7 (1930), 1–29; H. S. Offler, 'England and Germany at the Beginning of the Hundred Years' War', *English Historical Review*, 54 (1939), 608–31; F. Trautz, *Die Könige von England und das Reich 1272–1377* (Heidelberg 1961), 344–408; H. Stoob, 'Kaiser Karl IV. und der Ostseeraum', *Hansische Geschichtsblätter*, 88 (1970), 163–214; S. C. Rowell, 'Unexpected Contacts: Lithuanians at Western Courts, c.1316-c.1400', *English Historical Review*, 111 (1996), 557–77; *Kaiser Karl IV.: Staatsman und Mäzen*, ed. F. Seibt (Munich 1978), 152–89; H. Thomas, 'Frankreich, Karl IV. und das Grosse Schisma', in *Bündnissysteme und Außenpolitik im späten Mittelalter*, ed. P. Moraw, Zeitschrift für historische Forschung, Beiheft 5 (Berlin 1988), 69–104; F. Kafka, 'Karel IV. a anjouovsko-piastovské dědictví', *Sborník historický*, 36 (1989), 5–57; and F. Šmahel, *Cesta Karla IV. do Francie, 1377–78* (Prague 2006).

10. Charles announced his diplomatic journey to France in the summer of 1377 and at the same time (at the latest before the end of that year) proposed the engagement of his daughter Anne to the young English King Richard II; Perroy, *Grand Schisme* (as in n. 2), 136.

11. On the marriage negotiations, see Perroy, *Grand Schisme* (as in n. 2), 129–65, and (more recently) N. Saul, *Richard II* (New Haven/London 1997), 83–107; A. Tuck, 'Richard II and the House of Luxemburg', in *Richard II: The Art of Kingship*, ed. A. Goodman and J. Gillespie (Oxford 2003), 205–29, and A. Reitemeier, *Aussenpolitik* (as in n. 3), 145–81.

12. *Foedera, Conventiones, Litterae, etc.*, III/3, ed. T. Rymer (The Hague 1745), 114, 129.

13. *Acta imperii* (as in n. 3), 637–42, nos. 977, 978 and 982, and 880–81, no. 1228. See also I. Hlaváček, 'K diplomatice úmluv Václava IV. s Karlem V. z r. 1380', *Zápisky katedry československých dějin a archivního studia*, 3 (1958), 55–61; J. Kejř, 'Příspěvky k dějinám pražské právnické univerzity', *Acta Universitatis Carolinae - Historia Universitatis Carolinae Pragensis (AUC-HUCP)*, 30 (1990), 9–24; K. Walsh, '"Ecce Arbor in Medio Terre". Ein irischer Prälat an der Prager Juristenuniversität, das "Purgatorium Sancti Patricii" und die Debatte um das Fegefeuer', in *Husitství-Reformace-Renesance*, ed. J. Pánek, M. Polívka and N. Rejchrtová, 3 vols (Prague 1994), I, 167–90.

14. Perroy, *Grand Schisme* (as in n. 2), 160.

15. On relations with the Valois, see, for example, J. Fantysová-Matějková, 'Lucembursko mezi Francií a Římskou říší: Cesta Václava I. k moci (1334–1354)', in *Korunní země v dějinách českého státu*, ed. L. Bobková, J. Fantysová-Matějková and J. Zdichynec (Prague 2003), 293–353; eadem, 'Vladařský lesk a sentiment: Francie a Karel IV. v letech 1355–1357', in *Lesk královského majestátu ve středověku*, ed. L. Bobková and M. Holá (Prague/Litomyšl 2005), 81–98.

16. Saul, *Richard II* (as in n. 11), 455; P. Strohm, 'Queens as Intercessors', in *Hochon's Arrow: The Social Imagination of Fourteenth-Century Texts* (Princeton 1992), 95–119.

17. See, for example, *CPR* (as in n. 5), Richard II (II, 411; III, 311, 462), and especially William Hontingfeld (a thief who received a pardon), *CPR*, Richard II (IV, 275), or Alicia Foster from Dover (who was condemned to death for 'divers felonies'), *CPR*, Richard II (III), 359).

18. Strohm, 'Queens' (as in n. 16), 106; Saul, *Richard II* (as in n. 11), 456. See also D. Gordon, *Making and Meaning: The Wilton Diptych* (London 1993), 22 fig. 4.

19. F. M. Bartoš published the necrology according to manuscript *APH* (as in n. 6), Knihovna metropolitní kapituly *(KMK)*, D.12, fols 217r–217v, in 'Z dávných styků našich s Anglií', *Časopis Musea království Českého*, 93 (1919), 203–04. In manuscript H.15 (*APH, KMK*, fols 90r–90v) the text begins on the first folio of the last quire, which also contains the description of Westminster Abbey, including the 'sepulchrum regine Anne qua fuit filia imperatoris Karoli IIII[ti] et Boemie regis' (fol. 92v), and an itinerary from Prague to Brussels (fol. 99r). It seems that at least the last quire of manuscript H.15 could be interpreted as a record by a Bohemian pilgrim of his journey to France and England.

20. Richard Abberbury, chamberlain; see S. Walker, 'Sir Richard Abberbury (c. 1330–1399) and his Kinsmen: the rise and fall of a gentry family', *Nottingham Medieval Studies*, 34 (1990), 120–27; Thomas More, receiver general, *CCR* (as in n. 5), Richard II (III, 99), and C. Given-Wilson, *The Royal Household and the King's Affinity* (London 1986), 93, 128; Richard de Waldegrave, steward of the lands of Queen Anne, *Calendar of Fine Rolls (CFR)*, Richard II (IX, 329–30), and Given-Wilson, *The Royal Household*, 185; William Karlell, attorney general in Ireland, *CCR*, Richard II (II, 313); John Parker, usher of her chamber, *CPR* (as in n. 5), Richard II (IV, 257); John Nell, groom of her wardrobe, *CPR*, Richard II (II,166, 299). See also A. Simpson, *The Connections between English and Bohemian Painting during the Second Half of the Fourteenth Century* (New York 1984), 45.

21. *Foedera* (as in n. 12), 131.

22. Simpson, *The Connections* (as in n. 20), 40. On Anne's journey through Flanders to Bruges, see also M. Vale, *The Princely Court: Medieval Courts and Culture in North-West Europe* (Oxford 2005), 331, and Reitemeier, *Aussenpolitik* (as in n. 3), 166–67.

23. *Foedera* (as in n. 12), 134. Reitemeier (*Aussenpolitik* as in n. 3), 44, 166, 446) states that it was Elisabeth, Landgräfin von Leuchtenberg. Walsh assumes that they were two different persons and that it was Johanna who returned home in February 1382; K. Walsh, 'Lollardisch-hussitische Reformbestrebungen in Umkreis und Gefolgschaft der Luxemburgerin Anna, Königin von England (1382–1394)', in *Häresie und vorzeitige Reformation im Spätmittelalter*, ed. F. Šmahel (Munich 1998), 92–93.

24. Przimislaus, duke of Těšín (*Techinensis*), the bannerets, knights, esquires and other subjects of King Wenceslas who came to England in the company of Queen Anne left England via Calais; *CCR* (as in n. 5), Richard II (II, 155).

25. Simpson, *The Connections* (as in n. 20), 44. See also Saul, *Richard II* (as in n. 11), 194.

26. Simpson, *The Connections* (as in n. 20), 46–48. See also Given-Wilson, *The Royal Household* (as in n. 20), 213, 225, and Appendix V, 286; Appendix VI, 290. There was also a foreigner with a Bohemian name (Wenceslas Dorsteynour) among the king's knights in 1403; ibid., Appendix VI, 288.

27. Nicholas Mountz, Nicholas Hornyk, Brother Jacob; Simpson, *The Connections* (as in n. 20), 46. See also Reitemeier, *Aussenpolitik* (as in n. 3), 166 n. 91, 406.

28. *The Diplomatic Correspondence of Richard II*, ed. E. Perroy (London 1933), 193, nos. 33–39. See also Walker, 'Sir Richard Abberbury' (as in n. 20), 129; Given-Wilson, *The Royal Household* (as in n. 20), Appendix V, 286; and Reitemeier, *Aussenpolitik* (as in n. 3), 72 n. 205.

29. N. B. Lewis, 'The Last Medieval Summons of the English Feudal Levy', *English Historical Review*, 73 (1958), 1–26 (here 7), and Appendix II, nos. 25 and 70. Hervey Berzebo is mentioned in connection with the duke of Těšín and his negotiators in England in 1381 in Simpson, *The Connections* (as in n. 20), 39. The question is whether he could be identified with Herman Bergo, a foreign knight of Richard II in 1386 (Given-Wilson, *The Royal Household* (as in n. 20), Appendix V, 284) and (probably) a relative of Sir Otes Bergo, who left the kingdom in October 1383 (Saul, *Richard II* (as in n. 11), 93 n. 37). In any event, Here Bergo was at the campaign with forty horses; Reitemeier, *Aussenpolitik* (as in n. 3), 332 n. 62.

30. See for example, Simpson, *The Connections* (as in n. 20), 43–44, and M. Nejedlý, '"V Praze jsou tři města, mnoho výstavných kostelů a lidé zbožní": Obraz českých zemí a jejich panovníků ve francouzsky psané literatuře 14. století', in *Evropa a Čechy na konci středověku*, ed. E. Doležalová, R. Novotný and P. Soukup (Prague 2004), 35–57 (here 53). Knight Hans Czechwicz appears in sources in connection with the Scottish campaign; Reitemeier, *Aussenpolitik* (as in n. 3), 332 n. 62.

31. *The St Albans Chronicle, Volume I: 1376–1394*, ed. J. Taylor, W. R. Childs and L. Watkiss (Oxford 2003), 736–37.

32. ibid., 688–89. See also Given-Wilson, *The Royal Household* (as in n. 20), 36, 75, 92–93, 128; R. G. Davies, 'Richard II and the Church', in *Richard II: The Art of Kingship*, ed. A. Goodman and J. Gillespie (Oxford 2003), 89–90; and M. J. Bennet, 'Richard II and the Wider Realm', ibid., 191. On Anne's dowry, see also *CCR* (as in n. 5), Richard II (II, 518–19).

33. The loan was a part of the marriage treaty; Perroy, *Grand Schisme* (as in n. 2), 159; Saul, *Richard II* (as in n. 11), 90–91; Tuck, 'Richard II and the House of Luxemburg' (as in n. 11), 219. The situation was ironically commented on by contemporary writers: 'Nam non modicam pecuniam refundebat rex Angliae pro tantilla carnis portione'; *The Westminster Chronicle*, ed. L. C. Hecor and B. F. Harvey (Oxford 1982), 24–25. See also *Polychronicon Ranulphi Higden monachi Cestrensis together with the English translations of John Trevisa and of an unknown writer of the fifteenth century*, ed. J. R. Lumby, 9 vols (London 1879–86), IX, 12.

34. *St Albans Chronicle* (as in n. 31), 690–91; *Westminster Chronicle* (as in n. 33), 160–63, 274–75; *Polychronicon* (as in n. 33), 80.

35. The royal couple even wrote to the pope asking him to annul de Vere's marriage with Philippa, granddaughter of Edward III and daughter of Countess Isabelle, who was supposed to marry Charles IV in 1349. The divorce was seen as a great offence by the nobility, especially by the duke of Gloucester, who turned against de Vere during the Merciless Parliament in 1388. See Simpson, *The Connections* (as in n. 20), 42–43; Trautz, *Die Könige von England* (as in n. 9), 354; A. Tuck, *Richard II and the English Nobility* (London 1973), 77–78; Saul, *Richard II* (as in n. 11), 183.

36. C. Evans, 'Margaret, Lady Felbrygge', *Blackmansbury*, 2 (1965), 3–7; J. D. Milner, 'Sir Simon Felbrigg, KG: The Lancastrian Revolution and Personal Fortune', *Norfolk Archaeology*, 37 (1978), 85–86; Given-Wilson, *The Royal Household* (as in n. 20), 165. The question remains whether she could be identified with 'Margarete de Boheme', who obtained a letter of passage in 1386; see Reitemeier, *Aussenpolitik* (as in n. 3), 174, 323.

37. See Perroy, *Grand Schisme* (as in n. 2), 149–63.

38. J. V. Polišenský, *England and Czechoslovakia* (Prague 1946), 10–11.

39. A. Sedláček, *Hrady, zámky a tvrze království Českého*, 15 vols (Prague 1882–1927), IV (1885), 104; and *Hrady, zámky a tvrze v Čechách, na Moravě a ve Slezsku*, 7 vols (Prague 1981–89), V (1986), 117.

40. *CPR* (as in n. 5), Richard II (II, 4).

41. *CPR* (as in 5) Richard II (V, 286); see also Reitemeier, *Aussenpolitik* (as in n. 3), 48, 72, 173 n. 135, 330, 346–47, 485; Simpson (*The Connections* (as in n. 20), 48) identifies him with Here Nikel Bergo.

42. Simpson, *The Connections* (as in n. 20), 47; Saul, *Richard II* (as in n. 11), 93, n. 36. Reitemeier, *Aussenpolitik* (as in n. 3), 330.

43. Anne wrote in one letter to brother Wenceslas that 'nostre eciam virgines et puelle, quarum duas mors sevissima iam substraxit, Altissimo laus et honor, apud singulos multa generose fulgent et constancia virginali et de permissione graciosa speramus L.I. et F. dimittuntur pro nostro solacio non modica superstare'; *Diplomatic Correspondence* (as in n. 28), 193, nos. 33–39. In another letter to Empress Elizabeth (post 1385) Richard mentions 'puellas alias nobis a vestra serenitate transmissas'; ibid., 36, no. 57.

44. Simpson, *The Connections* (as in n. 20), 45. Reitemeier, *Aussenpolitik* (as in n. 3), 336, 346, 485. For bibliography about Bořivoj, see Walsh, 'Lollardisch-hussitische Reformbestrebungen' (as in n. 23), 82–83, n. 31.

45. *Diplomatic Correspondence* (as in n. 28), 28–31, nos. 46–49. According to Simpson (*The Connections* (as in n. 20), 50, no. 3), he was back in England before 1395; see also Given-Wilson, *The Royal Household* (as in n. 20), 162, and Appendix V, 283, and Reitemeier, *Aussenpolitik* (as in n. 3), 337.

46. *CPR* (as in n. 5), Richard II (II, 365); Simpson, *The Connections* (as in n. 20), 45–46.

47. Wrocław (Polish), Breslau (German), Wratislavia, Vratislavia (Latin), in Lower Silesia, Poland. See *Diplomatic Correspondence* (as in n. 28), 20, no. 33.

48. Simpson, *The Connections* (as in n. 20), 48.

49. See I. Panic, *Ksiaze cieszynski Premyslaw Noszak (⁺ok. 1332/1336–†1410): Biografia polityczna* (Cieszyn 1996), 13, 31–32, 34–35, 46.

50. See *Diplomatic Correspondence* (as in n. 28), 21–24, nos. 35–39; 28–29, no. 46; 35–36, no. 57; 38–39, no. 62; 46–47, no. 71; 65–66, no. 99, 94–95, nos. 139–40; 130, no. 183; 161–63, no. 221. Some letters bear secondary evidence of mutual correspondence, for example, Richard II in a letter (post August 1385) to the Empress Elizabeth refers to 'epistola de data X^e die mensis ffebruarii nobis missa per familiarem vestrum Nicholaum de Libus'; ibid., 35–36, no. 57. See also P. Chaplais, 'English Diplomatic Documents', in *The Reign of Richard II*, ed. F. R. H. du Boulay and C. M. Barron (London 1971), 21–45.

51. *Diplomatic Correspondence* (as in n. 28), 38–39, no. 62.

52. ibid., 65–66, no. 99.

53. Richard wrote to Wenceslas in favour of 'dilectus noster R[obert] de V[ere], unus de militibus nostris, eidem serenitati vestre noverit intimare, quem utpote suis exigentibus meritis admodum nobis carum nostri intuitu suscipere dignemini intime recommissum'; *Diplomatic Correspondence* (as in n. 28), 94, no. 139. Robert de Vere died in exile in Leuven (Flemish-Brabant); Saul, *Richard II* (as in n. 11), 461 n. 115. Yet Richard had pardoned minstrel John de Wylton at the intercession of the king of the Romans and Bohemia and the Empress Elizabeth in 1384; *CPR* (as in n. 5), Richard II (II, 384); Simpson, *The Connections* (as in n. 20), 50; Reitemeier, *Aussenpolitik* (as in n. 3), 404.

54. Given-Wilson, *The Royal Household* (as in n. 20), 178.

55. *CPR* (as in n. 5), Richard II (III, 201); Simpson, *The Connections* (as in n. 20), 48.

56. 'Quare celsitudini vestre intimo deprecamur affectu quatinus super continencia premissorum et status altitudinis vestre quociens interveniencium oportunitas affuerit, nostra dignemini precordia recreare'; *Diplomatic Correspondence* (as in n. 28), 94, no. 139.

57. *Diplomatic Correspondence* (as in n. 28), 22–23, no. 37, and 193, nos 33–39. On John de Roches, see also Given-Wilson, *The Royal Household* (as in n. 20), Appendix V, 283.

58. Perroy, *Grand Schisme* (as in n. 2), 155, n. 7; A. Goodman, *John of Gaunt* (London 1992), 182–83. Reitemeier (*Aussenpolitik* (as in n. 3), 170 n. 113, 171 n. 123, 454 n. 141) suggests that he can presumably be identified with Boto von Isenburg.

59. The items left the country on the same boat, the *Fligut*, that took Johanna of Brabant back to the Continent at the end of February; *Foedera* (as in n. 12), 134. See also n. 23 above.

60. *CCR*, Richard II (IV, 7); Simpson, *The Connections* (as in n. 20), 50; Reitemeier, *Aussenpolitik* (as in n. 3), 446 n. 90.

61. Wenceslas sent a letter (dated 20 December 1389) to Richard II in which he regretted that he could not come to England due to his journey to Moravia and Hungary; *Diplomatic Correspondence* (as in n. 28), 211–12, no. 99. This was probably only a pretext, as he did not seem inclined to leave Prague and its surroundings at the time. For his itinerary, see I. Hlaváček, 'Studie k diplomatice Václava IV.: IV. Itinerář krále Václava. (1361–1419)', *Československý časopis historický*, 10 (1962), 76–79; idem, 'Itinerář Václava IV. jako pramen pro rekonstrukci fungování vládní moci i mobility panovnického dvora', in *K organisaci státního správního systému Václava IV* (Prague 1991), 33–72 (here 45).

62. On the Prussian part of the journey, see F. du Boulay, 'Henry of Derby's expedition to Prussia', in *The Reign of Richard II* (as in n. 50), 165–72.

63. The journey can be reconstructed according to travel accounts; *Expeditions to Prussia and the Holy Land made by Henry Earl of Derby, afterwards Henry IV, in the years 1390–91 and 1392–93. Being the accounts Kept by His Treasurer*, ed. L. Toulmin-Smith, Camden Society, new series, LII (London 1894), 56–63, 72–74, 188–211, 260, 262, 274–75, 279–80. On the Zittau road, see H. Krüger, *Das Älteste deutsche Routenbüchlein: Jörg Gails "Raißbüchlin"* (Graz 1974), 186–87; I. Vávra, 'Žitavská cesta', *Historická geografie*, 12 (1974), 27–83; J. Jíhlavec, 'Po stopách Žitavské cesty', ibid., 18 (1979), 383–94. On the socio-economic aspects of the journey between Frankfurt on the Oder and Vienna, see M. Suchý, '"Na cestě" in partibus Boemie: Svědectví cestovních účtů Jindřicha z Derby z roku 1392', *Numismatický sborník*, 22 (2007), 115–40.

64. The road to Žebrák went through Beroun (*Bernau*), where Karlstein is situated; *Expeditions* (as in n. 63), 57, 73, 274. See also A. Profous, *Místní jména v Čechách: Jejich vznik, původní význam a změny*, 4 vols (Prague 1947–57), I, 57–58, and Krüger, *Routenbüchlein* (as in n. 63), 80–82. Toulmin-Smith (*Expeditions*, 73, n. c) talks about a visit to Bernau, a village near Saaz (Žatec), or (according to Dr Pauli) Alt-Bernarticz near Pilsen (Plzeň), or Čáslav. For Wenceslas's itinerary, see I. Hlaváček, 'Studie k diplomatice' (as in n. 61), 79; idem, 'Itinerář Václava IV.' (as in n. 61), 45.

65. For Jošt's itinerary, see T. Baletka, 'Dvůr, rezidence a kancelář moravského markraběte Jošta (1375–1411)', *Sborník archivních prací*, 46 (1996), 259–532 (here 510), and V. Štěpán, *Moravský markrabě Jošt (1354–1411)* (Brno 2002), 325, 811. For the road from Prague to Brno, see J. Pošvář, 'Obchodní cesty v českých zemích, na Slovensku, ve Slezsku a v Polsku do 14. století', *Slezský sborník*, 62 (1964), 54–63 (here 60), and I. Vávra, 'Haberská cesta', *Historická geografie*, 3 (1969), 8–29.

66. Toulmin-Smith (*Expeditions* (as in n. 63), lvii, 193) interprets 'Weisskirch' as Henry's detour to Hranice na Moravě (north-east from Olomouc), but Holíč (Weissenkirchen in German), which lies on the old route from Brno to Hungary, is the more probable location; see Štěpán, *Moravský markrabě* (as in n. 65), 325, n. 142; R. Vermouzek, 'Dobytčí cesta', *Jižní Morava*, 28 (1992), 54–66; and *Itinerar König und Kaiser Sigismund von Luxemburg 1368–1437*, ed. J. K. Hoensch (Warendorf 1995), 57.

67. His itinerary is published in Štěpán, *Moravský markrabě* (as in n. 65), 125–26, 828.

68. Expenses for these gifts appear in the accounts; *Expeditions* (as in n. 63), 289.

69. *Expeditions* (as in n. 63), lvii, 190, 279–80. On Jošt's residence and possible gallery, see Baletka, 'Dvůr, rezidence a kancelář' (as in n. 65), 281–82.

70. *Expeditions* (as in n. 63), 188–94.

71. 'pro peperi, gingibre, canella, sugre, amigdalis confectis … pro carne bouum, multonum et vitulorum, porcis et salsis … pro aucis, caponibus, pullis, pulcinis, columbellis, malardez, et farina auenarum … pro vergus, vinegre, senape, et aliis diuersis salsis'; *Expeditions* (as in n. 66), 191. See also Suchý, '"Na cestě"' (as in n. 63), 125–27.

72. *Expeditions* (as in n. 63), 262.

73. 'pro emendacione diuersarum sellarum domini'; *Expeditions* (as in n. 63), 191.

74. 'pro emendacione j paris de vambras domini'; *Expeditions* (as in n. 63), 280.

75. 'pro i vlna de satyn … pro i pilche … pro i pare de botes furratis cum blanket pro domino'; *Expeditions* (as in n. 63), 280.

76. 'pro sotularibus … pro panno … pro factura ij gounarum pro dictis hensmen'; *Expeditions* (as in n. 63), 279–80. On henksmen, see ibid., xcvi, n. b.

77. *Expeditions* (as in n. 63), 279. See also Suchý, '"Na cestě"' (as in n. 63), 131–32.

78. 'Item domino Hugoni Herlee pro ij superaltaribus per ipsum emptis ibidem, XVIIj gr. Item pro imposicione dictarum petrarum in tabulis, et seruientibus episcopi laborantibus circa consecracionem earundem per manus dicti domini Hugonis ibidem, XV gr.'; *Expeditions* (as in n. 63), 279. On Hugo Herlee, see *Expeditions*, li, xcii. The claim that it was probably Archbishop Jan of Jenstein who performed the consecration is made in F. M. Bartoš, *Čechy v době Husově 1378–1415* (Prague 1947), 100.

79. 'Item eidem pro registro portiforii domini empto ibidem per manus eiusdem, VIII gr.'; *Expeditions* (as in n. 63), 279. See also Suchý, '"Na cestě"' (as in n. 63), 132.

80. 'Item Hanz Goldsmyth, pro XIIII colers, quorum IX sunt deaurati, ab ipso emptis apud Prake'; *Expeditions* (as in n. 63), 280. It interesting that 'Hanuss aurifaber domini imperatoris' is located in sources in Hradčanské Square (Hradčanské náměstí) in 1373; Tomek, *Základy* (as in n. 7), 139, no. 63. See also Suchý, '"Na cestě"' (as in n. 63), 132.

81. Gorfronio de Zewele appears in sources, in 1348 as a knight of King Edward (*Archivum coronae regni Bohemiae II*, ed. V. Hrubý (Prague 1928), 73–74, no. 67); in 1364 as Bernardus de Cedelicz, 'miles Wratislav. diec.' (F. Tadra, *Kulturní styky Čech s cizinou až do válek husitských* (Prague 1897), 164, pozn. 2); in 1380 as Bernardus van Sedles/Zetles (*Foedera* (as in n. 12), 101, and *Diplomatic Correspondence* (as in n. 28), 13, no. 18); in 1383 and 1384 as Bernard de Credelicz (*Acta imperii* (as in n. 3), 644, no. 984, and Perroy, *Grand Schisme* (as in n. 2), 164). Tadra (*Kulturní styky Čech*, 164, n. 2) states that he was Bohemian; Perroy (*Grand Schisme*, 145) connects him with Germany; and Given-Wilson (*The Royal Household* (as in n. 20), 283) suggests he came from The Netherlands. Simpson (*The Connections* (as in n. 20), 37) mentions the possibility of the south Bohemian town of Sedlec, but this possibility had already been excluded by Betts; R. R. Betts, 'English and Czech Influences on the Hussite Movement', in *Essays in Czech History* (London 1969), 138, n. 16. Trautz (*Die Könige von England* (as in n. 9), 372) is probably right when talking about 'Schlesier Bernhard von Zedlitz', especially when we consider that the duchy of Těšín (unlike south Bohemia) belonged to the diocese of Vratislavia (Wrocław). Reitemeier (*Aussenpolitik* (as in n. 3), 329) even mentions that, while Bernhard von Zedlitz was in Richard's service, Nikolaus von Zedlitz was in the service of King Wenceslas.

82. Walker, 'Sir Richard Abberbury' (as in n. 20), 128–29; on his diplomatic activity, see Reitemeier, *Aussenpolitik* (as in n. 3), 182–282, 495.

83. Simpson, *The Connections* (as in n. 20), 47. On his diplomatic activity, see Reitemeier, *Aussenpolitik* (as in n. 3), 188–222, 495–96.

84. *Diplomatic Correspondence* (as in n. 28), 97, no. 143.

85. ibid., 20–21, no. 34. For an attempt to see the letter in connection with Anglo-Scandinavian negotiations, see M. Suchý, 'Scandinavia and the Great Schism 1378: a study into international politics and cultural contacts' (unpublished M.Phil. thesis, University of Oslo, 2001), 43–47. See also A. Tuck, 'Some Evidence for Anglo-Scandinavian Relations at the End of the Fourteenth Century', *Mediaeval Scandinavia*, 5 (1972), 78–79, and E. Haug, *Provincia Nidrosiensis i dronning Margretes unions- og maktpolitikk* (Trondheim 1996), 166–67, 199–205. According to Reitemeier (*Aussenpolitik* (as in n. 3), 333), Johannes Lantgraf was the eldest son of Elisabeth, Lantgräfin von Leuchtenberg, who accompanied Anne of Luxembourg to England; see also n. 23 above.

86. The English chronicler especially disliked shoes 'with long pykes'; *Polychronicon* (as in n. 33), VIII, 497. The same disgust towards 'calceos rostratos et cum londissimis nasibus' was expressed by his Bohemian counterpart in Prague several decades earlier; 'Chronicon Benessi de Weitmil', *Fontes rerum bohemicarum* (as in n. 4), IV (1884), 536. For other examples of Bohemian fashion (clothes), see Reitemeier, *Aussenpolitik* (as in n. 3), 460–61 n. 178. The sources explicitly mention also saddles and a shrine in St Paul's. For saddles ('veille celle guyse de Boeme'), see M. V. Clarke, 'Forfeitures and Treason in 1388', in *Fourteenth Century Studies*, ed. L. S. Sutherland and M. McKisack (Oxford 1937), 118. For the shrine ('imperiale feretrum valde curiosum'), see *Westminster Chronicle* (as in n. 33), 516–17, and *Polychronicon*, IX, 280. See also Simpson, *The Connections* (as in n. 20), 44–45, and Bennet, 'Richard II and the Wider Realm' (as in n. 32), 200. Bohemian musicians Piere Organer and Haukyn Guyterner played (Bohemian music?) at Sheen in February 1384; Reitemeier, *Aussenpolitik* (as in n. 3), 404.

87. Simpson, *The Connections* (as in n. 20), 190; N. Saul, 'The Kingship of Richard II', in *Richard II: The Art of Kingship*, ed. A. Goodman and J. Gillespie (Oxford 2003), 43–45; G. Matthew, *The Court of Richard II* (London 1968), 22–23. V. J. Scattergood, 'Literary Culture at the court of Richard II', in *English Court Culture in the Later Middle Ages*, ed. V. J. Scattergood and J. W. Sherborne (London 1983), 29–43; P. Strohm, *Social Chaucer* (Cambridge 1989), 24–46; V. Krása, *Die Handschriften König Wenzels*, trans. H. Gaertner (Vienna 1971).

88. Clarke, 'Forfeitures and Treason' (as in n. 86), 120.

89. See n. 19.

90. Saul, *Richard II* (as in n. 11), 455–56.

91. She met one of 'the Seven' (John Montague, steward of the household), who was already in Calais in 1381; Perroy, *Grand Schisme* (as in n. 2), 154. For discussion and further bibliography, see K. B. Mc Farlane, *Lancastrian Kings and Lollard Knights* (Oxford 1972); Saul, *Richard II* (as in n. 11), 297–303; and K. Walsh, 'Lollardisch-hussitische Reformbestrebungen' (as in n. 23), 77–108.

92. Peter Payne, the English helper of Faulfiš and Kněhnic in Oxford, came to Prague to partake in the Hussite uprising at the beginning of 1415 at the latest. For discussion and further bibliography, see, for example, A. Hudson, 'From Oxford to Prague: The Writings of John Wyclif and his English Followers in Bohemia', *The Slavonic and East European Review*, 75 (1997), 642–57; A. Hudson, 'Accessus ad Auctorem: The case of John Wyclif', *Viator*, 30 (1999), 323–44; S. Petr, 'The new Floretum - Rosarium manuscripts found in libraries of Czech and Moravian chateaux', *Studie o rukopisech*, 30 (1995, for 1993–94), 29–43; M. Lambert, *Medieval Heresy*, 2nd edn (Oxford 1992), 243–83; and F. Šmahel, 'Curriculum vitae Magistri Petri Payne', in *In memoriam Josefa Macka* (Prague 1996), 141–60.

93. Hudson, 'From Oxford to Prague' (as in n. 92), 657.

94. Thomas, duke of Norfolk, was to cross Almain, Bohemia and Hungary before traversing the great sea on pilgrimage in 1398; *CPR* (as in n. 5), Richard II (VI, 420).

95. See D. M. B. de Mesquita, 'The Foreign Policy of Richard II in 1397: Some Italian Letters', *English Historical Review*, 56 (1941), 628–37; J. J. N. Palmer, 'England and the Western Schism, 1388–1399', *English Historical Review*, 83 (1968), 516–22; J. J. N. Palmer, 'English Foreign Policy 1388–99', in *Essays in Honour of May McKisack* (London 1971), 75–107; J. H. Harvey, 'Richard II and York', ibid., 202–17; Bennet, 'Richard II and the Wider Realm' (as in n. 32), 196–97; and Reitemeier, *Aussenpolitik* (as in n. 3), 182–254.

The Church of St Bartholomew at Kyje

ERIC FERNIE

The plain and undecorated character of the 13th-century church of St Bartholomew at Kyje near Prague is difficult to attribute to poverty, as its patrons were the bishops of Prague. Similarly, the defensive character of the design is contradicted by the fact that the building would be difficult, if not impossible, to defend. It is proposed here that the character of building is not explained by either poverty or defence, but by the fact that it is a bishop's chapel and as such a member of a type in which oddity is a sought-after characteristic.

THE church of St Bartholomew stands on what was a manor of the bishop of Prague east of the city in the village of Kyje (Figs 1–3). It is both magnificent and odd. It is only 22 m (72 ft) long and consists of a rectangular chancel, a two-bay nave, and a massive oblong western tower the same width as the nave. The tower has three original storeys: the ground floor, the gallery floor open to the nave, and a third above that, with access via wall passages. Every part of the church is groin-vaulted, apart from the third storey of the tower. There is very little architectural decoration. An inscription on the north wall of the chancel has been read as saying 'FUNDATOR. HVIVS. ECLE. IOHES. PRAG. EPSC.' (that is, 'FUNDATOR HUIUS EC(C)L(ESI)E IOH(ANN)ES PRAG(ENSIS) EP(I)SC(OPUS)'). As there were no fewer than four bishops called Jan between the mid-12th and early 14th centuries, the information does not help to date the building, but it does associate it with the bishops of Prague. A date in the 13th century is generally agreed, not least because the arch opening from the gallery into the nave is pointed, and it is difficult to find dated examples of the form in Bohemia before c. 1200, the earliest appearing to be, for example, Osek from c. 1207, Velehrad in Moravia begun in 1205, or Teplá consecrated in 1232. The chief additions are what is now the sacristy on the north side of the nave and the western porch and doorway. The fourth, topmost, storey of the tower was rebuilt in the 19th century. The church was extensively restored in the 1970s and 1980s. The key publications are the article by Dalibor Prix and Zuzana Všetčková in *Umění* (1993), which provide a complete historiography and a thorough analysis of the building, including explanatory drawings, and the invaluable book by Klára Benešovská, Tomáš Durdík and Zdeněk Dragoun, in English, on Romanesque architecture in the Czech Republic (2001).[1]

This church type consisting of a chancel, a nave and a west tower is common in Bohemia in the 12th and 13th centuries, as it is throughout the territories of the Latin Church in the Romanesque period. Chancels in Bohemia are most often given an apse, but rectangular east ends like that at Kyje are also common, as in St Ursula at Újezdec (Fig. 4). A short nave is almost the rule, some examples being only slightly longer than a square, as also at Újezdec. Passages and stairs in the thickness of the wall are very common. The groins at Kyje have been considered as both original and as additions.

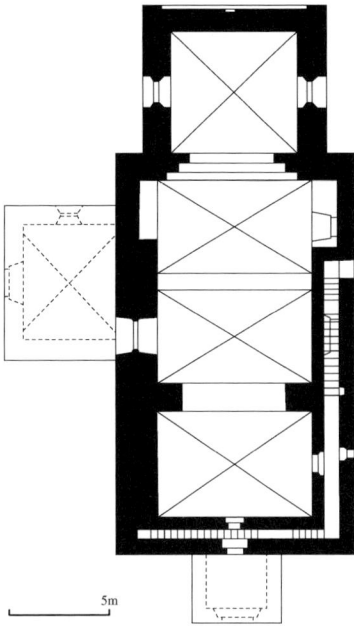

FIG. 1.   Kyje, St Bartholomew: ground-plan (Benešovská et al., *Architecture of the Romanesque* (as in n. 1), 84)

5m

FIG. 2.   Kyje, St Bartholomew: view from the south-west (Benešovská et al., *Architecture of the Romanesque* (as in n. 1), 85)

FIG. 3. Kyje, St Bartholomew: interior, to the east (Benešovská et al.,
Architecture of the Romanesque (as in n. 1), 85)

Although rib-vaults were introduced from the late 12th century over the main spans of the
large abbey churches, groin-vaults continued to be used in parts even of the large buildings
and as a matter of course in the smaller churches into the 13th century.[2]

In this paper I would like to explore three aspects of Kyje Church in particular,
namely the western gallery and tower; whether the church was built as a refuge; and
the role of the bishops of Prague in its design.

THE WESTERN GALLERY AND TOWER

A western gallery is a common feature of Bohemian Romanesque architecture, as for
example again at Újezdec, and suggests that the buildings were probably magnates'
churches, including those of bishops. The thesis that the westworks of the Carolingian
and Ottonian periods were built for the emperor has been discredited, but its
equivalent here can be defended for two reasons: because the magnates in question,
unlike the emperors, would have made frequent use of the gallery, and because such
provision might be expected where a system of parishes, which involved wider sources
of responsibility, was not widespread, even in the 13th century.[3]

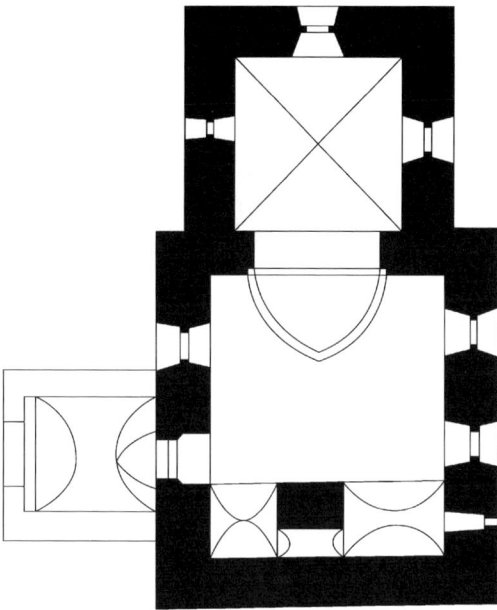

FIG. 4. Újezdec, St Ursula: ground-plan
(Benešovská et al., *Architecture of the
Romanesque* (as in n. 1), 174)

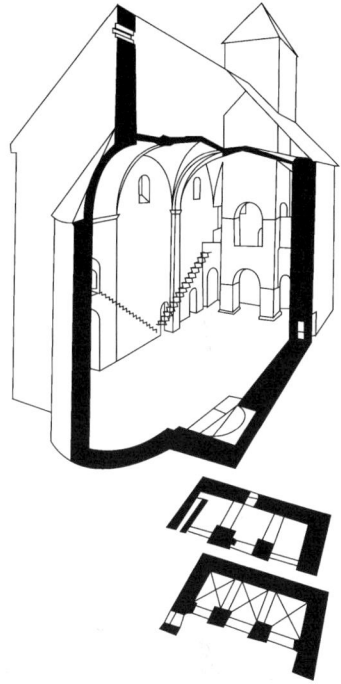

FIG. 5. Prague, St Martin in the Wall:
reconstruction (after Mencl, 'Panské
tribuny' (as in n. 8), fig. 100)

There are three chief ways in which a gallery is related to a tower in Bohemian churches of this date. In the first, the gallery is situated in the nave and the tower is placed over it, as at Újezdec and St Martin in the Wall (sv. Martin ve zdi) in Prague (Figs 4–5). As it is not evident from the plan that there is a tower, churches with this arrangement can be separated from the standard three-cell type. In the second, the gallery is at the west end of the nave as in the first type, but the tower is attached to the west face of the nave beyond it, as in the standard three-cell type, as for example at St James at Jakub near Kutná Hora, which has an inscription mentioning a consecration in 1165.[4] In the third, the gallery is situated in the tower, as at Kyje (Fig. 6). While a gallery set in the nave, as in the first two types, resembles a piece of furniture, like a box in the theatre, a gallery in a tower forms part of the structure and can be related to the great tower or keep, and hence with the power of magnates.

The gallery at Kyje is reached via a stair in the south wall of the nave. The entrance to the stair at ground level is currently internal, but the published plans also show an entrance from the outside, and there is a blocked archway visible on the exterior. Because of the restored state of the evidence it is difficult to be certain, but, if access to the gallery was provided from the outside, the arrangement would in that respect resemble Charlemagne's 8th-century palace chapel in Aachen and the 6th-century imperial church of H. Sergios and Bakchos in Constantinople, though the entrances in those churches led directly into the first floor.

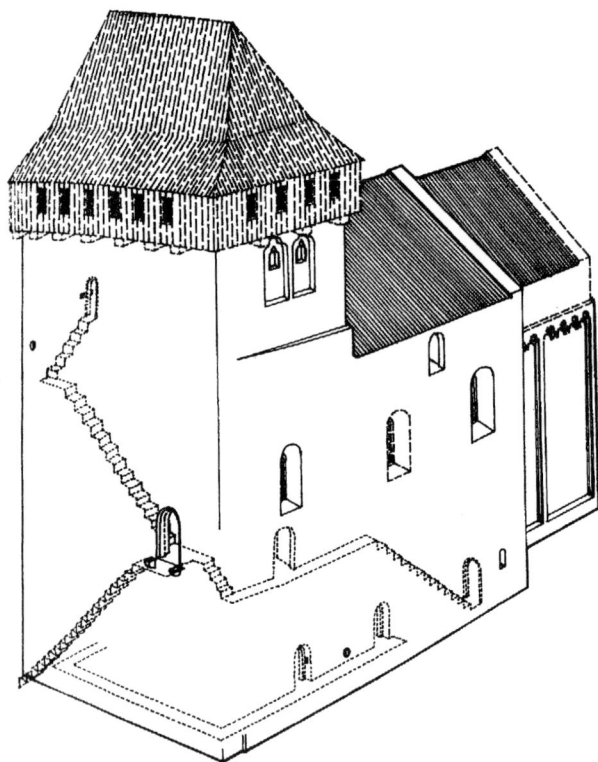

FIG. 6. Kyje, St Bartholomew: view from the south-west, reconstruction (Prix and Všetečková, 'Středověký kostel' (as in n. 1), fig. 6)

The doorway in the west wall at gallery level, with two corbels on the exterior to support a platform, has been explained in two very different ways. According to one view, it was an entrance approached by a flight of stairs either attached to the façade or freestanding to the west. Against this interpretation is the absence of evidence of an attached stair on the wall, or of supports for a free-standing one in the ground. The second explanation, and on the evidence the more likely one, is that the doorway was not an entrance but the means of access to a balcony, supported on the two corbels and used for presentation and display, as of relics, or for legal pronouncements.[5]

Every element I have discussed so far is common in the Bohemian small church type. The oblong west tower the same width as the nave is, on the contrary, very difficult to parallel. St Martin's in Prague is an example (Fig. 5). It is, however, very different from Kyje, as it belongs to the first of my three categories of gallery and tower arrangement, where the gallery is in the nave and the tower stands above it, that is, the nave is open right to the westernmost wall of the church. Contrariwise these two characteristics, the oblong shape of the tower and the position of the gallery, are common in village churches of the 12th and 13th centuries in eastern Saxony, as at Bernburg-Waldau, Dambeck, Thalheim and Melkow (Fig. 7). These buildings differ from Kyje in having a longer nave, an apse, and ceilings rather than vaults.[6]

THE CHURCH AS A REFUGE

THERE is disagreement over whether Kyje was designed as a refuge, with, for example, Grueber and Prix and Všetečková in favour, and Mencl and Merhautová against (Fig. 8). There are no fewer than five pieces of evidence in favour, namely (i) the appearance of the building; (ii) the jambs of all the doorways, which indicate that they were intended to be locked from the inside; (iii) the restricted access to the ground-floor room of the tower, which is only via a wall passage from the nave; (iv) the placing of the stairs in wall passages; and (v) a document of 1281, which describes a dispute at Potvorov over who went where when the tower was used as a refuge, together with the existence of similar physical arrangements at Čelákovice, Dolní Počernice, Malý Bor, and Planá by Marianské Lázně. The third storey of the tower, the one above the gallery, was therefore for the defence of the lord and his retinue, and the lofts of nave and chancel, with lockable doors, added to their options (Fig. 8).[7]

This sounds like an irrefutable case, but in my view the argument against is stronger. As Mencl and Merhautová have pointed out, the arrangement of the jambs of the doorways at Kyje could indicate nothing more than a need for general security, with the ground floor of the tower as a strong-room, while the wall passages could have been intended to avoid the visual clutter of staircases in the nave and elsewhere.[8] The fact that a building was used as a refuge does not mean it was designed to be one: any masonry

FIG. 7.   Melkow, brick church (after *Deutsche Kunstdenkmäler* (as in n. 6), pl. 190)

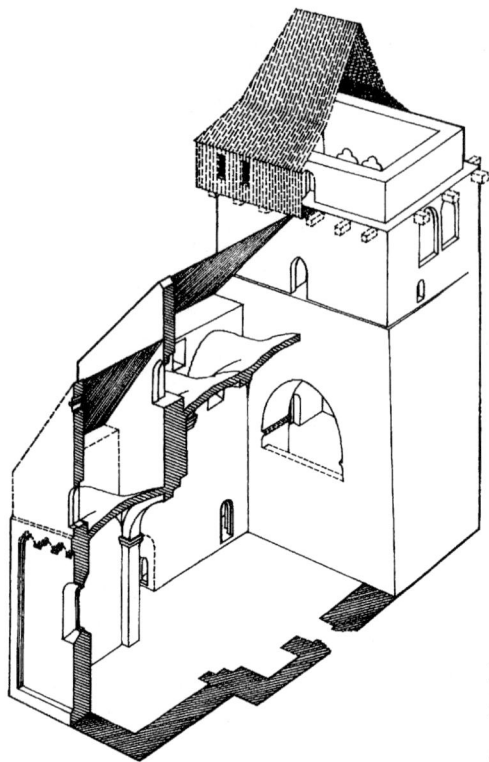

FIG. 8. Kyje, St Bartholomew: exploded reconstruction from the north-east (Prix and Všetečková, 'Středověký kostel' (as in n. 1), fig. 5)

building is clearly preferable to a wattle-and-daub hut or a wooden hall in the event of an attack. In a period of instability, rights to the most secure parts could have become codified, as at Potvorov.

The fact is that St Bartholomew is very badly designed for any sort of defence, especially in the upper parts of the tower. These are vulnerable to assault because of the easy access provided by the stepping up of the roofs of the chancel and nave right to the level of the third storey. The arrangement is the equivalent of building a donjon with a series of structures of increasing height against one of its walls. There is also the fact that the chancel steps in from the nave, forming areas hidden from the tower. Finally, the lofts have a fundamental weakness as refuges, because the roof covering, whether of thatch, tiles or slates, would have been easily removable.

The free-standing round towers of Ireland of the 10–13th centuries meet the requirements of a refuge, whatever other functions they may have had, while some churches, especially those in the south of France like Les Saintes-Maries-de-la-Mer in the Camargue, are properly defensible, with battlements all round, in consequence looking very different from other churches (Fig. 9).[9] If the third storey at Kyje could not be easily defended, what was its purpose? The usual function of the upper storeys of towers in medieval buildings was the hanging of bells, so, if the missing fourth storey housed the bells, the third storey would have been for the bell-ringers. The building would

FIG. 9. Les Saintes-Marie-de-la-Mer
Conway Library, Courtauld Institute of Art

have looked much as it does now (Fig. 2), but with arched double or triple bell-openings in the top storey.

This leaves the fact that the building looks as if it was designed for defence, which raises the question, if Kyje was not built to be defended, why does it look as if it was? All the elements of which the building is formed contribute to a sense of simplicity and massiveness, from the widely used ones like the rectangular chancel and the groin-vaults, to the unusual ones, like the tower being the same width as the nave. There is also the sparseness of the architectural decoration. On the exterior it is restricted to the chancel, with pilasters which might have carried a corbel table, and a north portal, of which there are fragmentary remains, and on the interior to the orders of the chancel arch (Figs 10 and 3). The contrast with Vinec, like Kyje attributed to the middle decades of the 13th century, is striking, as the whole exterior there is articulated by pilasters, shafts, and heavily moulded arched corbel tables (Fig. 11).

The restricted decoration could be taken as a sign of an early date, were it not for the pointed arch, which, with other elements, indicates the 13th century. Alternatively it might suggest that St Bartholomew was a poorly funded, out-of-the-way church using old-fashioned designers and unsophisticated craftsmen. This, however, is contradicted by the fact that it was built by a bishop of Prague, and that he and his successors were proud

FIG. 10. Kyje,
St Bartholomew: view
from the south-east
Concordia Pax, Prague

of the fact, as 14th-century wall-paintings in the chancel depict a number of them. In other words, the building, rather than being a standard magnate's church, was a bishop's chapel.

THE ROLE OF THE BISHOPS

THE difference between a magnate's church and a bishop's chapel may appear to be minimal, as a bishop is simply one kind of magnate, but the bishop's chapel is one of the most interesting types in the canon of church buildings, and one which I think might help to explain the odd character of St Bartholomew. Many examples of bishops' chapels are unusual, to the extent that one can claim it as a characteristic of the type. All the characteristics of St Bartholomew make it an unusual design, its simple, massive, old-fashioned aspect perhaps intended to be read as encapsulating the associated virtues.

30

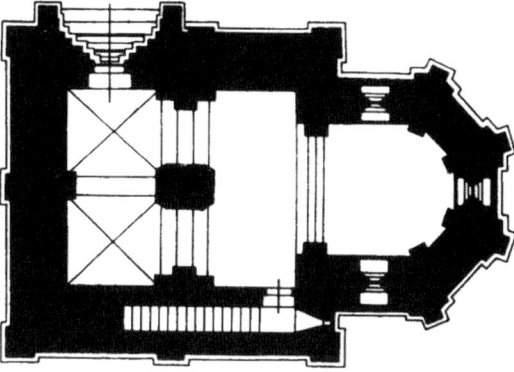

FIG. 11. Vinec, St Nicholas:
ground-plan and portal
(Benešovská et al., *Architecture of
the Romanesque* (as in n. 1), 150)

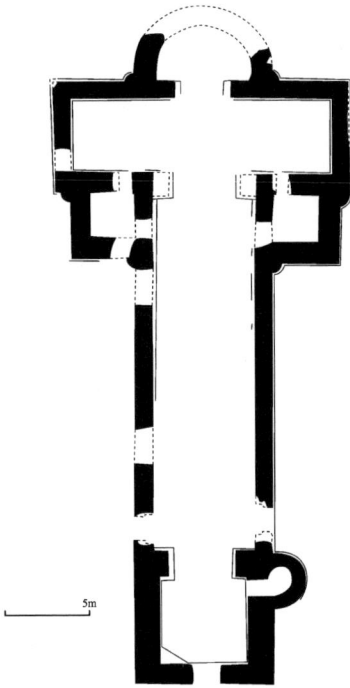

Fig. 12. North Elmham, bishop's chapel: ground-plan (Fernie, *The Architecture of Norman England* (as in n. 10), fig. 176)

The small church at Idensen in central Saxony built as his burial place by Sigward, bishop of Minden 1120–40, is a good example of a bishop's chapel. It shares features with the buildings in eastern Saxony already mentioned, namely an oblong west tower the same width as the nave, a chancel, and an apse. It differs from them, however, in having a transept, a very unusual feature in a small, longitudinal church, but the sort of sport one might expect in a bishop's chapel.

I cannot resist calling attention in this context to the unusual character of bishops' chapels in Norman England, and to one of the most unusual, that of the late 11th or early 12th century at North Elmham in Norfolk (Fig. 12). This had a west tower the same width as the nave (as at Kyje and Idensen), and a transept (as at Idensen), though in this case it is a miniature version of the continuous type of Old St Peter's. Of course there are no links between the Norman building and either Kyje or Idensen, but there could be a parallel use of features for other reasons chiefly related to prestige.[10]

* * *

To conclude, I do not pretend that this study is anything more than partial. Numerous questions remain, concerning, first, possible parallels in buildings such as those at Milevsko, Čelákovice, Dolní Počernice, Malý Bor, Planá by Marianské Lázně, and St Martin in the Wall in Prague, as well as other churches in the vicinity of the city, and concerning, second, elements I have commented on (such as wall passages), and others I have not (such as the arched recesses in the nave walls).

The concept of 'oddity' may appear to be a subjective intrusion from the modern age. I hope, however, that I have provided sufficient evidence first to support the view that the characteristic could have been actively sought, and second to establish the status of St Bartholomew not only as a bishop's chapel, but as a prime example of the genre.

ACKNOWLEDGEMENTS

It is a great pleasure to record my thanks to Dr Klára Benešovská, for information about the church at Kyje and other structures; to the custodians of the church for their kindness in facilitating my study of the building; and as always to Agnieszka Rożnowska-Sadraei and Zoë Opačić for access to the literature in Czech and for their very helpful comments on the paper. I would also like to thank Dalibor Prix, Richard Plant (especially for Idensen), and Andreas Puth for their helpful comments on the paper at the conference, and to record my thanks to the Leverhulme Trust for the Emeritus Fellowship, which among other things funded my research in the Czech Republic.

NOTES

1. D. Prix and Z. Všetečková, 'Středověký kostel sv. Bartoloměje v Praze 9-Kyjích do počátku husitských válek', *Umění*, 41 (1993), 231–61; K. Benešovská, P. Chotěbor, T. Durdík and Z. Dragoun, *Architecture of the Romanesque* (Prague 2001).

2. Benešovská et al. (as in n. 1), 174.

3. On westworks, see É. Fels, 'Études sur les églises-porches carolingiennes et leur survivance', *Bulletin Monumental*, 92 (1933), 331–65; 96 (1937), 425–69; and C. Sapin ed., *Avant-nefs et espaces d'accueil dans l'église entre le IVe et le XIIe siècle* (Auxerre 2002). On the parish system, see Z. Boháč, 'Vývoj diecézní organizace českých zemí', in *Traditio & Cultus: Miscellanea Historica Bohemica*, ed. Z. Hledíková (Prague 1993), 21–35.

4. Benešovská et al. (as in n. 1), 114.

5. For a parallel arrangement in Anglo-Saxon England, see M. Hare, 'The ninth-century west porch of St Mary's church, Deerhurst, Gloucestershire: form and function', *Medieval Archaeology*, forthcoming, 2009.

6. *Deutsche Kunstdenkmäler: Provinz Sachsen, Land Anhalt* (Darmstadt 1968), pls 12, 19, 190 and 323.

7. Prix and Všetečková (as in n. 1), 241; Benešovská et al. (as in n. 1), 154. The question of defence is the only basic point on which I find myself in disagreement with Prix and Všetečková.

8. V. Mencl, 'Panské tribuny v naší románské architektuře', *Umění*, 13 (1965), 29–62; A. Merhautová and D. Třeštík, *Románské uměni v Čechách a na Moravě* (Prague 1983), 258.

9. On the Irish towers, see R. Stalley, 'Sex, symbol, and myth: some observations on the Irish round towers', *From Ireland Coming*, ed. C. Hourihane (Princeton 2001), 27–47. Stalley argues against their having been built as refuges, but he also acknowledges (pers. comm.) that the possibility certainly remains open. On the Southern French defended churches, see S. Bonde, *Fortress-Churches of Languedoc: Architecture, Religion, and Conflict in the High Middle Ages* (Cambridge 1994).

10. E. Fernie, *The Architecture of Norman England* (Oxford 2000), 233–42.

Romanesque Prague and New Archaeological Discoveries

ZDENĚK DRAGOUN

This article presents a short summary of the development of Romanesque architecture in Prague, together with a description of the main features of the most recent archeological discoveries relating to the city's early-medieval buildings, both sacred and secular.

VISITORS and experts alike have been attracted to Prague because of the stylistic diversity of its buildings and its rich architectural history. Among the earliest buildings are those belonging to the Romanesque period, many of which have attracted attention in the past; the remains of others, found only below ground level, have had to await discovery for a number of years. These buildings have been recorded in scholarly literature, featured in the surveys of Romanesque architecture, and more recently been the subject of specialised studies devoted to the Romanesque architecture of Prague (Fig. 1).[1] The development of Romanesque architecture in Prague is also indicative of how this new style of building developed elsewhere in Bohemia, as it was first introduced in the capital, then rapidly spread to other parts of the country.

The appearance of the first stone structures of a pre-Romanesque character, in the 9th and 10th centuries, in Bohemia as a whole and in Prague in particular, is closely linked to the arrival of Christianity. Soon after the baptism in Moravia of the Bohemian Duke Bořivoj (868–89), the oldest stone sanctuary in Bohemia, the church of Our Lady, was erected in the 890s at the ducal seat of Prague Castle, in the form of a simple rectangular nave with an apse. The first phase of St George's, the second church in Prague Castle and also Bohemia's first monastic foundation, dates from the beginning of the 10th century; its present appearance however reflects the renovations made following a fire in 1140. St Vitus's Cathedral itself had two Romanesque predecessors — a rotunda established by Duke Wenceslas in the first third of the 10th century, and a Romanesque basilica with a transept and a double choir from the end of the 11th century. Before the middle of the 12th century, stone fortifications were erected around the castle stronghold, with a polygonal bastion on the south side in the immediate vicinity of the palace, and three tower gateways, the White Tower (Bílá věž), Black Tower (Černá věž), and South Tower (Jižní věž). The great multi-storey Romanesque ducal palace, including the chapel of All Saints, was part of that development.[2]

Prague's second stronghold, at Vyšehrad, underwent a similar development. Its origins have been dated to the second half of the 10th century, and the earliest phase of St Lawrence's church, built on a cruciform plan, probably dates from that period; this was replaced in the 11th century by a small basilica. The main church at Vyšehrad, dedicated to Sts Peter and Paul, was also a basilica with a double chancel.

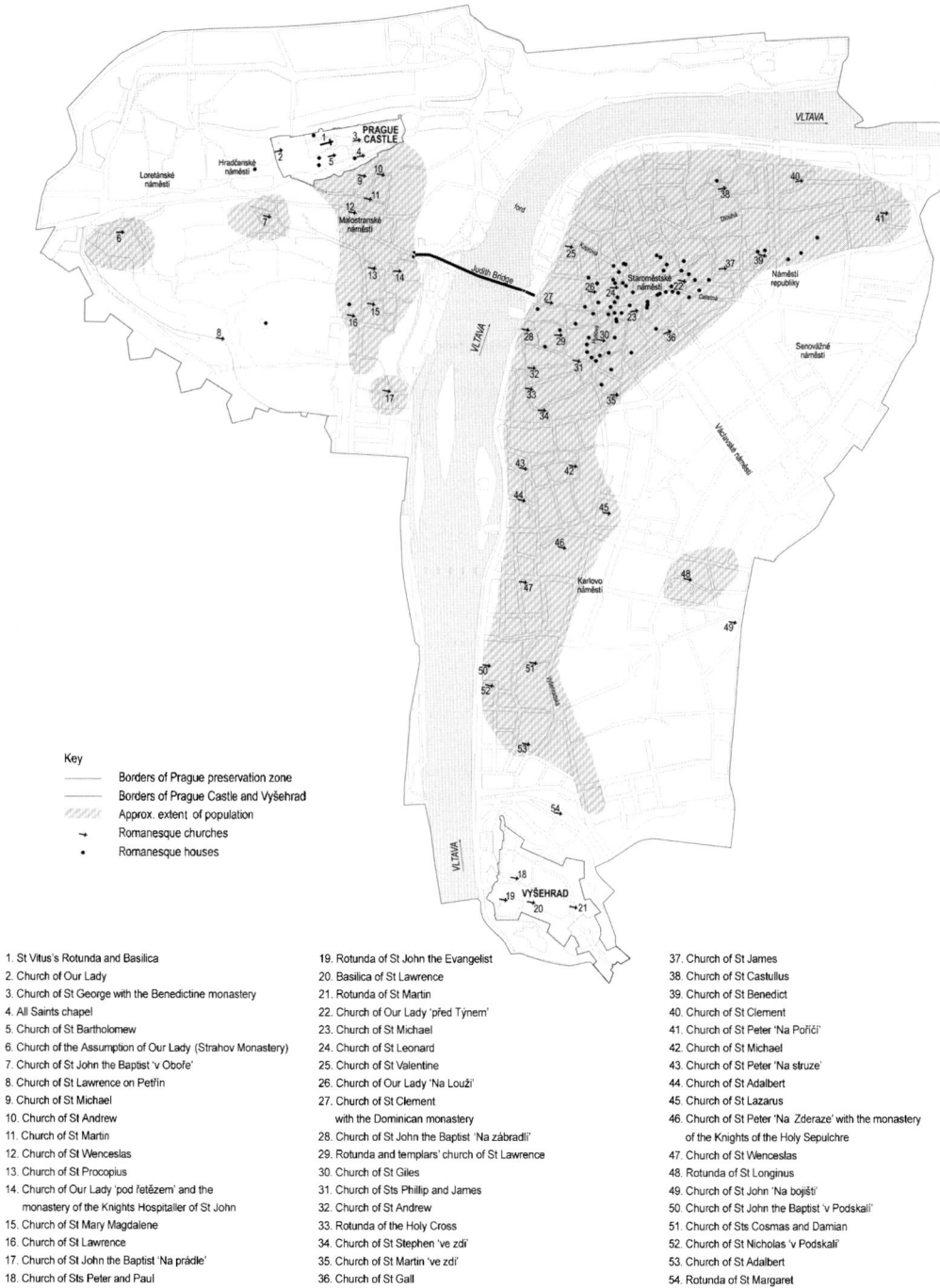

Key

—	Borders of Prague preservation zone
—	Borders of Prague Castle and Vyšehrad
▨	Approx. extent of population
→	Romanesque churches
•	Romanesque houses

1. St Vitus's Rotunda and Basilica
2. Church of Our Lady
3. Church of St George with the Benedictine monastery
4. All Saints chapel
5. Church of St Bartholomew
6. Church of the Assumption of Our Lady (Strahov Monastery)
7. Church of St John the Baptist 'v Oboře'
8. Church of St Lawrence on Petřín
9. Church of St Michael
10. Church of St Andrew
11. Church of St Martin
12. Church of St Wenceslas
13. Church of St Procopius
14. Church of Our Lady 'pod řetězem' and the monastery of the Knights Hospitaller of St John
15. Church of St Mary Magdalene
16. Church of St Lawrence
17. Church of St John the Baptist 'Na prádle'
18. Church of Sts Peter and Paul

19. Rotunda of St John the Evangelist
20. Basilica of St Lawrence
21. Rotunda of St Martin
22. Church of Our Lady 'před Týnem'
23. Church of St Michael
24. Church of St Leonard
25. Church of St Valentine
26. Church of Our Lady 'Na Louži'
27. Church of St Clement with the Dominican monastery
28. Church of St John the Baptist 'Na zábradlí'
29. Rotunda and templars' church of St Lawrence
30. Church of St Giles
31. Church of Sts Phillip and James
32. Church of St Andrew
33. Rotunda of the Holy Cross
34. Church of St Stephen 've zdi'
35. Church of St Martin 've zdi'
36. Church of St Gall

37. Church of St James
38. Church of St Castullus
39. Church of St Benedict
40. Church of St Clement
41. Church of St Peter 'Na Poříčí'
42. Church of St Michael
43. Church of St Peter 'Na struze'
44. Church of St Adalbert
45. Church of St Lazarus
46. Church of St Peter 'Na Zderaze' with the monastery of the Knights of the Holy Sepulchre
47. Church of St Wenceslas
48. Rotunda of St Longinus
49. Church of St John 'Na bojišti'
50. Church of St John the Baptist 'v Podskalí'
51. Church of Sts Cosmas and Damian
52. Church of St Nicholas 'v Podskalí'
53. Church of St Adalbert
54. Rotunda of St Margaret

FIG. I. Romanesque Prague at the beginning of the 13th century
Zdeněk Dragoun and Stanislava Babušková

On the south side the church precinct was linked by a stone footbridge to the area of the royal court, the likely site of a stone-built palace and the rotunda of St John the Evangelist mentioned in documents from 1258, 1264 and 1267. Another rotunda, situated in the eastern part of the fortress and dedicated to St Martin, has survived, albeit in slightly reconstructed form. The stone ramparts of this second royal seat have not been identified.[3]

Somewhat later — from the 11th century, and above all during the 12th century — Romanesque stone architecture also appeared in the area between the two strongholds on both banks of the Vltava. Several small churches, including at least two rotundas, were constructed within the settlement on the left bank. Most of these have not survived, and information about them is found solely in occasional references to them in documents; their locations are no longer precisely known. After the mid-12th century, there was major building development southwards on the left bank, including the construction of several new churches that are entirely Romanesque in appearance. One of them, St Lawrence's, in today's Malá Strana district, had a rectangular chancel that is unusual for Prague. A solitary Romanesque church with a rectangular nave and semicircular apse, also dedicated to St Lawrence, was erected on the top of Petřín Hill. In addition, after the mid-12th century, the Knights Hospitaller established a monastery on the left bank, and with it the church of Our Lady beneath the Chain (P. Marie pod řetězem) in the form of a smallish triple-aisled basilica, with the square courtyard of the commandery's buildings on the south side of the church.

It is still not entirely clear what sort of stone fortifications replaced the older defences below the castle on the left bank, which had consisted of an earth rampart reinforced with timber, and a front wall of timber or stone. The remains discovered of stone fortifications set into mortar are all regarded as the town ramparts built in 1257 on the site of an earlier settlement; some parts of that rampart nevertheless were built using the Romanesque ashlar technique, and one cannot therefore rule out the possibility that they are of earlier origin.

The stone buildings of the right bank are certainly later than those on the left, and date mainly from the second half of the 12th century. Within this area more than fifteen churches were built using Romanesque construction methods. Most of those identified are simple, single-cell churches with semicircular apses, although two rotundas are also documented. The centrally planned church of St John the Baptist 'Na zábradlí' was of an interesting design, having three apses, on the east, north and south sides, and a rectangular nave to the west, possibly in the form of a tower. Recent archeological surveys have also revealed the remains of its predecessor, a rectangular church with a single nave and an apse.[4] Basilical layout is adopted only at the church of St Castullus, although it must be pointed out that the Romanesque phases of the Old Town's most important churches, Our Lady before Týn (P. Marie před Týnem), St Nicholas and St Gall, are yet to be identified. Prior to 1235, a series of monastic institutions was established, sometimes attached to existing churches. The Agnes Convent (Anežský klášter) is a Přemyslid foundation dating from the beginning of the 1230s that already displays both Romanesque and Gothic features: brick sections of the wall — the oldest instance of brick Gothic architecture in Prague — are connected directly to the ashlar sections of the oldest buildings on the site.[5] The Old Town fortifications, also built in the 1230s, are regarded as being entirely Gothic in construction, because the walls are wholly of dressed stone.

One of the most important structures in Romanesque Prague was the Judith Bridge (Juditin most), over 500 m long, linking the settlement beneath the castle walls on the left bank to the inhabited areas on the right bank. The bridge was built between

1158 and 1172, and was in use until it was swept away in the floods of 1342. Access to the bridge from the left bank was between a pair of towers, while a tower gate was later added over the second pier from the Old Town side.[6] The same scheme was adopted for the Gothic Charles Bridge (Karlův most), which replaced the Romanesque structure in second half of the 14th century.

The large number of Romanesque dwellings is in many ways the most exceptional aspect of Prague's early-medieval architecture. Larger or smaller vestiges of over sixty-five two- and three-storey stone houses have survived, their dates of construction spanning the last third of the 12th and the first third of the 13th centuries. They include the central living quarters of extensive palatial structures with extremely varied ground-plans, built along the network of streets for the growing urban patriciate, as well as small storehouse-like stone structures located within plots surrounded by mostly timber buildings. Almost all the surviving remains are located within the Old Town of Prague. Their characteristic features include a lower floor in the form of a basement entered from the rear of the plot, not the street; minimal decorative architectural features; and the frequent use of vaulting in place of wooden ceilings (Figs 2–7).[7]

Outside the Old Town precinct in the area that would become the New Town lay a number of independent settlements, within which further Romanesque sanctuaries were established. Once again the dominant sacred form is the small rectangular structure with a semicircular apse, a design used, for example, for the votive church of St John the Evangelist 'on the Battleground' ('Na bojišti'), built to commemorate a battle between two Přemyslid pretenders to the princely throne in 1179. St Longinus's rotunda (originally dedicated to St Stephen) is among those to have survived in a remarkably good condition. The church of St Lazarus, which has not survived, had a rectangular nave and presbytery. The conventual house of the Knights of the Holy Sepulchre and the church of Sts Peter and Paul 'at Zderaz' ('Na Zderaze'), the only monastic complex to have been established during this period on the site of the New Town, close to the present Charles Square (Karlovo náměstí), has disappeared without a trace, so nothing is known of its Romanesque appearance.

Many notable Romanesque churches were built at a number of sites that are now part of the city of Prague, such as Břevnov, the first (male) Benedictine monastery in Bohemia, founded in 993, whose surviving 11th-century crypt belongs to an earlier phase of stone construction.[8] In 1140, a Premonstratensian monastery was founded in Strahov. Its buildings date from the second half of the 12th century, and beneath later alterations the older core of the monastery has survived to a large extent. It is one of the best-preserved Romanesque complexes in the country. The Romanesque precincts consist of the three-aisled basilica of the Assumption of the Our Lady with a north side chapel, a large cloister to the south of the church with a trapezoid pond at the centre, as well as the remains of other monastery buildings of indeterminate function. Remains of the Romanesque enclosing wall of the complex were also uncovered in a number of locations.[9] Also worth mentioning are the St Wenceslas basilica at Prosek and St Bartholomew's church at Kyje, whose architectural features, some apparently defensive in character, are discussed in this volume by Eric Fernie.

Romanesque structures in Prague cover a broad functional and typological spectrum, for which a range of more or less obvious influences and analogies may be identified, particularly in various parts of the neighbouring German empire. Domestic tradition is linked above all with the preference for centrally planned churches. In the 9th, 10th and 11th centuries, stone architecture was concentrated primarily in the princely strongholds or at sites associated with court patronage (e.g., Břevnov

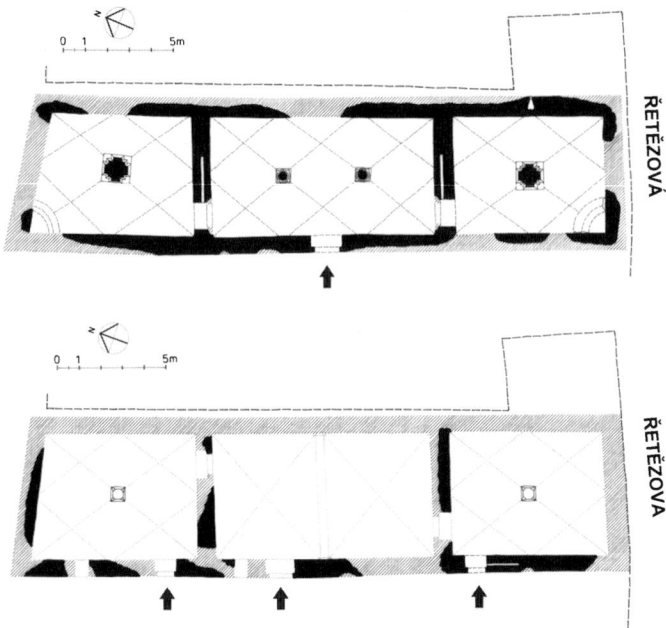

FIG. 2. Prague, Old Town: ground-plan of the ground and first floors of the Romanesque palace on plot no. 222/I, Řetězová Street (Řetězová ulice), with stoves in the corners of the side rooms. Black — preserved walling; hatching — reconstructed walling; broken line — outline of present building; arrows indicate direction of entrance

Stanislava Babušková

FIG. 3. Prague, Old Town: view of central hall of the lowest floor of the Romanesque palace on plot no. 222/I, Řetězová Street

Zdeněk Helfert

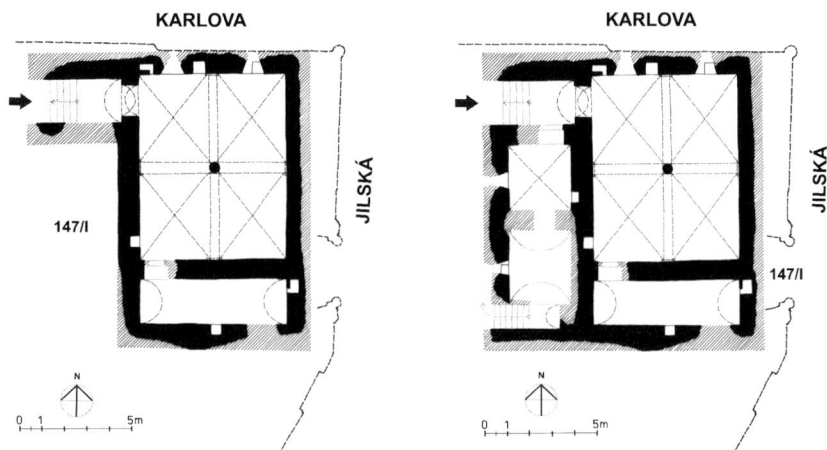

FIG. 4.   Ground-plan of the earlier and later building phases of the lowest floor of the Romanesque house on plot no. 147/I, Jilská Street (Jilská ulice). Two small rooms were added during the second phase; a staircase led from one of them to the first floor. All rooms had stone vaulting. Black — preserved walling; hatching — reconstructed walling; broken line — outline of present building; arrows indicate direction of entrance

Stanislava Babušková

Monastery, which, according to legend, was founded jointly by Duke Boleslav II and Bishop Adalbert). As we have seen, it was not until the 12th century, and in the latter half of that century in particular, that there was a huge expansion in building activity in Prague. During this period, dozens of churches, important monastic foundations, and the unique stone bridge were erected; at the end of it, residential stone-built structures appeared in the settlement beneath Prague Castle. This period is associated above all with the reign of Duke Vladislav II (1140–72), who was crowned king of Bohemia in Regensburg in 1158. It was during his reign that a company of masons came from the Rhineland to Prague to build Strahov Monastery — the first monks came to Strahov from Steinfeld in the Rhineland, and the second group, led by Abbot Gezo in 1143,[10] probably brought with them the masons responsible for the stone monastery — and their work may have influenced other Romanesque architecture in Prague, including the stone bridge. The Strahov Monastery and several dwellings of the suburbium on the right bank, as well as surviving relics of the Judith Bridge, use the same unit of measurement (multiples of the so-called 'Roman foot', 296 mm).

The visible remains of the Late Romanesque structures of the second half of the 12th century are now the main source for our impression of Romanesque Prague. The principal characteristic of the style is the use of light, almost white masonry in courses, modelling simple shapes and spaces. Indeed, the impact of Romanesque architecture in Prague stems from its clean lines and unadorned, severe elegance of expression. The decoration of individual tectonic elements remained, perhaps deliberately, of only peripheral concern.

Practically speaking, only archaeological excavation can now provide the new finds and fresh information that will clarify the extent and form of Prague's Romanesque

FIG. 5. Prague, Old Town: view of the main room of the lowest floor of the house on plot no. 156/I, Husova Street (Husova ulice). The room is vaulted with four quadripartite groin vaults with transverse arches resting on a central column. At the rear is the entry from the narrow side spaces. Two storage niches are visible in the wall, with a window with angled splays above left

Roman Maleček

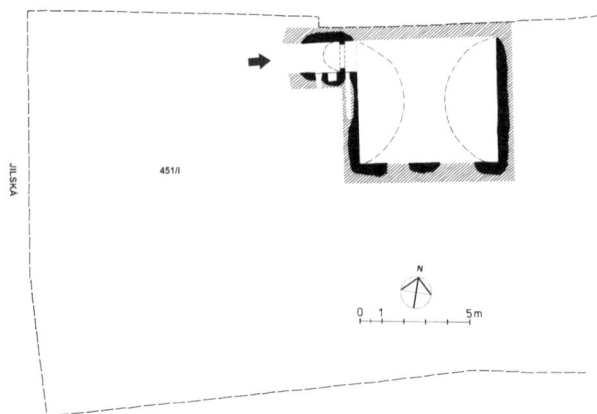

FIG. 6. Prague, Old Town: ground-plan of a single-cell house with covered entrance passage on plot no. 451/I, Jilská Street, which apparently served as a type of storage space that was more resistant to the common risk of fire. In the Romanesque period, the buildings on street level were made of wood. Black — preserved walling; hatching — reconstructed walling; broken line — outline of present building; arrow indicates direction of entrance

Stanislava Babušková

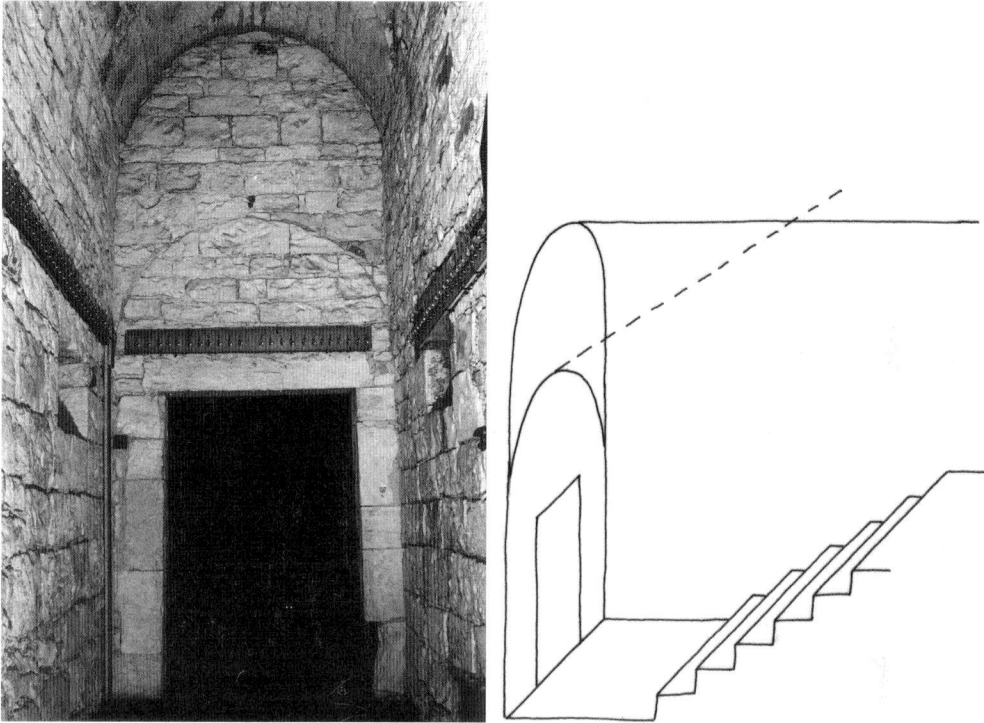

FIGS 7A–B.   Prague, Old Town: the covered entrance passage to the house on plot no. 646/I, Štupartská Street (Štupartská ulice). At the bottom is the rectangular entrance portal, with two semicircular vault arches above it. The presence of two arches is evidence of the original intention to vault the stairway with a sloping barrel vault. The vault was however constructed at a higher level and in a horizontal line, and a steeply rising set of steps was added in front of the portal

Drawing: Martin Müller; photograph: Jan Krupka

architecture. Two major finds have come to light in recent years, adding to our knowledge of both religious and domestic architecture. Within the former Jesuit complex at the centre of Malá Strana Square (Malostranské náměstí) the circular nave of the St Wenceslas rotunda, known from contemporary literary references (such as the Wenceslas legends) and depicted in historical sources (e.g., several etchings depicting the Passau invasion of Prague in 1611), has been uncovered (Fig. 8 & Col. Pl. IIIA in print edn). The exposed part of what was originally the main church of the settlement on the left bank beneath the castle dates from the end of the 11th and the beginning of the 12th centuries. The circular nave had an inner diameter of approximately 6.6 m, and an exterior diameter of over 8 m. The apse was completely destroyed during building alterations in the 1930s. The surviving wall belongs largely to the foundations, and only very limited portions of the sections that were above ground have been preserved. The rotunda had magnificent ceramic floor tiles of the so-called Vyšehrad type, whose basic pattern is a composition of hexagonal and triangular pieces. These were first discovered in the basilica of St Lawrence at

FIG. 8.   Prague, Malá Strana Square: the round nave of the St Wenceslas rotunda
Libor Smutka

FIG. 9.   Prague, Malá Strana Square: a Romanesque relief of terracotta tiles preserved in the north-eastern part of the nave in the St Wenceslas rotunda
Martin Pavala

Vyšehrad and probably date from the end of the 11th century. The hexagonal tiles in the rotunda were decorated with mythical creatures (lions and griffins); the triangular ones had a dark purple-brown or black glaze and thus contrasted with the rust-red areas of hexagonal tiles (Fig. 9 & Col. Pl. IIIB in print edn). There are indications that an even older structure, possibly also of a sacred character, stood on the site. One remnant of the older building is part of a circle of flat marlite stones, worked and fitted on the inside edge, in a single horizontal row; the rest of it probably remains preserved in the unsurveyed terrain that is now part of the later structure. Archaeological survey on the site also distinguished the remains of three successive wooden

Fig. 10. Prague, Old Town: reconstruction of the ground-plan of the Romanesque palace on the Square of the Republic

Martin Líbal

Fig. 11. Prague, Old Town: the northern room of the Romanesque palace on the Square of the Republic, with the wall of the staircase and the socle of the vault-supporting pillar

Petr Juřina

structures whose specific function and appearance cannot be determined.[11] The uncovered remains of the church will eventually be open to the public.

The other surprising find consisted of the remains of three Romanesque stone dwellings discovered during excavations on the site of the former army barracks on the Square of the Republic (Náměstí Republiky). The first dwelling was an extensive palace with many rooms and a latrine pit (Figs 10 and 11), the second a 'standard', single-space Romanesque house, and the third an extensive wooden house with a stone entrance passage to the lower floor (Figs 12 and 13). All three buildings excavated have the same orientation and form part of a homogeneously organised space (Fig. 14), which at this location extended beyond the limits of the Old Town. The buildings can be dated to the end of the 12th century, and their demise is linked to the construction of the Old Town fortifications in the 1230s.[12] These buildings will also be on public display as part of a shopping and administrative complex currently under construction.

FIG. 12. Prague, Old Town: an excavated wooden dwelling on the Square of the Republic, with remains of the walled entrance passage

Jaroslav Podliska

FIG. 13.   Prague, Old Town: remains of the walled entrance passage on the Square of the Republic, with the stone floor of the landing and a preserved threshold

Jaroslav Podliska

Some smaller recent finds help complete the picture of Romanesque Prague. During excavations of the church of St Mary Magdalene in Karmelitská Street (Karmelitská ulice) in Malá Strana, the scant remains of a wall of an earlier Romanesque church were discovered to the west of the Gothic presbytery.[13] In the house on plot no. 479/I on the Old Town Square (Staroměstské náměstí) an ashlar section of a house gable was found among the already well-known remains of a house within that plot.[14] In addition, remnants of the outer face of a previously unknown Romanesque house or its stone enclosure (Fig. 15) have been surveyed in Týnská Street (Týnská ulice).[15]

Archaeological surveys thus have not only led to an increase in the number of Romanesque stone buildings excavated, contributing to our knowledge of the significant position Prague occupied in Central Europe and beyond. The survey of the St Wenceslas rotunda recorded one of the important buildings of the earliest phase of the Romanesque and uncovered the remnants of an older structure that may be connected with the very beginnings of the cult of St Wenceslas. The relief tiles discovered have extended the range of known types of Romanesque tiles that were produced from the end of the 11th century. The Romanesque dwellings discovered outside the future boundaries of Prague's Old Town, which had entrances facing in the same direction, indicate that not only did the urban settlements of the 12th and early 13th centuries have many more stone houses than was previously assumed, but also that the urbanisation of the suburbium on the right bank was much more extensive than previously thought. The incidence of palatial buildings in places that were regarded as peripheral areas of settlement and the discovery of a second Romanesque latrine bay in Prague testify to the presence of higher social strata within an extensively built-up

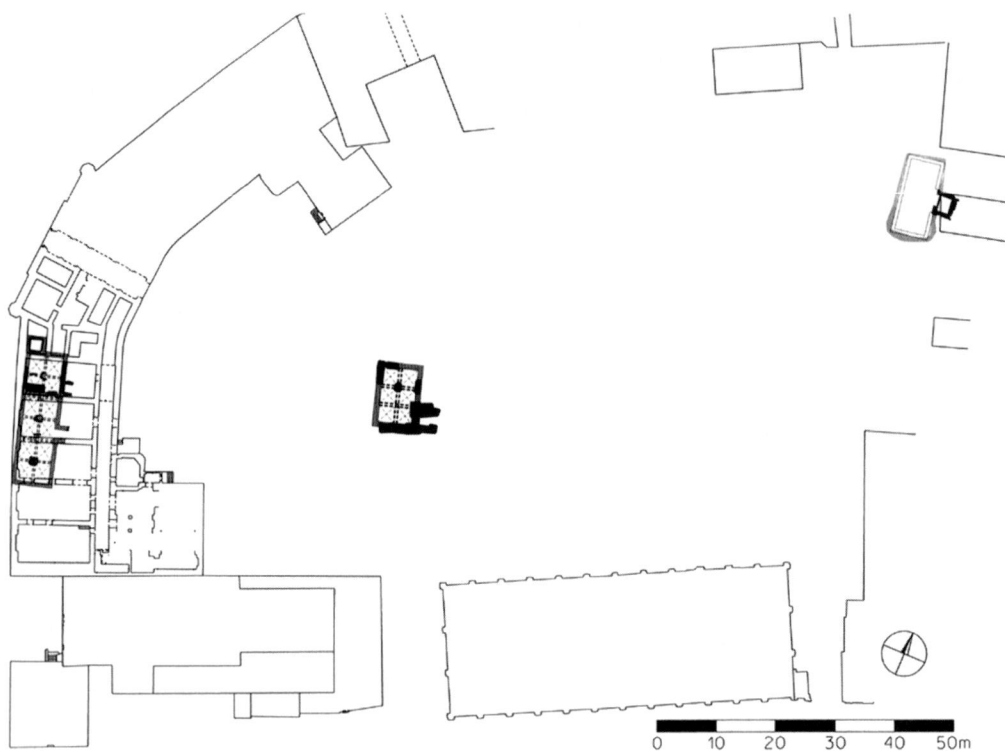

FIG. 14.   Prague, Old Town: the location of three Romanesque stone structures
(in solid black and grey) at the archaeological survey site at the George of Poděbrady barracks
on the Square of the Republic

Jan Růžička

FIG. 15.   Prague, Old
Town: Romanesque walling
discovered in Týnská Street

Egon Ditmar

46

area. The unique combination of stone and timber architecture augments the already wide range of medieval building types known for Prague. The examples briefly presented here indicate that there will be further finds of Romanesque buildings, and that our knowledge of Romanesque architecture in Prague will continue to grow and be enhanced.

NOTES

1. J. Čarek, *Románská Praha* (Prague 1947); V. Chaloupecký, J. Květ and V. Mencl, *Praha románská* (Prague 1948); A. Merhautová, *Raně středověká architektura v Čechách* (Prague 1971); A. Merhautová and D. Třeštík, *Románské umění v Čechách a na Moravě* (Prague 1983); Z. Dragoun, *Praha 885–1310: Kapitoly o románské a raně gotické architektuře* (Prague 2002).

2. Merhautová, *Raně středověká architektura* (as in n. 1), 200–34; K. Benešovská, P. Chotěbor, T. Durdík and Z. Dragoun, *Architektura románská* (Prague 2001, published in English as *Architecture of the Romanesque*), 56–63; Dragoun, *Praha 885–1310* (as in n. 1), 9–43.

3. Merhautová, *Raně středověká architektura* (as in n. 1), 237–40; Dragoun, *Praha 885–1310* (as in n. 1), 44–50; B. Nechvátal, *Kapitulní chrám sv. Petra a Pavla na Vyšehradě* (Prague 2004).

4. J. Podliska, 'Nové poznatky o kostela sv. Jana Křtitele Na Zábradlí na Starém Městě pražském', *Průzkumy památek*, 9/1 (2002), 83–100.

5. H. Soukupová, *Anežský klášter v Praze* (Prague 1989); Dragoun, *Praha 885–1310* (as in n. 1), 164–79.

6. Z. Dragoun, 'Juditin most', in O. Šefců ed., *Karlův most* (Prague 2007), 26–38.

7. Z. Dragoun, J. Škabrada and M. Tryml, *Romanesque Houses in Prague* (Prague/Litomyšl 2003).

8. Z. Dragoun, A. Merhautová and P. Sommer, 'Stavební podoba břevnovského kláštera ve středověku', in I. Hlaváček and M. Bláhová ed., *(993–1993) Milénium břevnovského kláštera* (Prague 1993), 67–137.

9. A. Kubíček and D. Líbal, *Strahov* (Prague 1955); Dragoun, *Praha 885–1310* (as in n. 1), 116–28.

10. A. Merhautová and P. Sommer, 'Strahovský klášter. Jeho založení a románská bazilika', *Umění*, 47 (1999), 154–68, here 156.

11. J. Čiháková and M. Müller, 'Zpráva o nálezu rotundy sv. Václava na Malostranském náměstí v Praze', *Zprávy památkové péče*, 66 (2006), 100–16.

12. P. Juřina, 'Objev kamenného románského paláce na Novém Městě pražském', *Forum urbes medii aevi*, 3 (2006), 170–77; V. Kašpar, J. Žegklitz, K. Svoboda and J. Poledne, 'Náměstí Republiky No. 1078/II a 1079/II - areál bývalých kasáren Jiřího z Poděbrad', in Z. Dragoun et al., 'Archeologický výzkum v Praze v letech 2003–04', *Pražský sborník historický*, 34 (2006), 363–66; J. Havrda, M. Kovář, M. Omelka and J. Podliska, 'Náměstí Republiky No. 1078/II a 1079/II - areál bývalých kasáren Jiřího z Poděbrad', ibid., 368–74.

13. J. Havrda and M. Tryml, 'Několik poznámek k provádění stavebněhistorického průzkumu z pohledu archeologa (na příkladu výzkumu v Karmelitské ulici na Malé Straně v Praze)', *Svorník*, 4 (2006), 169–74.

14. Z. Dragoun, 'Zjištění další části románské obytné stavby v domě No. 479/I na Staroměstském náměstí v Praze', *Průzkumy památek*, 11/1 (2004), 89–91.

15. J. Podliska, 'Praha 1 - Staré Město, Týnská ulička No. 1046/I', in Z. Dragoun et al., 'Archeologický výzkum v Praze v letech 2005–06', *Pražský sborník historický*, 35 (2007), 344–46.

The House at the Stone Bell:
Royal Representation in
Early-Fourteenth-Century Prague

KLÁRA BENEŠOVSKÁ

The House at the Stone Bell (Dům U kamenného zvonu, plot no. 605/I) in Prague's Old Town Square (Staroměstské náměstí) is the last remaining part of a magnificent town residence, which in the early 14th century occupied the entire area between the Goltz-Kinsky Palace (Palác Goltz-Kinských, today plot no. 606/I) on the north side and Týnská Street (Týnská ulice) on the south and east sides (plot no. 629/I). Two residential wings of the house were arranged along two sides of an inner courtyard. Facing the square was a corner tower with a massive ground floor and a façade decorated with sculpture. The tympanum above the entrance portal evidently contained an equestrian figure of a king (of which a fragment has been found), while the niches between the windows on the first storey housed a king and queen, enthroned and accompanied by two standing armed knights (partially preserved); above them on the second storey were probably statues of the four patron saints of Bohemia (now lost). The façade of the House at the Stone Bell therefore anticipated that more famous sculpted structure: Charles IV's Old Town Bridge Tower (Staroměstská mostecká věž).

The patron of this residence was manifestly the king of Bohemia, and the symbol of the house — the stone bell on its corner — connects the decoration of the façade with John of Luxembourg's conquest of occupied Prague in December 1310 and the accession of the Luxembourgs to the Bohemian throne. Archbishop of Mainz Peter of Aspelt, the counsellor of the last Přemyslid king, Wenceslas II (d. 1306), and of the young King John (in the period of 1310–14), also played an important role: the façade of the House at the Stone Bell bears many similarities to that of contemporary buildings in the lands of Peter of Aspelt's archdiocese, such as the Wernerkapelle in Bacharach and the Frauenkirche in Mainz, and it is known that Master Heinrich from Bohemia was employed by Peter after 1314.

SINCE its 'rebirth' in the 1960s, when remnants of its architecturally and sculpturally rich decoration began to emerge from beneath the neo-Baroque façade, the House at the Stone Bell on Prague's Old Town Square has proved a riddle for scholars.[1] It stood outside the familiar context of the autochthonous development of Bohemian art — that is, art fully anchored in local tradition — of the first half of the 14th century. The building's impact on our perception of Bohemian art in this period has been twofold: on the one hand it confirms the existence of close artistic links and similarities between Bohemian and western European courts, while on the other hand it displays local traits stemming from the tradition of Přemyslid court art.

The appearance of the House at the Stone Bell today does not correspond entirely to the original proportions of this lavish town residence from the first half of the 14th century (Fig. 1). The main tower-like section of the residence (hereinafter denoted the tower) faces the main square with its expressive and symbolic façade decorated with statues, fragments of which are currently on display in the chapel on the ground floor (as part of the collection of the Muzeum hlavního města Prahy (Prague Municipal Museum)). Behind this was a lower L-shaped block of two two-storeyed wings: a transverse wing running from north to south and encroaching deeply into the present plot no. 606a/I (Figs 2A, 2B), and a south wing that ran along the side street by the Týn Church (P. Marie před Týnem) and joined the tower of the residence at the corner. Jamb fragments of large windows found at first- and second-floor levels in the wall now facing the small inner courtyard suggest that windows originally opened onto an enclosed courtyard or a garden (Fig. 3). The entire palatial complex probably reached as far back as Týnská Street (Týnská ulice); this is confirmed by the fact that the first documented owners of all three neighbouring sites (plots no. 605/I, no. 629/I near Týnská Street, and no. 606a/I by the

FIG. 1. Prague, Old Town Square: the House at the Stone Bell, with the Týn Church on the right and the Goltz-Kinsky Palace on the left

Klára Benešovská

49

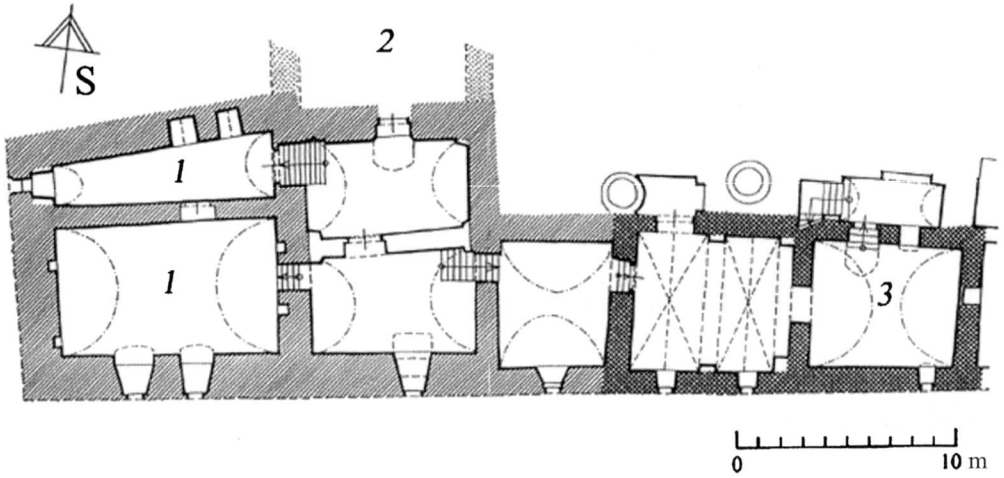

FIG. 2A. The House at the Stone Bell, plan of the basement: 1 — cellars under the tower; 2 — transverse wing; 3 — south wing, with the remnant of an older structure. Chronology: cross-hatching — 13th century; hatched — c. 1300 and after; white — later additions

Eva Vyletova

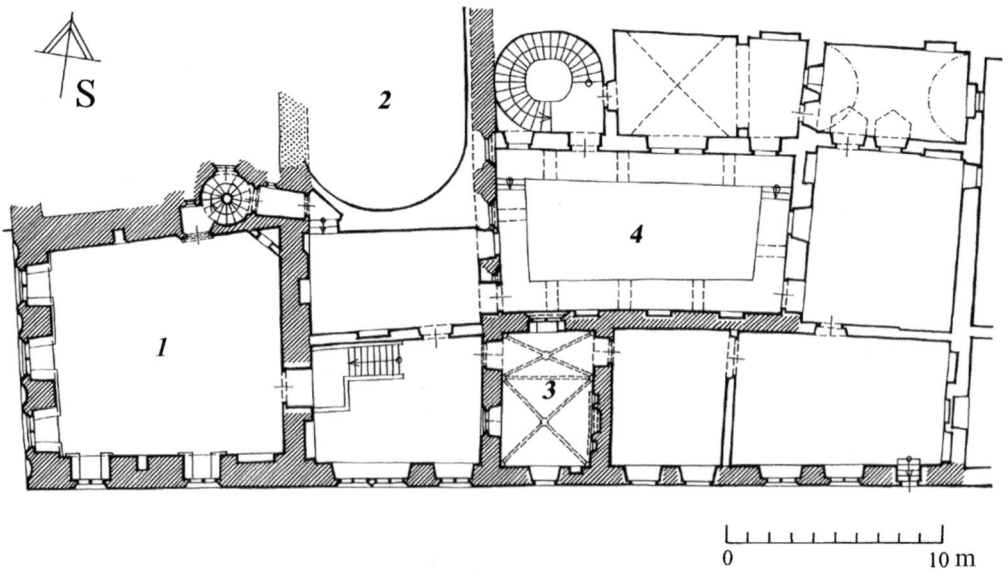

FIG. 2B. The House at the Stone Bell, plan of the first floor: 1 — hall in the tower; 2 — transverse wing; 3 — oratory in the south wing; 4 — location of the inner courtyard. Chronology: cross-hatching — 13th century; hatched — c. 1300 and after; white — later additions

Eva Vyletova

FIG. 3. The House at the Stone Bell, jamb fragments of the large windows in the inner-court façade, on first-floor level on the far side

Klára Benešovská

residence's east wing) were the descendants of Pesold of Cheb, the attested owner of plot no. 629 in 1359, who bought the palace in the second third of the 14th century and divided it up.[2] The distribution of spaces around the courtyard and the manner in which they related to neighbouring houses cannot be ascertained above ground-floor level, as the present form of the transverse and south wings shows that they have been significantly altered.

The layout of the basement spaces of the House at the Stone Bell shows that the position of the corner tower was taken into account during the digging of the cellars, as was that of the palace's transverse wing. The cellars of the transverse wing were tucked in behind the Romanesque cellars of the neighbouring house occupying plot no. 606a/I (now the Goltz-Kinsky Palace), and placed at a deeper level than those in the south wing; they had thick walls and small windows placed high under the vaults, taking into account the new level of the square, which was raised during the period 1270–80 at the latest. The south wing of the new structure covered parts of a ground floor and basement of an older building. Archaeological evidence shows that the older structure, which predates the building of the tower, extended as far as the east wall of the chapel at ground-floor level and the corresponding basement substructure of that block (Fig. 2A). Above ground level, the entire complex was constructed by a single workshop, following a uniform design: the mouldings of the window and portal jambs correspond on all levels of the building.

The sculptural programme of the tower's main façade, set within a unified architectural design whose proportions are based the principle of the Golden Section,[3] must have been planned from the outset, although it is now legible only on the first and second storeys. Stylistic similarities in the foliate and figural details of the architecture on the two upper storeys indicate that the entire programme is the work of one workshop.[4]

The tower was the dominant feature of the entire complex, with its two great halls, surmounted on the exterior by a crenellated passage (now replaced by a solid parapet) resting on consoles (the large masks currently on display in the interior), and a tall steep-sided roof, which can be seen on Philip van den Bosche's view of Prague in 1606 (Fig. 4). This architectural type has its origins in the residential towers of Early Gothic houses; these were common in Prague and frequently erected at the corners of living quarters. The towers of ostentatious patrician houses in Gothic towns were built not only for defensive purposes, but also as an expression of the owner's social standing and ambition. The defensive character of the corner tower is evident from its key architectural features: it is a solid, simple, rectangular structure with massive walls and without any extraneous external additions such as buttresses (they were unnecessary, since the two internal halls have flat ceilings rather than vaults), or any architectural articulation. The only exception to this prevailing sense of defensive purpose and aesthetic austerity was the west façade facing the public space of the square.

This geometrically meticulously conceived façade was adorned with sculptures originally set in niches flanking the first-floor windows. Placed under canopies and supported by consoles were the figures of a king and a queen seated on simple rectangular thrones, accompanied by two men-at-arms in their own spacious niches, holding shields and swords (Figs 5A–D & Col. Pl. IIB in print edn).[5] The statues on the second storey (possibly the four patron saints of Bohemia), if executed, have not survived. The niches were flanked by pinnacles and — like the windows — were surmounted by sharply

FIG. 4.   Philip van den Bosche's view of Prague, 1606: detail showing the Old Town Square with the House at the Stone Bell to the left of the Týn Church (64)

Ústav dějin umění, Akademie věd České republiky, Prague

pointed gables with elaborate crockets and terminating in cross-shaped finials. Not enough of the façade at ground level has been preserved to allow a full reconstruction, though it would seem that the main portal was also flanked by pinnacles and topped by a gable, as were the two flanking windows.

The placing of statues in the niches between windows has its origins in the sculptural tradition of cathedral façades and in particular their galleries of rulers. The use of canopies above the statues and of pointed windows with tracery, as well as of pinnacles and gables — all borrowings from the vocabulary of ecclesiastical architecture — was intended to underline the sacred connotations of the programme.[6] The recently unearthed sculpted fragments of a horse's leg may be part of an equestrian statue, executed in high relief and originally placed on the tympanum above the main portal. If they were, the sculptural programme can be reconstructed as having been composed along a vertical hierarchical axis: at ground level the statue of the king on horseback, a floor above the majestic enthroned figures of a royal couple accompanied by two standing men-at-arms, and above them the figures of four saints.[7] Undoubtedly, the main theme of the entire scene was the glorification of the ruler and his image (Fig. 6).

The origins of the programme's focal motif — that of the enthroned royal couple — can be traced back to Byzantium and ultimately to Antiquity.[8] But aside from the images of rulers accompanied by men-at-arms, appropriated from the Roman tradition of ruler representation by the Byzantine emperors and later modified by the Ottonian, Stauf and Capetian dynasties,[9] there was an important local tradition.[10] Symbolic references to imperial authority and to triumphal entries of Holy Roman emperors became a logical subject for façade iconography. This iconography of rulership could also be linked with the tradition of ruler images of the last Přemyslids, promoted on a long series of seals showing kings seated on a throne or mounted on horseback.[11] Parallels for the two men-at-arms are found in 14th-century chronicles, where they flank the enthroned figure of Charles IV, who is shown in the process of arbitration or the ritual of oath-taking in a public setting (for example, the illuminations of the *Croniche Sercambi*, Lucca, Archivio di Stato, MS 107, fol. 187v).[12] Furthermore, they also accompany the royal family in official portraits (for example, the statues of the Valois dynasty on the ceremonial staircase — *La Grande Vis* — once at the palace of Louvre).[13] Although these examples postdate the sculpted ensemble of the House at the Stone Bell, they nevertheless belong to the same tradition.

Traces of polychromy on the statues and other fragments show that the unplastered stone façade was originally painted, as were the sculptural details in the interior. The material used for the sculpture was soft Prague limestone, which facilitated detailed and precise workmanship and a delicate finish.[14]

The splendid façade of the palace was matched by a lofty interior. The entrance hall provided access to the south and transverse wings. Its north-east corner housed a spiral staircase that linked the entrance hall with both upper floors. The staircase was reached via an elevated 'platform' (possibly constructed there for the riders to dismount) and it provided access to the first- and second-floor levels of the transverse wing and to all the principal chambers of the complex. The jamb fragments of large rectangular windows embedded in the façade facing the inner courtyard (near the entrance to the later newel staircase) are the only evidence of the transverse wing's original external appearance. In the south wing a chapel and its antechamber have survived (Fig. 2A (3)), each accessed through a Gothic portal. The original appearance of the medieval interior can only be gleaned in the chapel, which is divided by a massive transverse arch into two bays vaulted

FIGS 5A–D. Museum hlavního města Prahy: statues of a king (centre left) and queen (centre right), from the façade of the House at the Stone Bell, both seated on flat thrones, and originally flanked by two men-at-arms with shields and swords (far left and far right)

Vlado Bohdan

with quadripartite vaults (Fig. 7). Judging by the ground-plan, the simple architecture devoid of ostentatious decorative elements, and the absence of a niche for liturgical vessels, it would seem that the space was not originally built as a chapel. If this space was ever in use as a chapel, the execution of the wall-paintings would have coincided (and been connected) with that role. The style of the paintings on the east and north walls constitutes a *terminus ante quem* for the architecture of the chapel of *c.* 1310 and thus also for the stylistically related first and second storeys of the building.[15]

The entire first floor of the tower was taken up by a great hall illuminated by three tall pointed windows looking onto the square, and two facing the side street (Figs 2B (1) and 8). The former contain rich tracery and have deep embrasures equipped with seats. The latter windows do not have seats; on the inside their straight tops follow the line of the wooden ceiling, while on the exterior they appear to be pointed with gables. The beams of the ceiling rested on a projecting string-course. Traces of the painted Decalogue inscription (*c.* 1320s–*c.* 1350s) survive on the north wall, and rectangular alcoves with wooden shelves are set into the south wall (Fig. 8). The ceremonial character of the hall is also suggested by a Gothic portal with delicately moulded jambs that leads to the spiral staircase. According to a proposed reconstruction the portal was flanked by pinnacles, decorated with openwork tracery, and framed with crockets culminating in a

C

D

cross-shaped finial. One of the consoles bears fragments of a relief, probably a lion's mane and an eye.

It is not clear whether it was possible to access this great hall directly from the south wing; it may have been accessed indirectly via the transverse wing and the spiral stair. Moving from the spiral staircase and through two small portals along a narrow corridor one could also reach a chamber in the transverse wing lit by three tall rectangular windows facing the inner courtyard that were divided with mullions and decorated with open or blind tracery. The splays of the windows have been preserved in parts. This chamber led to the rooms in the south wing. The first of these, situated immediately next to the tower, was probably the master's private chamber, where he could follow the service in the adjacent oratory through a rectangular window. The two-bay oratory also led into other parts of the south wing, and its north bay — which was probably separated from the south bay by a screen — has its own quadripartite vault and a tall pointed window with tracery and a seat that looked onto the courtyard (Fig. 2B (3)). The east wall of the oratory's south bay has three recesses. The middle one, with a projecting string-course below and a deep alcove with a gable above, housed an altar; the other two were used as niches for the sacrament and for liturgical vessels (Fig. 9). Two identical Gothic portals lead into the north bay of the oratory. Their placement on the outer face of the wall indicates that they were intended to lead into the oratory from both directions, and that the oratory was therefore used as the main thoroughfare of the south wing. On either side of the oratory were private chambers whose original medieval appearance (from the first half of the 14th century) eludes us.

KLÁRA BENEŠOVSKÁ

FIG. 6. The House at the Stone Bell: reconstruction of appearance in the first half
of the 14th century
Klára Benešovská and Dalibor Prix

The layout of the second floor corresponded to that of the first, with the great hall in the tower constituting the dominant feature of the plan, reflecting its importance, higher than that of the rooms of the transverse and south wings. The only difference is that the tall windows of the chamber on the first floor of the transverse wing adjacent to the tower have been supplanted on the second by smaller rectangular windows, suggesting a private use for this room. The second storey of the south wing was probably arranged in

FIG. 7. The House at the Stone Bell: chapel on the ground floor, view of the rib-vault and the east wall mural
Klára Benešovská

FIG. 8. The House at the Stone Bell: great hall on the first floor of the tower, to north-east
Vlado Bohdan

the same way as the floor below; at any rate, the first chamber next to the tower had a portal leading to the north side of the wing, which overlooked the courtyard. The rest of the medieval structure at this level is lost.

The great hall on the second floor of the tower had a flat wooden ceiling and was also illuminated by large pointed windows with tracery and furnished with alcove seats. Unlike the hall bellow, this chamber has in the south wall a tripartite niche consisting of one tall and two lower flanking windows, opposite the entrance to the spiral staircase (Fig. 10). According to Josef Mayer, the royal throne may have been placed in front of the

FIG. 9. The House at the Stone Bell: east wall of the private oratory on the first floor of the palace
Taťána Billerová

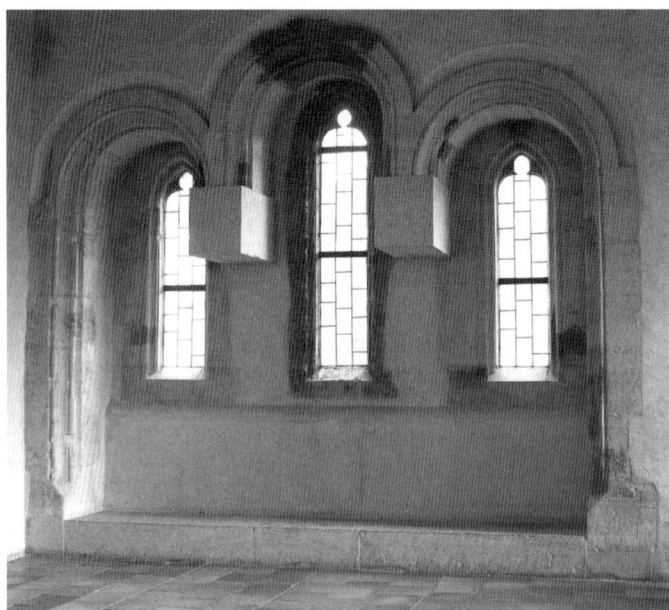

FIG. 10. The House at the Stone Bell: great hall on the second floor of the tower, south wall alcove
Klára Benešovská

central window under a baldachin.[16] Similar examples of this type of arrangement are found in contemporary manuscripts, for example, the *Liber viaticus* of Jan of Středa (Prague, Knihovna Národního muzea, XIII A.12, fol. 9v).[17] Another interpretation focuses on the incisions found on the stone arch of the tripartite niche, which may indicate

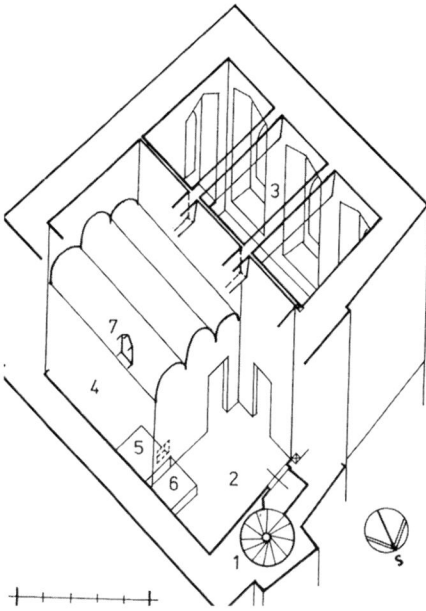

FIG. II. The House at the Stone Bell: speculative reconstruction of the proposed small wooden chamber attached to the south wall niche in the great hall on the second floor of the tower. 1 — entrance from the spiral staircase; 2 — antechamber; 3 — large chamber; 4 — heated chamber; 5 and 6 — position of the heater; 7 — opening for ventilation. Most of these functions cannot be verified

After Jiří Škabrada and Michal Rykl

that a wooden vault was attached above the panelling of a small wooden chamber installed in the main hall (known in German as a *Blockwerkkammer*) (Fig. 11).[18]

The functional layout of the complex, as far as it can be reconstructed from its present state, points to the owner's elevated status; this is further confirmed by the high quality of the sculpture and architectural detail. Correspondence of dress with contemporary fashion, as well as the hairstyle, the modelling of the outline of faces, and the elegance of their postures, place the four surviving statues in the context of court art of *c.* 1300 and early 14th century, formed in Parisian court circles from the middle of the 13th century and subsequently taken up and developed in the courts of other European rulers, church dignitaries and aristocracy. Seen in its Bohemian context, the sculpture is related to the court art of the last Přemyslids, in particular to its final flourishing in the years after the coronation in 1297 of Wenceslas II (1278–1305) and his acquisition of the Polish crown in 1300. In this period, emphasis was placed on the display of royal magnificence and *splendor regalis*. This heightened sense for regal display was also bolstered by the growth of the economy and especially by the discovery of fresh silver deposits near Kutná Hora.[19]

Seen in that light, the sculptural decoration of the House at the Stone Bell may have emerged from Wenceslas II's court circle, at the very end of his reign.[20] In 1303, there was a large fire in the royal palace in Prague Castle, and Wenceslas II had to move his court to the Old Town across the river, where he rented or briefly lived in the houses of local burghers. This is confirmed by the fact that the king died on 21 June 1305 in the house of Conrad the Goldsmith, not far from the Dominican monastery of St Clement (on the site of today's Clementinum).[21]

Historical evidence from the following period however supports a shift in the sculptures' date to the beginning of the reign of John, the son of Emperor Henry VII of Luxembourg and the father of Charles IV. After the death in 1306 of Wenceslas III (the

59

last Přemyslid on the Bohemian throne) and the brief interregnum that followed, John obtained the crown in 1310, when he received the hand of Wenceslas II's daughter Elizabeth in marriage.[22] The unusual attribute of the whole complex — the stone bell placed on its corner — can be related to the story of John's accession. It probably commemorates the dramatic entry of the new king into Prague in 1310, while the town was still in the hands of Henry of Carinthia's men. After a futile siege of the town, the gates were finally breached when Elizabeth's chaplain Berengar rang the bell of the Týn Church as a pre-arranged signal for John's forces to attack. Only then was John able to make his triumphal entry into the capital.[23] Almost immediately, the new king legitimised his position with two important legal acts: he convened the public royal court of law and the assembly of allegiance.[24] The public court was assembled three days after his arrival in Prague, on 6 December. It annulled the charters and privileges issued during Henry of Carinthia's reign (1306–10), and the citizens who had assisted him were put on trial. Significantly, the court convened in the town's main square, the present Old Town Square, in front of the house of Simeon Štuk,[25] which can probably be identified as the House at the Stone Bell, or as the building that previously occupied the site. The tradition of holding inaugural royal courts on that spot was recorded as late as the 15th century, and the house on the neighbouring plot (no. 606a/I) is sometimes called in the documents the house 'at the royal bench' ('ad sedem domini regis').[26] Presiding over the court in 1310 were John's counsellors, recommended to him by his father Emperor Henry VII, such as the archbishop of Mainz, Peter of Aspelt, and Count Berthold of Henneberg.[27] Peter of Aspelt had also been a counsellor and diplomat in the service of Wenceslas II and was well acquainted with local circumstances in Bohemia; he therefore seems the likeliest instigator (or perhaps overseer of the final stages) of work on the sumptuous palatial complex with its tower and sculptural programme.[28] The complex would have served as a residence for the young royal couple until the rebuilding of Prague Castle was completed. The decoration of the House at the Stone Bell could therefore be accurately dated to the period between 1310 and 1315.

Peter of Aspelt also provides an important architectural link: it is documented that he took with him from Prague to Mainz Master Heinrich, who was from 1314 *magister operis* of the church of Our Lady in Mainz (demolished between 1803 and 1807).[29] The style of the church was closely related to that of the key buildings in the new 'Mainz style', as the façade of the House of the Stone Bell also appears to have been.[30] However, the House at the Stone Bell equally belongs to the group of buildings of *c.* 1300 influenced by the lodges of Strasbourg and Cologne cathedrals. Similarities are found in the geometrical scheme of the façade, and the forms of the windows (especially their jambs, slender columns, foliate capitals and tracery) and of the gables and finials crowning the windows and the niches. The high quality and style of the Prague statues distinguishes them from the sculpture of the church of Our Lady, as far as can be judged from the surviving pre-restoration drawings and from the set of twenty-two statues in Mainz's Landesmuseum.[31]

In conclusion, the proposed hierarchical programme for the sculptural ensemble of the façade — with the equestrian figure of the king probably placed above the door and the enthroned royal couple accompanied by two men-at-arms on the first floor, culminating with Bohemian patron saints intended for the second storey — formed an impressive public statement with several layers of meaning. First, it fell within the tradition of ruler images previously found on the seals of the last members of the Přemyslid dynasty. On the House at the Stone Bell, King John of Luxembourg was represented both as *miles christianus*, a valiant and undaunted knight, and as a rightful ruler chosen by God, anointed and crowned, whose legitimate accession to the Bohemian throne would have been emphasised by the presence of the enthroned crowned figure of his Přemyslid queen next to him. The mensa-shaped thrones and the canopies above the statues underline the sacred nature of kingship and the iconographical likeness of the royal pair to the enthroned figures of Christ and the Virgin (in, for example, the Coronation of the Virgin iconography). The figures of the Bohemian patron saints in the niches above them would have appeared as inhabitants of the Heavenly Jerusalem, offering celestial protection to the royal couple. Secondly, the sculptural ensemble embodied the idea of a just government, guaranteed by the new ruler who was represented here also as *rex pacificus*, a wise ruler and a just judge. This idea was strengthened by the presence of the two accompanying knights, who were an indispensable part of the royal *entourage* during public gatherings.[32] Lastly, it acted as a permanent reminder of the inaugural court held probably on this place immediately after the triumphal entry of the new king into Prague in 1310.

The sculptural decoration of the façade of the House at the Stone Bell and its iconographic programme helps us understand the overlapping of the court and civic spheres in Bohemian art and the complicated ways in which the new 'avant-garde' Rhenish-Rayonnant architecture and the monumental sculpture emanating from the circles of the Paris court were received and adapted in early-14th-century Prague. The House at the Stone Bell should be seen as one of many such local examples (now lost to us) that had a profound influence on Charles IV's own fertile iconography of rulership found, for example, on the surviving façade of the Old Town Bridge Tower.

English version by Zoë Opačić

NOTES

1. On the discovery of the Gothic structure, see J. Mayer, 'Unikátní pražská památka', in *Dějiny a současnost*, 1 (1968), 21–25; J. Mayer, 'Dům U zvonu na Staroměstském náměstí v Praze', *Architektura ČSR*, 29 (1970), 178–86; J. Mayer, 'Dům U kamenného zvonu na Staroměstském náměstí', *Časopis společnosti přátel starožitností*, 102 (1994), 65–89.

2. V. V. Tomek, *Základy starého místopisu pražského*, 4 vols (Prague 1866–75), I, 23. See most recently J. Vítovský, 'Zeměpanská kurie s panovnickým trůnem, Eberlinovou mincovnou a palácem Přemyslovců a Jana Lucemburského na Starém Městě pražském', *Průzkumy památek*, 13/1 (2006), 110–44.

3. A. Charvátová and J. Mayer, 'Geometrická kompozice průčelí Domu U zvonu na Staroměstském náměstí v Praze', *Umění*, 22 (1974), 8–17.

4. K. Benešovská, 'Královští stavebníci na dvoře Jana Lucemburského' (habilitation thesis, Institute of Art History, Czech Academy of Sciences, Prague, 1989), 18–66; eadem, 'No. 605/I, Staré Město, Dům U kamenného zvonu', in P. Vlčed., *Umělecké památky města Prahy: Staré město-Josefov* (Prague 1996), 405–10; eadem, 'Les résidences du roi Jean de Boheme: leur fonction de représentation', in K. Benešovská ed., *King John of Luxemburg (1296–1346) and the Art of his Era*, Proceedings of the International Conference, Prague, 16–20 September 1996 (Prague 1998), 117–31.

5. The statues have been painstakingly pieced together by the restorer Jiří Blažej from a large number of fragments reused on the Baroque façade and in the interior; the process is described in J. Blažej, 'Cesta za podobou soch z průčelí domu U Kamenného zvonu', *Zprávy památkové péče*, 62 (2002), 73–116.

6. For a detailed analysis of this phenomenon, see N. Coldstream, *The Decorated Style: Architecture and Ornament 1240–1360* (London 1994), 37–39.

7. An identical composition hierarchically arranged in three tiers can also be seen in the two representations of the *Pribytku nebeskych* (heavenly hierarchies) in the Passional of Abbess Kunegunda (Prague, Národní knihovna, XIV A.17, fols 20r and 22v), which illustrate the 'De mansionibus caelestis' by the Dominican Kolda of Koldice. The architectural framing of the scenes in the manuscript closely resembles the tracery and decorative details of the House at the Stone Bell.

8. For a discussion of this iconography in the context of the enthroned imperial couple Otto I and his first wife Edith, see F. Möbius and H. Sciurie, *Symbolwerte mittelalterlicher Kunst* (Leipzig 1984), 112. Just as in the case of Otto and Edith, the presence of Queen Elizabeth Přemyslovna alongside John of Luxembourg was an important sign of the continuity of the Přemyslid line and the legitimacy of the accession of the new king of Bohemia.

9. For an in-depth discussion of this substantial topic, see K. Benešovská and Z. Všetečková, *Dům U kamenného zvonu ve středověku* (forthcoming).

10. Among other examples of monumental statues of enthroned rulers placed on public buildings of the Přemyslid era, one should mention in particular the late-12th-century figure of a ruler once above the arch of the Malá Strana Bridge Tower (Malostranská mostecká věž) that led onto the Judith Bridge (Juditin most), the first stone bridge in Prague and the predecessor of the famous Charles Bridge (Karlův most). The enthroned ruler may have been either Frederick I Barbarossa, who rewarded Vladislav II in 1158 with a royal title for his support in the Italian campaign, or more probably Vladislav II, the royal founder of the fortified district of Malá Strana on Prague's left bank. For the most recent bibliography, see P. Vlček ed., *Umělecké památky Prahy: Malá Strana* (Prague 1999), 121, and Zdeněk Dragoun's article in this volume.

11. On the enthroned king and queen in majesty, see most recently K. Benešovská, 'Podoby královského majestátu v Českých zemích kolem roku 1300', in B. Bukovinská and L. Konečný ed., *Ars longa: Sborník k nedožitým sedmdesátinám Josefa Krásy* (Prague 2003), 27–42.

12. *Croniche Sercambi: Le illustrazioni delle Croniche nel codice Lucchese (con i commenti di O. Banti e M. I. Testi-Cristiani)* (Genova 1978), fol. CLXXXVII, 15 cm; Benešovská, 'Les résidences' (as in n. 4), 128, fig. 40.

13. The architect of Charles V, Raymond du Temple, made in 1365 for the staircase known as 'la grande vis du Louvre' ten stone statues that represent members of the royal family, accompanied by two standing men-at-arms. See E. Viollet-le Duc, *Encyclopédie médiévale*, ed. G. Bernage, 2 vols (Paris 1978), I, 482; and H. Sauval, *Histoire et Recherches des Antiquités de la ville de Paris*, II (1724), 23. See also M. Whiteley, 'Deux escaliers royaux du XIVe siècle: les "Grands Degrez" du Palais de la Citè et la "Grande Viz" du Louvre', *Bulletin Monumental*, 147 (1989), 133–54.

14. Blažej, 'Cesta za podobou' (as in n. 5), 73–80.

15. Z. Všetečková, 'Nástěnné malby v přízemní kapli domu U zvonu', *Umění*, 38 (1990), 377–400; Vítovský, 'Zeměpanská kurie' (as in n. 2), 130–33.

16. J. Mayer, 'Dům U kamenného zvonu na Staroměstském náměstí', *Časopis přátel starožitností*, 102 (1994), 65–97; K. Benešovská in *Staré město-Josefov* (as in n. 4), 405–10.

17. J. Mayer, 'Dům U bílého zvonu na Staroměstském náměstí v Praze', *Umění*, 36 (1988), 97–126. This form of representation is also part of an older iconographic tradition that includes the enthroned Henry II accompanied by two knights and allegorical figures in the Sacramentary of Henry II (Munich, Bayerische Staatsbibliothek, Clm 4456, fol. 11v), which itself continues the visual tradition of Ottonian emperors. From a period more contemporary with the Bohemian rulers in question one could cite the representation of Ludwig the Bavarian in the now lost *Münchener Rechtshandschrift*; see R. Suckale, *Die Hofkunst Kaiser Ludwigs der Bayern* (Munich 1993), 245.

18. J. Škabrada and M. Rykl, 'Die Wohnung im zweiten Stock des Turmes des Hauses "zur Glocke" in Prag', *Zprávy památkové péče*, 56 (1996), 12–16.

19. J. Šusta, *Poslední Přemyslovci a jejich dědictví 1300–1308* (Prague 1926), 1–103; J. Šusta, *České dějiny, II/1: Soumrak Přemyslovců a jejich dědictví* (Prague 1935), 482–554; K. Charvátová, *Dějiny cisterckého řádu v Čechách 1142–1420, I: Fundace 12. století* (Prague 1998), 107–19.

20. Benešovská, 'Královští stavebníci' (as in n. 4), 64; Vítovský, 'Zeměpanská kurie' (as in n. 2), 132.

21. Wenceslas II's death is described in the 'Chronicon Aulae Regiae'; *Fontes rerum Bohemicarum*, ed. J. Emler, 8 vols (Prague 1873–1932), IV (1884), 1–337, here 98.

22. The active role played by the abbots Oto of Zbraslav and Heidenreich of Sedlec as well as Elizabeth herself in securing John as a future king is vividly described in the 'Chronicon Aulae Regiae' (as in n. 21), 144–50 and 165–69. For a recent summary of the historical circumstances of the Luxembourg dynasty's involvement with the kingdom of Bohemia, see J. Spěváček, 'Neue Gesichtspunkte zur Beurteilung der Politik sowie der historischen Rolle Königs Johann von Böhmen', in *King John* (as in n. 4), 11–18, and I. Hlaváček, 'Johann von Luxembourg und die böhmischen Städte: Bemerkungen zu Johanns Itinerar', ibid., 19–27. See also M. Margue with J. Schroeder, *Un itinéraire européen: Jean l'Aveugle, comte du Luxembourg et roi de Bohème 1296–1346* (Brussels 1996), with full bibliography.

23. For John of Luxembourg's entry into Prague, see the 'Chronicon Aulae Regiae' (as in n. 22), 98 and 172; Benešovská, 'Les résidences' (as in n. 4), 129.

24. 'Chronicon Aulae Regiae' (as in n. 22), 175.

25. Benešovská, 'Les résidences' (as in n. 4), 125, n. 32.

26. J. Teige, *Základy starého místopisu Pražského*, II (Prague 1915), 22.

27. 'Chronicon Aulae Regiae' (as in n. 22), 171–77.

28. Peter of Aspelt (*c.* 1250–1320), from 1296 Wenceslas II's *protonotarius* and chancellor, left Bohemia after the death of the last Přemyslid king, Wenceslas III, in 1306, and returned in 1310 with the new king, John of Luxembourg, and his queen, Elizabeth Přemyslovna; D. Dvořáčková-Malá, 'Petr z Aspeltu mezi Přemyslovci a Lucemburky', in L. Březina ed., *Ve znamení zemí Koruny české: sborník k šedesátým narozeninám Prof. PhDr. Lenky Bobkové, CSc.* (Prague 2006), 27–34.

29. F. Falk, 'Interessanter Baukontrakt aus Mainz vom Jahre 1314', *Kirchenschmuck*, 24 (1868), 54–55; Vítovský, 'Zeměpanská kurie' (as in n. 2), 142–43.

30. See most recently P. Crossley, 'The Wernerkapelle in Bacharach', in U. Engel and A. Gajewski ed., *Mainz and the Middle Rhine Valley: Medieval Art, Architecture and Archaeology, BAA Trans.*, xxx (Leeds 2007), 167–92, and M. C. Schurr, *Gotische Architektur im mittleren Europa 1220–1340: Von Metz bis Wien* (Munich/Berlin 2007), 251–53, 328.

31. B. Dengel-Wink, *Die ehemalige Liebfrauenkirche in Mainz: Ein Beitrag zur Baukunst und Skulptur der Hochgotik am Mittelrhein und in Hessen*, Neues Jahrbuch für das Bistum Mainz 1990 (Mainz 1990), 201–88.

32. The presence of the two accompanying knights derives from the classical and Byzantine tradition of representing the emperor in majesty; see W. C. Schneider, 'Imperator Augustus und Christomimétés', in A. Wieczorek and H.-M. Hinz ed., *Střed Evropy okolo roku 1000*, 3 vols (Prague 2002), III, 281–85 (published in German as *Europas Mitte um 1000*, 3 vols (Stuttgart 2000)). See also nn. 9–14.

Our Lady in Nuremberg, All Saints Chapel in Prague, and the High Choir of Prague Cathedral

PAUL CROSSLEY

The high choir of Prague Cathedral — the triforium, clerestory and high vault — is usually extolled for the ingenuity and originality of its decorative forms. But it also reflects certain general attitudes or approaches to architectural design: a close correspondence between external and internal forms; a handling of wall planes in terms of layering and recession; and a conscious contrast between a relatively simple and robust arcade storey and delicate, intricately fashioned upper levels. This paper argues that such general approaches to design are prefigured (or paralleled) in two buildings founded by Emperor Charles IV, and associated with or designed by Peter Parler: the now much-damaged chapel of All Saints in Prague Castle and the Westwerk of the church of Our Lady in Nuremburg. While the creative relationship between the Prague chapel and the cathedral is difficult to disentangle (both were under construction in the 1370s), the Nuremberg church, particularly its western upper chapel of St Michael dating to the mid-1350s, anticipates much of Peter Parler's thinking in Prague twenty years later. Both buildings also shared a common function, for they belonged to an elite group of colleges of priests (mansionaries) founded by Charles IV in honour of the Virgin Mary. The most senior of these institutions served as an imperial chantry at the very centre of the choir of Prague Cathedral — a fact that may have led Parler to look at Our Lady in Nuremberg as an appropriate source of inspiration for the architectural setting of the mansionaries' college in Prague.

IT is universally acknowledged that the high choir of Prague Cathedral — the triforium, clerestory and high vault — counts as the supreme creation of one of the most inventive architects of the Middle Ages, Peter Parler of Gmünd. Begun in c. 1370 and completed by 1385, the high choir shows him at the height of his powers: playful, virtuoso, revelling in modernity, adopting convention only to undermine it. In general appearance and in specific detail the Prague choir as completed by Peter Parler is a late homage to the idea of a Rayonnant Great Church, of the kind first conceived a century and a half earlier at Saint-Denis and developed in Germany in the nave of Strasbourg and the choir of Cologne cathedrals.[1] Charles IV of Luxembourg, Peter's patron, was an *ex officio* honorary member of the Cologne chapter. Heinrich, Peter's father, had held the position of warden of the masons (*Parlier*) at Cologne Cathedral, and the young Peter may have worked there as a journeyman, meeting and marrying the daughter of a Cologne stonemason.[2] In the western bays of the choir of Prague Cathedral, Peter Parler adopts Cologne's massive bundle piers and prominent vault responds resting on broad, diamond-shaped plinths; and like Cologne, he places a multi-light clerestory above a glazed triforium supported by double batteries of delicately detailed flying buttresses (Figs 1, 2).[3]

Into this self-consciously retrospective framework Peter inserted a set of decorative and spatial novelties that mark a prodigious enlargement of the vocabulary of Continental Rayonnant architecture. His clerestory windows amount to the first consistent display of curvilinear tracery on the Continent. His net vault, the first of its kind in Central Europe, transforms the conventional Gothic vault from a series of discrete canopies over clearly demarcated bays into a continuous, densely patterned ceiling. The bay-denying horizontality of the vault complements the longitudinal accents of the elevation below it — the prominent triforium balustrade and the famous zigzagging projections and recessions of the triforium and clerestory. All these devices undermine the two fundamental aesthetic principles of the conventional Rayonnant elevation, supremely exemplified by Cologne: flatness and verticality (Fig. 1).

These disruptive novelties may have been triggered by the demands of imagery. Sometime in the early 1370s, it was decided to insert, above the (now suppressed) entrances to the triforium passages, the famous cycle of portrait busts of Charles IV, his family, his architects, and the Prague archbishops and clerical building administrators (Fig. 2, between A and B).[4] A conventional Rayonnant triforium grill, such as that at Saint-Denis or Cologne, aligned with the inner plane of the wall, would have obscured the busts behind it; but by setting the triforium arches back towards the outer plane of the high wall the busts are brought clearly into view, and then made more insistently visible by the angled projections of the clerestory window sills above them. Above these slanting sills lie the correspondingly slanted aedicules in the clerestory (Fig. 1), their framed glazed panels suggesting that their original purpose may have been to frame standing figures in stained glass, perhaps a cycle of Bohemian kings modelled on the great gallery of kings inserted into the base of Cologne's clerestory in *c.* 1300.[5]

The chain of events set in motion by this need to display figural imagery in the upper parts may have been decisive in the shaping of the high choir. By recessing the central sections of the triforium and clerestory, yet connecting them back to the vault responds with slanting motifs, Parler differentiated in depth and design the four central lights of the triforium and clerestory from the two outer lights that frame them and jut forward. As a result, the clerestory forms a 'window-within-a-window' motif, with the two outermost lights terminating in single, downward-drooping mouchettes, and the four inner lights, framed by thicker mullions, crowned by full dress tracery (Fig. 1). In recessing the triforium, Peter Parler placed its columns and arcades almost exactly half-way between the inner and outer planes of the high wall, and exactly opposite the openings into the triforium passages. For reasons of support, the clerestory windows had in turn to be recessed, and placed directly above the triforium arcade, on the same vertical axis. The bilateral position of triforium grill and clerestory, half-way between the inner and outer faces of the high wall, seems to have triggered Peter Parler's emphasis on symmetry between interior and exterior (Fig. 2). There is symmetry of circulation at triforium level, by walking either behind (A) or in front of the columns (B, the latter pathway requiring a balustrade for security), and there is symmetry at clerestory level, where the slanting aedicules inside the choir (E) are exactly matched outside it by identical aedicules (C), which once conveyed the exterior clerestory passage (Ai) through openings at the bay divisions. There is no precedent for this bilateral exactness. Never in a Gothic Great Church have inside and

FIG. 1. Prague Cathedral, choir: interior to the north
Christopher Wilson

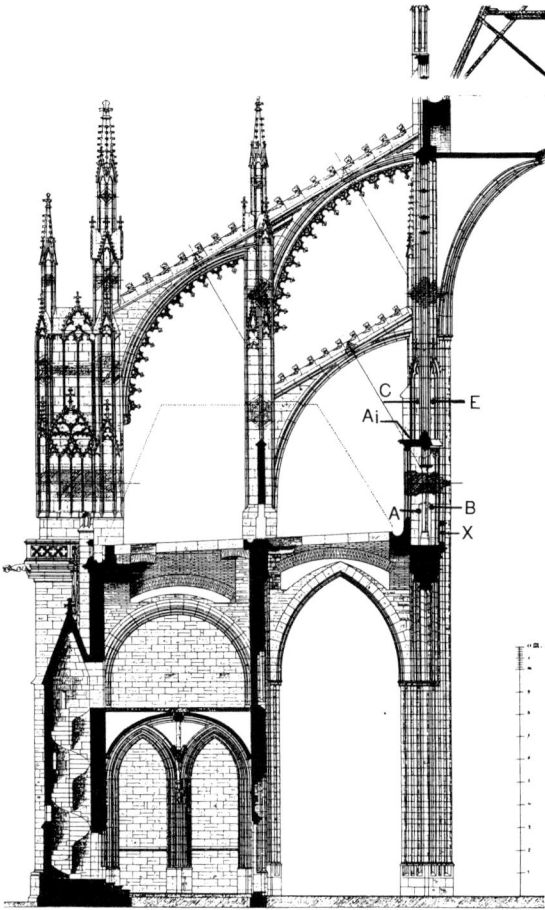

FIG. 2. Prague Cathedral, choir: cross section.
X — triforium parapet; A — outer half of triforium; B — inner half of triforium; Ai — triforium roof and base of exterior clerestory passage; C — framing arch into the clerestory passage openings; E — oblique tracery panels on interior of clerestory; F — pinnacles flanking the clerestory windows (after Antonín Podlaha and Kamil Hilbert, *Metropolitní chrám sv. Víta v Praze* (Prague 1906))

outside, inner and outer planes of wall, been so consciously integrated and realigned.[6] But symmetry in the domain of depth is matched by deliberate contrast in the dimension of height. In the choir's western bays, completed according to Parler's designs, the lower, arcade, storey of the elevation — with its sculptural clusters of piers and its flat, undecorated, spandrels — contrasts deliberately, and in a manner typical of Rayonnant basilican architecture, with the glass-house delicacy of the upper parts. It is as if a Rayonnant chapel — for example the Sainte-Chapelle — has had its floor removed and been set like a crown on the top of the structure (Fig. 1).[7] Prague's idiosyncrasies enhance this contrast of modes, by shifting the glazed upper parts back from the inner wall plane of the arcade storey, by emphasising the longitudinal continuity of the clerestory and triforium, and by the insistent triforium parapet that ruthlessly separates lower and upper parts at exactly half way up the elevation. Here was a true 'chapel-clerestory', hoisted up on the podium of a basilica.

It would be wrong to infer from this narrative of Peter Parler's creativity that the busts were the sole efficient cause of his design, and that practical choices led to aesthetic solutions in a purely internal process of visual reasoning. Faced in the early 1370s with the

supreme structural challenge of building the upper parts of a great church, Peter Parler —
along with the Gothic architects who later argued over high vaults at Milan or Gerona —
must have invoked authority and usage.[8] What were Peter Parler's necessary models for
the high choir? What churches or chapels provided the inspiration for those distinctive features of the upper parts that our analysis has singled out: the curvilinear tracery, the equal
interchange between exterior and interior, and the handling of wall planes in terms of
layering and recession? Answers to these questions cannot avoid a dose of conventional
source-spotting — the identification of literal borrowings — but they also aim to uncover
the syntax as well as the vocabulary of Peter Parler's thinking; they offer a possible insight
into the fundamental aesthetic principles that may have underpinned his selection of
forms and shaped his solutions to particular problems.

The Decorated architecture of the English West Country, known to the young Peter
by drawings or first-hand experience, must be counted among his deliberations. The
similarities between the Prague choir and the choirs of Wells and Bristol cathedrals
and Ottery St Mary are too close to be dismissed as parallel coincidences.[9] But of
Parler's more local resources, in his homelands of Cologne and the Upper Rhine, there is
remarkably little by way of precedent, even in buildings associated with the founders of
the ubiquitous Parler clan of architects: Peter's father, Heinrich, and his uncle, Johann
of Gmünd. The eastern choir bays of the Lower Rhenish cathedral of Xanten, a filiation
of Cologne, provide a precedent for a balustrade fronting a passage whose openings
are surmounted by sculpture, but little else that anticipates Prague.[10] The choir of
Augsburg Cathedral, associated by Marc Carel Schurr with Heinrich Parler, was finished
with a pathetically stunted clerestory as late as 1396.[11] Johann's remodelling of the
Romanesque choir in Basel Cathedral from 1357 was perforce in the form of a veneer of
flat tracery grids running down over the old Romanesque gallery openings, with not a
trace of the layering and depth found in Peter Parler's later work.[12] And the most
promising potential source for the Prague high choir, Peter Parler's own basilican choir
at St Bartholomew's in Kolín on the Elbe, begun in 1360 and consecrated in 1378,
shows little of Prague's complexity: no balustrade, no net vault, no recessions, no diagonal
breaks, no pronounced horizontality, no mirroring of interior and exterior (see Fig. 1,
p. 102).[13]

Two buildings in Parlerian circles may, however, have caught Peter Parler's
attention as resources for the design problems posed by his high choir. Neither has
been much discussed in relation to the cathedral, yet we know that one was designed
by Peter and the other perhaps at least overseen by him, and that both were well
placed chronologically to offer him inspiration. The first is the Frauenkirche in
Nuremberg, a church-cum-royal-chapel, begun c. 1350 but officially founded by Emperor
Charles IV, Peter Parler's patron, in 1355.[14] Consisting of an apsidal choir, a square hall
nave articulated by four centrally placed round columns, and a western porch with a
chapel of St Michael above it, the Frauenkirche was begun in the years after 1349,
probably in 1350, and was consecrated and structurally completed in 1358 (Fig. 3).[15]
Peter's contribution to this building, before Charles called him to Prague in 1356, is
still uncertain. Stylistically, the whole church belongs more to Heinrich Parler's work
in Augsburg and in the nave and choir of the Holy Cross church at Schwäbisch Gmünd,[16]
and recently Stefan Roller has cast serious doubt on the traditional attributions of
the Frauenkirche's western portal sculpture to the young Peter.[17] But there can be no
doubt that the Frauenkirche was known to Peter, and it is not inconceivable, given
its proximity to Heinrich Parler's work, that aspects of the building, especially its
later, western parts, may have been built with Peter's participation, perhaps even

FIG. 3.   Nuremberg: the Frauenkirche, from the north-west
Conway Library, Courtauld Institute of Art

under his wardenship as a young *Parlier* of the masons.[18] Something in Peter's early work must have impressed Charles IV, and there were few better opportunities for the young architect to catch the eye of his future patron than in Charles's own foundation.

Particularly important in this context is the little St Michael's chapel above the west porch of the Frauenkirche — among the last sections of the church to be completed, and all the more likely to encapsulate Peter's approach to architectural design at the moment when, in 1356, he was called to Prague.[19] Although overlooked in reference to Prague, this little traceried oratory anticipates some of the characteristics of the Prague high choir. It is, in the first place, a polygonally apsed glass-house 'chapel-clerestory' (but with a floor), hoisted onto the podium of an arcade storey (the portals of the porch), and separated from it by a prominent balustrade (Figs 1, 3, 4, & Col. Pl. IB in print edn). The exterior of this 'chapel-clerestory' and the porch below were repaired and 'restored' in *c.* 1820–30 and more extensively rebuilt in 1879–81, but much of the chapel's pre-restoration state is preserved in pre-1820 drawings.[20] It is the closest anticipator of a number of features in Prague's exterior clerestory. The spandrels of the St Michael chapel's easternmost windows form recessed panels, a feature found later on the exterior of the Prague clerestory, but absent from the more conventional Rayonnant exteriors with gabled clerestories.[21] Like Prague, these windows are flanked by tall pinnacles, whose finials terminate just below the upper cornice (Figs 2 (F), 4) — again, a feature absent from Cologne or from any advanced Rayonnant clerestory in southern Germany or the Rhineland, where the heads of the flyers do not abut pinnacles but rest on aedicules or solid buttresses, and where pinnacles in this position only appear above the parapet of the roof.[22] In its two canted bays St Michael's chapel also sports curvilinear tracery in the form of 'chasing' mouchettes, while its eastern windows have a window-within-a-window motif, with (like Prague) downward-drooping mouchettes over the outer lights

FIG. 4.   Nuremberg: the Frauenkirche, St Michael's chapel
Andreas Puth

(Figs 1, 4, & Col. Pl. IB in print edn).[23] If we add to this list the chapel's cresting in the form of the popular Nuremberg motif of curtains of tracery hanging from semicircular arches (compare the so-called 'bridal portal' of St Sebaldus, *c.* 1360, or the hanging tracery once over the high altar of the east choir of the same church), we have a precedent for the unique use of this type of decoration in the soffits of the flyers of the Prague high choir.[24] Worth noting too is the treatment of each exterior bay of the chapel as a series of layers, arranged in depth from outside to inside: first the buttresses, then the diagonally set pinnacles, then the window jambs and windows (Fig. 4 & Col. Pl. IB in print edn). Following Parler's principle that exterior and interior forms can be interchangeable, this, writ small, is a plausible blueprint — with the expected variations — for the Prague interior choir (Fig. 1). There the Nuremberg buttresses have become vault shafts, and their diagonally placed pinnacles have been replaced by slanting aedicules, followed in both cases by window jambs and, finally, windows. Given these similarities, it comes as no surprise that commentators have noted the influence of the Frauenkirche elsewhere in Prague Cathedral, notably in Peter Parler's re-use of the Y-shaped arches of its porch for his great window (now suppressed) in the base of the south tower, topped, in Prague as in Nuremberg, by a balustrade.[25] And is it a coincidence that the St Michael's chapel is the first fully modern Rayonnant version in the empire of what the Germans call a *Chörlein* (a miniature choir), popular as an oriel in Nuremberg in the later 14th century and resurfacing in Prague in the 1370s and 1380s in the oriels of the Old Town Hall and the Carolinum, Wenceslas IV's college for Prague University?[26]

Historical and patronal ties between Nuremberg and Prague add weight to these visual parallels. The stated purpose of Charles IV's foundation of the Frauenkirche in July 1355, and its dedication to the Virgin ('ad honorem gloriose semperque virginis Marie Genitricis Dei') was to say the daily office and canonical hours of the Virgin, and (less formally) to honour the anniversaries of Charles IV and his family.[27] To do this Charles set up a small college of priests, consisting of a precentor (*vicarium principal*) and two *mansionarii* (mansionaries, resident canons or vicars choral). The connections of the Nuremberg college to Prague were close, both institutionally and personally. The names of two of the earliest Nuremberg vicars have come down to us, both of whom held office at the Prague court: 'our beloved and reverend chaplain and courtier [*Hofgesinde*] Bartholomew' and (from 1361) 'our dear Johann Saxo, registrar [*registrator*] of our imperial chancellery'.[28] The Nuremberg mansionaries belonged to an elite club of Marian or mansionaries' colleges — founded by Charles or his bishops — in Prague, Wrocław, Magdeburg, Brno and Terenzo near Parma, all with the express purpose of enhancing Marian devotion through the extended recitation of the office of the Virgin.[29] The Italian college was founded near the site of Charles's Augustinian 'conversion experience' on the feast of the Assumption in 1333 — a terrifying vision of genital amputation, which (he was convinced) had been vouchsafed to him by the Virgin herself, as a warning against sexual excess. It set in train these propitiatory foundations, and cemented Marian devotion at the life-long centre of Charles's piety.[30]

All these institutions were modelled on the largest of these Marian colleges, that of the twenty-four mansionaries in Prague Cathedral. Founded in 1343, dedicated to the Virgin, and occupying the western (St Mary's) choir of the old Romanesque church, the college was moved into the still incomplete choir of the new cathedral in or a little before 1365.[31] In their new choir, also dedicated to the Virgin, the mansionaries occupied a most unusual position. The cathedral canons were pushed eastwards to occupy the two bays around St Vitus's altar, the *chorus major* (Fig. 5 (A)), while the

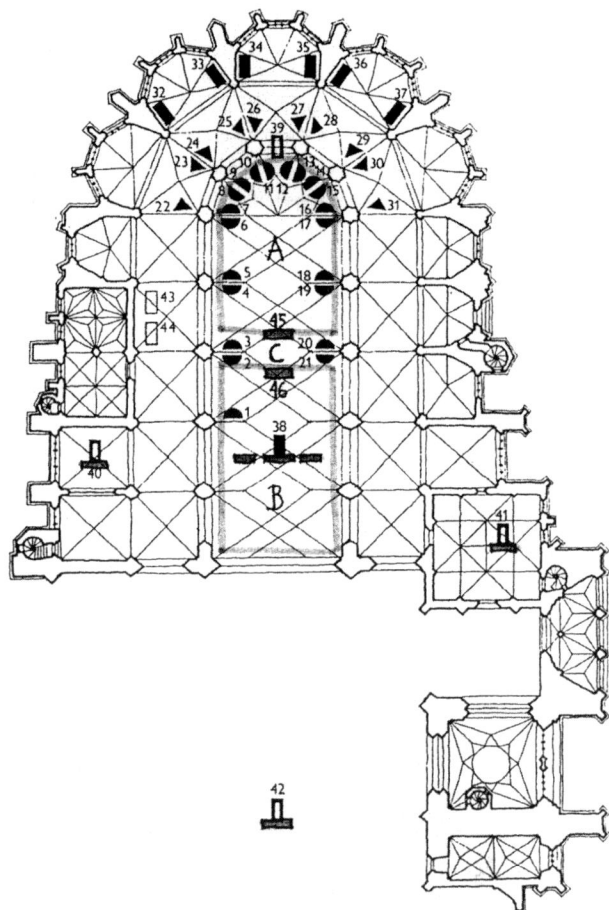

FIG. 5. Prague Cathedral: ground-plan showing altars.
A — canons' choir; B — choir of the Virgin;
C and 45 — altar of St Catherine *intra choros*;
38 — tomb of Charles IV, with the altars of St Nicholas, St Louis and the Holy Innocents;
39 — altar of St Vitus; 46 — altar of the Virgin

Klára Benešovská

mansionaries enjoyed a large, separate two-and-three-quarter-bay *chorus minor* in the western bays, dominated by the altar of the Virgin, and sheltering the tombs of Charles IV, his first two wives, and his first son Wenceslas (who died prematurely in 1353) — soon to be joined by other members of the royal family. In effect, the mansionaries' space became a royal chantry and a collegiate choir to complement the chapter's (Fig. 5 (B)).[32] When Peter Parler began the clerestory and triforium of the choir in the early 1370s, he started — according to the building accounts — at this western end of the choir, more precisely at the eastern crossing, and moved eastwards.[33] It is not inconceivable that questions of decorum may, at that moment, have turned Peter Parler's and Charles IV's minds to the Frauenkirche, especially when the Nuremberg foundation, unlike any of its sisters (except Terenzo), was placed directly under the control of the precentor of the Prague mansionaries ('precentori chori S. Mariae in ecclesia Pragensi').[34] Like the Frauenkirche, the new high choir could now be seen as the crowning architecture of a mansionaries' chapel and a royal memorial chantry, but one conceived on a much grander scale, as befitting the capital status of the Prague college. And, at the same time, Peter Parler's intimate knowledge of the Nuremberg church may have inspired him to borrow many of the Frauenkirche's most advanced Rayonnant features. Such a functional explanation must not be pressed too far, for it was not — as a proper decorum might expect — the day-to-day liturgical home of the mansionaries in Nuremberg, their austere choir, that Peter Parler chose to imitate and develop for his new upper parts, but the 'chapel-clerestory' of St Michael's oratory, which has the look of the emperor's pew, though it never seems to have been used as such.[35] Yet such category leaps are quite consistent with the accidents of inspiration, and with the powerful presence of Nuremberg in Charles's political and personal life to the end of his reign. It is very likely that the imperial relics were exhibited from the Frauenkirche's western balcony in celebration of the baptism (in St Sebaldus) of Charles's long-awaited heir, Wenceslas, in 1361.[36] In the same year, the wording in Charles's charter appointing Johannes Saxo to one of the church's three prebendaries refers to the church as a 'royal chapel' (*capella regia*), an honour shared only by the All Saints chapel in Prague Castle and the *capella regia* at Karlstein Castle.[37] The lasting status of the Frauenkirche, and its elevated and eye-catching western chapel, point to the network of possible connections, triggers and associations along which architectural ideas may have passed between Nuremberg and Prague Cathedral just before and after 1370, when Peter Parler was pondering on the design of his novel upper choir.

Indeed, one of these *capelle regie* may have been the second possible source for the peculiar treatment of the high choir in Prague: the chapel of All Saints in Prague Castle, attributed to Peter Parler in the inscription over his bust in the cathedral triforium.[38] Occupying a salient position off the east wing of the imperial palace the chapel fell victim to a devastating fire in 1541 and an anaemic restoration in 1579/80. But reliable reconstructions of the 1960s and recent excavations from 2001 have revealed a building of exceptional quality and invention, commensurate with its high status (Figs 6–10).[39] In 1339, as Margrave of Moravia, Charles IV re-founded the chapel with a provost, dean and eleven canons, and generously endowed it with relics and reliquaries, including a particle of the Crown of Thorns. Indeed, one of the new chapel's main functions was to act as a treasury to shelter important parts of the royal relic collection.[40] Its provost was *ex officio* the Bohemian chancellor. It belonged, as we have seen, with the

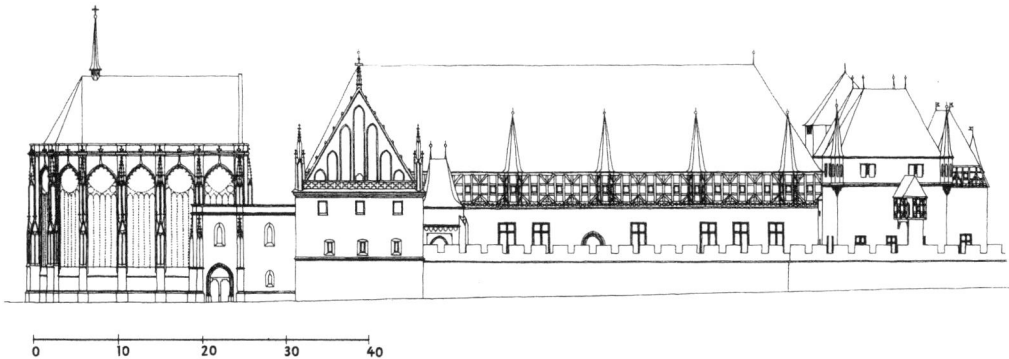

FIG. 6. Prague Castle and All Saints chapel: reconstruction by Dobroslava Menclová

FIG. 7. Prague Castle, All Saints chapel: reconstruction of exterior by Dobroslava Menclová and Václav Mencl

FIG. 8. Prague Castle, All Saints chapel: reconstruction of interior by Jan Sokol

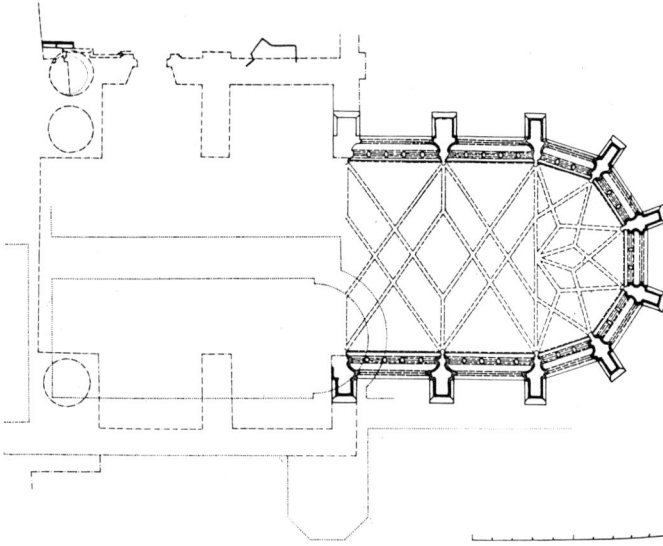

FIG. 9. Prague Castle, All Saints chapel: ground-plan (Sokol, 'Parléřův kostel' (as in n. 39))

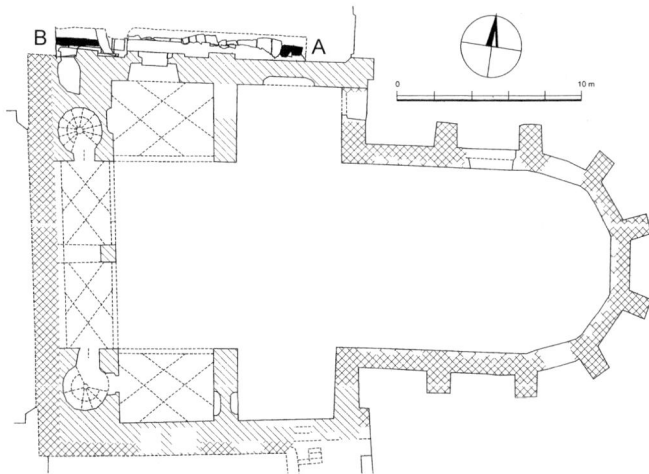

FIG. 10. Prague Castle, All Saints chapel: plan of the 2001 excavations

After Jan Frolík and Petr Chotebor

Frauenkirche in Nuremberg and the 'royal' chapel at Karlstein Castle, to an elite group of three *capelle regie* founded by Charles IV in connection either with relics or soul-masses or both.

The links with the Frauenkirche may have been more than institutional, since recent excavations in the east wing of Prague Castle have uncovered the lower parts of the exterior north wall of the chapel, once thought by Menclová to be fragments of a porch,[41] but now believed to be the northern section of a square nave, never completed, and opening on to the polygonally apsed choir (Fig. 10). This plan is strikingly like

Nuremberg's (without the *Westwerk*), and the square or near-square nave suggests that the Prague chapel may have been designed to accommodate four centrally placed pillars as part of a hall structure — a speculation given some weight by recent excavations of the royal chapel of St Sigismund and Our Lady in Buda Castle, founded by Charles IV's son (Sigismund IV), under construction in 1410, which show a short squarish hall nave opening into a chapel choir.[42] The sources for the Hungarian chapel, hitherto seen as Nurembergian, may well have come directly from the Prague exemplar.

But for the cathedral high choir the most important aspect of All Saints chapel was its three-bay apsidal sanctuary. Described by the chronicler Václav Hájek, who saw it before the fire, as 'a beautiful work built at great expense by Charles IV ... decorated at great expense with stone carvings ... and magnificent glass',[43] it was a Sainte-Chapelle of precocious delicacy and luminosity, a tribute to Charles's abiding fascination with its archetype in Paris, which had dazzled him as a boy, during his sojourn in Paris from 1323 to 1330, and would continue to colour his own blend of glamorous sanctity and royal myth. On 4 January 1378, as a gout-ridden old man in the last year of his life, he was carried into the Sainte-Chapelle to venerate the Passion relics with 'great devotion' (*grant devocion*) at an exhibition especially prepared for him.[44]

The parallels between the All Saints choir and the high choir in Prague are closer than those between the latter and the Frauenkirche, but they will always remain parallels, not provable sources, since although we know that the chapel was in use by 1382, its starting date is unrecorded. Designed 'c. 1370', the All Saints chapel was therefore coterminous with the high choir, and it shared with it many of its aesthetic principles and some of its actual forms. It copied (or anticipated?) the choir's ground-breaking use of a net vault, and the geometry of its apse (five sides of a decagon) (Figs 8, 9). It also exhibited the high choir's fascination with glass-house structures whose walls are conceived in depth in order to exploit visual layering and to experiment with new types of glazed peripheries. In the cathedral's high choir the plane of the clerestory is clearly distinguished from the plane of the vault responds, that is, the bay divisions (Fig. 1). Similarly, the windows of the All Saints chapel were set on a different plane to the bay divisions, in this case the buttresses. In the chapel this common premise leads to different, indeed opposing, results. Far from being recessed, like the cathedral clerestory, towards the outer wall plane, the chapel's windows were drawn onto the innermost plane of the wall, and were framed on the exterior by huge casements that did not splay outwards, as is normal with window jambs, but turned inwards, to join the salient buttresses (Figs 7, 9). By thus uncoupling the windows from the buttresses, Parler could stretch each window bay *behind* its two buttresses to create colossal five-light openings, with each window drawn so closely towards the inner plane of the wall that the vault responds were reduced to single, thin shafts that barely interrupted the chapel's flat and almost continuously glazed envelope (Figs 8, 9). The effect must have been prodigious. Not since the apses of Saint-Urbain at Troyes or of Saint-Martin aux Bois had any structure reduced its interior to such taut cages of glass, held tensely in place by the thinnest of mullions and responds. In the cathedral choir Peter Parler separated window plane from bay division in order to recess and narrow the window composition; in the All Saints chapel he did the same thing in order to produce an opposite effect — one of unparalleled glazed expansion. A second Parlerian principle, the interchangeability of interior and exterior effects, comes into operation on the chapel's *exterior* elevations (Fig. 7). Here, the cathedral's *interior* play with recession and framing was given full rein. The most eye-catching devices on the exterior of the chapel — the ones calculated to draw our attention to it from the city beneath it — were the large ogee arches crowning the window apertures, and the curtains of tracery hanging from them, casting deep shadows onto the back plane of the windows. Here, as in the cathedral choir (Fig. 1), tracery was recessed into extreme depth and then framed by a foreground of complex linear motifs, either vaults shafts and aedicules (in the cathedral) or curtained and hooded arches (in the chapel).

Comparisons of this unspecific kind, aimed more at uncovering general attitudes to design than identifying particular formal similarities, may seem a soft-centred method of stylistic analysis. But I would argue that such approaches are forced on us by the evidence of changing patterns of design in later Gothic architecture. By the middle of the 14th century, when lodges were building up their own extensive collections of plans and making them available to other architects, Paris had lost its architectural pre-eminence in Europe, and regional and national versions of Gothic were flourishing in such far-flung centres as Naples, Barcelona and Prague itself. The exact copying of revered models was a thing of the past. Masons no longer needed to travel to acquaint themselves with the most fashionable ideas. Cologne's 13th-century reworking of Amiens, or Strasbourg's of Saint-Denis, were no longer *de rigueur*. In the decades either side of 1300, architectural influence had become something less literal, less overtly dependent on its sources, more elusive and — in conceptual terms — more structural. Linguists might define it as the change from borrowing new words to adopting a new syntax, though a more useful distinction might be Ferdinand de Saussure's classic differentiation between *langue* and *parole*.[45] *Parole*, the outward vocal apparatus or individual utterance, belongs to the world of literal borrowing, the overt commerce of speech; *langue* opens up to us the rules and conventions of a whole language by uncovering its deeper structures and substrata. In this paper I have concentrated as much on the *langue* as on the *parole* of Peter Parler's language. How else can we produce a reasoned, if always idealised, reconstruction of the problems and situations posed to the great Gothic architects by the exigencies of their tasks, and of the solutions that they brought to bear in solving them? A foray into *langue* must count as at least one method of explaining the mysteries of architectural causation.

ACKNOWLEDGEMENTS

For generous help in the preparation of this paper I am profoundly indebted to Klára Benešovská, Timothy Juckes, Marc Carel Schurr, Andreas Puth, and Zoë Opačić (who invited me to speak at the conference). I would also like to thank warmly Dr Gerhard Weilandt for sending me a copy of Katharina Blohm's dissertation on the Frauenkirche and Stephan Schuler's *Salbuch*. Without their practical and inspirational support this article would certainly be the poorer.

NOTES

1. The literature on the choir of Prague Cathedral is enormous. The best recent summaries on questions of dating, function, meaning and stylistic pedigree are K. Benešovská, I. Hlobil et al., *Peter Parler and St Vitus's Cathedral 1356–1399* (Prague 1999); M. C. Schurr, *Die Baukunst Peter Parlers: Der Prager Veitsdom, das*

Heiligkreuzmünster in Schwäbisch Gmünd und die Bartholomäuskirche zu Kolín im Spannungsfeld von Kunst und Geschichte (Ostfildern 2003); idem, 'Saint-Guy de Prague: une Cathédrale Gothique "À la Française"? Réflexions sur les Sources de son Architecture', *Bulletin Monumental*, 162/4 (2004), 273–87, esp. 277–78.

2. B. Schock-Werner, 'Die Parler', in A. Legner ed., *Die Parler und der Schöne Stil 1350–1400: Europäische Kunst unter den Luxemburgern*, 5 vols (Cologne 1978–80), III, 7–8; J. Vítovský, 'Die Künstlerfamilie "Parler" in neuem Licht', in R. Strobel and A. Siefert ed., *Parlerbauten: Architektur, Skulptur, Restaurierung (Internationales Parler-Symposium Schwäbisch Gmünd 17.–19. Juli 2001)* (Stuttgart 2004), 149–54. Much of our information about Peter Parler's family and his work in Prague is dependent on the inscription above his bust in the triforium of Prague Cathedral. For a translation and transcription of this, see Benešovská and Hlobil, *Peter Parler* (as in n. 1), 152–55. The text of all the inscriptions may also be found in the Appendix to Professor Bartlová's article in this volume, which however, casts doubt on the reliability of these inscriptions as medieval documents. If she is correct, we shall have substantially to revise much of the little that we know about Peter Parler and his work in both Swabia and Bohemia.

3. For the closest analysis of the connections between Prague and Cologne, see C. Freigang, 'Köln und Prag. Der Prager Veitsdom als Nachfolgebau des Kölner Domes', in L. Honnefelder, N. Trippen and A. Wolff ed., *Dombau und Theologie im mittelalterlichen Köln: Festschrift zur 750-Jahrfeier der Grundsteinlegung des Kölner Doms und zum 65. Geburtstag von Joachim Kardinal Meisner*, Studien zum Kölner Dom, VI (Cologne 1998), 49–86.

4. For a discussion of the busts and of recent literature on the topic, see C. Freigang, 'Werkmeister als Stifter. Bemerkungen zur Tradition der Prager Baumeisterbüsten', in B. Klein and H. Wolger von dem Knesebeck ed., *Nobilis Arte Manus: Festschrift zum 70. Geburtstage von Antje Middeldorf Kosegarten* (Dresden/Kassel 2002), 244–64.

5. U. Brinkmann and R. Lauer, 'Die mittelalterlichen Glasfenster des Kölner Domchores', in *Himmelslicht: Europäische Glasmalerei im Jahrhundert des Kölner Dombaus (1248–1349)* (Cologne 1998), 23–33.

6. A fuller discussion of this bilateral organisation of circulation at Prague is given in P. Crossley, 'Peter Parler and England. A Problem Revisited', *Wallraf-Richartz-Jahrbuch*, 64 (2003), 53–82, esp. 69–71. See also idem, 'Peter Parler and England - A problem revisited', in *Parlerbauten* (as in n. 2), 155–79. I find the origins of the distinctive 'undulating' elevation in Prague in the English West Country. Schurr traces it to Regensburg Cathedral nave; see Schurr, 'Saint-Guy de Prague' (as in n. 1), 277–78.

7. A point first made, in the context of the choir of Le Mans, by R. Branner, *St Louis and the Court Style in Gothic Architecture* (London 1965), 81.

8. The Gerona expertise of architects, held in 1417, referred to certain rules of thumb for calculating the necessary size of buttresses (see P. Frankl, *The Gothic: Literary Sources and Interpretations through Eight Centuries* (Princeton 1960), 84–86), while at Milan the warring factions each invoked their own building traditions (see J. White, *Art and Architecture in Italy 1250–1400* (Harmondsworth 1966), 336–50).

9. For this and earlier literature, see Crossley, 'Peter Parler and England' (as in n. 6), passim.

10. The similarities are noted in Freigang, 'Köln und Prag' (as in n. 3), 83–84.

11. Schurr, *Die Baukunst Peter Parlers* (as in n. 1), 44–51; and idem, 'Heinrich und Peter Parler am Heiligkreuzmünster in Schwäbisch Gmünd', in *Parlerbauten* (as in n. 2), 29–38. For the building history of Augsburg choir, see A. Chevalley, *Der Dom zu Augsburg*, Die Kunstdenkmäler von Bayern, Neue Folge, I (Munich 1995), esp. 110–19.

12. P. Kurmann, 'Neues Bauen in altem Rahmen: Das Basler Münster des Johannes von Gmünd', in *Parlerbauten* (as in n. 2), 87–94.

13. J. Kuthan, 'Zu Parlers Chor der St. Bartholomäuskirche in Kolín an der Elbe', in *Parlerbauten* (as in n. 2), 141–48; and Marc Carel Schurr's article in this volume.

14. G. Bräutigam, 'Gmünd - Prag - Nürnberg. Die Nürnberger Frauenkirche und der Prager Parlerstil vor 1360', *Jahrbuch der Berliner Museen*, 3 (1961), 38–75; idem, 'Die Nürnberger Frauenkirche. Idee und Herkunft ihrer Architektur', in H. Schlegel and C. Zoege von Mannteuffel ed., *Festschrift für Peter Metz* (Berlin 1965), 170–97; idem, 'Nürnberg als Kaiserstadt', in F. Seibt ed., *Kaiser Karl IV.: Staatsmann und Mäzen* (Munich 1978), 339–43. The fullest account is now K. Blohm, 'Die Frauenkirche in Nürnberg (1352–1358). Architektur, Baugeschichte, Bedeutung' (unpublished dissertation, Technische Universität, Berlin, 1992). The 1355 foundation charter refers to it as 'novam ecclesiam seu capellam'; see Blohm, 'Die Frauenkirche', 134.

15. The exact beginning of the building of the Frauenkirche is not known. It was started sometime between the Jewish pogrom, which erupted towards the end of 1349 (when the synagogue was destroyed to make way for the Frauenkirche on the same site) and the first endowment in the form of a chantry mass documented on the 19 February 1352. The document refers to the church as being under construction ('in der newen capelln in man bawet'). Bräutigam, 'Gmünd - Prag - Nürnberg' (as in n. 14), 39, and Blohm, 'Die Frauenkirche' (as in n. 14), 132–34.

16. Schurr, *Die Baukunst Peter Parlers* (as in n. 1), 134–35.

17. S. Roller, 'Die Nürnberger Frauenkirche und ihr Verhältnis zu Gmünd und Prag. Beobachtungen und Überlegungen zur frühen "Parler-Skulptur"', in *Parlerbauten* (as in n. 2), 229–38.

18. His status only as a warden or *Parlier* would explain why the church was not attributed to him in the inscription above his bust in the Prague Cathedral triforium.

19. I am not convinced by Vítovský's suggestion that Heinrich Parler, Peter's father, was the principal architect in Prague from 1356 to 1366; see Vítovský, 'Die Künstlerfamilie' (as in n. 2), 150–51.

20. Blohm discusses the 19th-century restorations in detail, and draws our attention to drawings of the exterior of the west front and the St Michael's chapel by Johann Jacob Schwarz in 1736, and Georg Christoph Wilders in 1816; see Blohm, 'Die Frauenkirche' (as in n. 14), 3–20 and figs 9, 10, 11. These are critical in reconstructing the original 14th-century appearance of the façade.

21. Note, however, that recessed *interior* spandrels appear in the nave arcade of Regensburg Cathedral, dating to the 1330s; see Schurr, *Die Baukunst Peter Parlers* (as in n. 1), 107; and idem, 'Saint-Guy de Prague' (as in n. 1), 277. C. Wilson (*The Gothic Cathedral: The Architecture of the Great Church 1130–1530* (London 2000), 230–31) suggested that the source for Prague's panel motif might be the exterior eastern wall of the choir of Wells Cathedral.

22. The pre-restoration existence of the pinnacles in the Frauenkirche is confirmed by Wilders's 1816 drawing of the west façade; see Blohm 'Die Frauenkirche' (as in n. 14), 7–8 and fig. 10. The Prague pinnacles are clearly visible in Schurr, *Die Baukunst Peter Parlers* (as in n. 1), figs 8, 10, 11; and Benešovská and Hlobil, *Peter Parler* (as in n. 1), figs on 112, 113, 122. Compare the cathedrals of Regensburg, Strasbourg and Cologne, where pinnacles only appear above the level of the roof parapet.

23. The mouchettes appear in some of the pre-1820 drawings; see Blohm, 'Die Frauenkirche' (as in n. 14), figs 9, 10, 11. They do not however provide evidence for the present window-within-a-window motifs, nor the drooping mouchettes. The most informative drawings, by Wilders in 1816, show the easternmost window as a simple design, with two-lights supporting a quatrefoiled oculus. But the drawing is suspiciously summary, as if the artist had deliberately ignored the window, as he did with other details in his drawings of the façade. This leaves open the possibility that the easternmost windows could reflect the original designs.

24. For the St Sebaldus curtains, see G. Weilandt, *Die Sebalduskirche in Nürnberg: Bild und Gesellschaft im Zeitalter der Gotik und Renaissance*, Studien zur internationalen Architektur- und Kunstgeschichte, XLVII (Petersberg 2007). Other sources for the Prague hanging motif can be found in the portals of the choir of Augsburg Cathedral (*c.* 1350), the sedilia of the St Catherine's chapel in Strasbourg (1340s), and the north portal of the choir of Freiburg Minster (*c.* 1360); see Schurr, *Die Baukunst Peter Parlers* (as in n. 1), 105, n. 399. All this depends on our dating of these curtains to the original 14th-century façade and not to Adam Krafft's remodelling of the upper parts of the St Michael's choir, in 1506–09, to make way for the clock. Blohm ('Die Frauenkirche' (as in n. 14), 151–52) believes that no reconstruction of the original upper parts is possible, given the complete lack of medieval stonework in these areas. In the easternmost bays, where there are no blind arches, the roof sits closely above the apex of the windows. If we conclude from this that the original roof line was the same in the western, polygonal, bays, then the roof line would have been too low to accommodate the curtained arches. However such curtains belong stylistically to the 14th century, not to the early 16th.

25. Bräutigam, 'Die Nürnberger Frauenkirche' (as in n. 14), 184, 187.

26. A. Timmermann, 'Two Parlerian Sacrament Houses and their Microarchitectural Context', *Umění*, 47 (1999), 400–12, esp. 403–05.

27. The foundation charter is in Blohm, 'Die Frauenkirche' (as in n. 14), 220–21, and printed in G. Dobner, *Monumenta historica Boemiae*, 6 vols (Prague 1764–85), III (1774), 346ff. See also F. Kavka, *Vláda Karla IV. za jeho císařství (1355–1378)*, 2 vols (Prague 1993), I (1355–64), 16–17.

28. For a transcript of the whole charter, see Blohm, 'Die Frauenkirche' (as in n. 14), 158–60, 226.

29. For all these foundations, see Blohm, 'Die Frauenkirche' (as in n. 14), 153–66.

30. *Karoli IV Imperatoris Romanorum Vita ab Eo Ipso Conscripta et Hystoria Nova de Sancto Wenceslao Martyre. Autobiography of Emperor Charles IV and his Legend of St. Wenceslas*, B. Nagy and F. Schaer ed. and trans. (Budapest/New York 2001), ch. VII, 58–65; Z. Hledíková, 'Fundace českých králu ve 13. století', *Sborník historický*, 28 (1998), 5–55, esp. 10–11. For Charles's Marian devotions, see F. Machilek, 'Privatfrömmigkeit und Staatsfrömmigkeit', in Seibt ed., *Kaiser Karl IV.* (as in n. 14), 87–101. For Charles IV's vision in Terenzo specifically, see O. Odložilík, 'The Terenzo dream of Charles IV', *Orbis medievalis: Festgabe für Anton Blaschka* (Weimar 1970), 163–73.

31. The date of the consecration of the new altar to the Virgin in the Gothic choir. The space was almost certainly covered with a provisional roof, since the upper parts of the choir were not begun until the early 1370s. The move from the half-surviving Romanesque cathedral to the uncompleted Gothic eastern choir is clearly plotted by K. Benešovská, 'Die Prager Kirche zur Zeit des Erzbischofs Arnestus von Pardubice', *Miscellanea musicologica*, 37 (2003), 29–46, esp. 35–38.

32. K. Benešovská, 'Aménagement des Tombeaux Royaux dans la Cathédrale de Prague à l'Époque des Luxembourg', *Hortus Artium Medievalium*, 10 (2004), 65–74.

33. The eastern arch of the crossing — the triumphal arch into the choir — was closed in 1373, allowing work to continue at triforium and clerestory levels, moving eastwards, north before south, to close with the turning of the high vault on 12 July 1385. See Benešovská and Hlobil, *Peter Parler* (as in n. 1), 73, and Schurr, *Die Baukunst Peter Parlers* (as in n. 1), 65–67.

34. Blohm, 'Die Frauenkirche' (as in n. 14), 159, 220.

35. Blohm, 'Die Frauenkirche' (as in n. 14), 192–98. See also E. Eichhorn, 'Der Sebalder Engelschor. Ein Beitrag zur mittelalterlichen Sakralarchitektur Nürnbergs', in H. Baier ed., *600 Jahre Ostchoir St. Sebald - Nürnberg 1379–1979* (Neustadt an der Aisch 1979), 94–116, esp. 106–10. He properly questions Bräutigam's notion of the Frauenkirche as a 'copy' of Aachen Minster, and relates the nave of the Frauenkirche to the late Romanesque castle chapel.

36. The earliest source for this plausible supposition is Siegmund Meisterlein's Nuremberg chronicle of *c.* 1488. See Blohm, 'Die Frauenkirche' (as in n. 14), 180–82; H. Kühne, *Ostensio Reliquiarum: Untersuchungen über Entstehung, Ausbreitung, Gestalt und Funktion der Heiltumsweisungen im römisch-deutschen Regnum*, Arbeiten zur Kirchengeschichte, LXXV (Berlin/New York 2000), 130–32.

37. 'Quod cum in nova capella regia Civitatis Nurembergensis . . .'. See Blohm, 'Die Frauenkirche' (as in n. 14), 167–68, 226; and N. Grass, 'Zur Rechtsgeschichte der abendländischen Königskirche. Einwirkungen französisch-böhmischer Sakralkultur auf die Capella regia Austriaca', *Festschrift Siegfried Bader* (Cologne/Graz 1965), 159–84, esp. 164–69. The chapel at Karlstein referred to as *capella regia* is the chapel of the Lesser Tower. The phrase occurs in Charles's request to Innocent VI in 1357 for visitors to the 'royal chapel' in the Lesser Tower. See J. Fajt ed., *Magister Theodoricus: Court Painter to Emperor Charles IV* (Prague 1998), 96. Although the charter does not specify the exact location of the chapel, the date of 1357 makes it certain that the reference is to the college of priests founded at the chapel of Our Lady to which the small oratory of St Catherine (then dedicated to the Passion of Our Lord) was also attached.

38. Benešovská and Hlobil, *Peter Parler* (as in n. 1), 153.

39. J. Sokol, 'Parléřův kostel Všech Svatých na Pražském Hradě', *Umění*, 17 (1969), 574–82; J. Kaigl, 'Kostel Všech Svatých na Pražském Hradě pred požárem v roce 1541 (Příspěvek k historické topografii Pražského Hradu)', *Zprávy památkové péče*, 52/2 (1992), 1–8; J. Homolka, 'Paris - Gmünd - Prag. Die königliche Allerheiligenkapelle auf der Prager Burg', in *Parlerbauten* (as in n. 2), 135–39.

40. Grass, 'Zur Rechtsgeschichte' (as in n. 36), 166–68.

41. D. Menclová, *České hrady*, 2 vols (Prague 1972), II, 126–32 and figs 177, 178. Her reconstructions of the chapel, based on Vaclav Mencl's, are a little fanciful in their details, especially of the window tracery.

42. A. Vegh, 'Skulpturenfunde aus der Zeit Sigismunds aus dem Umfeld des Königspalastes von Buda', in I. Takács ed., *Sigismundus Rex et Imperator: Kunst und Kultur zur Zeit Sigismunds von Luxemburg 1387–1437* (Augsburg 2006), 219–24, esp. fig. 1 (where the chapel is marked as 'B2'), and fig. 6. It should be pointed out, however, that the Buda nave was four bays long, not three, and had six not four pillars. See also K. Benešovská, 'Le bouleversement de la mise en scène du pouvoir. L'art en Bohême à l'époque des rois Wenceslas IV (1378–1419) et Sigismond de Luxembourg (1420–1437)', in M. Pauly and F. Reinert ed., *Sigismund von Luxemburg: Ein Kaiser in Europa*, Tagungsband des internationalen historischen und kunsthistorischen Kongresses in Luxemburg, 8.–10. Juni 2005 (Mainz 2006), 263–83, esp. 272 and n. 26.

43. Václav Hájek z Libočan, *O neštiastné příhodie, kteráž jse stala skrze oheň v Menším Miestie Pražském a na Hradie Swatého Wacslawa i na Hradčanech etc., Leta M.D. XXXXI.*; quoted in Sokol, 'Parléřův kostel' (as in n. 38), n. 3, 581–82.

44. R. Delachenal ed., *Les Grandes Chroniques de France: Chronique des règnes de Jean II et de Charles V* (Paris 1916), 193ff. For the whole episode, see P. Kováč, 'Notes on the Description of the Sainte-Chapelle in Paris from 1378', in J. Fajt ed., *Court Chapels of the High and Late Middle Ages and their Artistic Decoration* (Prague 2003), 162–70. The Parisian parallels with the All Saints chapel are underlined by Kaigl, 'Kostel Všech svatých' (as in n. 38), passim.

45. J. Culler, *Ferdinand de Saussure* (Ithaca/New York 1986).

The Choir Triforium of Prague Cathedral Revisited: The Inscriptions and Beyond

MILENA BARTLOVÁ

Twenty-one portrait busts in the choir triforium of St Vitus's Cathedral in Prague are surmounted by inscriptions giving the name, status and deeds of the person represented. It has been known for some time that the inscription above the bust of the architect and sculptor Peter Parler contains puzzling errors. This contribution undertakes an analysis of the inscriptions as a single written source. Mistakes were found in one third of the inscriptions, as well as surprising omissions. Stratigraphic analysis of the polychromy revealed that the ochre ground under the inscriptions was also painted over the polychromy of the busts, which in turn had been painted over the deteriorated sculptures. The inscriptions should therefore not be considered a definitive source for the 14th century and may have been written in their present form in the 18th century in an attempt to restore the original lettering. The inscription above the bust of Charles IV has been one of the main sources for scholars who wished to attribute the arrangement of some parts of the cathedral to the emperor's personal invention. This article, however, argues in favour of the cathedral chapter as the true builder of the great church.

A visitor to the choir triforium of Prague's St Vitus Cathedral will encounter a row of sculptural portraits that has no parallel (Fig. 1 & Col. Pl. IA in print edn).[1] The portraits are barely visible from the ground, and access to them is rather inconvenient. Aside from the general unwillingness of the custodians in the cathedral to permit visitors entry, the constricted gallery can be reached only via a narrow winding staircase in the north-western tower, built in the late 19th century during the reconstruction and completion of the cathedral. Owing to the fact that the passages through the piers in the gallery were walled in at the same time to improve tectonic stability, gaining access to the portraits is not best suited for the corpulent among visitors, who now have to squeeze through curved narrow passages running behind each pier. Before the late 19th century, access was even more arduous, as it was possible to ascend to the gallery solely via an openwork staircase attached to the great south tower; it remains unclear, however, how the staircase's upper end was connected to the gallery level of the then still incomplete transept.[2] The dating of the busts relies on the documented progress of the building and is generally situated in the latter part of the 1370s. Authorship of them has long been attributed to Peter Parler, but recent opinion is in favour of a larger number of sculptors' being involved, leaving to Peter himself only some of the portraits — notably not his own — and the general design.[3]

Each portrait bust is accompanied by a monumental inscription, painted directly above it, stating the identity of the person depicted, who in most cases is also

FIG. 1.   Prague Cathedral: choir triforium, looking north-west
Martin Frouz

identifiable by the coats of arms flanking the bust (Figs 2, 3). The state of conservation is far from uniform. All the inscriptions are in place, but some are barely
legible while others are quite clear. The inscriptions that have been exposed to direct
sunlight are in the worst condition. Historians have been interested in the inscriptions
since the end of the 18th century, and that interest has led to several attempts to make
the inscriptions more visible.[4] In the 1850s, the Cologne Cathedral conservator Franz
Bock had them expertly copied at a ratio of 1:1 (see the Appendix at the end of this
article). Because the visibility of the inscriptions varies, the single most important
source for all scholars interested in their form and content is still the reproductions of
these copies, published in 1906.[5] After the restoration by Alena and Vlastimil Berger,
undertaken between 1972 and 1976, the inscriptions were again more visible and, to
some extent, legible. Together with the sculpted and painted coats of arms they
inform us that the twenty-one portraits in the triforium gallery are those of Charles
IV, king of Bohemia and emperor of the Holy Roman Empire; members of his family;
the three archbishops and the cathedral canons who had served as directors of the
building project; and, famously, the two principal architects of the cathedral —
Matthias of Arras and Peter Parler. The busts are set into the piers, over the passages
that led through them. Charles, his wives, and his parents occupy the central position,
in the apex of the choir apse, followed on the northern and southern sides of the choir
by other members of Charles's family, the archbishops, the canons, and the two
architects. The remaining places in both clerestories are filled with five sculptures of
the same size, representing a cat fighting with a dog; a gryphon; a head of a man in

FIG. 2.   Prague Cathedral, choir triforium:
bust of Anne of Schweidnitz
Martin Frouz

FIG. 3.   Prague Cathedral, choir triforium:
bust of Johanna of Bavaria
Martin Frouz

foliage; a grotesque male head; and a head of a monster.[6] Similar passages cut through the buttresses on the exterior of the choir polygon, situated directly above the internal triforium, are surmounted by ten figural busts representing Christ, the Virgin, and the eight patron saints of Bohemia. The remaining external passages along the choir's southern and northern sides are decorated with allegorical animals, monsters, and a heraldic lion.

The inscriptions in the triforium have hitherto not been studied together as one group, although such an approach is undoubtedly warranted by their uniform appearance and manner in which they were executed. Baroque historiographers — who are going to play an important role in our story later on — were interested in the information the inscriptions provide about the first three archbishops of Prague. Canon Johann Thomas Berghauer was the first to publish any of the inscriptions: three of them appeared in the 1720s. Modern interest has focused almost exclusively on Peter Parler and on his predecessor, Matthias of Arras (Figs 4, 5, 6). This interest dates back to the second decade of the 19th century, when one of the first medieval art historians, Sulpice Boisserée, asked the leading Czech historian Josef Dobrovský to verify the reading of Parler's bust inscription published a generation earlier by Franz M. Pelzel, according to which Peter Parler came to Prague from Bologna.[7] The text written

FIG. 4.   Prague Cathedral, choir triforium: bust of Matthias of Arras
Martin Frouz

above Parler's sculpted portrait has been drawing the most attention ever since, because it is the main source of biographical information about this important artistic personality.[8] Compared with the information gained from other sources however it contains three errors: the surname of Peter's father is not given in its conventional form, but as '*Arler*'; Peter's place of origin is given as '*Polonia*' instead of the correct '*Colonia*', and the date of the of the completion of the cathedral's high choir is given as 1386, instead of the correct 1385. Furthermore, Peter Parler had little if any involvement in the construction of the stone bridge in Prague now known as the Charles Bridge (Karlův most).[9]

Art historians have had to deal with these problems. Otto Kletzl suggested in 1928 that the dubious '*P*' in '*Polonia*' appeared because the whole inscription was a forgery, perpetrated in the early 19th century by Václav Hanka, a leading representative of the Czech emancipation movement famous for his forgeries of Slavonic names in medieval manuscripts, who is also believed to have had a leading part in the writing of two epic poems later unveiled as Romantic fabrications of the Ossian type. The intention of the forger(s) was presumably to make Peter Parler a Slav by assuming that his roots were in Poland.[10] Kletzl was, however, mistaken: Pelzel had read the strange and unique spelling '*Arler*' before 1781, so the inscription must have already been in place in its current form then, and the '*P*' in '*Polonia*' simply a misdeciphered '*b*'. In 1817, the most critical of the historiographers of the Czech Enlightment, Josef Dobrovský,

FIG. 5. Prague Cathedral, choir triforium: inscription above the bust of Matthias of Arras

Milena Bartlová

FIG. 6. Prague Cathedral, choir triforium: bust of Peter Parler

Martin Frouz

recorded the inscriptions meticulously in the form they have today. He mentioned that they were in poor condition as a result of old age, and this suggests that they could not have been executed recently. In spite of this, the hypothesis of Romantic, nationalistic forgeries has been revived by the Castle archivist Marie Kostílková in the 1980s and 1990s.[11]

Art historians have mostly tried to restore the credibility of this rare source of biographical data on a master mason by opining that the mistakes crept in because the texts were composed and the inscriptions executed not at the time at which the busts were completed, that is in the 1370s, but only during the period when Václav of Radeč was director of the building project and after the completion of the vault mentioned in his inscription, that is between 1389 and 1392.[12] Less frequently expressed has been the alternative opinion that the inscriptions we see today are in fact slightly mistaken restorations of the damaged originals, faithful to them to a large extent and executed some time after the iconoclastic episode of the Hussite Wars, but still during the Late Gothic period. The Polish origin of the Jagiellonian dynasty who ruled Bohemia at that time might thus explain the 'Polonia' mistake.[13] Some art historians have claimed that the doubtful historical reliability of the inscriptions is irrelevant, since other methods, namely formal analysis, and, above all, iconology can provide sufficiently good results.[14] Historians proper could hardly subscribe to such an approach, not to mention those art historians who may have less confidence in iconology as a method.[15] In any event, both groups would habitually rely on other pieces of information gained from the inscriptions, an approach that should be also discarded if the inscriptions are deemed irrelevant.

New insights into the problem were formulated in several ways in the context of this study. The first was the critical analysis of the sources for the contents of all twenty-one inscriptions, taken as a whole.[16] The second was an attentive reading of the extensive reports filed by the restorers who attended to the busts and inscriptions between 1972 and 1976.[17] Further to this, two more expert opinions were canvassed. According to an epigraphist, the script is of a 14th-century type. However, the proposition that the inscriptions were the work of one hand could not be corroborated. The inscriptions contain many errors as regards medieval usage of conventional abbreviations, and two of them contain rounded points that were not in use before the 16th century.[18] Analysis of the language yielded similar results: the Latin is generally correct, and the relatively small number of odd errors could be attributed to general negligence on the part of the scribe.[19] Analysis of the content has brought to light the fact that grave errors in dates and names are to be found not only in the Peter Parler's inscription, but in one third of the inscriptions, that is in seven out of the total of twenty-one. Charles's third wife, Anne of Schweidnitz, is reported in the inscription as being 'from Bosnia, in the kingdom of Dalmatia', one of the strangest errors, since no such kingdom existed. Duke Wenceslas of Luxembourg died in 1383, not 1380 as stated in the inscription. The first and second directors of the building lodge, Busco Leonhardi and Nicholas nicknamed the Squab, have the dates of their deaths shifted by twenty-two years and three years respectively. Most notably, Charles IV's age of death is mistakenly given as sixty-four instead of sixty-two. In the inscription concerning Matthias of Arras, Charles is said to have been elected Holy Roman Emperor in Avignon in 1342, whereas he only accepted his candidature there in 1344, and was only formally elected at Rhens in 1346.

If such mistakes were not enough, the inscriptions contain several conspicuous omissions. These concern first of all Wenceslas IV, Bohemian and Roman king, and Jan of Jenstein, archbishop of Prague, who held their respective offices at the time at which it is supposed the inscriptions were executed. Jenstein is credited only with rebuilding the tower of the archbishop's castle at Keyserberg (Kyšperk, Supí Hora) in northern Bohemia, while the inscription over Wenceslas's head recalls nothing more than his royal titles and the fact that he is the son of Charles IV. This inscription is, in fact, one of the shortest, and thus clearly fits the young appearance of the portrait, made in the late 1370s — but it is hardly fitting to Wenceslas's position in later years. Furthermore, the title of cardinal has been omitted from the inscription of Archbishop Jan Očko of Vlašim, the first Bohemian prelate on whom this title was bestowed. More surprisingly, the solemn laying of the foundation stone of the cathedral on 21 November 1344, celebrated together with the arrival of the papal pallium for the first archbishop of Prague, is not mentioned in any of the inscriptions, even though it is the single most notable moment concerning the building in other contemporary reports. This omission is all the more surprising, since out of the fourteen people mentioned as being present at the solemnities of laying the foundation stones of the choir (in 1344) and of the nave (in 1386) on the memorial panel now placed at the southern entrance of the cathedral (the original position of which has not been established to my knowledge), ten have their busts in the triforium. A minor but potentially important mistake can be found in the inscription of Johanna of Bavaria, the first wife of King Wenceslas IV. Her death on 31 December is placed in 1386, although until the middle of the 15th century the beginning of the New Year was set at 25 December and the correct dating therefore should be 1387, which can be, in fact, found in contemporary sources.

Taken together, these data do not allow a critical historian any option other than to pronounce the triforium inscriptions to be unreliable as a historical source for the 14th century. Any information gained from them can be considered correct only in so far as it can be corroborated from another, unrelated source. This would be true even if the inscriptions were written in the 14th century. This dating was called into question by the mistakes and omissions outlined above, but it is clearly excluded by the results of a stratigraphic analysis of the layers of paint. This shows that the monochrome ochre paint under the inscriptions was also painted over all the busts, covering the remains of a rich polychromy that had, in turn, been painted over the already damaged sculptures.[20] The visual effect achieved thereby was to unify the surface of the busts and their backdrop, so as to conform to the monochrome aesthetic — which is certainly not medieval — that unifies the building's surfaces and stone sculptures. The ochre base coat of the inscriptions lies directly on the secondarily abraded surface of the building blocks, though scattered traces of gold and silver were found underneath.

So who wrote what we can see now on the triforium, when and why? The answer cannot be anything else than an accumulation of hypotheses. The 'when' will have to fit between the 1680s, when the correct 'Colonia' may have been read by Bohuslav Balbín, and the *terminus ante quem* in the late 1770s, when the inscriptions were read and recorded by Pelzel in their present form, as mentioned above.[21] The very first report on the existence of the inscriptions and recording of three of them comes from Canon Johann Thomas Berghauer, who characterised them in 1723 as 'vetustate cxccsa ct laccrata' ('ruined and mutilated through old age'). He was unable to decipher the 'Arras' in the inscription relating to the first architect.[22]

The solution to this detective search may be the following series of hypotheses. Originally, inscriptions stating the name, status, memorable deeds, and (in most cases) also date of death were painted above the busts in gold and silver lettering. These were presumably not composed and written in a single campaign, but may either have been added gradually, or perhaps written together sometime after the busts were completed but before 1392. The rather unusual form of the inscriptions, which are not chiselled in stone as may have been expected, may have been dictated by the need to add new data later. The inscriptions had been badly damaged by the early 18th century, and at some point before the 1770s their remains were abraded in order to replace them with newly written, uniform and complete-looking inscriptions. Where the original text was not properly legible it was either shortened, or information was drawn from other available sources; for example, the tombstone in the cathedral might have been used as a source for Matthias of Arras. The type of script used may have been learned from medieval manuscripts.

It was possible to compare the texts of the inscriptions with other written sources only in the cases of the three archbishops of Prague. I would like to suggest nevertheless that the texts in their current form may have been composed with knowledge of the book *Proto-martyr poenitentiae*, written by the Baroque hagiographist and historiographer Johann Thomas Berghauer mentioned above in 1723, but printed in Augsburg only in 1736.[23] In his transcription of the text above the bust of Arnošt of Pardubice Berghauer indicated that many words were missing, but only one of these is lacking from the inscription we see today. Indeed, the inscription now contains two additional lines of text not recorded by Berghauer, the wording of which is nevertheless consistent with the information about the archbishop compiled by Berghauer from other sources while acquiring material for the hagiography of John of Nepomuk, the late-14th-century martyr canonised in 1729. The handiwork could have been that of Johann Ferdinand Schor, the architect, theoretician and fresco painter, who was the author of the last pre-modern project for the completion of the cathedral, for which he employed Gothicising forms in the design.[24] His intention may have been to confirm the image of the faithful, catholic and at the same time truly Czech past of the church where John of Nepomuk was active.

Be that as it may, for medieval art history it is enough to state the unreliability of the triforium inscriptions as historical evidence. This should mean that information obtained from the inscriptions that cannot be corroborated by another, independent source (such as chronicles, or legal and church records, for example) should not be used as a basis for historical argument. The inscription over the bust of Charles IV states, among other things, that he 'fundavit novam pragensem ecclesiam de sumptuoso opere ut apparet ac sumptibus propriis laboravit' ('founded the new Prague church with the sumptuous fabric that can be seen, and built it at his own expense') (Fig. 7). This is, in fact, the main basis for the assumption that plays a key role in most art-historical interpretations of Prague Cathedral, and which was succinctly formulated by Hans Seldmayr in often-cited words, that St Vitus's Cathedral was, metaphorically, Charles's *Eigenkirche*.[25] Other sources however, namely the foundation charter of the cathedral and contemporary chronicles, tell us something different: the new church was founded by Charles's father, John of Luxembourg, in 1341, in lasting memory of himself and his family.[26] Although King John must have acted in agreement with his son and designated successor, he issued the charter during Charles's long absence from Bohemia and he named him only once in the charter, in a long list of names of relations whose services of commemoration were to be performed in perpetuity once the new church had been completed and paid for using all the financial resources that had been allocated for its construction.

If our understanding of the situation is to remain in agreement with the practice of the period and with the testimony of the sources, we should consider the metropolitan chapter of St Vitus's Cathedral to have been the true builder of the cathedral.[27] This

FIG. 7.   Prague Cathedral, choir triforium: bust of Charles IV with inscription
Martin Frouz

would conform not only with the chapter's responsibilities in general but also with the specific situation in Prague, where the chapter was traditionally financially and institutionally quite independent and relatively strong, even in its relations with the (arch)bishop.[28] When Arnošt of Pardubice wrote a new statute for the chapter in 1350, he carefully identified a balance of incomes and spending for the building project, because 'nos et capitulum nostrum nimis sumptibus fabricae ecclesiae nostrae occurrere debeamus', that is both the archbishop and his chapter had to meet the enormous costs of building the fabric of the church.[29] In addition, the order of visitations in 1358 suggests that the canons had to seek the emperor's approval when selecting a new sacristan, not because the emperor would have any special or founder's rights in the cathedral, but because he 'has augmented the treasure immensely, and thus has a real interest in the matter'.[30] We seem to arrive at the conclusion that the social motives and symbolical structures deployed in the building and decoration of the St Vitus's Cathedral in Prague did not differ in any profound sense from those that were usual elsewhere.[31]

Charles IV gave many special gifts to the church and he certainly may have played an important role in its design, although the kings of Bohemia were never in any formal sense patrons of the church. Their strong presence in Prague Cathedral stems from the fact that the church shares the narrow Castle Hill (Hradčany) with the royal palace, an unusual situation, which on the Continent was only matched by Cracow.[32]

This, however, should not provide justification for completely dismissing any role played by the chapter in the conception of the architectural project, or any notion that the structure of the great church embodied both spiritual values and practical concerns. St Vitus's was the space for coronation rites and it also became the place for royal burials. Besides those functions, however, the cathedral also served as a bishop's seat and, first and foremost, as the space for performance of the chapter's liturgy. This primary function can be seen to be embodied in the relative dimensions of the choir, which had to accommodate spaces occupied previously by the two choirs of the Romanesque basilica in order to maintain the sophisticated liturgy of the chapter developed over the centuries (Fig. 8).[33] St Vitus's Cathedral has also been an important pilgrimage site of the most popular local patron saint, St Wenceslas, since the 11th century. His chapel functioned almost as a separate unit from liturgical, practical and financial points of view, and this was, naturally, mirrored in its architecture: a 'building within a building', both in ground-plan and elevation. I would like to argue that the architects' task for the cathedral was not so much to embody ideological constructs, but to rise to the challenge of incorporating all these practical functions into an artistically convincing and coherent whole.[34]

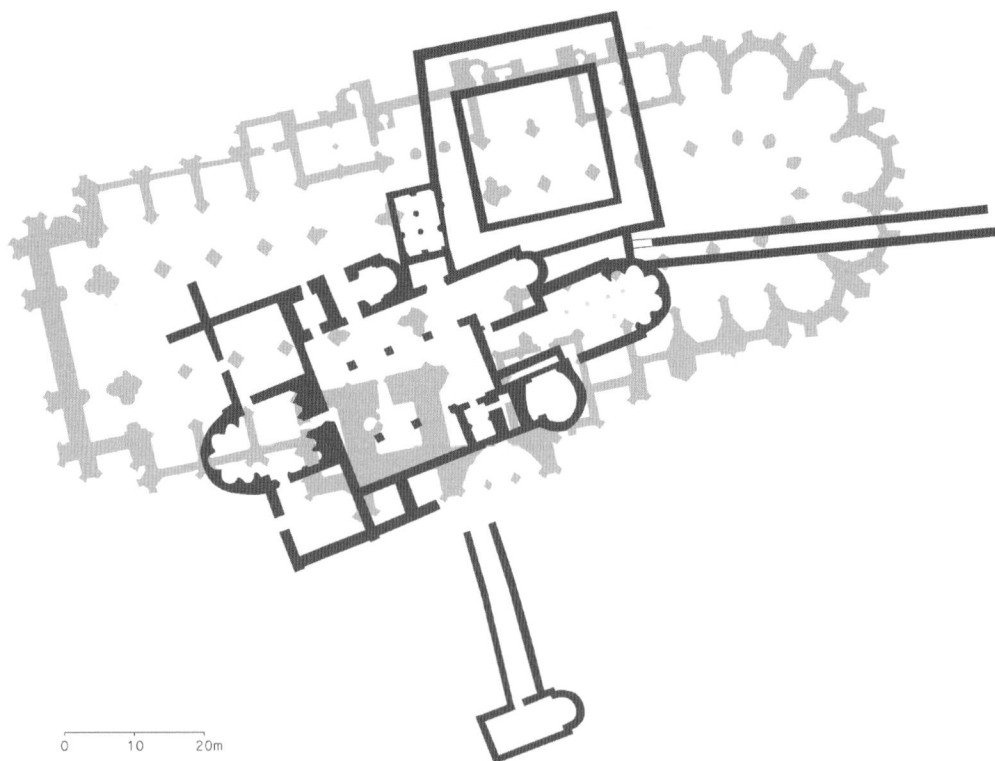

FIG. 8. Superimposed ground-plans of Prague Cathedral (in grey) and the basilica previously on the site (in black)

Jana Maříková-Kubková

An alternative point of view suggested here could also bring a fresh insight into the question of the original function of the series of portraits on the Prague Cathedral triforium, a question long debated, but never satisfactorily solved. A recent explanation (in my opinion the most successful to date) has suggested a memorial function for the gallery related to the burials in the church.[35] As Paul Crossley convincingly shows in his contribution to this volume, the architect has done a great deal to ensure at least partial visibility of the busts from the ground, and thus angels alone were not the sole intended viewers of these visual messages.[36] Although the whole symbolical concept of the choir was challenged by the rediscovery only in 2005 of the real location of the royal tomb directly in front of the main altar,[37] the busts and their inscriptions seem to have played an important commemorative role. The restorer's report informs us that between each head and the inscription above there was originally an iron implement, which probably supported a source of light.

Still, problems arise if the key to the presence of those commemorated by their portraits is considered to be exclusively membership of the Luxembourg dynasty. Not only would the archbishops, canons and architects somehow have to be sidelined, but too many members of the dynasty are missing. Among the most striking absences from the triforium series are John's second wife, Beatrix of Bourbon, and all of Charles's children apart from Wenceslas. Most significantly, Sigismund is mentioned in the triforium only in the inscription above Elizabeth of Pomerania, his mother and Charles's fourth wife, as the king of Hungary and elector of Brandenburg, alongside his siblings John, duke of Görlitz, and Anne, queen of England. These omissions are naturally attributable to the fact that the series was instigated in the 1370s. When considered necessary, however, extensions to the original programme were possible, as is testified to by the addition of the bust of Václav of Radeč some time in the 1390s. This is hewn not from sandstone like the other busts, but from the local marlite limestone, a material frequently used for the sculpture of the so-called Beautiful Style.

The difficulties with this interpretation may be avoided if we consider the criterion for the inclusion not to be membership of the Luxembourg dynasty, but whether the individual contributed in some way to the building and decoration of the church. In this way, it was not a dynasty being commemorated, but the church's benefactors.[38] The insertion of the busts into the buttresses may have embodied metaphorically the role of the benefactors as 'pillars of the church', similar to the arrangement of the figures in the western choir in Naumburg, often cited in this connection, or to the anonymous men and women in the outer buttresses of the parish church in Sebeş (Mühlbach/Nagysebes), in Transylvania (medieval Hungary, now Romania) (Fig. 9). This point of view may also help to explain the unusual inclusion in a sacred space of the portraits of two architects, who were not ordained. Robert Suckale has recently proposed that the differences in sculptural quality of the triforium busts suggest that the best workmanship — identifiable perhaps with the busts sculpted personally by Peter Parler — was reserved for the canons, especially for the director of the building lodge who at the time of the realisation of the series was Beneš Krabice of Weitmile (Figs 10, 11).[39] I believe there is no problem now in proposing that the whole triforium design was overseen by representatives of the chapter, who were also responsible for the selection of those commemorated by the busts.[40]

As Paul Ricoeur has observed, an inscription is a fixation of meaning. In terms of their reliability and credibility, inscriptions generally rate highly in history and art

FIG. 9. Sebeş, parish church: detail of the buttress with an eroded bust of a benefactor

Milena Bartlová

history because of their apparent unambiguousness, simplicity and clarity. For precisely the same reason, however, they may be a prime tool for constructing a desired memory. An important example may be the highly convincing analysis by Volker Herzner, who has shifted the famous inscription on the frame of the Ghent altarpiece to the late 16th century.[41] In our case, there also seems to be a divide between the meaning originally intended and the one understood by a modern reader. The inscriptions on the triforium were, in fact, one of the important tools in the construction of an exceptional image to which we have become accustomed: that of Charles IV acting as a unique individual, a ruler both learned and deeply spiritual, who engaged in the building of the great church not only as benefactor, but also as conceiver and designer, and who collaborated with the architect to such a degree that we may call him a co-author of the project.[42] It is, however, possible that what was initially intended to be maintained in the cathedral for centuries was not so much the memory of a singular spiritual hero, but the memory of a group of men and women who had contributed to it (albeit a group headed by Charles IV). The shift of founder's honour of premium *memoria* from John to Charles (that is from father to son) must have occurred already during the latter's lifetime. The location of Charles's burial place directly in front the main altar of the church was the most visible manifestation of this shift, made easy by John's wish to be buried in Luxembourg; the siting of his bust in the central position in the triforium and the demotion of King John to a secondary place must have also played a crucial role. An entry in the *Series Regum Bohemiae*, written in the last third of the 14th century, uses wording similar to that of the triforium inscription to state that the emperor started to build the new, magnificent cathedral structure with his own means.[43] The intention of magnifying Charles — and proportionally diminishing John in the process — may have been that of the king himself, but also of the chapter. We should not forget that the *Chronicles* by Beneš Krabice of Weitmile, which constitute the principal source of information on

FIG. 10.   Prague Cathedral, choir triforium: bust of Archbishop Jan Očko of Vlašim

Martin Frouz

FIG. 11.   Prague Cathedral, choir triforium: bust of the Canon Beneš of Weitmile

Martin Frouz

the building of the cathedral, were written with the clearly stated aim of representing Charles IV in the most direct light of both spiritual and worldly glory.[44] Only a slight shift of vantage point sufficed to reach quite an opposite point of view; thus according to the *Chronicles* written from the perspective of the Prague (arch)bishopric by Canon Francis of Prague, Arnošt of Pardubice was both the founder and builder of St Vitus's Cathedral.[45]

Generally speaking the neo-Gothic reconstruction and completion of the cathedral is not highly valued, but its authors seem to have understood the original intention of the triforium series quite precisely, if intuitively. Because the busts in the triforium of the new nave, complete with inscriptions chiselled in stone (Fig. 12), were only finished after Czechoslovakia was inaugurated in 1918, the artistic committee of the Jednota pro dostavění hlavního chrámu sv. Víta (Union for the Completion of the Metropolitan Cathedral of St Vitus) soon decided that the busts of representatives of the Habsburg dynasty, who contributed finances to the building, were to be deleted from the programme as originally planned and replaced with portraits of several members of the Union previously omitted.[46]

APPENDIX

THE INSCRIPTIONS IN THE CHOIR TRIFORIUM OF PRAGUE CATHEDRAL

TRANSCRIPTS by Šárka Lenochová, 'Nápisy v triforiu katedrály sv. Víta na Prahzském hradhe' (as in n. 7), based on Bock, 'Die Inschriften und Büsten' (as in n. 5) and Podlaha and Hilbert, Metropolitní chrám (as in n. 5). In transcribing these heavily abbreviated texts, emendations commonly made have been adopted, including the resolution of abbreviations, the addition of omitted letters, and in some cases the correction of erroneous letters.

FIG. 12. Prague Cathedral, nave triforium: bust of Kamil Hilbert, 20th century

Martin Frouz

Wenceslas of Radeč

Wenczeslaus de Radecz, canonicus / Pragensis et decanus ecclesie sancti Apollinaris / Pragensis, director fabrice quintus, / qui totum chorum Pragensem / testudinari procuravit de / pecuniis fabrice.

Matthias of Arras

Mathias, natus de Arras civitate / Francie, primus magister fabrice huius ecclesie quem Karo / lus IIII. pro tunc marchio Moraviae cum / electus fuerat in regem Romanorum in Avinione / abinde adduxit ad fabricandam ecclesiam / istam, quam a fundamento incepit anno domini M / CCC XLII. Et rexit usque ad annum LII in / quo obiit.

Peter Parler

Petrus, Henrici parleri de Polonia, magistri de Gem / unden in Suevia, secundus magister huius fabrice, quem impera / tor Karolus IIII. adduxit de dicta civitate et fecit eum ma / gistrum huius ecclesie, et cum tempore fuerat annorum XXIII et incepit regere anno domini / M CCC LVI et perfecit chorum istum anno domini M CCC LXXXVI, quo / anno incepit sedilia chori illius et infra tempus prescriptum etiam incepit / et perfecit chorum Omnium sanctorum, et rexit pontem Multauiae, et incepit a / fundo chorum in Colonya circa Albiam.

Andreas Kotlík

Andreas, dictus Kotlik, canonicus / et altarista sancti Dionysii in ecclesia / Pragensi, director fabrice IIII. Obiit / Anno domini M CCC LXXX.

Beneš Krabice of Weitmile

Benesius, dictus Crabiczie / canonicus Pragensis studiosus / director fabrice tercius. Obiit / anno domini M CCC LXXV, die / XXVII mensis Julii.

Wenceslas Luxembourg

Dominus Wenczeslaus, dux / Luczemburgensis et Brabancie / frater Karoli et Iohannis marchionis / Moraviae. Hic morit Anno / domini M CCC LXXX sepultus.

John Henry Luxembourg

Iohannes, frater Karoli, marchio [sic] / Moraviae, morit anno domini M CCC / LXXV die XII mensis Novembris / Hic construxit monasterium / fratrum heremitarum in Brunna / ibidem sepultus. Item monasterium / Cartusiensie prope Brunna.

Blanche of Valois

Margareta dicta Blanczie, Romanorum et / Boemie regina illustrissima, que construxit / et dotavit altare sancti Ludovici, regis Francie / in choro novo sancte Marie in ecclesia Pragensi, quam / eciam donavit dicte ecclesie cortinas / nobilissimas de axemito rubeo et / albo cum armis diversis auro sutis / et alias strifeas sericeas preciosas / cum casula bona. Obiit dies sancti Petri / ad vincula.

Anne of the Palatinate

Anna Romanorum et Boemie regina, que / construxit et dotavit altare sancti Nicolai / in medio chori sancte Marie in ecclesia Pragensi / qua eciam donavit ecclesie predicte duas / casulas cum perlis solempnisimas / Coronamque suam pro dechore sepulchri / beatissimi Wenceslai imperatoris pie donavit cum / cortinis camere sue. Obiit in / purificacione sancte Marie.

Anne of Schweidnitz

Anna de Bosna de regno / Dalmacie, mater domini / Wenczeslai regis Romanorum / et Boemie.

Elizabeth of Pomerania

Elizabet de Stetina, filia ducis / Bohuslai, mater Sigismundi / regis Ungariae et marchionis / Brandenburgesi, Johannis ducis / Gorliczensis et Anne regine / Anglie.

Charles IV Luxembourg

Karolus IIII, imperator Romanorum et / Boemie rex, hic fundavit novam Pragensem ecclesiam / de sumptuoso opere ut apparet ac sumptibus / propriis laboravit hic eciam impetravit a sede / apostolica ecclesiam Pragensem erigi in metropolitanam / per Clementem papam VI, et archiepiscopum legatum apostolice / sedis fieri procuravit per dominum Urbanum papam / Vtum, collegium Omnium sanctorum in castro / et mansionarios in ecclesia Pragensi / instituit ct dotavit, studium Pragense / instutuit [sic], pontem novum per Multauiam laborari / precepit. Amator cultus divini et cleri precipuus / Moritur Prage anno domini M CCC LXXVIII die / penultima novembris etatis sue anno LXIIII.

John 'the Blind' Luxembourg

Iohannes, filius Henrici imperator / comes Lutzemburgensis, rex Boemie / VIII, duxit Elizabet filiam / regis Venceslai. Hic moritur in / bello in Francia per regem Anglie Anno / domini M CCC XLVI in die Ruffi. Hic / fundavit monasterium carthusiense / prope Pragam.

Elizabeth Přemyslovna

Elisabeth, regina Bohemie, mater / ilustrissimi [sic] principis domini Karoli / Romanorum et Bohemie regis. Obiit / in die sanctorum Cosme et Damiani / martirum.

Wenceslas IV Luxembourg

Wenczeslaus, primus Romanorum / et Boemie rex, comes Lucemburgesis [sic] / natus serenissimi principis, domini / Karoli IIII, Romanorum Imperatoris.

Johanna of Bavaria

Iohanna Romanorum et Boemie regina / illustrissimi domini Alberici, ducis / Holandrie, filia, uxor prima / serenissimi principis domini Wenceslai / Romanorum et Boemie regis. Obiit / anno domini M CCC LXXXVI in vigilia / circumcisionis domini.

Arnošt of Pardubice

Arnestus, primus archiepiscopus Pragensis, fundavit et / dotavit ac perfecit ad plenum monasterium sancte / Marie canonicorum regularium in Glacz. Item monasteria eisudem / ordinis Zatzka et in Rokicano ac hospitale in Broda Boemi / cali fundavit, perfecit et dotavit. Hic moritur in Rudnicz anno domini / M CCC LXIIII die ultimo mensis Juni, sepultus / in Glacz. Primus officium correctoris ad reprimendam [sic] / insolencíam clericorum instituit.

Jan Očko of Vlašim

Iohannes, II archiepiscopus Pragensis, primus legatus, dotavit / altaria sancte Marie in capella Omnium sanctorum. Sanctorum Erharde / et Otilie in ecclesia Pragensi. Item construxit dota / vit hospitale sancte Marie sub Wissegrado. Item / hospitale sancti Anthonii et sancte Elisabeth in / Hradczano pro clericis pauperibus infirmis / Hic moritur anno domini M CCC LXXX / die XII mensis Ianuarii. Orate pro (eo).

Jan of Jenstein

Ioannes, tertius archiepiscopus / Pragensis apostolici sedis legatus / secundus, olim episcopus misnensis. Hic re / dificavit castrum Keisperg cum / magnis muris et turrim forti / castro fundavit.

Nicholas Holubec

Nicolaus, dictus Holubecz / canonicus Pragensis, secundus / director fabrice Pragensis. Hic / obiit anno domini M CCC LV.

Bušek of Velhartice

Busco Leonardi, archidiaconus / Curimensis, canonicus Pragensis / primus fabrice director / Obiit anno domini M CCC L.

ACKNOWLEDGEMENTS

The research for this article was undertaken in the context of the 'Sources-Land-Culture' project (MSM0021622426) at the Faculty of Arts, Masarykova univerzita, Brno.

NOTES

1. The bibliography on this topic is very extensive, and many important publications will be cited below. For a recent discussion, see M. C. Schurr, *Die Baukunst Peter Parlers: Der Prager Veitsdom, das Heiligkreuzmünster in Schwäbisch Gmünd und die Bartholomäuskirche zu Kolin im Spannungsfeld von Kunst und Geschichte* (Ostfildern 2003).

2. I am indebted to Petr Chotěbor for the technical information.

3. R. Suckale, 'Über die Schwierigkeiten, Peter Parler Skulpturen zuzuschreiben', in *Parlerbauten: Architektur, Skulptur, Restaurierung. Internationales Parler-Symposium Schwäbisch Gmünd 17.–19. Juli 2001*, Landesdenkmalamt Baden-Württemberg, Arbeitsheft 13 (Stuttgart 2004), 197–206; J. Fajt ed., *Karl IV. Kaiser von Gottes Gnaden* (Berlin 2006).

4. Good surveys of the interventions are given in O. Kletzl, 'Sulpiz Boisserée und Joseph Dobrovský: Ein Briefwechsel als Beitrag zur Parlerforschung', *Witiko*, 1 (1928), 231–49, and V. Kotrba, 'Kdy přišel Petr Parléř do Prahy?', *Umění*, 16 (1971), 109–31.

5. F. Bock, 'Die Inschriften und Büsten der Gallerie im Dome von St. Veit zu Prag', *Mittheilungen der K. K. Central-Commission*, 2 (1857), 185–86; A. Podlaha and K. Hilbert, *Metropolitní chrám sv. Víta v Praze*, Soupis památek historických a uměleckých v království českém, I (Prague 1906), figs 132–52.

6. P. Kalina, 'Příspěvky k výkladu architektonické skulptury na Svatovítské katedrále', *Umění*, 40 (1992), 108–23.

7. F. M. Pelzel, *Geschichte Kaiser Karls IV., Königs von Böhmen*, 2 vols (Prague 1781), II, 533; Kletzl 'Sulpiz Boisserée' (as in n. 4); unpublished notes by Josef Dobrovský in the archives of the Památník národního písemnictví (Museum of Czech Literature), Prague, reproduced and transcribed in Š. Lenochová, 'Nápisy v triforiu katedrály sv. Víta na Pražském hradě' (unpublished MA thesis, Faculty of Education,

Charles University, Prague, 2005). The principal conclusions of Lenochová's work will appear in the forthcoming issue of *Castrum Pragense.*

8. P. Vlček ed., *Encyklopedie architektů, stavitelů, zedníků a kameníků v Čechách* (Prague 2004), 478–79 (entry by J. Vítovský).

9. The bridge was designed and built by Magister Oto; see J. Vítovský, 'Stavitel Karlova mostu Oto', *Zprávy památkové péče*, 54 (1994), 1–6; idem, 'K datování, ikonografii a autorství Staroměstské mostecké věže', *Průzkumy památek*, 1/2 (1994), 15–44.

10. Kletzl, 'Sulpiz Boisserée' (as in n. 4); idem, 'Ein Briefwechsel G. Th. Legis-Gluckseligs mit Wenzel Hanka', *Witiko*, 2 (1939), 198–200.

11. In the 1970s–80s, Marie Kostílková reportedly wrote an analysis of the inscriptions in which she considered them to be a 19th-century forgery. The text was available to Ivo Hlobil, but it has not been published, and I have not been able to trace it in any public archives or library. The excerpts published as a chapter in K. Benešovská, I. Hlobil et al. (*Petr Parléř: Svatovítská Katedrála 1356–1399* (Prague 1999), 149–57, published in English as *Peter Parler and St Vitus's Cathedral 1356–1300*) are not consistent. Kostílková's opinion was made public in a television programme broadcast by the Czech channel TV2 on 22 September 1995; transcripts were published by K. Nesměrák, 'Václav Hanka a triforium katedrály sv. Víta', in *Almanach rukopisné obrany*, 4 (1997), 42–50. (I am indebted to Š. Lenochová for this information.) For a brief reply and refutation, see I. Hlobil, 'Nápisy v triforiu Svatovítské katedrály', *Dějiny a současnost*, 17 (1995), 56–57.

12. V. Birnbaum, 'Kdy přišel Petr Parléř do Prahy?' *Umění*, 2 (1929), 51–56; Kotrba, 'Kdy přišel Petr Parléř do Prahy?' (as in n. 4).

13. J. Homolka, 'Ikonografie katedrály sv. Víta v Praze', *Umění*, 26 (1978), 564–75; idem, 'Zu den ikonographischen Programmen Karls IV.', in A. Legner ed., *Die Parler und der Schöne Stil 1350–1400: Europäische Kunst unter den Luxemburgern*, 5 vols (Cologne 1978–81), II, 607–18; M. V. Schwarz, 'Peter Parler im Veitsdom. Neue Überlegungen zum Prager Büstenzyklus', in M. Winner ed., *Der Künstler über Sich in Seinem Werk* (Weinheim 1992), 55–72.

14. I. Hlobil, 'Sochařství', in A. Merhautová ed., *Katedrála sv. Víta* (Prague 1994), 66–95. The independence of stylistic criticism from written sources is noted, for example, by T. Flum, 'Die Parler: ein Stolperstein der Kunstgeschichte', in B. Boerner and B. Klein ed., *Stilfragen zur Kunst des Mittelalters* (Berlin 2006), 151–63.

15. See P. Crossley, 'Medieval architecture and meaning: the limits of iconography', *Burlington Magazine*, 130 (1988), 116–21; more generally, see V. C. Raguin, K. Brush and P. Draper ed., *Artistic Intergration in Gothic Buildings* (Toronto 1990). For the methodological approach, see also P. Binski, *Becket's Crown: Art and Imagination in England 1170–1300* (New Haven/London 2004).

16. This was the principal subject of Lenochová's unpublished dissertation (see n. 6).

17. A. and V. Berger, 'Triforium chrámu sv. Víta. Průzkum nápisů. Zprávy z restaurování' unpublished restoration report (Prague 1972); Q. and J. Adamec, 'Zprávy z restaurování portrétních byst vnitřního triforia katedrály sv. Víta', unpublished restoration report (Prague 1974); both typescripts are available in the archives of the Department of Art Collections, Prague Castle. See also the interview with V. Berger reprinted in Nesměrák, 'Václav Hanka' (as in n. 11).

18. I am indebted to Jiří Roháček at the Ústav dějin umění (Akademie věd České republiky) (Institute of the History of Art at the Czech Academy of Sciences) in Prague for his expert opinion.

19. Analysis of Latin was kindly undertaken by Iva Adámková of Masarykova univerzita, Brno.

20. Adamec, 'Zprávy z restaurování' (as in n. 17).

21. Kletzl, 'Sulpiz Boisserée' (as in n. 4): Boisserée speculated that Balbin must have read 'Colonia', because he thought that Prague Cathedral was modelled on Cologne Cathedral. A 'description of the colours of the triforium busts' recorded in *Kurze Beschreibung der Metropolitan. Kirche St. Veit* (1798, 120; Knihovna Národního muzea, VI F.36), and cited in I. Kořán, 'Mariánský oltářík svatovítského pokladu a mariánské obrazy katedrály' (*Umění*, 54 (2006), 316–26), deals with the coats of arms.

22. J. T. A. Berghauer, *Proto-martyr poenitentiae ... divus Johannes Nepomucensis ... a tenebris vindicatur* (Augsburg 1736), 103. Kletzl and also, after him, Kotrba and Lenochová mention a report on the inscriptions by Hilarius of Litoměřice written in the 1460s. This is, however, based on a misunderstanding; Hilarius did not write specifically about the busts. I am indebted to Marek Suchý of the Archiv Pražského Hradu (Prague Castle Archives) for recognising this error, for locating Berghauer's book, and for his support and co-operation.

23. V. Vlnas, *Jan Nepomucký: Česká legenda* (Prague 1993), 202.

24. M. Šroněk, 'Katedrála v 18. století', in A. Merhautová ed., *Katedrála sv. Víta* (Prague 1994), 185–97; 'Schor', in *Nová encyklopedie českého výtvarného umění* (Prague 1995), 739 (entry by M. Šroněk).

25. Hans Sedlmayr, 'Die gotische Kathedrale Frankreichs als europäische Königskirche', in idem, *Epochen und Räume* (Vienna 1959), 182–99. The key role of the inscriptions in the argument is very clear in Paul Crossley, 'The Politics of Presentation: The Architecture of Charles IV of Bohemia', in S. Rees Jones ed., *Courts and Regions in Medieval Europe* (York 2000), 99–172 (esp. 110).

26. J. Emler ed., *Regesta diplomatica nec non epistolaria Bohemiae et Moraviae*, 4 vols (Prague 1855–92), IV (1892, covering 1333–46), 411–12. The chronicler and canon Beneš Krabice of Weitmile had erroneously given the charter the date of the laying of the foundation stone, 1344; see J. Emler ed., *Fontes rerum bohemicarum*, 8 vols (Prague 1873–1932), IV (1884), 495.

27. This point of view has already been proposed by J. Bureš, 'Peter Parlers Chor in Kolin und seine Beziehung zur Prager Bauhütte im Lichte der schriftlichen Quellen', *Gesta*, 28 (1989), 136–46. P. Kalina has made the same suggestion indepedently in *Praha 1310–1419* (Prague 2004, 167–98), and in 'Architecture and Memory: St Vitus's Cathedral in Prague and the Problem of the Presence of History', in J. Fajt and A. Langer ed., *Kunst als Herrschaftsinstrument: Böhmen und das Heilige Römische Reich unter den Luxemburgern im europäischen Kontext* (Munich/Berlin forthcoming). Kalina reaches similar conclusions to mine starting from a comparison with other cathedral projects in Europe. For a general survey of the topic, see G. Binding, *Baubetrieb im Mittelater* (Darmstadt 1993), 31–100.

28. Z. Hledíková, 'Pražská metropolitní kapitula, její samospráva a postavení do doby husitské', *Sborník historický*, 19 (1972), 5–46.

29. *Statuta Metropolitanae Ecclesiae Pragensis*, ed. A. Podlaha (Prague 1905), 20–21.

30. Hledíková, 'Pražská metropolitní kapitula' (as in n. 28), 17.

31. Cf. W. Brückle, 'Stil als Politikum: Inwiefern?', in Boerner and Klein ed., *Stilfragen* (as in n. 14), 229–56.

32. Hans Sedlmayr saw a similar situation not in Cracow, but in Westminster, Roskilde and Batalha; see Sedlmayr, 'Die gotische Kathedrale' (as in n. 25), 195. The parallels between Prague and Cracow were elaborated by Paul Crossley in 'Bohemia sacra et Polonia sacra. Liturgy and History in Prague and Cracow Cathedrals', *Folia Historiae Artium*, n.s., 7 (2001), 49–68.

33. J. Maříková-Kubková and D. Eben, 'Organizace liturgického prostoru v bazilice sv. Víta', *Castrum Pragense*, 2 (1999), 227–40; F. and M. Machilek, 'Der Liber breviarius der Prager Kathedralkirche in der Universitätsbibliothek Würzburg', *Umění*, 41 (1993), 375–85.

34. Crossley ('Politics of Presentation' (as in n. 25)), follows much the same line of argument as the one presented here, only to conclude that the initiative must be credited to Charles IV personally. Unfortunately, I was able to read this article — my thanks go to Zoë Opačić for providing me with a copy — only after the conference where this paper was first presented, and also after my critical analysis of Charles's assumed personal artistic capacities and interests was published. See M. Bartlová, 'Hledání řádu. Karel IV. a výtvarné umění', in *Ve znamení zemí Koruny české: Sborník k 60. narozeninám prof. L. Bobkové* (Prague 2006), 348–61, where I analyse the role of a paradigm in interpreting historical data.

35. M. V. Schwarz, 'Peter Parler im Veitsdom' (as in n. 13); idem, 'Felix Bohemia, sedes imperii', in idem ed., *Grabmäler der Luxemburger: Image und Memoria eines Kaiserhauses* (Luxembourg 1997), 123–54; idem, 'Kathedralen verstehen. St. Veit in Prag als räumlich organisiertes Medienensemble', in E. Vavra ed., *Virtuelle Räume: Raumwahrnehmung und Raumvorstellung im Mittelater* (Berlin 2005), 47–68.

36. Schwarz, 'Kathedralen verstehen' (as in n. 35), 67–68.

37. Jana Maříková et al., 'Předběžná zpráva o průzkumu staré královské hrobky v chóru katedrály sv. Víta na Pražském hradě', *Castrum Pragense*, 6 (2005), 99–124; K. Benešovská, 'Ideál a skutečnost. Historické a badatelské peripetie kolem královského pohřebiště v katedrále sv. Víta v Praze v době Lucemburků', *Epigraphica et sepulcralia*, 1 (2005), 19–48. Michael Schwarz was the only art historian to reconstruct the true original position of the tomb, in his latest text devoted to St Vitus's Cathedral, and his conclusions have been confirmed by a recent archaeological survey; see Schwarz, 'Kathedralen verstehen' (as in n. 35).

38. This point of view develops suggestions made by R. Hausherr, 'Zu Auftrag, Programm und Büstenzyklus des Prager Domchores', *Zeitschrift für Kunstgeschichte*, 34 (1971), 21–46, and C. Freigang, 'Werkmeister als Stifter. Bemerkungen zur Tradition der Prager Baumeisterbüsten', in *Nobilis arte manus: Festschrift zum 70. Geburtstag von Antje Kosegarten* (Dresden 2002), 244–64.

39. Suckale, 'Die Schwierigkeiten' (as in n. 3); cf. also idem, 'Die Porträts Kaiser Karls IV. als Bedeutungsträger', in M. Büchsel and P. Schmidt ed., *Das Porträt vor dem Erfindung des Porträts* (Mainz 2003), 191–204.

40. Christian Freigang argues for a prominent role for the canons as *magistri fabrice* in 'Werkmeister als Stifter' (as in n. 38).

41. Volker Herzner, *Jan van Eyck und der Genter Altar* (Worms 1995), 152–99.

42. This concept was formulated first by R. Hausherr in 'Zu Auftrag' (as in n. 38). The most important discussions of the concept are Homolka, 'Ikonografie katedrály' (as in n. 13); idem, 'Zu den

ikonographischen Programmen' (as in n. 13); and Crossley, 'Politics of Presentation' (as in n. 25). For a critical discussion of this concept, see my 'Hledání řádu' (as in n. 34).

43. The excerpt is cited by W. W. Tomek, *Základy starého místopisu pražského*, 4 vols (Prague 1866–75), III/5 (1872), 105. I am indebted to Marek Suchý of the Prague Castle Archives for identifying the codex as H9. Together with the triforium inscription, these seem to be the sole two sources identifying Charles as the builder of the cathedral.

44. 'Chronicon Benessii de Weitmil', in Emler ed., *Fontes rerum Bohemicarum* (as in n. 26), IV, 459–548.

45. *Chronicon Francisci Pragensis*, ed. J. Zachová (Prague 2005), 351. For a recent evaluation, see Jiří Kuthan, 'Arcibiskup Arnošt z Pardubic jako stavebník', in *Arnošt z Pardubic 1297–1364: Osobnost - okruh - dědictví* (Wrocław/Prague/Pardubice 2005), 175–94.

46. Archival files of the Jednota pro dostavění hlavního chrámu sv. Víta in the Prague Castle Archives. I am indebted to Martin Halata for his support during my research in the Prague Castle Archives.

Peter Parler's Choir of St Bartholomew in Kolín and the Art of 'Articulation'

MARC CAREL SCHURR

Peter Parler's choir of the parish church of St Bartholomew in Kolín is the architect's most important work alongside St Vitus's Cathedral in Prague. He rose to the challenge of designing a building that simultaneously repeats the main architectural features of the cathedral yet clearly indicates its lower ecclesiastical rank in a most brilliant way. On the one hand, by using the same key stylistic features and the same type of construction Parler ensured that the similarities were obvious enough to demonstrate a close architectural and institutional relationship between the cathedral and the parish church. On the other hand, if one looks at the details of St Bartholomew's choir, many of its forms are clearly distinct from those used for the corresponding elements of the cathedral. This paper proposes to call this extremely skilful application of subtle nuances within the same basic style 'articulations' of the same stylistic vocabulary. These articulations were used to express a difference in status and in function.

ON the northern wall of the choir of St Bartholomew in Kolín (Fig. 1), there is an inscription that tells us that 'this structure was begun on 30 January 1360, under the reign of Emperor Charles IV, king of Bohemia, by master Peter of Gmünd' (Fig. 2).[1] Master Peter of Gmünd was none other than Peter Parler, the emperor's architect, who was responsible for the construction of the new Gothic cathedral on Castle Hill (Hradčany) in Prague.[2] There, the choir of St Bartholomew is mentioned once again, in the triforium of the cathedral, directly above the bust of Peter Parler, in an enumeration of the master's works: the cathedral of St Vitus, the chapel of All Saints in the royal palace, the bridge over the River Vltava, and, finally, the choir of St Bartholomew.[3] Another inscription, on one of the piers in the choir of St Bartholomew, vanished today but handed down to us by the chronicles, gives us the year of the choir's consecration: 1378, the year of Charles IV's death.[4] Obviously the construction was not completely finished in that year, as sources continue to report on building works until the end of the 1380s.[5] Perhaps it was the emperor's bad health that caused the relevant authorities to hasten consecration of the uncompleted structure in 1378. Although it is unclear who commissioned the new choir,[6] the lost inscription is a first hint at a personal involvement of Charles IV. This hint is confirmed by a chronicle dating from 1735 that speaks of a stained-glass window in the choir; this window is lost today, but according to the source it contained a representation of Charles IV.[7]

According to the Prague Cathedral triforium inscription Parler's choir at Kolín was constructed anew from the foundations ('incepit a fundo chorum in colonya circa albiam'); it replaced an older one damaged in the great fire of 1349, which nearly

FIG. 1. Kolín, St Bartholomew: choir looking north-east

Marc Carel Schurr

FIG. 2.   Kolín, St Bartholomew: inscription on the north wall of the choir
ambulatory, next to the sacristy
Marc Carel Schurr

destroyed the whole city.[8] Kolín was an important place: its leading citizens were
involved with the nearby silver mines of Kutná Hora, and the city's tenth was an
important contribution to the royal treasury. Not only was the king of Bohemia the
master of the city, he was also the founder patron of the parish church.[8] Thus, there
was at least a formal obligation for him to contribute to the reconstruction of the
choir.[9]

This alone might be enough to explain some donations by the emperor, but
probably not the commitment of his highly prized and extremely busy master builder.
Moreover, the affiliation of the priest Andreas of St Bartholomew to the chapter of
the royal chapel of All Saints in Prague Castle[10] would not in itself account for this.
After all, Peter Parler would have needed the permission of the Prague Cathedral
chapter to accept the assignment in Kolín;[11] in reality, this would also have meant
gaining approval from the emperor. As we know from the chronicle of Beneš Krabice
of Weitmile, although officially the chapter was the client for whom the new cathedral
in Prague was built, Charles IV was deeply involved in all kinds of decisions and
personally bore the cost of its construction, according to the inscription above his bust
in the triforium.[12] Of course, the good connections of the priest of St Bartholomew
with the imperial court may have influenced the choice of an architect who came from
that milieu, and the burghers, who contributed regularly to the construction,[13]
certainly wanted to have their church built by the best available architect. Yet Peter
Parler's affiliation to the emperor[14] was much too close to allow him to accept other
projects without his consent. The final decision to give the assignment to Master Peter
must therefore have been Charles IV's.

Such a decision would have made sense for the emperor and king of Bohemia. As I will try to show, it was in Charles IV's interest to exercise his rights as the heir to Přemysl Otakar II (1253–78), the founding patron of the parish church. This also entailed performing the duties of the founding patron, including the maintenance or renovation of the building itself,[15] in a way that was obvious to everyone in the city. This had become necessary, because at the time most of the upcoming cities in the empire were trying to emancipate themselves from the power of their masters.[16] Typically, an important step towards greater autonomy was to acquire the rights of the founding patron of the parish church, which usually belonged to the founder of the city and his heirs. Cities in Alsace and Swabia especially took advantage of the political instability in these regions caused by the fall of the Hohenstaufen dynasty.[17] By rebuilding their parish churches anew, often in a grand style and without any contribution from the founding patron, cities like Ulm, Reutlingen or Schwäbisch Hall were able to represent themselves as the *novi fundatores* of their churches, and to claim successfully the transferral of the rights of the founding patron into the hands of the city council.[18] These rights included the *ius praesentandi*, the right to choose the parish priest and all the chaplains; the reception of all the revenues generated by the ecclesiastic activities; and, most importantly, the supervision and administration of all the properties of the church.

It is easy to see how Charles IV, having witnessed this development in southern Germany with his own eyes, had no interest in allowing similar things to happen in Bohemia, where all the major cities were by and large still in the possession of the king. This was also true of Kolín, which was of special importance to the king because of the high revenues it generated. The burghers were well aware of that. When the father of Charles IV, John of Luxembourg, arrived in Bohemia in 1310, the city of Kolín refused to swear the pledge of allegiance for more than a year and, of course, to give any kind of financial support.[19] Finally, when Charles IV was crowned in 1347, the Luxembourg dynasty only entered their second generation as kings of Bohemia after the demise of the Přemyslids in 1306, and Charles would have been concerned that wealthy cities such as Kolín or Kutná Hora might attempt to profit from the vulnerable position of the Luxembourg dynasty in the same way as the cities in Alsace and Swabia had been doing.

Charles must thus have decided to forestall any challenges to his role as master of the city and founding patron of its church by supporting the reconstruction of the devastated choir. By sending his master builder from Prague, Charles IV not only demonstrated his generosity and his willingness to fulfil his pledges, he also created an opportunity to visualise the relationship between the king and his subjects in Kolín. Peter Parler used an architectural vocabulary associated with royal display and ideology while at the same time simplifying it in order to articulate the building's lower order in ecclesiastical hierarchy (Figs 1, 3). Through architecture he staged the meaning of kingship, but also the validity of ecclesiastical hierarchy. If ever there was a need to demonstrate the 'mediality'[20] of medieval architecture, the choir of Kolín would be the perfect example.

Peter Parler achieved this effect by using two complementing strategies: simplification and carefully modified articulation of the stylistic vocabulary. Both the general shape and style of the Kolín choir were derived from St Vitus's Cathedral in Prague. Although the existing nave was built as a hall church, Peter Parler opted for a different type of structure when he designed the new choir for St Bartholomew, erecting a basilica with a clerestory, an ambulatory, and radiating chapels (Figs 5 and

FIG. 3.   Prague Cathedral: choir looking east

Marc Carel Schurr

6). For a parish church this was quite an ambitious layout and may have been considered pure extravagance by many contemporaries. Admittedly, during the second half of the 14th century the growing need among rich families for individual chapels led to the construction of radiating chapels even in the case of simple parish churches, as both economic and religious developments resulted in an increasing number of private chapel foundations;[21] the choirs of the parish churches of cities such as Lübeck, Freiburg im Breisgau and Schwäbisch Gmünd provide the proof of this devotional trend. In Kolín, wealthy citizens had founded individual altars during the 1360s and 1370s, as is evident from several sources.[22] Obviously, there was a need to make provision for a chain of individual altar chapels, which may account for the construction of an ambulatory with radiating chapels. But the impressive clerestory with its huge, tracery-filled windows and the use of flying buttresses on the exterior (Figs 1, 4) have nothing to do with the citizens' desire to set up their foundations within the choir.

As the characteristic Y-shape of the buttresses clearly indicates, the choir of St Vitus's Cathedral in Prague was the model for the new choir in Kolín (Figs 4, 5). The two-storied elevation of a basilical choir with flying buttresses, visible from a

FIG. 4. Kolín, St Bartholomew: choir from the north
Marc Carel Schurr

FIG. 5. Prague Cathedral: choir from the east
Marc Carel Schurr

considerable distance, was an unmistakable symbol of the city's affiliation to the kingdom and church of Bohemia. Even the flat roofs of the aisles may very well be derived from Prague Cathedral: the present hipped roofs over the aisles are much steeper than the originals, whose exact form is unknown. However, there are also subtle differences. The buttresses at Kolín share the same general shape with those at Prague, but they are reduced in complexity and dimensions. The clerestory windows incorporate eye-catching curvilinear tracery with six main lights beneath, but in Kolín the main lights lack the idiosyncratic arrangement of the Prague clerestory, whereby a four-light inner 'window' is flanked by two outer lights, and the richness of the Prague moulding profiles is replaced by austere sharp-edged mullions and tracery forms.

The same contrast between sumptuous extravagance of general design and simplicity of execution also dominates the interior of the choir of St Bartholomew (Fig. 1). Just as in Prague (Fig. 3), Peter Parler created a pseudo-triforium — a motif that was then quite rare in Central European parish churches and reserved essentially for the great cathedrals like Cologne, Strasbourg or Prague. There is no triforium in a true sense — no passage, not even blind arcades — there are just the mullions of the clerestory windows that are extended over the bare surface of the wall below. The triforium of Prague Cathedral is only hinted at; it is, so to speak, reduced to a minimum. In Kolín, the 'triforium' is simplified to such a degree that it might escape the attention of a casual viewer or that art historians might even doubt its existence. But this doubt is eliminated in the face of another building that must have served as a model for Peter Parler when he designed the interior of Kolín's choir: the nave of St Florentius in Niederhaslach, Alsace (Fig. 7), not far from Strasbourg and designed around 1310 by the son of Strasbourg Cathedral's Master Erwin,[23] uses the very same device to represent the cathedral's triforium. Two generations later, Matthäus Ensinger, the son of another famous master of the Strasbourg lodge, Ulrich von Ensingen, returned to this device, when his nave for Bern's minster had to equal the triforium of the church in the neighbouring rival city of Fribourg.[24]

There are other hints besides that the church of Niederhaslach was very well known to the workshop of St Vitus's Cathedral in Prague, especially its first architect Matthias of Arras. For instance, the highly original design of the buttresses, where the finials seem to penetrate the cornice of the next storey (Fig. 8), can be found on the radiating chapels of St Vitus's (attributed to Matthias), and also in Niederhaslach on the chapel of St Mary (Fig. 9). The latter was dedicated in 1344, the year the foundation stone for the new cathedral was laid in Prague.[25]

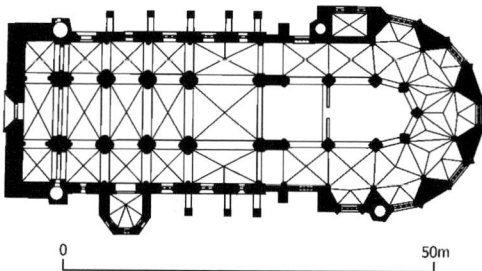

0   50m

FIG. 6. Kolín, St Bartholomew: ground-plan
Marc Carel Schurr

FIG. 7. Niederhaslach, St Florentius: choir looking north-east

Marc Carel Schurr

Other examples of simplification on a high artistic level are the vaults and piers in the choir of St Bartholomew. Compared with the splendid decorated vaults of St Vitus's Cathedral, the quadripartite rib vaults of the Kolín nave look rather old-fashioned. However, there are triradials in the ambulatory, and the ribs of the vaults of the nave intersect with the responds that seem to run straight through the vaults (Fig. 10). These details are highly original and could almost be called avant-garde. The same goes for the piers, which at first glance seem to replicate the classicism of the strong round shafts of St Vitus's in Prague, itself reminiscent of the great cathedrals of the 13th century (Figs 1, 3). Yet on closer examination, the piers of St Bartholomew are extremely complex structures, a combination of rectilinear and rounded profiles, resulting in planar and convex surfaces. The appearance of simplicity of these pillars is deceptive. The irregular shape of their cross-section clearly demonstrates this (Fig. 11), as do the elimination of capitals and the elegant flow of the mouldings (Fig. 10). These pillars are indeed simple and reduced, but they are refined and sophisticated at the same time.

Equally sophisticated is the way Peter Parler found to overcome the narrowness of the choir, which was dictated by the dimensions of the existing western parts of the church. Instead of trying to construct an even-sided arcade with an arch at the apex of the apse, which would have resulted in ridiculously small bays, he placed a pier right on the central axis (Fig. 1). By giving an odd number of sides to the choir, Peter Parler maintained the majestic rhythm of the wide nave arcades, retaining a sense of

FIG. 8. Prague Cathedral: detail of a buttress
Marc Carel Schurr

FIG. 9. Niederhaslach, St Florentius:
detail of a buttress
Marc Carel Schurr

monumental spaciousness. A subtle balance between an overall impression of cathedral-like grandeur and a certain modesty of execution characterises the architecture of St Bartholomew in Kolín. Despite the lavishness of some details, especially the tracery, the principal forms are kept simple and reduced, often appearing startlingly modern.

Yet the differentiation between the parish church and the cathedral was achieved not only by simplification and reduction, but also by the means of style. Peter Parler did not really change his style, as this would have destroyed the desired impression of affiliation. Instead, he made a distinction, not by using a wholly different vocabulary of forms, but rather by changing the articulation of his vocabulary. It is evident in the case of Kolín and Prague that there is a difference in status between the two churches, or what Robert Suckale described as 'different levels of style', according to the hierarchical distinctions in the antique and medieval theories of rhetoric.[26] However, there are other similar and comparable cases, where there is no implication of hierarchical distinction, only functional differences on the same level of importance.[27] It would be

FIG. 10.   Kolín, St Bartholomew: capital zone
of the choir's vaults
Marc Carel Schurr

FIG. 11.   Kolín, St Bartholomew:
cross-section of one of the choir's piers
Katarina Papajanni

misleading to talk about different levels of style in that context, whereas the term 'articulation' could be applied to this phenomenon in a more general sense without indicating a value judgement. I would therefore like to propose the term 'articulation' as a better expression to describe such formal distinctions that are made within the same general stylistic framework.

In order to expand on what the term articulation means in this context, I shall set out an example of different articulations of the same style in relation to two equally important but functionally different parts of the same building. If one compares the high choir of St Vitus's Cathedral with the chapel of St Wenceslas on the choir's south side, both built by Peter Parler, the difference in their appearance will be immediately obvious, despite the fact that they share key stylistic features. For example, the windows of St Andrew's chapel (known also as the Martinic chapel) in the choir's south aisle and of the chapel of St Wenceslas have a tracery pattern that consists of Peter Parler's most characteristic motif, the mouchette (in German *Fischblase*) (Figs 12, 13). These are pointed figures with one concave curve above and one s-shaped double curve below, usually known as divergent mouchettes, similar to the mouchettes of the Flamboyant style. No architect on the European Continent used these figures to such extent as Peter Parler, who made the *Fischblase* a true leitmotif of his tracery patterns. Both windows share the general design: a quatrefoil in the centre

FIG. 12.   Prague Cathedral, St Andrew's chapel: window tracery
Marc Carel Schurr

flanked by two mouchettes pointing downwards and to the side. There is no doubt that the two windows draw on the same stylistic vocabulary, but in the articulation of this vocabulary they differ drastically. Whereas the window of the chapel of St Wenceslas has a more sharply pointed arch and the slenderness of all its members and the sharpness of the profiles create a dynamic overall impression, the window of the St Andrew's chapel seems proportionally balanced and majestic, resplendently displaying the lavishness and elegance of its tracery.

The same aesthetic values apply to the interiors as a whole (Figs 3, 14). In the chapel of St Wenceslas, the shafts are sharp-edged, creating the impression of elegant lines drawn on the taut parchment-like surface of the wall. Without the interruption of capitals, they run dynamically directly into the vaults, forming a decorative rib-pattern. In the choir, however, the vault and arcades are carried on massive round shafts with bases and capitals. The wall of the upper storey is not the flat expanse of the chapel of St Wenceslas, where the windows look as if they were literally cut through the thin stonework. The clerestory of Prague Cathedral is by contrast a thick-wall structure with deep jambs and mural passages on the triforium level below. Together with the massive shape of the triforium piers and the columns this seems like an allusion to the great High Gothic cathedrals of the 13th century. In the choir of St Vitus, an atmosphere of ecclesiastical and royal splendour is evoked, as opposed to the more mystical mood of the chapel of St Wenceslas.

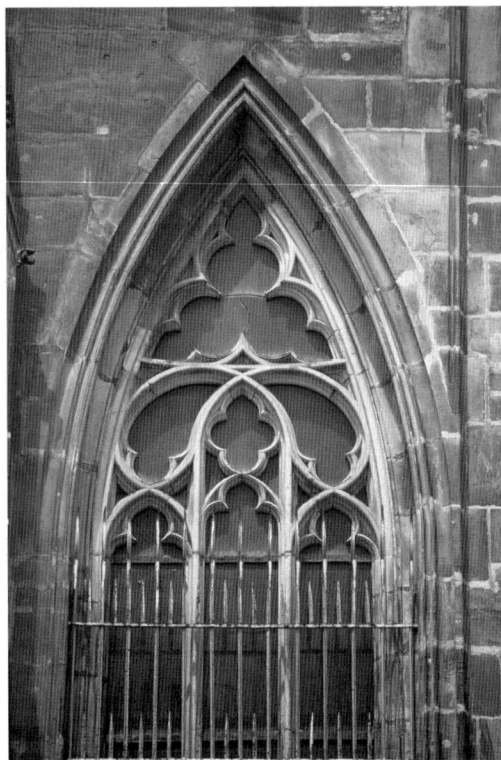

Fig. 13. Prague Cathedral, chapel of
St Wenceslas: window tracery
Marc Carel Schurr

The two share the same basic style, but differ in their articulation of it, and neither can be said to be of a higher or lesser rank. The choir of St Vitus was meant for the archbishop and his chapter, but at the same time was the architectural setting for the coronation of the king. The royal crown, on the other hand, belonged to St Wenceslas and was kept in the St Wenceslas chapel on the reliquary bust of the saint; the rest of the royal insignia were locked in a separate sacristy accessible only via a staircase in the St Wenceslas chapel.[28] Thus, the chapel of St Wenceslas not only contained the relics of the most important patron saint of the kingdom of Bohemia, but also the symbols of royal power. All this made the chapel a part of the cathedral with special functions of its own, so that it could rightly be called a 'church within a church'.[29] This justified the use of a different articulation of the architectural style, which was intended to signify these different functions, but surely not a hierarchical subordination.

Play with different articulations however was not an invention of Peter Parler's. It seems to have originated in the heyday of the Rayonnant style in the middle of the 13th century. Competing masters such as Pierre de Montreuil and Jean de Chelles in Paris challenged each other by using different formal approaches, as is shown by the transepts of Notre-Dame de Paris.[30] In a similar way, the master who was responsible for the design of the new Gothic nave of the minster in Strasbourg tried to surpass the splendid architecture that was under construction in Cologne, where the cathedral's new choir had been begun shortly before.[31] The strategy he adopted was simply the application of a different articulation.[32] For example, all the shafts and columns in the

FIG. 14.   Prague Cathedral, chapel of St Wenceslas: vault
Marc Carel Schurr

tracery of the windows as well as in the triforium of Cologne Cathedral are rounded. Just to show the difference of his building, the master of the Strasbourg nave provided the corresponding parts of the windows in the aisles and the triforium with a highly unusual, rectangular shape. In Cologne, even the spandrels between the openings of the triforium are pierced, and the triforium itself seems to be connected to the clerestory as if they were both part of one huge window filled with stained glass. In Strasbourg, the masons articulated the vocabulary of the Rayonnant style differently and filled the spandrels between the openings of the triforium with beautifully sculpted animals and foliage. Above the triforium, they placed an angular, strongly protruding cornice, which clearly separates the triforium from the clerestory windows.

The principle of contrasting articulations was adopted in a brilliant manner at Niederhaslach. Once more, the collegiate church of St Florentius seems to have delivered an important inspiration for Peter Parler's work in Prague.[33] In the nave, the architect used a sharp-edged, linear articulation very similar to the one adopted by Peter Parler for the chapel of St Wenceslas in Prague. In contrast to the nave of St Florentius in Niederhaslach, the church's chapel of St Mary, just like Peter Parler's choir in St Vitus, is provided with rounded shafts and true capitals. Like the chapel of St Wenceslas in Prague, the chapel of St Mary seems to have been a separate part of the church with distinct functions, accessible only through a portal that opens onto the south aisle. Unfortunately, we do not know much about the liturgical function of the chapel at Niederhaslach, which was originally dedicated to the Holy Cross.[34] As it contains a superb sculptural group showing the Entombment of Christ, it could be suggested that special relics of the Passion of Christ were kept in the chapel. The group may also have functioned as a repository for the host (the host would have been placed in the hollow of Christ's chest), and this eucharistic and devotional function may have justified the use of a different articulation of the architectural style in order to express the unique quality of the place — again, not necessarily a different rank. An aside, but one not without interest to our topic, is that the style of the sculpture seems closely related to that of the sculptures made between 1350 and *c.* 1380 in Schwäbisch Gmünd and (especially) Augsburg, and both of these sites are demonstrably connected to the Parler family.[35]

In Kolín, Peter Parler retained many of the peculiarities of the lavish architecture he had created for St Vitus's Cathedral in Prague. Thus, he employed again the sumptuous mouchettes of the cathedral for the clerestory windows in Kolín (Fig. 1). He even developed the design further by creating dynamic whirling patterns, which would become a characteristic of Late Gothic architecture in Central Europe. But a closer look at the tracery also reveals how he used the articulation of these forms to set the cathedral's architecture apart from that of the parish church. Here the intention was to indicate the different rank of the two, and the elegant, but simple and uniform shape of the mullions and tracery patterns in Kolín express the necessary distance from the richer and more complex mouldings of their counterparts in Prague. Indeed, the king could not have wanted the royal and ecclesiastical splendour of Prague to be rivalled, so it would have been felt that the forms of the parish church ought not to come too close to those of the cathedral. On the other hand, the king must have desired that the affiliation of the parish church to the cathedral and the imperial court be visualised; this meant that there had to be easily recognisable similarities in the architecture of both buildings. Peter Parler resolved the dilemma by staying within the same stylistic idiom, but using articulation to make a clear distinction in rank between the cathedral and the parish church.

The use of articulation is nothing other than the architect's reaction to the functions of architecture as a medium. This 'medial function' could be the representation of a mixture of institutional affiliation and hierarchical grading, as in Prague and Kolín, but also a sophisticated distinction of liturgical functions, as in the chapel of St Wenceslas and the choir of St Vitus. By means of a subtle change of articulation, Peter Parler was able to express a whole palette of different primary and secondary meanings in the medium of Gothic architecture.

NOTES

1. K. B. Mádl, *Topographie der Historischen und Kunst-Denkmale im Königreiche Böhmen, I: Der politische Bezirk Kolin* (Prague 1896); K. B. Mádl, *Soupis památek historických a uměleckých v Království českém, sv. I: politický okres Kolínský* (Prague 1897); J. and L. Kamarýt, *Kolínský chrám: Stavebně historický popis* (Kolín 1988); D. Líbal, *Katalog gotické architektury v České republice do husitských válek* (Prague 2001), 186–91.

2. A. Merhautová ed., *Katedrála sv. Víta v Praze* (Prague 1994); K. Benešovská, I. Hlobil et al., *Petr Parléř: Svatovítská Katedrála 1356–1399* (Prague 1999, published in English as *Peter Parler and St Vitus's Cathedral 1356–1399*); M. C. Schurr, *Die Baukunst Peter Parlers* (Ostfildern 2003).

3. Schurr, *Baukunst Peter Parlers* (as in n. 2), 13–15.

4. For the chronicles, see W. W. Tomek ed., 'Paměti král. města Kolína', in *Časopis Českého Musea*, 22/1 (Prague 1848), 383–400, 510–31, 611–19.

5. J. Burcš, 'Peter Parlers Chor in Kolin und seine Beziehung zur Prager Bauhütte im Lichte der schriftlichen Quellen', *Gesta*, 28/2 (1989), 136–46.

6. J. Kuthan, 'K Parléřovu chóru kostela sv. Bartoloměje v Kolíně nad Labem', in *Pro Arte: Sborník k poctě Ivo Hlobila*, ed. D. Prix (Prague 2002), 127–39; J. Kuthan, 'Zu Parlers Chor der St. Bartholomäuskirche in

Kolin an der Elbe', in *Parlerbauten: Architektur, Skulptur, Restaurierung. Internationales Parler-Symposium Schwäbisch Gmünd 17.–19. Juli 2001*, Landesdenkmalamt Baden-Württemberg, Arbeitsheft 13 (Stuttgart 2004), 141–48.

7. Chronicle of Antonín Formandl, deacon of St Bartholomew in Kolín, reprinted in J. Vávra, *Dějiny královského města Kolína nad Labem* (Prague 1888), 45. See also Bureš, 'Peter Parlers Chor in Kolin' (as in n. 5), 145; Kuthan, 'Zu Parlers Chor' (as in n. 6), 141–43; F. Matouš, *Mittelalterliche Glasmalerei in der Tschechoslowakei*, CVMA Czechoslovakia (Prague 1975), 44–49.

8. The triforium inscriptions are reassessed in the article by Milena Bartlová in this volume.

9. On Charles IV's relationship with Kolín and its main church, see Vávra, *Dějiny královského* (as in n. 7), 5. On the rights and responsibilities of founder patrons more generally, see K. J. Philipp, *Pfarrkirchen: Funktion, Motivation, Architektur* (Marburg 1987), 18–24.

10. Kuthan, 'Zu Parlers Chor' (as in n. 6), 141–42.

11. On the role of the chapters, see W. Schöller, *Die rechtliche Organisation des Kirchenbaues im Mittelalter, vornehmlich des Kathedralbaues: Baulast, Bauherrenschaft, Baufinanzierung* (Cologne/Vienna 1989).

12. 'fundavit novam pragen. ecclesiam … ac sumptibus propriis laboravit'. See also Schurr, *Baukunst Peter Parlers* (as in n. 2), 74–88. For a reassessment of the inscriptional evidence, see Milena Bartlová's contribution in this volume.

13. Kuthan, 'Zu Parlers Chor' (as in n. 6), 142.

14. Schurr, *Baukunst Peter Parlers* (as in n. 2), 16–17, 84–85.

15. Philipp, *Pfarrkirchen* (as in n. 9), 21–24.

16. For an overview, see H. Boockmann, *Die Stadt im Spätmittelalter*, 2nd edn (Munich 1987); B. Kirchgässner and E. Naujoks, *Stadt und wirtschaftliche Selbstverwaltung*, Stadt in der Geschichte, XII (Sigmaringen 1987); E. Ennen, *Die europäische Stadt des Mittelalters*, 4th edn (Göttingen 1987); E. Engel, *Die deutsche Stadt des Mittelalters* (Munich 1993); B. Kirchgässner and H.-P. Becht ed., *Stadt und Handel*, Stadt in der Geschichte, XXII (Sigmaringen 1995).

17. For the historical development, see T. Mayer ed., *Grundfragen der alemannischen Geschichte*, Vorträge und Forschungen, I (Darmstadt 1962); H. Büttner, *Schwaben und Schweiz im frühen und hohen Mittelalter*, Vorträge und Forschungen, XV (Sigmaringen 1972); E. Maschke and J. Sydow ed., *Südwestdeutsche Städte im Zeitalter der Staufer*, Stadt in der Geschichte, VI (Sigmaringen 1980).

18. Philipp, *Pfarrkirchen* (as in n. 9), passim.

19. Tomek ed., 'Paměti král. města Kolína' (as in n. 4), 383–86.

20. For the term 'mediality' and the 'medial turn' in the history of art, see H. Bredekamp, 'Bildmedien', in H. Dilly et al. ed., *Kunstgeschichte: Eine Einführung*, 6th edn (Berlin 2003), 355–78; M. V. Schwarz, *Visuelle Medien in der christlichen Kunst: Fallstudien aus dem 13. bis 16. Jahrhundert* (Vienna/Cologne/Weimar 2002); H. Belting, *Bildanthropologie* (Munich 2002), 143–88.

21. An excellent case study is delivered by A. Grewolls, *Die Kapellen der norddeutschen Kirchen im Mittelalter: Architektur und Funktion* (Kiel 1999).

22. Bureš, 'Peter Parlers Chor in Kolin' (as in n. 5), 145; Kuthan, 'Zu Parlers Chor' (as in n. 6), 142, n. 8.

23. M. C. Schurr, *Gotische Architektur im mittleren Europa 1220–1340: Von Metz bis Wien* (Munich/Berlin 2007), 217, 233–35, 268, 346–47.

24. P. Kurmann and B. Kurmann-Schwarz, 'Die Architektur und die frühe Glasmalerei des Berner Münsters in ihrem Verhältnis zu elsässischen Vorbildern', in *Bau- und Bildkunst im Spiegel internationaler Forschung: Festschrift zum 80. Geburtstag von Edgar Lehmann* (Berlin 1989), 194–209; M. C. Schurr, 'Die Münster von Freiburg i. Üe., Strassburg und Bern im Spiegel der europäischen Baukunst um 1400 — Gedanken zur Legende der Junker von Prag', in *Zeitschrift für Schweizerische Archäologie und Kunstgeschichte*, 61 (2004), 95–116.

25. R. Recht, *L'alsace gothique de 1300 à 1365* (Colmar 1974), 155–68; P. Kurmann, 'Niederhaslach, la nef de l'église Saint-Florent', *Congrès Archéologique de France*, 162 (2006), 79–89.

26. R. Suckale, 'Peter Parler und die Stillagen', in *Die Parler und der Schöne Stil 1350–1400: Europäische Kunst unter den Luxemburgern*, ed. A. Legner, 5 vols (Cologne 1978–81), IV, 175–83.

27. Schurr, *Baukunst Peter Parlers* (as in n. 2), 127–33.

28. On the special functions of the St Wenceslas chapel, see P. Crossley, 'Bohemia sacra. Liturgy and History in Prague Cathedral', in *Pierre, lumière, couleur: Études d'histoire de l'art du Moyen Âge en l'honneur d'Anne Prache*, ed. F. Joubert and D. Sandron (Paris 1999), 341–65, and idem, 'Politics of Presentation: The Architecture of Charles IV of Bohemia', in *Courts and Regions in Medieval Europe*, ed. S. R. Jones, R. Marks and A. J. Minnis (York 2000), 99–170. The main work on the St Wenceslas chapel, sadly unpublished, is still Lucy Ormrod, 'The Wenceslas Chapel in St Vitus' Cathedral, Prague. The marriage of imperial iconography and bohemian kingship' (Ph.D. thesis, Courtauld Institute of Art, University of London, 1997).

29. Schurr, *Baukunst Peter Parlers* (as in n. 2), 85.

30. D. Kimpel, *Die Querhausarme von Notre-Dame zu Paris und ihre Skulpturen* (Bonn 1971); D. Kimpel and R. Suckale, *Die gotische Architektur in Frankreich 1130–1270* (Munich 1985), 410–21.

31. Schurr, *Gotische Architektur* (as in n. 23), 77–97.

32. Schurr, *Gotische Architektur* (as in n. 23), 95.

33. Schurr, *Baukunst Peter Parlers* (as in n. 2), 113–15, 132.

34. Recht, *L'alsace gothique* (as in n. 25), 156.

35. Schurr, *Baukunst Peter Parlers* (as in n. 2), passim.

Prague – Vienna – Košice:
The Church of St Elizabeth in Košice
and Vault Design in the Generation
after Peter Parler

TIM JUCKES

The reconstruction of the parish church of Košice (Kaschau in German, Kassa in Hungarian), which began around 1390 and continued into the second half of the 15th century, was one of the most important church-building projects in northern Hungary (present-day Slovakia) in the late-medieval period. Apart from the scale and representative ambition of the design, the reconstructed church's unusual artistic character confirms its exceptional value for architectural history, not only within Hungary, but in the Central European region as a whole. The present essay explores the church's potential as an art-historical source by concentrating on a single, yet highly instructive part of the design — the high vaults. These consist of a rich array of stellar patterns of the so-called 'bent-rib' type (in German Knickrippensterne) *that provide evidence for close relations with a series of projects in early-15th-century Prague and Vienna. The essay examines the processes by which such artistic ideas spread across the region, from two of Central Europe's most important lodges to Košice. It also shows that the Košice work was no straightforward rendition of established forms, but rather that it adds a further dimension to our understanding of developments in Prague and Vienna. From this a picture emerges of how the wealth and patronal ambitions of a north Hungarian town enabled a location on the late-medieval periphery to become a plausible site for innovative experiments in architectural design.*

ST Elizabeth's was the parish church of Košice, today in eastern Slovakia, but part of Hungary in the Middle Ages. By the late 14th century, Košice had become the most important urban centre in north-eastern Hungary, a wealthy free royal town with extensive privileges and a tradition of close relations with the Hungarian kings. The town's late-medieval prosperity was accompanied by its growing ambitions as a patron of art and architecture. This is nowhere more apparent than in the rebuilding of its parish church, where work began *c.* 1390, following a fire at the old church, and continued for much of the following century (Fig. 1 & Col. Pl. VIII in print edn).[1]

Apart from the inherent interest of an eventful building history with several plan changes, the church's architecture also has art-historical implications that reach far beyond the boundaries of medieval Hungary. From the diagonally set chapels terminating its five-aisle ground-plan to the richly layered crowns of its main portals

FIG. 1.   Košice, St Elizabeth's: aerial view from south, with charnel chapel of St Michael
(Buran ed., *Gotika* (as in n. 13), 207)

or the virtuoso double-spiral staircase in the south transept, the Košice work suggests close contact with leading regional lodges, especially those in Vienna and Prague, and an ability to take established motifs in new directions. The intention here is to explore the church's potential value as an art-historical source by reference to a single, but particularly revealing aspect of the design — the high vaults in the nave, transepts and liturgical choir (that is, the two bays east of the crossing).

Before their late-19th-century reconstruction, the high vaults at St Elizabeth's showed an unusual series of *Knickrippensterne* ('bent-rib stars'), stellar patterns of the so-called 'bent-rib' type, where the paired diagonal ribs appear to bend around a central figure (Figs 2, 3, 11A).[2] At Košice, the stellar patterns took the form of four-point stars (with the exception of a single eight-pointer in the south transept), and the central figures of various shapes — a rhombus, hexagons of slightly different types, an irregular octagon, a square, a Greek cross, and an eight-point stellar form. Within the central figures were further patterns, some simple, some complex: a single, longitudinal lierne rib (choir, east bay); a cross form with bifurcating arms (choir, west bay); a St Andrew's cross (nave, east bay); four quadrilaterals locked around a small central square (nave, west bay); a rotated square divided into a grid (north transept); and two eight-point rhomboid stars (crossing and south transept). Each figure was described by ribs with roll-and-fillet mouldings, whose sharpened profiling sprung 'unannounced' — that is, without a capital zone — from the simple roll mouldings of the arcade piers and aisle responds. Further variations still were found in the south porch and gallery. The porch had a hanging vault with a suspended keystone and flying ribs (Fig. 11A). Its plan showed a star vault with a central quadrilateral figure (a rhombus) enclosing a cross form. The gallery also had a star vault with a central quadrilateral figure, but here the figure was square, its sides running parallel to those of the bay. In the centre of this a Greek-cross form was applied, its north–south line running to the edges of the bay.

The Košice designs represent an interesting episode in the development of a Late Gothic motif, that of the *Knickrippenstern*, which first appeared on the Continent in late-14th-century Prague and Vienna, before becoming established in southern

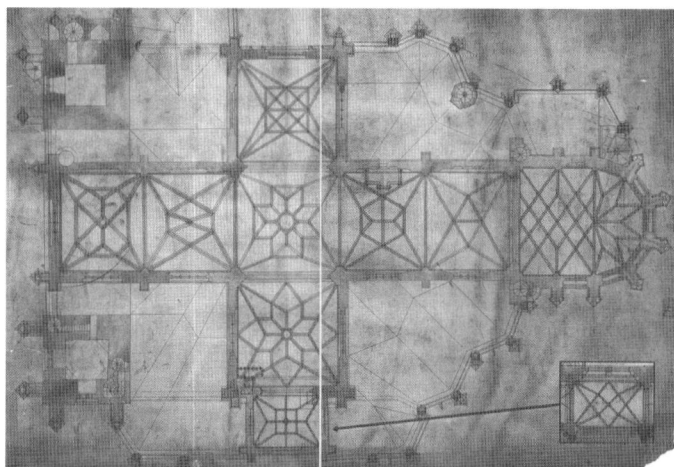

FIG. 2. Košice, St Elizabeth's: ground-plan of pre-restoration church, *c.* 1877, high vault level with south porch vault (bottom right)

Budapest, Kulturális Örökségvédelmi Hivatal, K8894 (with kind permission)

FIG. 3A.   Košice, St Elizabeth's: interior
looking east towards the sanctuary.
Watercolour by Viktor Myskovszky,
c. 1860–78, present location unknown
(József Mihalik, *A kassai Szent Erzébet
templom* (Budapest 1912), fig. 43)

FIG. 3B.   Košice, St Elizabeth's: interior looking
west towards the organ gallery, before 1877
*Budapest, Kulturális Örökségvédelmi Hivatal, P63120
(with kind permission)*

Germany and Austria in the 15th century.[3] There had been star vaults in Central
Europe for some time — particularly in the state of the order of Teutonic Knights
and Silesia — but never of the *Knickrippenstern* type, never with the diagonal ribs
'bending' or 'refracting' around a central figure. Two of the earliest known manifestations of the bent-rib type are found in the south tower at Prague Cathedral: the
chapter library showed two relatively simple central rhomboid figures, whilst the
Hasenberg Chapel had a circular figure, around which the diagonal ribs bifurcate to
form eight points like the radiating arms of a star (Fig. 4). These designs most likely
came from Peter Parler, but were executed by his sons soon after 1397.[4] At around the
same time, related forms appeared in Vienna. The south tower of St Stephen's shows
a simplified version of the star-with-central-ring motif, which was completed by
around 1400 (Fig. 6A).[5] By 1394, work had already begun on another important
Viennese project, the nave of St. Maria am Gestade (1394–1414) (Fig. 5).[6] Here are
found the rhomboid figure of the Prague chapter library in the north-east side chapel,
octagons in the high vault, and a slender hexagon enclosing a central quadrilateral in
the eastern bay.

   In the decades after the work at St. Maria am Gestade, the Vienna lodge
experimented further with vault designs of this type. In the nave of St Stephen's, the

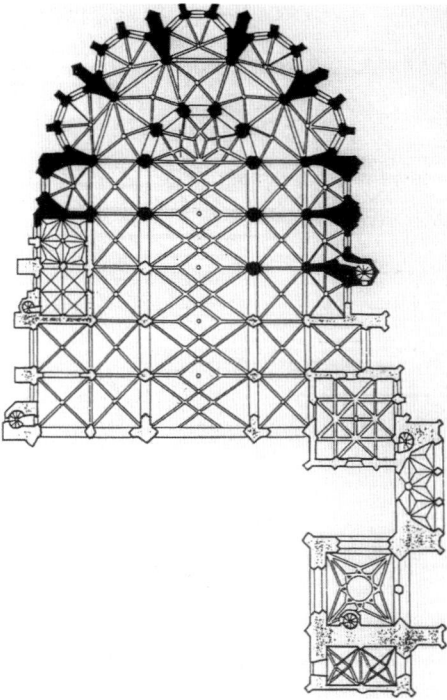

FIG. 4A.   Prague Cathedral: ground-plan
(Marc Carel Schurr, *Die Baukunst Peter
Parlers* (Ostfilden 2003), pl. 20)

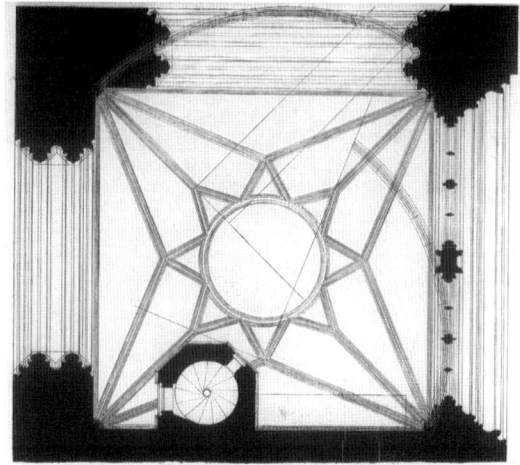

FIG. 4B.   Prague Cathedral, Hasenberg Chapel:
ground-plan with vault, *c.* 1906 (Antonín Podlaha
and Kamil Hilbert, *Metropolitní chrám sv. Vita v
Praze* (Prague 1906), 76)

motif of the bent-rib star was combined with a net vault (*c.* 1446–70s) (Fig. 6).[7] It can
be read either as a series of alternating figures (essentially two different octagonal
forms), or as a net uniting the whole nave. Other designs of the lodge from this period
show different combinations of net and star forms, some with a greater emphasis on
the net, some stressing the isolated central figure. For instance, the design for the high
vault of the choir at Steyr (Upper Austria, *c.* 1443–70s) is almost a pure net (Fig. 7A),[8]
but it is still related to the bent-rib designs: each bay has a central quadrilateral figure,
around and within which the diagonal ribs continue to 'bend'.

By the time of Steyr, the *Knickrippenstern* motif had arrived in Upper Austria and
Bavaria. Its occasional appearances in major Parler-influenced projects in this area,
particularly those associated with Hans von Burghausen and Stephan Krumenauer,
helped ensure that the bent-rib star became a common element of the vault design of
rural churches by the mid-15th century.[9] By the end of the century and during the
early 1500s, many further variations on the form appeared in a range of Bavarian and
Austrian projects. At the same time, the form also spread further west (to the
Rhineland and beyond) and east (particularly to the state of the Teutonic Knights and
Silesia, but with scattered examples elsewhere, including northern Hungary).[10]

As this survey suggests, the Košice forms represent a relatively isolated series
of experiments with the bent-rib-star motif in north-eastern Hungary. In terms of

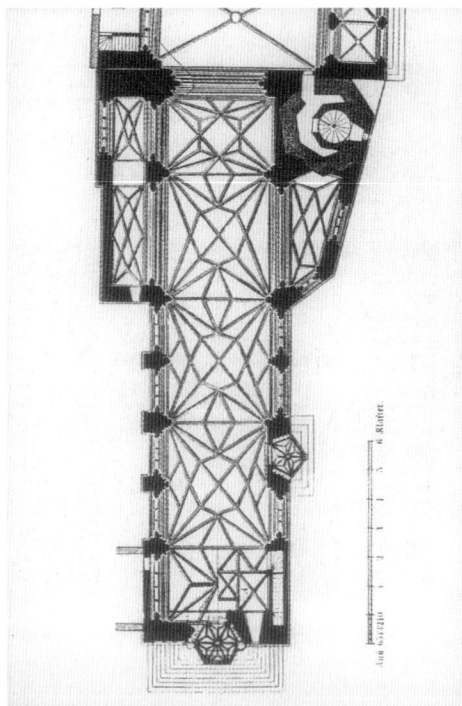

FIG. 5A.   Vienna, St. Maria am Gestade:
plan of nave (Eduard von Sacken,
*Österreichs kirchliche Kunstdenkmale der
Vorzeit: St. Maria Stiegenkirche in Wien*
(Vienna 1856), pl. 8)

FIG. 5B.   Vienna, St. Maria am Gestade:
nave vault

Tim Juckes

establishing the design's precise location within a regional development, a first aspect to address is the date of completion for the Košice work. On the basis of the stylistic evidence alone, several scholars have been inclined to date the Košice vaults to the mid-15th century and sometimes later still.[11] The logic of the building history, however, makes clear that St Elizabeth's was vaulted well before this. As Ernő Marosi has emphasised, a decorative inscription in the south transept at St Elizabeth's provides strong evidence that the body of the church was covered by the early 1440s.[12] Indications of the advanced state of work by this stage can also be found in the execution of mural paintings in the church's side aisles (c. 1420–50); the commissioning of a monumental Calvary in wood, presumably for the triumphal arch (c. 1430–50); and a reference to two functioning altars within the church, along with their respective priests (1457).[13] That the nave, transepts and liturgical choir (including the vaults) had been completed by this time is further supported by the continuation of work elsewhere in the church: the sanctuary with its net vault (by c. 1450); the north-west tower (by c. 1462); the south-west tower (after 1466); the south side chapels (1470s); as well as important furnishings, such as the sacrament house (by c. 1471) and high altar (c. 1474–77).[14] Whilst none of this provides a concrete date for the completion of the high vaults themselves (as distinct from the roofing), it seems

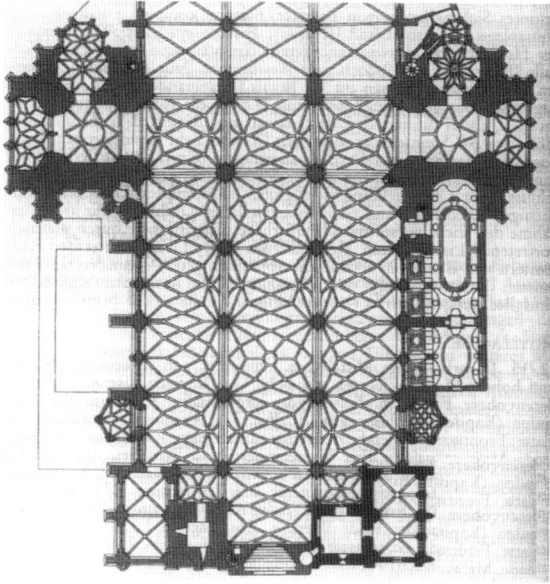

FIG. 6A.   Vienna, parish church of St Stephen:
ground-plan of nave

Collection of the author

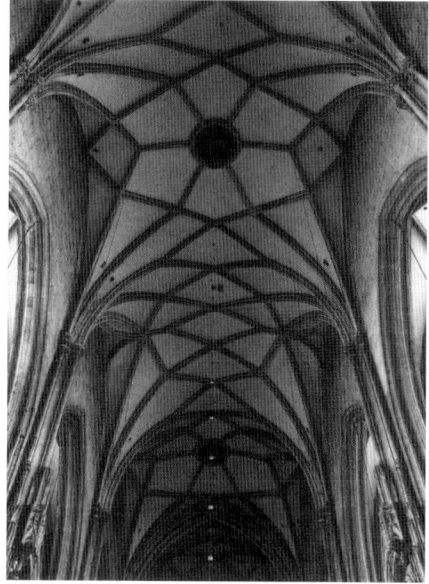

FIG. 6B.   Vienna, St Stephen's:
nave vault

Tim Juckes

highly unlikely that so much money would have been lavished on towers or furnishings at a time when the majority of the new church remained unvaulted. There is also stylistic evidence connecting the bent-rib stars with the lower parts of the church. As noted above, the south porch shows a bent-rib plan that corresponds with the high-vault motifs (Figs 2, 11A). The north portal, meanwhile, has microarchitectural baldachins with an elaborate series of miniature vaults, some of which are also remarkably close to the high vaults in their bent-rib star designs (Fig. 8). The Košice lodge was clearly already thinking about figured vaulting as the portals neared completion (1410s–20s).[15]

The north portal baldachins provide further evidence for the Košice lodge's approach to design. The insistence on variety, even in a (barely visible) micro-architectural context, reaffirms the eclectic impression made by the high vault. Then there are additional motifs that expand the lodge's known repertoire and suggest that its leading master was a well-travelled member of the early-15th-century architectural avant-garde.[16] The westernmost (right-hand) baldachin has a square figure related to its neighbours, but showing certain novelties — slightly curving ribs with tracery elements towards the middle of the vault (Fig. 8B). Both the application of tracery and the curvilinearity of the ribs were highly unusual for their time. Indeed, this appearance of tracery in a vault design, albeit for a baldachin, is among the earliest known examples on the Continent.[17]

A final instance of vault design that surely stems from the same workshop is found at the Franciscan church of St Nicholas in Košice. Alongside the church's west portal and its sculptural reliefs, the bent-rib star vaults of the choir immediately suggest a

FIG. 7A. Steyr, parish church of Sts Giles
and Coloman: ground-plan of the choir
(Koch, 'Die Baugeschichte' (as in n. 8), fig. 2)

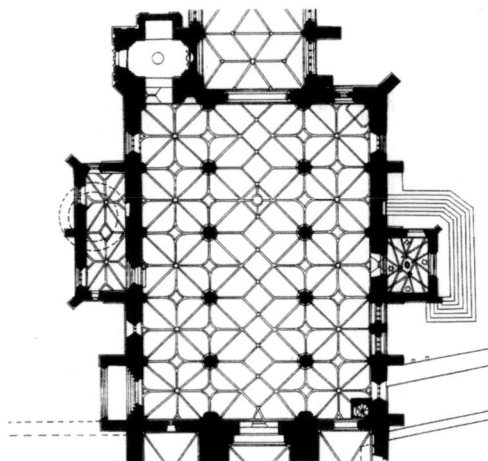

FIG. 7B. Bratislava, parish and collegiate
church of St Martin: ground-plan of the nave
(M. Pichová in Buran ed., *Gotika* (as in
n. 13), 230)

FIG. 8A. Košice, St Elizabeth's, north
portal: east jamb, west baldachin
Tim Juckes

FIG. 8B. Košice, St Elizabeth's, north
portal: west jamb, west baldachin
Tim Juckes

connection with the parish church (Fig. 9).[18] A first aspect to mention are the supports
and their relationship to the vaults. As was the case at St Elizabeth's, plain roll-
mouldings are contrasted with the sharpened profiles of the ribs, which spring from
their capital-less piers. More striking still is the choice of figures within the vault

FIG. 9.   Košice, Franciscan church: choir vault
János Krcho (with kind permission)

bays. The Franciscans' west bay shows an octagonal figure containing a four-point rhomboid star reminiscent of the crossing and south transept bays at St Elizabeth's. The middle bay shows further variety: a four-point star with an irregular central figure, whose overlapping forms connect with the polygonal eastern bay. The bent-rib star is here blended into a net form.

This interest in combined net and bent-rib star patterns suggests the need to look more closely at the relationship with the Vienna lodge. It has already been mentioned that the decades following the completion of St. Maria am Gestade (1414) saw further experimentation with hybrid net-star vaulting, most notably at St Stephen's and Steyr (Figs 5, 6, 7A). Further evidence that the masons concerned were thinking in these terms comes from drawings associated with the lodge. One design shows three different figures in isolation (Fig. 10A).[19] The central one of the three, an octagon, is reminiscent of the St Stephen's nave motif, but the handling of the ribs within the figure is much closer to Steyr's central choir: the pairs of diagonal ribs diffract and run parallel across the polygon. The close relationship to Steyr is underscored by the variation in the bay shown on the right-hand side of the drawing, where the octagon is almost quadrilateral and so nearly identical to the Steyr form.

This combination of net and star forms — sometimes inclining more towards a net, sometimes more towards free-standing central figures — produced some interesting

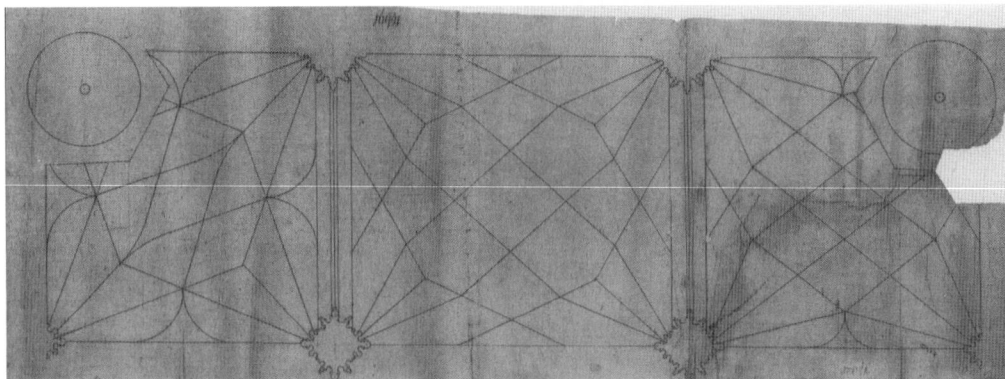

FIG. IOA.   Unidentified design for a vault, *c.* 1440–70. Black ink on paper, 207 x 559 mm
Vienna, Akademie der Bildenden Künste, Kupferstichkabinett, no. 16941 (with kind permission)

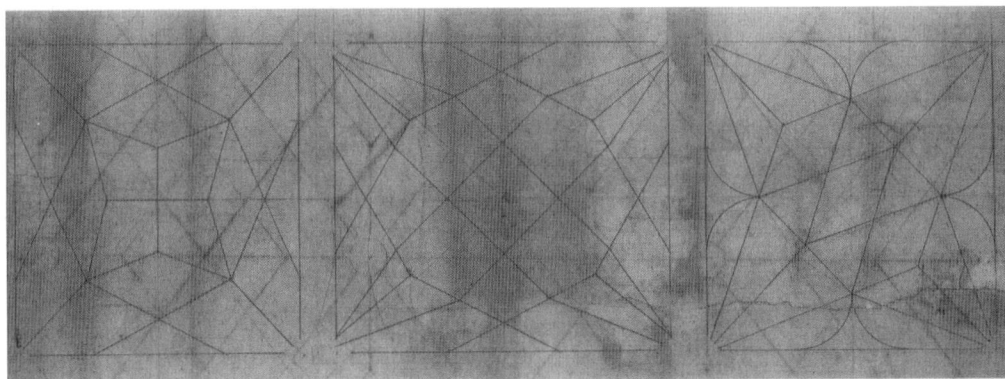

FIG. IOB.   Unidentified design for a vault (detail), *c.* 1440–70. Black ink on paper, 380 x 554 mm
Vienna, Akademie der Bildenden Künste, Kupferstichkabinett, no. 17019v (with kind permission)

parallels to the Košice designs. When one of the St Stephen's nave bays is isolated (the easternmost bay before the crossing for example, Figs 6A, 6B), its relationship to the unusual form in the westernmost bay of Košice's nave becomes clear: both can be read as irregular octagonal figures within which are pairs of springing rhombi whose points meet at the centre of the bay. The octagonal figures are not identical, but the inner motif and its disposition around a small central form are very similar.

The drawing already mentioned, and another closely related to it (also in Vienna), provide further stylistic evidence of a Vienna–Košice connection (Fig. IOB).[20] On a general level, they show bent-rib stars in which the figure itself is made the focus of its bay: there are bay-linking elements, but the net character of the design is not strong. In both drawings, there are instances where the rhomboid net within the polygon runs diagonally across the bay rather than longitudinally along it, as it tended to in a conventional net or even in the designs of St Stephen's or Steyr. In the bays depicted in the Vienna drawings, the polygon is treated as a field for further patterns, independent of any aisle-encompassing net. This is a similar handling to that at St Elizabeth's, where each figure has been removed entirely from the net and receives an inner pattern distinct from the bays on either side. Another general similarity is the combination of different polygonal forms — some regular, some irregular — within a single set of variations: as at Košice, there are quadrilaterals, hexagons and octagons. The play with a hexagon in the right-hand bay of the second drawing provides a point of comparison for the Košice hexagons (Fig. 10B). But perhaps most striking is the left-hand bay of the second drawing, which is the same as — and so provides a rare parallel for — the Košice Franciscan vault's west bay.

The evidence suggests then that the Košice forms are closely related to Viennese designs in a time of experimentation with net and star vaults. The extent of the Vienna lodge's activity in this period and the unique collection of masons' drawings associated with it make it possible to appreciate the range of experiments taking place and to locate the Košice design within this process. The crucial moment appears to come with the Vienna lodge's development of the design for the nave of St Stephen's, a process that the Košice's master of works may have witnessed first-hand. He presumably also knew the earlier work at St. Maria am Gestade, although the design of St Elizabeth's clearly represents a later stage in the development of the bent-rib motif. Its sophisticated detail and unbridled eclecticism mark it out as a member of the next generation.

To this increasingly vivid picture of artistic connections between Vienna and Košice can be added a final strand of evidence — the hanging vault of the south porch at St Elizabeth's (Fig. 11A). Vaults of this type, where the ribs split away from the web and descend before rejoining to hold a suspended keystone were also unusual in the early 15th century. The development of the form, however, shows similarities to the history of the bent-rib star. Early examples come once again from Prague Cathedral, where the old sacristy in the choir's north aisle contained by 1362 two designs using this construction.[21] By 1396, the St Catherine chapel in St Stephen's, Vienna, showed this vault type applied to an octagonal space (Fig. 11B).[22] Whilst the Košice work may have drawn on either (or even both) of these sources, one motif suggesting knowledge of the Vienna lodge design is the crocketing on the flying ribs at St Elizabeth's, which occurs in the St Catherine chapel, but is absent from Prague.

As for the chronological aspect of the Prague–Vienna–Košice relationship, the hanging vaults suggest a tidy process of stylistic diffusion, whereby a mid-14th-century Prague form recurred in 1390s Vienna and then early-15th-century Košice. With the bent-rib stars, the situation is more complex: on the one hand, the earliest forms appeared in Prague and Vienna roughly simultaneously; on the other, it seems that the vaults at St Elizabeth's were completed before some of their closest Viennese relations.

The former point is the more easily explained. It can be put in the context of close artistic relations between Prague and Vienna around 1400, perhaps best exemplified by the careers of masters Wenceslas Parler and Peter of Prachatitz.[23] The latter point — the relatively early date of the Košice work — seems more surprising and calls for further analysis. It should be emphasised that the evidence for the dating is reasonably clear. As was shown, the vaults at St Elizabeth's must have been finished by the 1440s. The nave vault for St Stephen's, however, is normally dated to the period after 1446, when Hanns Puchspaum was named master of works and contracted to provide a design for the work remaining to be done at the church, including the vaults.[24] It is not entirely clear when the Vienna nave was finally vaulted. Construction continued

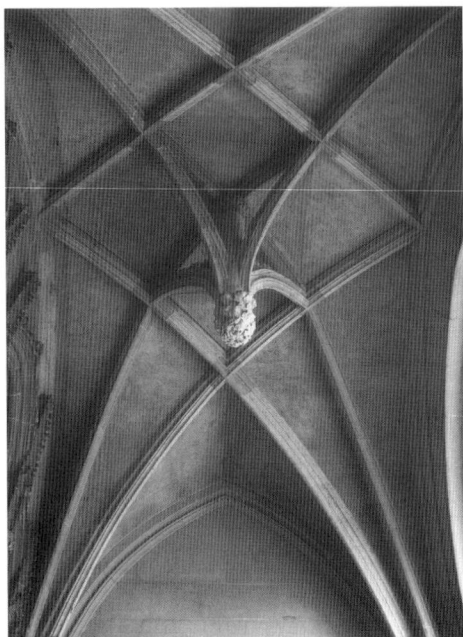

FIG. 11A.   Košice, St Elizabeth's:
(reconstructed) south porch vault

Tim Juckes

FIG. 11B.   Vienna, St Stephen's: St Catherine's
chapel, vault

*Vienna, Institut für Kunstgeschichte, Fotosammlung
(with kind permission)*

after Puchspaum's death (*c.* 1454) and, as Johann Josef Böker has stressed, it did not necessarily see the execution of his original plan.[25] At Steyr, work began around 1440–43, again with Puchspaum as the documented *Baumeister*.[26] As with St Stephen's, however, the project was not finished until several decades later and may also have involved alterations to the original plan.[27] With the nave of St Martin's in Bratislava (consecrated 1452), another vault design associated with the Vienna lodge, the completion of work came within Puchspaum's lifetime (Fig. 7B).[28]

The slightly earlier date for the Košice designs raises the question of whether the Vienna lodge was not already experimenting with hybrid *Knickrippenstern*-net designs in the 1420s and 1430s, or even slightly before. Whilst Böker has recently stressed the importance of Laurenz Spenning's time as master of works (*c.* 1454–77) for developments in vault designs of this type in Vienna, there are a number of indications that the process had already gathered momentum at an earlier stage.[29] The first is the aforementioned appearance of bent-rib star motifs both within the framework of the St Stephen's project (south tower, around 1400) and at St. Maria am Gestade (by 1414).[30] A second area to consider is the building history of St Stephen's itself. Progress on the outer walls of the nave was advanced as early as the 1420s (at least on the south side), but only completed by 1440.[31] It seems, then, that work on the final stages of the nave proceeded fairly slowly; the request for Puchspaum's vault design six years later, in 1446, adds to this impression. In these circumstances, it would be strange if Puchspaum's predecessors as masters of works, Peter and Hans von Prachatitz and Master Helbling, had not given some thought to the vault of the new nave — even if it is unclear what sort of designs they had in mind.[32]

A final point of reference connecting the vaults at St Stephen's and Steyr with the work of the pre-Spenning period comes from the closely related nave project in Bratislava (Fig. 7B). The evidence for the completion of work here by the early 1450s is clearer than Böker suggests.[33] A series of legacies for specific parts of the building allow the progress of work to be followed from the piers and roof (1435–36)[34] to the vaults (1443 and 1448),[35] before the consecration of the church in 1452.[36] Nor can there be any confusion with work on the choir, since the sources make equally clear that this was a separate project — anticipated as early as 1448, but started only slightly later (*c.* 1459–61) and nearing completion in the mid-1470s.[37]

All this makes it difficult to accept that a dynamic period for vault design in Vienna was dominated by the personality of a single mason — whether he be Hanns Puchspaum or Laurenz Spenning. The Košice work only strengthens the case, helping in many ways to bridge the gap between St. Maria am Gestade and St Stephen's, and suggesting the Vienna lodge's sustained engagement with new vaulting techniques throughout the first half of the 15th century. Nor is it necessarily surprising that the design of St Elizabeth's was completed before many of the Vienna lodge projects on which it appears to have drawn: whilst the St Stephen's nave project dragged on, progress at St Elizabeth's was fairly rapid. In this way, it seems that Košice offered its master of works an opportunity to experiment with new forms in the 1420s and 1430s before they could be executed in Vienna itself. This can be placed alongside numerous other instances of the town's desire to embrace the latest art and architectural fashions — a recurring theme of the building history at St Elizabeth's. The early dating for the vaults can also be related to the experimental quality of the Košice bent-rib forms *per se*. There is a real sense of a master trying out new ideas here, and growing in confidence as he did so. Nor was the vaulting by any means the only design element at St Elizabeth's that exhibits stylistic and technical precocity.[38]

Thus the example of St Elizabeth's shows how the late-medieval periphery could turn pioneer and become a plausible venue for innovative architectural design. In the context of the present essay, which has concentrated on the masonic side of church planning, it should also be emphasised how far the Košice master was compelled to work within the parameters laid down by the town. As the functional aspects of the church's early-15th-century replanning make clear, his international perspectives as an architect were always tempered by local priorities.[39] In the case of the vaults, however, it remains striking how far the town left the master free and how he seems to have relished the opportunity, using every last baldachin to develop the bent-rib star form. This sense of an ambitious and demanding patron nonetheless providing a master with favourable circumstances in which to exercise his eclectic creativity is a characteristic feature of architecture in Košice at this time.

ACKNOWLEDGEMENTS

This article was written within the framework of research for my doctoral thesis, which was made possible by an Arts and Humanities Research Council (AHRC) award in the ring-fenced subject area 'History of Architecture and the Built Environment'. My more recent fieldwork was also generously supported by the University of London's Central Research Fund (CRF). As for the vaults themselves, I derived great encouragement and many further ideas from discussions at the conference in Prague, where I presented this material for the first time. I would also particularly like to thank my supervisor at the Courtauld Institute of Art, Prof. Paul Crossley, and my co-supervisor in Bratislava, Dr Dušan Buran (Slovenská Narodná Galéria), for all their assistance and advice with the text.

NOTES

1. On the church and its rebuilding with further literature, see V. Mencl, 'Die Kaschauer Kathedrale', *Südost-Forschungen*, 8 (1943), 110–55; E. Marosi, 'Die zentrale Rolle der Bauhütte von Kaschau. Studium zur Baugeschichte der Pfarrkirche St. Elisabeth um 1400', *Acta Historiae Artium*, 15 (1969), 25–75; S. Tóth, 'Kaschau, Elisabethkirche, von der Westfassade her betrachtet', *Művészettörténeti Értesítő*, 42 (1993), 113–39; T. Juckes, 'St. Elizabeth's in Košice. Town, court and church-building in late medieval Hungary' (unpublished Ph.D. thesis, University of London, 2008).

2. The present-day church's high vaults are largely neo-Gothic, dating from the restoration of 1877–96. Art-historical analysis of the original design thus relies on pre-restoration surveys and photographs.

3. On the development of the *Knickrippenstern*, see K. Clasen, *Deutsche Gewölbe der Spätgotik* (Berlin 1958), 31 89; N. Nussbaum and S. Lepsky, *Das gotische Gewölbe: Eine Geschichte seiner Form und Konstruktion* (Darmstadt 1999), 216–59, especially 234–37. On the English antecedents for the bent-rib star vault in the work of William Joy in the 1330s–40s, most notably in the presbytery side aisles at Wells Cathedral (*c.* 1329–37) and the transepts at the collegiate church of Ottery St Mary (after 1337), see P. Crossley, 'Peter Parler and England. A problem revisited', *Wallraf-Richartz-Jahrbuch*, 64 (2003), 53–82, here 64–69.

4. The chapel contained the tombs of archbishops Olbram of Škvorec (d. 1402) and Zbyněk Zajíc of Hazmburk (d. 1411), and its altar was dedicated in 1415. See K. Benešovská, I. Hlobil et al., *Peter Parler and St Vitus's Cathedral 1356–1399* (Prague 1999), 125–30.

5. J. Böker, *Der Wiener Stephansdom: Architektur als Sinnbild für das Haus Österreich* (Salzburg 2007), 111–16.

6. The inscription above the triumphal arch of the nave states that the work was begun in 1394 and finished by 1414. Both dates are supported by other sources: the laying of the foundation stone took place on 2 June 1394, whilst in 1413–14 there are documentary references to the nave's eastern side chapels and the chapel in its west gallery as functioning entities. Furthermore, the inscription was clearly added after the vault was completed. It was intended to commemorate the nave's patrons, and there seems little reason to cast doubt on the information it provides. On the basis of stylistic evidence, E. Hassmann suggested that the vault, though begun before 1414, was only completed sometime after — by around 1450. A still later date, in the third quarter of the 15th century, was recently posited by Böker, drawing on his new chronology for St Stephen's. The fabric of St. Maria am Gestade, however, shows no sign of plan changes of this type, nor does the stylistic evidence by any means preclude the construction of the vault by a single master. The variation in the figures could easily be deliberate, particularly in the light of the eclecticism of the closely related Košice work. There is also the documentary evidence mentioned above for the completion of the nave side-chapels, which contain simple bent-rib star forms. For the sources and a full art-historical analysis with further literature, see E. Hassmann, *Meister Michael: Baumeister der Herzoge von Österreich* (Vienna 2002), 216, 224–25, 346–48, and Böker, *Stephansdom* (as in n. 5), 214, 224–25.

7. On St Stephen's, see in particular Böker, *Stephansdom* (as in n. 5), 133–253. The building history is discussed below.

8. On Steyr, see R. Koch, 'Die Baugeschichte der Stadtpfarrkirche von Steyr im Mittelalter', in *Stadtpfarrkirche Steyr: Baugeschichte und Kunstgeschichte*, ed. R. Koch and B. Prokisch (Steyr 1993), 23–54.

9. Nussbaum and Lepsky, *Das gotische Gewölbe* (as in n. 3), 235–36, 240–41. Examples of Burghausen-Krumenauer projects with bent-rib star forms are Salzburg, former parish (now the Franciscans') church, choir (*c.* 1408–*c.* 1450); Wasserburg, St James, nave and choir (consecrated 1448); Landshut, St Martin, nave, side chapels (by *c.* 1430); and Landshut, Holy Ghost, west porch (*c.* 1465). Early examples of the bent-rib form from smaller projects include Tamsweg, St Leonard, western nave chapel (1430–34); and Unter-Eching, St Emmeram (consecrated 1443).

10. Hungarian examples are Levoča, St James, south porch (*c.* 1450–75), and Prešov, St Nicholas, south porch (*c.* 1509–11). For these and further examples, see Juckes, 'St. Elizabeth's in Košice' (as in n. 1), 110. For the Polish buildings, see Nussbaum and Lepsky, *Das gotische Gewölbe* (as in n. 3), 236, n. 857; and D. Hanulanka, *Sklepienia późnogotyckie na Śląsku* (Wrocław 1971), 65–92.

11. Nussbaum and Lepsky, for instance, recently put the vaults towards the end of the 15th century; see Nussbaum and Lepsky, *Das gotische Gewölbe* (as in n. 3), 236, nn. 854, 857. For further examples and full literature, see Juckes, 'St. Elizabeth's in Košice' (as in n. 1), 110.

12. This decorative inscription, prominently positioned in the church's interior above the south portal, commemorates the crowning of Ladislas the 'Posthumous' in 1440 and only makes sense in the context of the disputed succession following the death of his father, Albert II, in 1439. It was a means by which the town proclaimed its loyalty to Ladislas in the civil war that was only resolved after the death of Władysław I Jagiełło in 1444. See E. Marosi, 'Tanulmányok a kassai Szent Erzébet templom középkori építéstörténetéhez', *Művészettörténeti Értesítő*, 18 (1969), 32–33.

13. Juckes, 'St. Elizabeth's in Košice' (as in n. 1), 49–50, 151–53. For the altars, see Archív mesta Košíc (Košice Town Archive), Schvarzenbachiana 298. On the murals, see I. Ciulisová, 'Gotická nástenná mal'ba dómu v Košiciach', *Ars*, 22 (1989), 33–39. On the Calvary, see particularly M. Bartlová's catalogue entry in *Gotika: Dejíny slovenského výtvarného umenia*, exhibition catalogue, ed. D. Buran (Bratislava 2003), 700–01.

14. On the later work at the church, with further literature, see E. Marosi, 'Tanulmányok a kassai Szent Erzébet-templom építéstörténetéhez III', *Művészettörténeti Értesítő*, 20 (1971), 261–91; Juckes, 'St. Elizabeth's in Košice' (as in n. 1), 161–76.

15. Confirmation of the portals' completion comes from Košice-influenced work elsewhere in Hungary. The nave portals of the parish churches in Transylvanian Cluj (1420s–1430s) and Sighişoara (1429 on) were executed by masters who had first-hand knowledge of the distinctive Košice designs. See Juckes, 'St. Elizabeth's in Košice' (as in n. 1), 119–29, 181–93.

16. The written sources relating to the main phases of the rebuilding provide limited information about the structure of the town's lodge or the masters that headed it. The first documented master of works ('werkmaister zu khassaw') was the long-serving Master Stephan, who was active in Košice *c.* 1460–87. Whilst no masters' names can firmly be connected with the St Elizabeth's project before this date, the evidence does suggest that Stephan's was an established post. As for the architecture, the church's fabric shows several plan and style changes that can be related to the arrival of new master-masons in the town. The most dramatic alterations to the original design were undertaken at the beginning of the second phase of work (*c.* 1405–40), which included the execution of the vaults under discussion here. See Juckes, 'St. Elizabeth's in Košice' (as in n. 1), 69–73, 76–159, 197–98.

17. It is roughly contemporary with Madern Gerthener's north porch vault at St Bartholomew's in Frankfurt (*c.* 1415–23); see F. Fischer, *Die spätgotische Kirchenbaukunst am Mittelrhein 1410–1520* (Heidelberg 1962), 17. The earliest tracery vaults of this type, however, seem to come from early-14th-century England, where important examples occur at Bristol (collegiate church of St Augustine, choir vault, *c.* 1298–1322; St Mary Redcliffe, southern side aisles of the nave, *c.* 1300–10) and Wells (cathedral, presbytery vault, *c.* 1329–37). See Nussbaum and Lepsky, *Das gotische Gewölbe* (as in n. 3), 188, 193–94.

18. On the Franciscan church, see H. Haberlandová, 'Stredoveký kostol frantiskánov v Košiciach', *Ars*, 17 (1984), 81–95; J. Krcho and G. Szekér, 'Adalékok a kassai ferences templom középkori építéstörténetéhez,' in *Művészettörténet - Müemlékvédelem*, ed. A. Harris (Budapest 1994), 333–58; Juckes, 'St. Elizabeth's in Košice' (as in n. 1), 42–43, 114–15, 119, 131, 142–43. There are no firm dates for the completion of the choir.

19. Akademie der Bildenden Künste (ABK, the Academy of Fine Arts), Kupferstichkabinett, no. 16941. The date of the drawing (and its close relative, no. 17019v) is uncertain. Böker suggested a connection to St Othmar's, Mödling (after 1454). The evidence, however, is problematic: the vaults at Mödling were destroyed during the Turkish wars, and their original form cannot be reconstructed. See J. Böker, *Architektur der Gotik* (Salzburg 2005), 259–61.

20. ABK, no. 17019v. See Böker, *Architektur* (as in n. 19), 326–28.

21. Benešovská and Hlobil, *Peter Parler* (as in n. 4), 38–42. A possible precedent for Prague is the St Catherine chapel in Strasbourg (consecrated 1349), but the exact form of this (lost) design is unknown.

22. On the St Catherine chapel, see Böker, *Stephansdom* (as in n. 5), 102–05, 107–11.

23. Wenceslas Parler (d. 1404) became master of works at St Stephen's after arriving from Prague around 1400. Peter of Prachatitz (d. 1429) succeeded him, but was also named master of works at Prague Cathedral in 1418. See R. Perger, 'Baumeister des Wiener Stephansdomes im Spätmittelalter', *Wiener Jahrbuch für Kunstgeschichte*, 23 (1970), 66–107, here 87–88; and Böker, *Stephansdom* (as in n. 5), 114, 118.

24. Puchspaum's contract (a source that is now lost, but was transcribed and published by Andreas Heyinger in 1722) stated that he was to provide 'ein ganze Visirung, und die ingeantwurdung des Paus, und gewelben des Tomhaus, der Kirchen, und was daran zu pauen ist' ('A complete design [...] and the vaulting of [...] the church, and what needs to be built there'). See Perger, 'Baumeister des Wiener Stephansdomes' (as in n. 23), 92; and Böker, *Stephansdom* (as in n. 5), 167. I would like to thank Regina Cermann, Sonja Führer and Susanne Rischpler for advice on the interpretation of the Puchspaum contract, as well as other sources translated in the notes below.

25. Böker, *Stephansdom* (as in n. 5), 133, 157–83, 206–26.

26. A burgher of the town gave money for the construction of the church's choir in 1440 ('Zu Hülff deß Chorbaues in d(er) Phorkirchen Zu Steyr', 'to help build the choir in the parish church at Steyr'). The 17th-century chronicler Valentin Preuenhueber, meanwhile, drawing on sources that no longer survive, stated that work on the new church began in 1443 under Hanns Puchspaum ('Der erste Baumeister, so den Anfang von dieser Gebäu gemacht, hat Hannß Puxbaum geheißen', 'The first master of works, who made a start on this building, was called Hanns Puchspaum'). For both sources, see Koch, 'Die Baugeschichte der Stadtpfarrkirche von Steyr' (as in n. 8), 23–54.

27. Böker, *Stephansdom* (as in n. 5), 166–67, 179.

28. On Bratislava, see particularly J. Bureš, 'Problém klenby Bratislavského dómu', in *Zo starších výtvarných dejín Slovenska*, ed. K. Kahoun (Bratislava 1965), 67–79; J. Bureš, 'Die Meister des Pressburger Doms', *Acta Historiae Artium*, 18 (1972), 85–105; J. Žáry, A. Bagin, I. Rusina and E. Toranová, *Der Martinsdom in Bratislava* (Bratislava 1990), 39–76. The dating of the nave vaults will be discussed further below.

29. The most detailed statement of Böker's views on the Puchspaum-Spenning question is Böker, *Stephansdom* (as in n. 5), 133–319.

30. See above, n. 6.

31. Böker, *Stephansdom* (as in n. 5), 142–57.

32. Peter von Prachatitz was master of works 1404–29, Hans von Prachatitz 1429–35, and Mathes (?)Helbling 1435/37–44. See Perger, 'Baumeister des Wiener Stephandomes' (as in n. 2), 88–91.

33. Böker states that Puchspaum only received the commission for the vaults in 1452, but his source is unclear, and the date is not found in other literature on Bratislava. It also contradicts the documentary evidence discussed here. See Böker (*Stephansdom* (as in n. 5), 170 n. 535), where he refers to two books, neither of which confirms his assertion.

34. The 1435 will of Andreas Pernhertel mentions 'tzway Fuder Wein zu aynem pheyler' ('two tuns of wine for a pier'). In the same year, the will of Linhart Langwiser left money for the roof, which had clearly not yet been built: 'zu dem Dachwerich tzwayhundert Gulden in Golt, un mein Maynung ist also, das man das golt nicht schol dargeben unt das man an hebt zu pawn' ('200 gulden in gold for the roof, and it is my intention that the gold should not be given until building work begins'). For the sources and building history, see Bureš, 'Problém klenby Bratislavského dómu' (as in n. 28), 69, n. 21.

35. In 1443, a tailor, Augustin, made a bequest 'zu den Gewelb zu sand Merten kirichen zu prespurg' ('to the vaults of St Martin's church in Bratislava') and then further 'zu sand merten chirichen zum paw und zum gewelb' ('for building works and vaults in St Martin's church'). In 1448, Simon Irher left 'zu dem paw sannd merten pfarrkirchen X flor. p. VII h., die sein aufgebracht Als der alt virczker dy teglich hat geben den aribatern da man dy bedacht kirchen Gewelbt hat' ('for the building work at the parish church of St Martin, 10 florins [. . .?] given daily to the workers whilst the mentioned church was being vaulted'). See Bureš, 'Problém klenby Bratislavského dómu' (as in n. 28), 69, n. 22.

36. Bureš, 'Problém klenby Bratislavského dómu' (as in n. 28), 69, n. 23.

37. In 1448, the same Simon Irher mentioned above left money for the choir, but also made it clear that work had not yet begun: 'zu den paw sand merten chirchen dy man dann solt zwanzigen auf arbait darraihen wann man den char anhueb ze pawn' ('for building work at St Martin's, to be spent on work [. . .] when they begin to build the choir'). A further will shows that the choir had still not been begun in 1456. By 1461, however, it seems that work was under way. The near completion of the choir is shown by a 1476 inscription on a vault boss and a 1478 payment for the stalls. See Bureš, 'Die Meister des Pressburger Doms' (as in n. 28), 86, 95–96.

38. The south transept staircase, for instance, employed an interlocking double-spiral construction, whose virtuoso form appears to have been unique for its time and was not repeated until its famous application at Graz Castle under Emperor Maximilian I in 1499–1500. On the staircase, see Juckes, 'St. Elizabeth's in Košice' (as in n. 1), 143–46.

39. On the question of the church's patronage and the impact of the town's requirements on the St Elizabeth's design, see Juckes, 'St. Elizabeth's in Košice' (as in n. 1), 57–69, 95–99, 152–59, 174–98.

'The Example of Prague in Europe'? The Case of the 'Habsburg Windows' from St Stephen's in Vienna in the Context of Dynastic Rivalry in Late-Fourteenth-Century Central Europe

ANDREAS PUTH

The artistic connections between 14th-century Prague and Vienna and the ways in which they reflect the rivalry of the Luxembourg and Habsburg dynasties have long been recognised and analysed by scholars. The architectural and sculptural relationships between St Vitus's Cathedral in Prague and St Stephen's in Vienna have frequently occupied centre stage in this discussion. Yet in many ways the general gist of this debate has been one-sided, on the artistic as well as the patronal level. Just as key architectural features of St Stephen's are seen as deriving from St Vitus's in Prague, the political and artistic programme of the Habsburg dukes in this era has been characterised by the term imitatio. *Attention in this context has traditionally focused on Duke Rudolf IV (1358–65), who was married to Emperor Charles IV's eldest daughter. His institutional foundations in Vienna and his strategies of dynastic self-aggrandisement have been interpreted as an attempt to follow the pattern set by his imperial father-in-law's patronage, which he had witnessed at first hand. This paper will be concerned with an artistic ensemble commissioned by Rudolf's younger brother Albrecht III (1365–95), also a son-in-law of Charles IV. The so-called 'Habsburg windows' made for the chapel of St Bartholomew in St Stephen's offer an appropriate case study for a careful re-examination of Habsburg dynastic imagery in the late 14th century and the ways in which it was allegedly inspired by the Luxembourg genealogy once in the imperial castle at Karlstein. Discussing them with regard to the genealogical idea they visualise, their architectural setting, and their chronological and workshop contexts, it will be argued that the windows should be dated to the late 1380s and situated in the immediate context of Albrecht's growing rivalry with the king of the Romans and of Bohemia, Wenceslas IV, and his eventual participation in schemes to depose Wenceslas IV so as to regain the Roman-German crown for the Habsburg dynasty.*

IN their distinctive ways St Vitus's Cathedral in Prague and St Stephen's in Vienna (Fig. 1) dominate their respective cities' skylines to this day. The general conception of St Stephen's magnificent south tower, with its integrated porch and a skeletal-ribbed

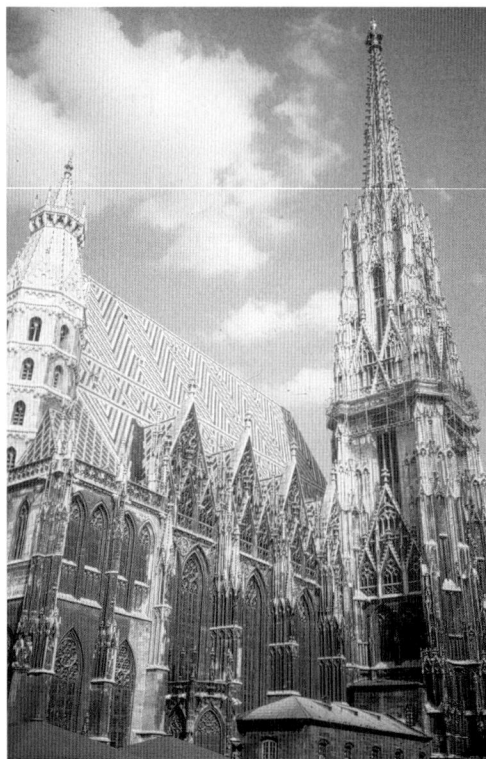

FIG. I.   Vienna, St Stephen's: view from the south-west

Andreas Puth

chapel as well as architectural and sculptural details on its second storey, echo similar features at St Vitus's, links that can be further substantiated by the recorded employment of Master Wenzel as master mason of the Vienna lodge in 1403/04; he is usually identified as Peter Parler's son, Wenzel, who had been in charge of Prague Cathedral until 1397/98.[1] These Prague-derived features, it has been argued, followed in the wake of a wider political as well as artistic programme instigated by the Habsburg Duke Rudolf IV (1358–65) that may be characterised as *imitatio* of Charles IV.[2] Rudolf (Figs 2, 10) founded a collegiate chapter dedicated to All Saints, first established in his birth chamber in the castle of Vienna and then transferred to the city's parish church of St Stephen as part of a long-term strategy to wrest control over the church from the bishops of Passau and establish an own diocese with St Stephen's as its cathedral.[3] In 1359, he and his wife Katharina (Catherine) laid the foundation stone for the enlargement of the church that was to be the new Habsburg mausoleum[4] and to be distinguished by ambitious dynastic imagery. In 1365, he founded the University of Vienna, seventeen years after Charles IV had established a university in Prague. Yet in his desire to elevate the Habsburg dynasty to the rank he thought befitted it within the empire, he did not shy away from seeking open conflict with the emperor.[5] The careful forging of ancient privileges granted to the dukes of Austria, not least by Caesar and Nero (the claiming of the title 'archduke' to equal the rank of the electors with their 'arch-offices', and the invention of regalia, most notably the

134

FIG. 2. Vienna, Wien Museum: Rudolf IV,
statue from the corner tabernacle of the
double chapel of Sts Eligius and Bartholomew
Wien Museum

archducal coronet, clearly modelled after the imperial ones) were only some of the
schemes by which Rudolf claimed quasi-royal status for himself, his dynasty, and the
territories they ruled, Austria being characterised as the 'clipeus et cor sacri Romani
imperii' ('shield and heart of the Holy Roman Empire').

In their programmatic article that lends its title to my paper, Jiří Fajt and Robert
Suckale address the questions that such a political programme raises for the issue of
artistic patronage.[6] The 'imitation of Prague models in Vienna' — institutionally as
well as artistically — can, they suggest, 'be an expression of grudging dependency as
well as of admiration'. The idea of style as an expression of political allegiance,

employed by the same authors with regard to other Central European territories in the era of Charles IV and indeed proposed as a general model for formal analysis of works of art, clearly does not apply in this case. But Fajt and Suckale also acknowledge the activity of artists in Vienna who were 'in all respects equal to Prague'. Indeed, the sculptures produced for St Stephen's in the early 1360s by the so-called 'first ducal workshop' — comprising the ducal statues on the lateral portals, the effigies of Rudolf and Katharina, and the dynastic cycle later inserted on the south tower and the corners of the western double chapels (Fig. 2) — are of outstanding quality and were, as the eminent art historian Gerhard Schmidt has demonstrated, inspired by northern French models. Their influence, in turn, has been observed in St Vitus's, on the celebrated statue of St Wenceslas now occupying the socle above the St Wenceslas chapel altar.[7] Connections between Prague and Vienna, it thus seems, are more complex than the idea of *imitatio* would suggest.

Turning to a remarkable ensemble that owes its existence to the patronage of Rudolf's younger brother Albrecht (Albert) III (1365–95, Fig. 3), this paper will be concerned with precisely those questions touched upon briefly with regard to Rudolf IV. For Albrecht III also married a daughter of Charles IV — Elizabeth — but, unlike his brother, remained a close ally of his father-in-law.[8] He is known to have commissioned works from Bohemian artists, most notably the enigmatic gospel book

FIG. 3. St. Erhard in der Breitenau (Styria), pilgrimage church: donor panel with Duke Albrecht III, Elizabeth of Luxembourg and Beatrix of Hohenzollern
Vienna, Bundesdenkmalamt

from Jan of Opava (Johann von Troppau) in 1368.[9] The ensemble under conside-
ration here, the so-called 'Habsburg windows' commissioned by Albrecht III for
the chapel of St Bartholomew in St Stephen's, has traditionally been seen as a late
conclusion to the dynastic imagery initiated at St Stephen's by Rudolf IV; the Luxembourg genealogy at Karlstein Castle was generally identified as its model and chief
inspiration, and its stylistic appearance was also seen as Bohemian.[10] Having not been
studied in detail since Eva Frodl-Kraft's *Corpus Vitrearum* volume on Vienna was
published in 1962, the windows provide an ideal opportunity to challenge
received wisdom in the light of the methodological questions raised above. In disas-
sociating Albrecht's patronage more clearly from Rudolf's than is usually done, and
adding a clear political motivation to the profile of a prince largely seen as *princeps
sapiens*, literary patron, and bibliophile, this paper offers a new interpretation for this
rather spectacular ensemble.[11] According to Gerhard Schmidt, it easily matches in
quality anything that was produced at the Valois, Luxembourg or Visconti courts at
that time, and it belongs to the same international milieu evoked so vividly by Andrew
Martindale in his lecture on 'heroes, ancestors, relatives and the birth of the
portrait'.[12]

To a late-14th-century audience, St Stephen's in Vienna would have looked completely unlike the famous south-west vista of the church familiar to the modern viewer
(Fig. 1). Its established building chronology has been thrown into question in recent
years, with particularly dramatic implications for the state of the works at the time of
Rudolf IV's death and the succession of his younger brothers Albrecht III and Leopold
III in 1365. According to the traditional interpretation, the third Romanesque church
on the site, a building of impressive size built *c.* 1220–60, was gradually replaced
in several campaigns throughout the 14th and 15th centuries. A new triple-aisled
hall choir was begun in 1304 and probably in use by the 1330s. In 1359, Rudolf
and Katharina laid the foundation stone for the enlargement of the church. This
enlargement has been interpreted as comprising a new nave with two lateral portals
including donor statuary, the south tower, and the two double chapels added to the
Romanesque west façade, which was kept and survives to this day. New dendrochronological evidence, to be discussed below, now appears to contradict Arthur Saliger's
attempt to date this rebuilding scheme to the 1340s and interpret it as allegedly
expressing the ambitions of Duke Albrecht II (1330–58) to regain royal status for the
Habsburgs, including the provision for housing the imperial relics and regalia in
the upper south-western chapel of St Bartholomew — a suggestion that is contrary to
the historical assessment of Albrecht II's policies in any case.[13] Johann Josef Böker,
however, has recently argued for a Rudolfine scheme comprising the choir (begun
only in 1359, according to his chronology), a single south tower, and merely single-
storey chapels flanking the west façade, one of which was originally intended as site of
Rudolf's burial, and both as settings for the donors' portals that would have faced
eastwards before their later re-insertion into the 15th-century nave walls.[14]

It is these western chapels adjoining the Romanesque west towers that are of
concern here (Fig. 4). On the north side are the Chapel of the Cross — originally
also dedicated to St Morandus — and the relic treasury above; on the south side the
chapels of St Eligius below and of St Bartholomew above. Documentary evidence
suggests that the St Eligius chapel was in liturgical use by 1366, when St Leonard's
altar, hitherto on the Romanesque western gallery, was transferred here.[15] Most
authors concluded that the western gallery had previously been a space exclusive to
the rulers — in loose association with traditional connotations of a *Westwerk* — and

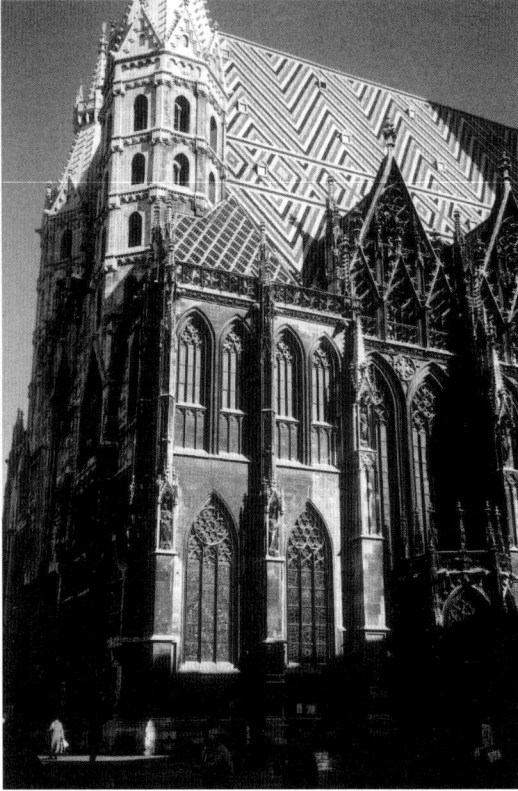

FIG. 4.   Vienna, St Stephen's: double chapel of St Eligius and St Bartholomew
Andreas Puth

that its function as a princely oratory was transferred to the double chapels when the gallery was turned into the chapter house of the college of All Saints established at St Stephen's by Rudolf IV in 1365. The placement of the 'first ducal workshop' statues of Rudolf and Katharina in the corner tabernacles of the south-western and north-western double chapels may underline this. In 1390, the St Eligius chapel is referred to as a 'ducal chapel' for the first time.[16] The chapel above it was dedicated to St Bartholomew in 1437 at the explicit 'command and wish' of Duke Albrecht V (elected King Albrecht II of the Romans in 1438) and is later referred to as 'royal chapel' or 'upper royal chapel'. As late as 1513, the lower north-western chapel is also mentioned as a 'ducal chapel'.[17] This terminology suggests both double chapels as a whole to have been intended as ducal oratories, their two-storey structure (if conceived from the outset) evoking — albeit in a different setting — a distinguished tradition of palace and castle chapels, and thus vital to Nikolaus Grass's interpretation of St Stephen's as 'capella regia austriaca'.[18] It should nevertheless be emphasised how unusual such a combination of features at the west façade actually is. While double-storey princely oratories attached to the main body of churches are not rare as such in the later Middle Ages, they are more usually situated close to the liturgical choir rather than the west end.[19] Also, the concept of the *Westwerk* as seat of the ruler within a church has itself been fundamentally called into question in recent years, and Beat Brenk's call for a more careful distinction between 'westworks' as liturgical spaces on the one hand and elevated private oratories on the other hand (and, accordingly, for much more caution in applying the special case of Charlemagne's Aachen chapel to other buildings) deserves particular attention in this context.[20]

It is in St Bartholomew's chapel that Joseph Ogesser, in his 1779 monograph on St Stephen's, recorded the Habsburg windows *in situ*, before they were taken out in the early 19th century and deposited largely in the Historisches Museum der Stadt Wien (now Wien Museum; some panels are preserved in the Österreichisches Museum für Angewandte Kunst in Vienna).[21] There is no reason to suggest that the upper chapel had not long been completed by the time of the first explicit mention of it in 1437: its architecture and the imagery on its internal keystones point firmly to a 14th-century date as well as a previous dedication to the Archangel Michael, the traditional patron saint of 'westwork'-related spaces. This view is supported by dendrochronological evidence uncovered during the restoration campaign in 2002, which strongly suggests a post-1369/70 date for the construction of the chapel.[22]

The upper chapel is externally clearly differentiated from the lower by its tight rhythm of two three-light traceried windows per bay, each above a dado with panel tracery. This system is made possible by the quinquepartite vaulting of the chapel's two interior bays (Fig. 5), a system pioneered on a much grander scale in the aisles of the hall choir of the Cistercian abbey church at Heiligenkreuz (Niederösterreich, 1280–95).[23] Shafts with triple pear-shaped mouldings rise uninterruptedly to the wall-arches and ribs, meeting in two keystones depicting St Michael slaying the dragon and St Michael weighing the souls. On the eastern wall, to the left of the altar, is an opening communicating with the largely 15th-century south aisle of the church. According to Ogesser's 1779 account, the west window depicted St Michael with three female saints beneath;[24] the two south windows of the western bay depicted twelve Habsburg princes;[25] and the two windows of the eastern bay showed (in the westernmost) the Adoration of the Magi and (in the easternmost), the Stoning of St Stephen, the patron saint of the entire church.[26] All figures and narrative scenes are distributed within elaborate and imaginative architectural settings that project and recede spatially, rendering each window a compositional unit.

Apart from St Stephen's Window, where two angular tabernacle towers with galleries, column-framed balconies, and spires form a dramatic setting for the

FIG. 5.   Vienna, St Stephen's: chapel of St Bartholomew, interior looking west
Andreas Puth

FIG. 6.   Vienna, Wien Museum:
first Habsburg window, photomontage (edges of panels cropped)
Bundesdenkmalamt, Wien

appearance of Christ the Saviour with a sceptre in the centre while St Stephen suffers his martyrdom beneath, it is undoubtedly the two Habsburg windows that are the most spectacular visual elements of this chapel in its original form (Fig. 6 & Col. Pl. IV in print edn). Thin columns support cusped arcades beneath elaborate friezes and also, in a rather classical manner, straight 'architraves' (on the second window, Fig. 7 & Col. Pl. VA in print edn). The spaces revealed behind, mostly covered by diamond patterns, house the seated princes, the central ones frontally enthroned, the flanking ones at an angle, one of them almost in profile. They are identified by inscriptions

FIG. 7.   Vienna, Wien Museum: second Habsburg window, without bottom-left panel of Friedrich II

Bundesdenkmalamt, Wien

FIG. 8.   Vienna, Wien Museum: Albrecht I from the first Habsburg window

Wien Museum

Count Rudolf IV of Habsburg 1218-91
King <u>Rudolf I</u> of the Romans 1273-91
m.
(1) Gertrud (as queen: Anna/Anne) of Hohenberg d. 1281
(2) Isabella (as queen: Elisabeth/Elizabeth) of Burgundy d. 1323 (no issue)

Rudolf II	Mathilde	**Albrecht (Albert) I**	Agnes
c.1270-90	c.1251-1304	1255-1308 (assassinated)	c.1257-1322
m. Agnes of Bohemia d. 1296	m. Duke Ludwig (Louis) II of Bavaria d. 1294	**King of the Romans 1298-1308**	m. Duke Albert II of Saxony d. 1298
		m. Elizabeth of Görz-Tyrol d. 1313	

Johann (John) 'Parricida'	Agnes	Rudolf III	Albrecht (Albert) II	**Friedrich (Frederick) I**
1290-1313	1280-1364	c.1281-1307	1298-1358	1289-1330
assassin of Albert I	m. King Andrew III of Hungary d. 1301	King of Bohemia 1306/07	m. Johanna of Pfirt (Joanna of Ferrette) d. 1351	**King Frederick III of the Romans**
		m.		**1314-1322/30**
		(1) Blanche of France d. 1305		m. Isabella (Elizabeth) of Aragon d. 1330
		(2) Elizabeth of Poland		(issue: 3 daughters)
		(widow of Wenceslas II) d. 1335		

Rudolf IV	Margarete (Margaret)	<u>Friedrich III.</u>	Albrecht (Albert) III	Leopold III
1339-65	1346-66	1347-62	1349/50-95	1351-86
m. Catherine of Luxembourg d. 1395	m.		m.	m. Viridis Visconti d. 1414
	(1) Meinhard III of Tyrol d. 1363		(1) Elizabeth of Luxembourg d. 1373	
	(2) John Henry of Luxembourg,		(2) Beatrix of Hohenzollern d. 1414	
	Margrave of Moravia d. 1375			

Albertinian Line   Leopoldinian Line

Albrecht IV	Wilhelm (William)
1377-1404	1370-1406
m. Joanna of Bavaria d. 1410	m. Joanna of Naples d. 1435

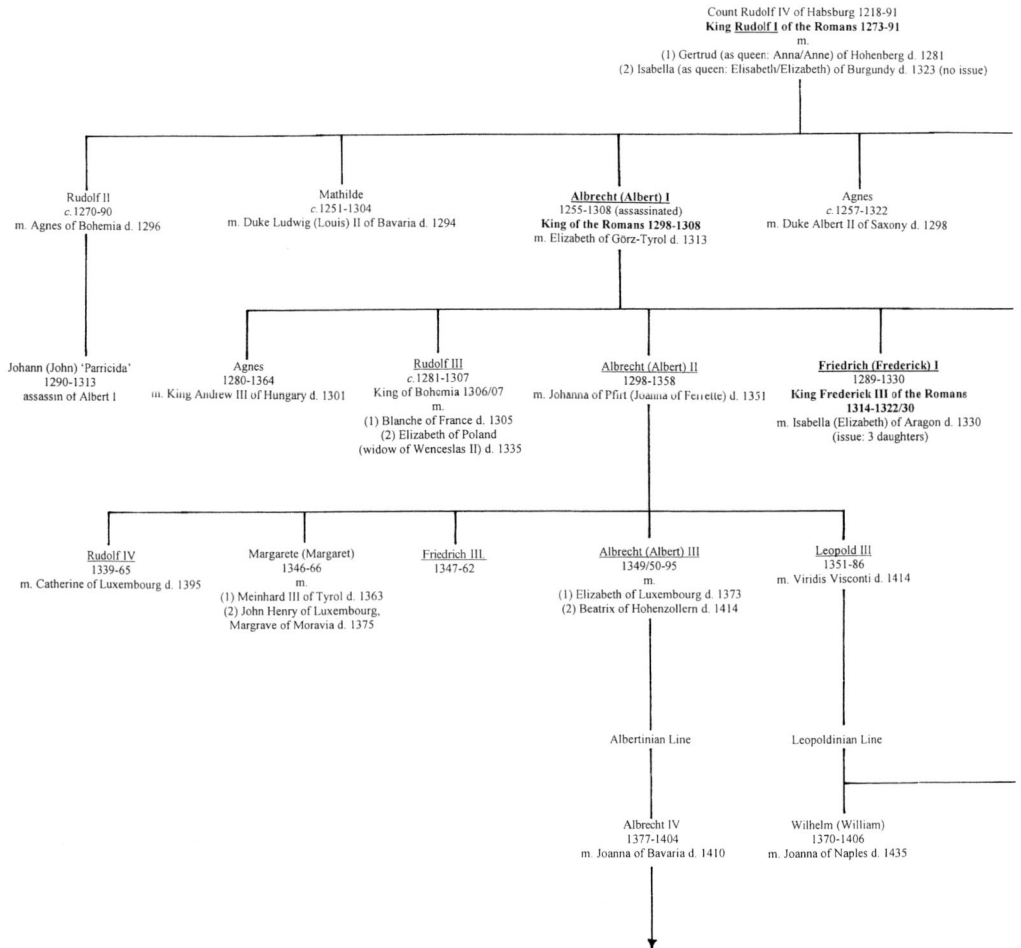

From 1282 onwards, all male Habsburgs were jointly dukes of Austria and Styria, and thereafter lords of those territories acquired subsequently (such as Carinthia, 1335, and Tyrol, 1363); in the Neuberg treaty of 1379 the territories were split between Austria (Albertinian line) and Styria, Carinthia, Tyrol, Carniola, and the Upper Rhenish lands (Leopoldian line).

Names in bold refer to Habsburgs who were kings of the Romans. Underlined names refer to those princes that are, or were, represented in the Habsburg windows. Albrecht III, the patron of the windows, was in all likelihood also depicted.

Hedwig/Heilwig
c.1259-85/6
m. Margrave Otto VI of Brandenburg d. 1309

Clementia
c.1262-93
m. Charles I Martel of Anjou,
titular king of Hungary d. 1295

Hartmann
1263-81

Guta
1271-97
m. King Wenceslas II of Bohemia d. 1305

Leopold I
1290-1326
m. Catherine of Savoy d. 1336

Katharina
1295-1323
m. Duke Charles of Anjou-Calabria d. 1328

Heinrich (Henry)
1298-1327
m. Elizabeth of Virneburg d. 1343

Otto
1301-39
m.
(1) Elizabeth of Bavaria d. 1330
(2) Anna (Anne) of Bohemia d. 1338

Katharina
d. 1349
m. (1) Enguerrand VI de Coucy d. 1346

Friedrich II
1327-44

Leopold II
1328-44

Leopold IV
1371-1411
m. Catherine of
Burgundy d. 1425

Ernst (Ernest)
1377-1424
m.
(1) Margaret of Pomerania d. 1407 (no issue)
(2) Cimburgis of Masovia d. 1429

Friedrich IV
1382-1439
m.
(1) Elizabeth of the Palatinate d. 1408
(2) Anne of Brunswick-Göttingen d. 1432

Margaret
c. 1370-after 1400
m. John of Moravia, Duke of Görlitz d. 1396

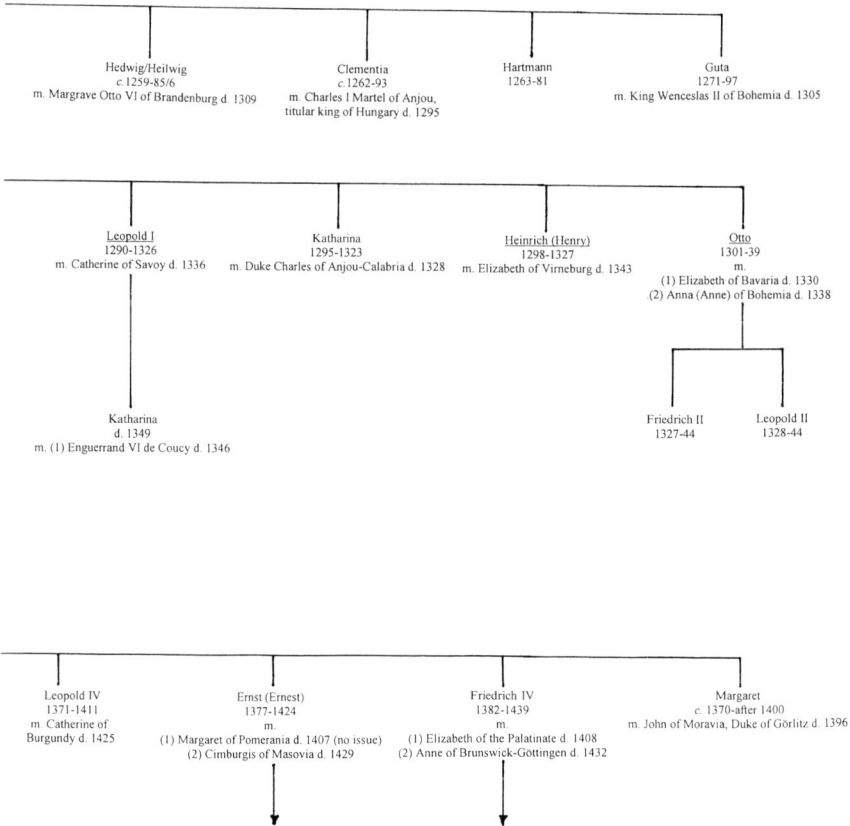

FIG. 9.   Selective family tree of the Habsburgs from Rudolf I to Albrecht III
Andreas Puth

143

on the 'architraves' above their images. The architecture of what was the left-hand window recedes in the central niche at the upper level, where King Albrecht I is enthroned (Fig. 8), giving way to a tripartite section where an axially placed arch is framed and surmounted by a double-storey system of walkways and balustrades, ending in three towers with open balconies. The right-hand window focuses on a central column-and-lintel canopy surrounding Otto I, which is integrated rather incongruously with the pointed arcades that were once on the ground storey, and the tall arches above the outer figures, which support the fanciful towers on either side (Fig. 7 & Col. Pl. Va in print edn). Overlapping the window lights, two dome-like niches continue the innermost section, framing an even taller tower set at an angle. All balustrades are formed of rows of quatrefoils. This is not micro-architecture faithfully reproducing large-scale built structures, but something altogether more fanciful. By the first half of the 14th century, the *gläserner Bauriss* — architectural drawing in glass, to quote Peter Kurmann — had reached its apogee in the Upper Rhine, with multi-tier tabernacles dominating window ensembles such as that in St Catherine's chapel in Strasbourg Cathedral (1340/45), the effect of which was enhanced by elements of three-dimensional representation;[27] the painted architecture of the Passion Window in the choir of St Stephen's in Vienna, perhaps in place by 1340, has been compared to Strasbourg models.[28] However, significant changes in architectural representation on stained glass took place at this time, ultimately influenced by spatial illusionism in Italian Trecento painting. This culminated in the arrangement of figures within monumental settings of quasi-perspectively conceived fantasy architecture such as that in the Habsburg windows. Their design shows remarkable parallels to a group of windows originating in Nuremberg workshops in the 1370/80s (at St Sebaldus's and St Martha's) and subsequently found elsewhere, notably at Ulm Minster and St Mary's in Erfurt.[29] However, this fantasy architecture in Vienna houses historical Habsburg rulers (Figs 6, 7, 9, & Col. Pls IV, Va in print edn): the three elected and crowned kings of the Romans Rudolf I (1273–91), Albrecht I (1298–1308, Fig. 8), and Friedrich der Schöne (Frederick the Fair, 1314–22/30); the male offspring of Albrecht I: Albrecht II (d. 1358), Rudolf III, the short-lived King of Bohemia (d. 1307), Heinrich I (d. 1327), Leopold I (d. 1326), and Otto I (d. 1339); and the male offspring of Albrecht II: Rudolf IV (d. 1365, Fig. 10), Friedrich III (d. 1362), Leopold III (d. 1386, lost but recorded in 1779),[30] and probably Albrecht III (d. 1395, proposed as the second of the two missing figures). All the figures are slender, animated, swathed in swirling draperies, and individually characterised. All hold sceptres and wear either their royal crowns or ducal ermine hats, displaying the royal eagle, the Bohemian lion, or the Austrian shield *gules a fess argent*.

What is so striking about this genealogy, if we can call it that? Firstly, it is selective. Since the Habsburgs exercised their lordship jointly and numbered every single one of their offspring — even if they died in infancy — it is striking that they should limit this sequence strictly to those males surviving into maturity (which for them was at the age of fourteen) and not belonging to the family branch of Albrecht I's murderer, thereby focusing on the male offspring of Albrecht I and Albrecht II (Fig. 9).[31] For the sake of coherence within this pictorial system, they omitted those not represented even from the dynastic numbering, thus turning Rudolf III into Rudolf II, Rudolf IV into Rudolf III, and so forth. In that sense, a different dynastic reality was created in these windows. Secondly, it is striking that this genealogy should make no obvious reference to Rudolf IV's dynastic aggrandisement. All dukes wear the traditional velvet-and-ermine ducal hats. If this glazing programme were indeed somehow derived from Rudolf's other dynastic imagery at St Stephen's — which, as discussed above, has frequently been suggested — a more striking reference to his adoption of archducal regalia might be expected. After all, the statues of Rudolf's parents Albrecht II and Johanna of Pfirt (Joan of Ferrette), which were made during Rudolf's reign and later inserted on the south tower, proudly display the archducal coronet, despite the fact that it was only invented by Rudolf and ran completely contrary to his father's conciliatory politics.[32] There is no retrospective appropriation of ranks and regalia in these windows then, merely the princely sceptres held by all regardless of their rank, which refer in this context rather to Christ's sceptre on St Stephen's Window and hence to the relationship between heavenly power and earthly rule. The only way in which Rudolf IV, the founder of the collegiate chapter at St Stephen's and initiator of the rebuilding of the church in which he was buried, stands out from all other Habsburgs is by being seated in profile (Fig. 10).

Fig. 10. Vienna, Wien Museum: Rudolf IV from the second Habsburg window

Wien Museum

145

Returning to the significance of the insignia, or the lack thereof, it is surely important to emphasise that none of the known representations of the windows' patron, Albrecht III, depicts him with the regalia invented by Rudolf IV, whether on the donor window in the pilgrimage church of St. Erhard in Styria (*c*. 1390; Fig. 3, discussed further below), in the lavish manuscript of the German translation of Durandus's *Rationale officium divinorum* (1385/95),[33] or on the wing of the Schloss Tirol altarpiece (1370–72),[34] where it is Albrecht's wife, Emperor Charles IV's daughter Elizabeth, who wears the imperial crown (echoing those worn by Christ and the Virgin in the Coronation of the Virgin scene on the same altarpiece). Karel Stejskal's attempt to prove that the glass atelier employed for the Habsburg windows used as a model older Bohemian ruler iconography still found in manuscript illuminations of the 1360s–80s (such as in the Milíčín Bible) — the primary piece of evidence being the fact that the represented Habsburg rulers do *not* wear Rudolf's archducal coronet but old-fashioned ducal hats, such as those on the miniatures in question — would therefore appear to have missed the point.[35]

The third, and probably most striking, aspect of this 'genealogy' is its limitation to a relatively recent past. In this respect, it stands out from the widespread type of genealogy of rulers that established dynastic lineage, transcending history by fixing it in the mythological past. Claiming descent from Troy was a particularly popular strategy to proclaim ancient kingship and chivalric ideals, formulated for Capetian France as well as Plantagenet England by the late 12th century and cast in stone by Philippe le Bel's (Philip the Fair's) sculpted sequence of forty-one rulers in the Palais de la Cité in Paris, largely completed by the time of the king's death in 1314, but leaving seventeen niches to become a prospective as well as retrospective genealogy.[36] It began with Pharamond, descended directly from King Priam of Troy, and was selective in omitting those rulers who could not easily be fitted into the dynastic sequence from Clovis to Charlemagne and Hugo Capet, or who had not resided in Paris, which itself had been founded by Trojan exiles. Charles IV's Luxembourg genealogy at Karlstein — painted *c*. 1355–57 and now only surviving in two late-16th-century manuscript copies — adopted the myth of the Trojan origin of the Franks.[37] Through his Luxembourg and Brabant ancestry, and in the writing of his chronicler Giovanni Marignola, Charles's idea of his place in universal history was anchored even further in the past: through fifty-five steps his lineage was depicted as going back through Priam of Troy, Jupiter, Saturn and Nimrod eventually to Noah's son Cham and Noah himself, the latter being seen as a type of Christ and therefore of particular significance for Charles's idea of sacred kingship. The diplomat and chronicler Edmund de Dynter vividly recalled how Charles's son Wenceslas had shown him his genealogy and proudly claimed his descent from the Trojans and Charlemagne.[38] The Luxembourg genealogy has long been identified as a decisive conceptual influence on the Habsburg windows in Vienna, and particular types of seated and animatedly gesticulating figures at Karlstein have been seen as having been adopted in Vienna.[39] Yet the suggested conceptual influence has to be qualified if it is to remain meaningful at all. Firstly, the genealogical concept of the windows is so strikingly different. It is consistent with the lack of any sustained effort on the part of the Habsburgs during the late 13th and throughout the 14th centuries with regard to the invention of a distinguished dynastic lineage. The sudden elevation of the 'small count' Rudolf of Habsburg to the German-Roman kingship in 1273 and the Habsburgs' acquisition of Austria and Styria after 1278 contrasted so dramatically with the family's previous obscurity that only humanist scholarship and imperial resources in the time of

Maximilian I (1493–1519) were able to overcome the difficulties and to link the Habsburgs with Troy too.[40] But neither do these windows adopt a tradition that had by then been established in the Austrian lands for some time, shown by the so-called Babenberg genealogy in the fountain house at Heiligenkreuz of *c.* 1290, in which the monastic founder and saintly margrave Leopold stands at the beginning of a depiction of his lineage.[41] Instead, the Habsburgs depicted themselves in this chapel as *stirps regalis*, emerging in history as kings through Albrecht III's great-grandfather Rudolf I, his grandfather Albrecht I, and his uncle Friedrich der Schöne; another uncle, Rudolf III, provided the crown of Bohemia.

Next to depictions of heavenly kingship (embodied by the image of Christ the Saviour) and of Christian kingship (personified by the Three Magi), the Habsburg windows genealogy is a programme specific to a 'private', ducal, oratory. In this respect it is rather reminiscent of certain aspects of Charles IV's idiosyncratic chapels at Karlstein, where salvific notions of kingship — embodied by Charles and his wives themselves — are depicted in several ways: in the oratory now dedicated to St Catherine Charles and Anne of Schweidnitz give 'feudal pledge' to the Virgin and Child (in the altar niche) and jointly venerate the True Cross (in the tympanum above the door); on the oratory's outside wall, Charles receives relics (notably of the Crown of Thorns) from other rulers and deposits them in the cross of the Bohemian kingdom; and finally he is shown as a magus in the Holy Cross Chapel's Adoration.[42] This distinction of setting — which is crucial in terms of the audience that would have been able to see the imagery — needs to be emphasised, as it marks a clear difference to Charles's genealogies set in palace halls: the Luxembourg genealogy at Karlstein and the likewise lost Přemyslid genealogies beginning with the eponymous founder of the dynasty in Prague Castle and at Tangermünde (the latter additionally praising legitimate German-Roman kingship in the guise of the electors, the emperor himself, his imperial grandfather, and his son Wenceslas as elected king of the Romans in 1376).[43] In the sense that painted architectural illusionism can also play a distinguishing role in the staging of sacred kingship, the relic scenes at Karlstein's chapel of Our Lady and their setting also recall the architectural 'stages' in St Bartholomew's chapel in St Stephen's, and these should therefore not be interpreted as quasi-secular, palatial settings.[44] The design of the Habsburg windows demonstrates the general 14th-century phenomenon of visualising the divine dignity of rulership by merging the sacred with the secular; at the same time, they form part of a careful distribution of the imagery within the chapel, placing the princes together with the eschatological representation of St Michael (in the west window) in its western bay, while the Adoration of the Magi and Christ the Saviour mark the distinction of the eastern bay with the altar.

Jean-Marie Moeglin has analysed the ambiguities that characterise Austrian historiography under the early Habsburgs.[45] The break from the Babenbergs to the Habsburgs (1246/78) and the initial resistance shown to the Upper Rhenish dynasty in its new territories did not result in attempts to construct genealogical links between the two; rather, efforts were directed at inventing an ancient history of the territory of Austria, with previous rulers and dynasties distinguished by the legitimacy of their respective successions. This had been the underlying principle of Rudolf's forged privileges that had supposedly been granted to the rulers of Austria by Caesar and Nero and would indeed be the characteristic feature of the Austrian chronicle written for Albrecht III during the last years of his reign, *c.* 1389–94.[46] The chronicle is a fairy-tale sequence of ninety-five lordships over Austria, extending over 2,975 years —

beginning 810 years after the deluge, reaching the Romans in the sixty-fifth lordship and the Babenbergs in the eighty-second. The land itself changes its name fifteen times during this period. The mythical princes in the chronicle are frequently related to emperors and they usually marry wives either from Hungary or Bohemia, thereby establishing Austria within its wider regional context and referring to the artistic as well as political parameters of Albrecht III's rule. The antiquity of the territory contrasts with the 'youthful' dynasty: in emphasising dynastic change, the importance of two rulers is underlined: of Rudolf I — as the first Habsburg king and military victor over Austria's and Styria's temporary ruler, King Přemysl Otakar II, in 1278 — and Albrecht I, who was formally enfeoffed as duke of Austria and Styria by his father in 1282. Indeed, the chronicle praises the 'edel sam dieser fürsten ze Österreich' ('the noble seed of the princes of Austria') leading directly from Albrecht I to Albrecht III.[47] The Habsburg windows therefore provide an apt visualisation of Habsburg dynastic thinking in the late 14th century; the concern with a more distant past appears to be reflected in other products of Albrecht's patronage, most conspicuously Jan of Opava's gospel book.[48]

There is no scope here for a detailed discussion of the stylistic problems raised by the Habsburg windows and indeed generally by painting in Austria towards the end of the 14th century. Bohemian models have been located — perhaps not entirely satisfactorily — in the workshops of the Master of Třeboň Altarpiece (c. 1380) and the illuminators at the court of Wenceslas IV.[49] Yet Eva Frodl-Kraft demonstrated long ago close analogies in terms of style and pictorial technique between the windows and a group of high-quality wall-paintings in Styria; these are now dated to c. 1390/95 and discussed very much in terms of the International Gothic, as are indeed the Bohemian examples in question. The difficulties inherent in this style and the resulting attempts to sort out Bohemian, 'western' (that is, Franco-Flemish), and Italian influences can therefore only be alluded to here.[50] Nevertheless, in trying to establish a plausible context for Albrecht III's commissioning of these images of Habsburg lordship with special emphasis on the dynasty's royal credentials, an attempt to advance rather precise dates for the windows needs to be made at this point.

The dating of the entire ensemble in St Bartholomew's chapel between c. 1370 and c. 1380[51] is informed by the assumption that the windows were executed over a considerable period of time: the more 'old-fashioned' ones (Adoration of the Magi, Archangel Michael) harking back to a stylistic mode formed by Master Theodoric in Karlstein at the beginning of the 1360s, the later ones (notably the Habsburg windows) forming the starting-point for the so-called 'second ducal workshop' of glass-painters that produced a series of ensembles for aristocrats close to the ducal court.[52] These ensembles are dated to c. 1390, in line with the inscription of the commemorative donor image of Albrecht III and his wives Elizabeth of Luxembourg (d. 1373) and Beatrix of Hohenzollern (m. 1375) in the pilgrimage church of the Styrian mining village of St. Erhard (Fig. 3).[53] As Albrecht is described here as Duke of Styria, the window is taken to postdate the death in 1386 of his brother Leopold, to whom Styria and all western Habsburg territories had been ceded in 1379. The windows at St. Erhard and the Cistercian abbey of Viktring in Carinthia (also dated to c. 1390 onwards)[54] are seen as the most advanced ensembles from this glazing workshop. Accordingly, if the Habsburg windows indeed provided the 'starting point' for these ensembles, they should be dated earlier. But did they? Given the variety of stylistic modes within St Bartholomew's chapel, they should be dated earlier — which, one assumes, would have been the most high-profile commission for glass-painters in Austria at this time — it may be appropriate to be cautious about models of thinking founded on the notion of stylistic progress and of artistic brilliance invariably instigated by patrons of the highest rank. The 'second ducal workshop' windows are easily distinguished by an iconographic and formal repertoire employed across the entire group. The Habsburg windows naturally stand apart from the religious imagery of the other ensembles; nevertheless, there are great similarities in the architectural settings and undoubted continuities in the painting style. Differences (above all, the window's dramatic contrasts of dark and bright colours) may well be explained by the different circumstances of Habsburg windows' patronage and the particular type of imagery demanded here. Gerhard Schmidt's stylistic dating of the Habsburg windows to the 1380s puts them much closer to the remaining output of the entire workshop.[55]

Keeping this in mind and examining anew Albrecht III's rather overlooked reign in the 1380/90s, it is conspicuous that he harboured serious ambitions to reclaim the German-Roman kingship for the Habsburgs, even though historical evidence for these schemes remains somewhat hazy. His first open conflict with King Wenceslas IV arose in 1387/88 over the appointment of a new bishop of Passau, an issue of considerable sensitivity to the Habsburgs as the diocese covered all of Austria.[56] As Wenceslas's reign in the empire and Bohemia got into serious trouble during the 1380s and a Bohemian aristocratic opposition began to rise against him, Albrecht exploited dynastic strife within the Luxembourg dynasty and joined forces with Wenceslas's brother Sigismund and his cousin Jodocus (Jošt) of Moravia, forming an alliance with the latter from 1388 onwards, and with the rebel aristocrats in 1393.[57] The rebels probably wanted to make use of Albrecht's ambitions rather than genuinely support a Habsburg kingship. Nevertheless, the Swabian imperial cities agreed in 1394 to help Albert 'towards the empire' should the throne become vacant. Wenceslas was captured by his opponents and imprisoned for several months, spending some days in a castle in Upper Austria. While the Rhenish electors — led by the archbishop of Mainz and Count Palatine Ruprecht II, who had assumed the imperial vicariate — succeeded in frustrating this attempt to topple Wenceslas, they could not prevent the Bohemian situation from flaring up again. Some of the leading noblemen, the Rožmberks and the Poděbrads among them, formed a new alliance with Jodocus of Moravia and Albrecht, who formally declared war on Wenceslas in July 1395. Before embarking on a military campaign in Bohemia, Albrecht fell ill and died in his hunting lodge at Laxenburg outside Vienna.

While details of Albrecht's strategy remain unclear and historians appear to be very cautious in their assessment of these events, I would argue that the imagery of the Habsburg windows should be taken into account as a piece of historical evidence too. Albrecht III's commissioning of the Habsburg windows can hardly be disassociated from his active opposition to Wenceslas and his pursuit of political schemes to reclaim the imperial crown for the Habsburg dynasty, documented from the late 1380s onwards. This is entirely consistent with the possibility of dating the windows to the late 1380s, following the stylistic and workshop implications hinted at above. Albrecht III's contemplation of such dynastic fulfilment would have found its appropriate expression in this visualisation of a lineage descending from King Rudolf I that prominently displayed three crowned rulers at its beginning (Fig. 6 & Col. Pl. IV in print edn). With Albrecht I in the upper centre of the first window and Albrecht III in the lower centre of the second, the composition would have visualised the dynastic praise of the 'edel sam' of the Austrian princes from one distinguished Albrecht to another.

ACKNOWLEDGEMENTS

This article is based on a chapter of my forthcoming doctoral dissertation, 'Imitatio Caroli, Imitatio Rudolfi? Reassessing Habsburg dynastic representation, c. 1360–c. 1470', supervised by Professor Paul Crossley at the Courtauld Institute of Art, to whom I owe deep gratitude for his ongoing support, patience, and penetrating criticism. Completion of the thesis is most generously being made possible by the award of an Ochs Scholarship of the British Archaeological Association. To the audience at the Prague conference I am indebted for valuable questions and comments. In Vienna, Dr Arthur Saliger was most helpful in facilitating my access to St Bartholomew's chapel while it was undergoing restoration. At the Bundesdenkmalamt, the late Prof. Dr Ernst Bacher and Dr Elisabeth Oberhaidacher-Herzig asked searching questions and thereby prompted me to question my methodological approach in the long run. In writing and improving this article, my debt to Dr Zoë Opačić is immense.

NOTES

1. In their close reading of the written sources and the fabric two articles in the *Wiener Jahrbuch für Kunstgeschichte* (23 (1970)) remain fundamental: M. Zykan, 'Zur Baugeschichte des Hochturmes von St. Stephan', 28–65; and R. Perger, 'Die Baumeister des Wiener Stephansdomes im Mittelalter', 66–107, here 87–88. The older scholarship on St Stephen's is surveyed in the well-illustrated account by R. Feuchtmüller, *Der Wiener Stephansdom* (Vienna 1978); M. Zykan, *Der Stephansdom*, Wiener Geschichtsbücher, XXVI–XXVII (Vienna/Hamburg 1981); and in G. Brucher, 'Architektur von 1300 bis 1430', in *Gotik*, ed. G. Brucher, Geschichte der bildenden Kunst in Österreich, II (Munich/London/New York 2000), 230–97 (esp. 234–35, 237–40, and nos. 34, 56). See now, however, also the monograph by J. J. Böker, *Der Wiener Stephansdom: Architektur als Sinnbild für das Haus Österreich* (Salzburg/Vienna/Munich 2007), which argues for a dramatically different building chronology. Böker's principal arguments were incorporated already in R. Bork, *Great Spires: Skyscrapers of the New Jerusalem*, 76. Veröffentlichung der Abteilung Architekturgeschichte des Kunsthistorischen Instituts der Universität zu Köln (Cologne 2003), 184–218. See further Tim Juckes's article in this volume.

2. Programmatic are R. Feuchtmüller, 'Die "Imitatio" Karls IV. in den Stiftungen der Habsburger', in *Kaiser Karl IV.: Staatsmann und Mäzen*, ed. F. Seibt (Munich 1978), 378–86, and the same author's contributions in *Die Parler und der Schöne Stil 1350–1400: Europäische Kunst unter den Luxemburgern*, ed. A. Legner, 5 vols (Cologne 1978–81), II, 415–21. *Imitatio* is still a leitmotif in the biography by W. Baum, *Rudolf IV. der Stifter: Seine Welt und seine Zeit* (Graz/Vienna/Cologne 1996). For a judicious reassessment, see A. Sauter, *Fürstliche Herrschaftsrepräsentation: Die Habsburger im 14. Jahrhundert*, Mittelalter-Forschungen, XII (Ostfildern 2003), 232–37.

3. St Stephen's was not elevated to cathedral status until 1469.

4. Parallels between the dynastic burial sites in St Vitus's and St Stephen's have been pointed out by K. Benešovská, 'Ideál a skutečnost (Historické a badatelské peripetie kolem královského pohřebiště v katedrále sv. Víta v Praze v době Lucemburků)', in *Epigraphica & Sepulcralia I*, ed. D. Prix and J. Roháček (Prague 2005), 19–48, here 28–29.

5. Excellent recent surveys of Rudolf IV's political agenda are to be found in A. Niederstätter, *Österreichische Geschichte 1278–1411: Die Herrschaft Österreich, Fürst und Land im Spätmittelalter* (Vienna 2001), 145–71, and Sauter, *Fürstliche Herrschaftsrepräsentation* (as in n. 2), 157–237.

6. J. Fajt and R. Suckale, 'The example of Prague in Europe', in *Prague: The Crown of Bohemia 1347–1437*, ed. B. D. Boehm and J. Fajt, exhibition catalogue (New York 2005), 47–57 (the quotation at 52); an extended version of this article is 'Die europäischen Dynastien - Nachahmung oder Konkurrenz', in *Karl*

IV. *Kaiser von Gottes Gnaden: Kunst und Repräsentation des Hauses Luxemburg 1310–1437*, ed. J. Fajt, exhibition catalogue (Munich/Berlin 2006), 422–39 with nos. 138–51.

7. G. Schmidt, 'Peter und Heinrich IV. Parler als Bildhauer', in idem, *Gotische Bildwerke und ihre Meister* (Vienna/Cologne/Weimar 1992), 175–228 (here 200–02); idem, 'Die Wiener Herzogswerkstatt und die Kunst Nordwesteuropas', ibid., 142–74; Fajt ed., *Karl IV.* (as in n. 6), nos. 72–73. Surveys of the entire cycle at St Stephen's are also provided by L. Schultes, 'Plastiky v chrámu sv. Štěpána - Od Rudolfa IV. k Maximiliánovi I.', in *Vídeňská Gotika: Sochy, sklomalby a architektonická plastika z dómu sv. Štěpana ve Vídni*, exhibition catalogue (Vienna 1991), 77–90 (here 77–80) and nos. 4–9; G. Schmidt, 'Die Skulptur', in *Gotik* (as in n. 1), 298–317 (here 308–11); and L. Schultes, 'Die Plastik - Vom Michaelermeister bis zum Ende des Schönen Stils', ibid., 344–96 (here 353–58, nos. 96–101).

8. Niederstätter, *Österreichische Geschichte* (as in n. 5), 172–93; C. Lackner, *Hof und Herrschaft: Rat, Kanzlei und Regierung der österreichischen Herzoge (1365–1406)*, Mitteilungen des Instituts für Österreichische Geschichtsforschung, Ergänzungsband 41 (Vienna/Munich 2002), esp. 26–28.

9. Vienna, Österreichische Nationalbibliothek, cod. 1182; *Karl IV.* (as in n. 6), no. 138; U. Jenni, M. Theisen and K. Stejskal, *Die illuminierten Handschriten und Inkunabeln der Österreichischen Nationalbibliothek: Mitteleuropäische Schulen III (ca. 1350–1400)* (Vienna 2004), 65–87, no. 3 (entry by U. Jenni).

10. E. Frodl-Kraft, *Die mittelalterlichen Glasgemälde in Wien*, CVMA Österreich, I (Graz/Vienna/Cologne 1962), 50–65 (on which all factual evidence concerning the glazing is based here); cf. E. Bacher, 'Malovaná okna z bývalé královské, resp. knížecí kaple chrámu sv. Štěpána', in *Vídeňská Gotika* (as in n. 7), 91–96 and nos. 36–39; E. Oberhaidacher-Herzig, 'Glasmalerei. Besonderheiten - Auftraggeber - Werkstätten', in Brucher ed., *Gotik* (as in n. 1), 411–32 (here 428, no. 181). Characteristic in treating these windows as conceptually belonging to Rudolf's patronage are the entries by G. Schmidt in *Die Zeit der frühen Habsburger: Dome und Klöster 1279–1379*, ed. F. Röhrig, exhibition catalogue (Wiener Neustadt 1979), 473–74, no. 271; and in Sauter, *Fürstliche Herrschaftsrepräsentation* (as in n. 2), 226–27. See ibid., 247–62, for Albrecht III as *princeps sapiens*.

11. Böker (*Stephansdom* (as in n. 1), 142) now implies a similar interpretation, though without engaging with the glass in detail.

12. G. Schmidt, 'Bildende Kunst: Malerei und Plastik', in Röhrig ed., *Die Zeit der frühen Habsburger* (as in n. 10), 82–97 (here 87). A. Martindale, *Heroes, Ancestors, Relatives and the Birth of the Portrait*, The Fourth Gerson Lecture (Maarssen/The Hague 1988), does (at 31, 33–34) include the portrait panel of Rudolf IV in his wide-ranging discussion, but makes no reference to the Habsburg windows.

13. A. Saliger, 'Zur Problematik der Fürstentore des Wiener Stephansdomes', *Umění*, 45 (1997), 26–31; idem, 'Zur kunsthistorischen Wechselwirkung parlerischer Aktivitäten in Prag und in Wien', in *Parlerbauten: Architektur, Skulptur, Restaurierung*, ed. A. Sieffert and R. Strobel (Stuttgart 2004), 109–15; idem, 'Aspekte zur künstlerischen Einmaligkeit der Heiligkreuzkapelle auf Burg Karlstein bei Prag', in *Court Chapels of the High and Late Middle Ages and their Artistic Decoration*, ed. J. Fajt (Prague 2003), 103–13 (here 107–09 for the alleged function of St Bartholomew's chapel). For Albrecht II, see Niederstätter, *Österreichische Geschichte* (as in n. 5), 132–46.

14. H.-J. Böker, 'Parlerisches am Wiener Stephansdom', in Sieffert and Strobel ed., *Parlerbauten* (as in n. 13), 103–07; idem, *Stephansdom* (as in n. 1), esp. 55–95, 133–57. It is beyond the scope of this paper to engage in detail with the problems raised by Böker's chronology.

15. For this and what follows, see N. Grass, 'Der Wiener Stephansdom als Capella Regia Austriaca', in *Festschrift Karl Pivec*, ed. A. Haidacher and H. E. Mayer (Innsbruck 1966), 91–129 (here 105, 108–10); V. Flieder, *Stephansdom und Wiener Bistumsgründung: Eine diözesan- und rechtsgeschichtliche Untersuchung* (Vienna 1968), 181–82.

16. For the documentary evidence relating to both south-western chapels, see also Frodl-Kraft, *Glasgemälde* (as in n. 10), 53.

17. Flieder, *Bistumsgründung* (as in n. 15), 182.

18. Grass, 'Capella Regia Austriaca' (as in n. 15), esp. 101–10; the chapter had officially been founded by Rudolf in Vienna Castle (the *Hofburg*) and attached to the chapel set up in his birth and childhood chambers, but was in all probability intended to be moved to St Stephen's from the outset and never actually existed in the castle (Flieder, *Bistumsgründung* (as in n. 15), 137–44). Böker (*Stephansdom* (as in n. 1), 134, 137) interprets the upper south-western chapel as a structure added to the lower chapel at a later date and not in accordance with the original scheme; he attributes it as an early work to the ducal architect Master Michael of Wiener Neustadt (whose activity is documented certainly by 1394). For an exhaustive study of Master Michael and a clear exposition of the historiographical myths that have evolved around him, see E. Hassmann, *Meister Michael: Baumeister der Herzöge von Österreich* (Vienna/Cologne/Weimar 2002), esp. 30–74, 77–92, 105–13. Contrary to Böker's assertion (*Stephansdom* (as in n. 1), 142), Hassmann did not assume the upper chapel to have been completed by 1366, but rather by *c.* 1380 (*Meister Michael*, 395); she

explained similarities between architectural features of the double chapels and structures documented for, or attributable to, Master Michael by the likelihood of his training in the Vienna lodge in the 1360/70s (ibid., 193–97, 387–89, 395–98, 506, 511–13).

19. For French examples at Champmol (furnished by 1394) and Vincennes (after 1385), see R. Prochno, *Die Kartause von Champmol: Grablege der burgundischen Herzöge 1364–1477* (Berlin 2002), 137–66 (where, at 137, it is shown that the term *oratoire* could be used for the entire double-storey structure at Champmol as well as for each chapel separately), 241–42. The choir of the Carthusian abbey church at Gaming in Lower Austria (begun 1341), the burial site of Duke Albrecht II, is flanked by two double-storey structures combining a ground-floor sacristy and chapter-house respectively with oratories above. For a survey of double-storey chapels in Lower Austria, see R. Wagner-Rieger, 'Gotische Kapellen in Niederösterreich', in *Festschrift Karl Maria Swoboda zum 28. Januar 1959*, ed. O. Benesch at al. (Vienna 1959), 273–307 (here 285–89).

20. B. Brenk, 'Wer sitzt auf der Empore?', in *Sinopien und Stuck im Westwerk der karolingischen Klosterkirche von Corvey*, ed. J. Poeschke (Münster 2002), 71–86. For a clear and critical historiographical analysis of the 'westwork' problem, see also K. Krüger, 'Zur liturgischen Benutzung karolingischer "Westwerke" anhand von bauarchäologischen Zeugnissen und Schriftquellen zu Liturgie und Altarstellen', in *Architektur und Liturgie: Akten des Kolloquiums vom 25. bis 27. Juli 2003 in Greifswald*, ed. M. Altripp and C. Nauerth (Wiesbaden 2006), 125–42. Böker (*Stephansdom* (as in n. 1), 36–37, 39–40, 43–44) locates feudal associations in St Stephen's west façade and interprets the gallery as a 'princely box', though pointing out that it is not a 'westwork' in the architectural sense. For the placement and pictorial labelling of royal pews within churches, see now also C. Wilson, 'Calling the tune? The Involvement of King Henry III in the Design of the Abbey Church at Westminster', *JBAA*, 161 (2008), 59–93, here 64–69.

21. J. Ogesser, *Beschreibung der Metropolitankirche zu St. Stephan in Wien* (Vienna 1779), 134–35; Frodl-Kraft, *Glasgemälde* (as in n. 10), 50–52.

22. Böker, *Stephansdom* (as in n. 1), 134.

23. For a recent analysis of the Heiligenkreuz hall choir and its architectural significance, see M. Thome, *Kirche und Klosteranlage der Zisterzienserabtei Heiligenkreuz: Die Bauteile des 12. und 13. Jahrhunderts*, Studien zur internationalen Architektur- und Kunstgeschichte, LII (Petersberg 2007), 240–74.

24. Frodl-Kraft, *Glasgemälde* (as in n. 10), fig. 102.

25. ibid., figs 79–80.

26. ibid., figs 106–07.

27. P. Kurmann, '"Architektur in Architektur": der gläserne Bauriss der Gotik', in *Himmelslicht: Europäische Glasmalerei im Jahrhundert des Kölner Dombaus (1248–1349)*, ed. H. Westermann-Angerhausen, exhibition catalogue (Cologne 1998), 34–43; R. Becksmann, 'Architecture, sculptures et verrières de la chapelle Sainte-Catherine de la cathédrale de Strasbourg: un ensemble artistique au seuil du gothique tardif', in *Bulletin de la Cathédrale de Strasbourg*, 25 (2002), 113–34.

28. Frodl-Kraft, *Glasgemälde* (as in n. 10), 39–42, pls 46, 48, 57. For the development of stained glass in Austria from *c.* 1340 onwards, see Oberhaidacher-Herzig, 'Glasmalerei' (as in n. 10), cat. nos. 176–80.

29. H. Scholz, *Die mittelalterlichen Glasmalereien in Mittelfranken und Nürnberg extra muros*, CVMA Deutschland, X/1, 2 vols (Berlin 2002), 57–63, with further references; see also the same author's forthcoming article 'Prag oder Nürnberg? Die Luxemburger Fensterstiftungen in Nürnberg und Franken und die Frage ihrer künstlerischen Verortung', in J. Fajt and A. Langer ed., *Kunst als Herrschaftsinstrument: Böhmen und das Heilige Römische Reich unter den Luxemburgern im europäischen Kontext* (Munich/Berlin forthcoming).

30. Frodl-Kraft, *Glasgemälde* (as in n. 10), pl. IIIa.

31. The sequence was discussed ibid., 56 with no. 25. It is significant that the inscription on the cenotaph with the effigies of Rudolf and Katharina in the choir of St Stephen's only refers to the offspring (*proles*) of Albrecht II and Johanna von Pfirt; Schultes, 'Die Plastik' (as in n. 7), cat. no. 101.

32. Schultes, 'Die Plastik' (as in n. 7), no. 99.

33. Vienna, Österreichische Nationalbibliothek, cod. 2765; A. Fingernagel, M. Roland et al., *Die illuminierten Handschriften und Inkunabeln der Österreichischen Nationalbibliothek: Mitteleuropäische Schulen II (ca. 1350–1400)* (Vienna 2002), 149–78, no. 31 (entry by M. Roland). See also Evelin Wetter's paper in this volume. The relevant depictions are on fols 1r, 30v, 42r and 57r.

34. N. Wolf, *Deutsche Schnitzretabel des 14. Jahrhunderts* (Berlin 2002), 152–65; Sauter, *Fürstliche Herrschaftsrepräsentation* (as in n. 2), 242–45; Fajt and Suckale, 'Die europäische Dynastien' (as in n. 6), 430–31.

35. K. Stejskal, 'Die Rekonstruktion des Luxemburger Stammbaums auf Karlstein', *Umění*, 26 (1978), 535–63 (esp. 546–48); the Milíčín Bible is Prague, Národní knihovna, A I.1. See now also K. Stejskal, 'Die Wandzyklen des Kaisers Karl IV. Bemerkungen zu Neudatierungen und Rekonstruktionen der im Auftrag Karls IV. gemalten Wandzyklen', *Umění*, 46 (1998), 19–41 (here 36–37, where a putative Přemyslid genealogy

on Vyšehrad — rather than the revised reconstruction of the Luxembourg genealogy at Karlstein advanced in his earlier article — is proposed as a model for this pictorial tradition).

36. For the cycle, see U. Bennert, 'Art et propagande politique sous Philippe IV le Bel: le cycle des rois de France dans la Grand'salle du Palais de la Cité', *Revue de l'art*, 97 (1992), 46–59; for the significance of the Troy myth, see W. Brückle, 'Noblesse oblige. Trojasage und legitime Herrschaft in der französischen Staatstheorie des späten Mittelalters', in K. Heck and B. Jahn ed., *Genealogie als Denkform in Mittelalter und früher Neuzeit*, Studien und Texte zur Sozialgeschichte der Literatur, LXXX (Tübingen 2000), 39–65. For a genealogical roll of the kings of Britain, dated to *c*. 1300 and depicting the succession of kings from Jason and Aeneas via Brutus to Edward I in the tradition of Geoffrey of Monmouth's *Historia Regum Britanniae* (1130s), and its context, see J. Alexander and P. Binski ed., *The Age of Chivalry: Art in Plantagenet England 1200–1400*, exhibition catalogue (London 1987), 200–01, cat. no. 10 (entry by L. F. Sandler); and R. R. Davies, *The First English Empire: Power and Identities in the British Isles 1093–1343* (Oxford 2000), 39–43.

37. J. Neuwirth (*Der Bilderzyklus des Luxemburger Stammbaums aus Karlstein* (Prague 1897), 19–24) carefully traces the interrelationship between Marignola's chronicle and the pictorial sequence; more recently, see the contributions in J. Fajt ed., *Magister Theodoricus, Court Painter to Emperor Charles IV: The Pictorial Decoration of the Shrines at Karlštejn Castle*, exhibition catalogue (Prague 1998): J. Homolka, 'The Pictorial Decoration of the Palace and Lesser Tower at Karlštejn Castle', 45–93 (here 51–59, where Stejskal's iconoclastic questioning of the pictorial records is refuted), and J. Fajt and J. Royt, 'The Pictorial Decoration of the Great Tower at Karlštejn Castle. Ecclesia Triumphans', 107–205 (esp. 135–37). See also I. Rosario, *Art and Propaganda: Charles IV of Bohemia, 1346–1378* (Woodbridge 2000), 27–30; Z. Opačić, '*Karolus Magnus* and *Karolus Quartus*: Imperial Role Models in Ingelheim, Aachen and Prague', in *Mainz and the Middle Rhine Valley: Medieval Art, Architecture and Archaeology*, ed. U. Engel and A. Gajewski, BAA Trans., xxx (Leeds 2007), 221–46 (here 233–38 for Augustinian and Carolingian models of Charles's view of history and the ways in which these may have informed his genealogical projects); and Milada Studničková's paper in this volume.

38. For specific discussions of the Dynter chronicle, see Neuwirth, *Bilderzyklus* (as in n. 37), 2–5; Martindale, *Heroes* (as in n. 12), 5–9; and Homolka, 'Palace and Lesser Tower' (as in n. 37), 51. Descent from Charlemagne was also important in the genealogical thinking of the Bavarian Wittelsbachs, who ultimately traced their ancestry to the Armenian Bavarus; J.-M. Moeglin, 'Dynastisches Bewusstsein und Geschichtsschreibung. Zum Selbstverständnis der Wittelsbacher, Habsburger und Hohenzollern im Spätmittelalter', *Historische Zeitschrift*, 256 (1993), 593–635 (here 599–600).

39. For the conceptual influence of the Luxembourg genealogy on the Habsburg windows, see Frodl-Kraft, *Glasgemälde* (as in n. 10), XXVII, 52, 57, 60; eadem, 'The Stained Glass from Ebreichsdorf and the Austrian "Ducal Workshop"', in *The Cloisters: Studies in Honor of the Fiftieth Anniversary*, ed. E. C. Parker (New York 1992), 384–407 (here 402). The adoption of figure types (notably that of Charles the Bald for Rudolf IV) is suggested by G. Schmidt, 'Die Malerei', in Brucher ed., *Gotik* (as in n. 1), 466–89 (here 476–77) and endorsed by Fajt and Suckale, 'Die europäischen Dynastien' (as in n. 6), cat. no. 139 (entry by J. Fajt).

40. A. Lhotsky, 'Apis Colonna. Fabeln und Theorien über die Abkunft der Habsburger. Ein Exkurs zur *Cronica Austrie* des Thomas Ebendorfer', in idem, *Aufsätze und Vorträge II: Das Haus Habsburg*, ed. H. Wagner and H. Koller (Munich 1971), 7–102; G. Althoff, 'Studien zur habsburgischen Merowingersage', *Mitteilungen des Instituts für österreichische Geschichtsforschung*, 87 (1979), 71–100.

41. E. Frodl-Kraft, *Die mittelalterlichen Glasgemälde in Niederösterreich I*, CVMA Österreich, II/1 (Vienna/Graz/Cologne 1972), 113–25; Thome, *Heiligenkreuz* (as in n. 23), 218–20.

42. Homolka, 'Palace and Lesser Tower' (as in n. 37), 60–66, 77–79; Fajt and Royt, 'Great Tower' (as in n. 37), 178–80. Note, however, the sequence of kneeling Habsburg princes beginning with Rudolf I inserted *c*. 1358/64 into the fourteen aisle windows of the church of the Franciscan double convent at Königsfelden (Switzerland), the commemorative centre of the dynasty's ancestral lands in the Upper Rhine. For the entire ensemble, see now B. Kurmann-Schwarz, *Die mittelalterlichen Glasmalereien der ehemaligen Klosterkirche von Königsfelden*, CVMA Schweiz, II (Bern 2008).

43. For Prague Castle, see J. Neuwirth, *Der verlorene Cyclus böhmischer Herrscher in der Prager Königsburg*, Studien zur Geschichte der Gothik in Böhmen, IV (Prague 1896); for Tangermünde, E. Wetter, 'Die Lausitz und die Mark Brandenburg', in *Karl IV.* (as in n. 6), 340–49 (here 346–48); both are also discussed in a wider context by Opačić, '*Karolus Magnus*' (as in n. 37), 236–37.

44. As suggested by Oberhaidacher-Herzig, 'Glasmalerei' (as in n. 10), no. 181. Quasi-sacred tabernacles also formed the setting for the Habsburg representations in the Königsfelden aisle windows (*c*. 1358/64); see Kurmann-Schwarz, *Königsfelden* (as in n. 41). Architectural illusionism also plays a crucial role in the setting of Edward III of England and his family in the 1350s altar wall-paintings of St Stephen's chapel in Westminster; E. Howe, 'Divine Kingship and Dynastic Display: The Altar Wall Murals of St Stephen's Chapel, Westminster', *The Antiquaries Journal*, 81 (2001), 259–303. For this and what follows, see also the

general comments in A. Puth, '"Christus dominus de hoc seculo": Charles IV, advent and epiphany on the south transept façade of St Mary's in Mühlhausen', in *Kunst als Herrschaftsinstrument* (as in n. 29).

45. J.-M. Moeglin, 'La formation d'une histoire nationale en Autriche au Moyen Âge', *Journal des savants* for 1983, 169–218; idem, 'Dynastisches Bewusstsein' (as in n. 38), 616–30.

46. J. Seemüller ed., *Österreichische Chronik von den 95 Herrschaften*, Monumenta Germaniae Historica: Deutsche Chroniken und andere Geschichtsbücher des Mittelalters, VI (Hanover/Leipzig 1909).

47. ibid., 180.

48. See above, n. 9. The classic study remains G. Schmidt, 'Johann von Troppau und die vorromanische Buchmalerei', in *Studien zur Buchmalerei und Goldschmiedekunst des Mittelalters: Festschrift für Karl Heinrich Usener*, ed. F. Dettweiler et al. (Marburg 1967), 275–93.

49. Frodl-Kraft, *Glasgemälde* (as in n. 10), XXVII–XXX, 56–58 (also for what follows); Schmidt, 'Die Malerei' (as in n. 39), 468.

50. For these wall-paintings, in Bruck, St Dionysen and Utsch, see E. Lanc and M. Porta, *Corpus der mittelalterlichen Wandmalereien in der Steiermark I* (Vienna 2002), 50–58, 418–52, 627–30. More recently, Eva Frodl-Kraft also emphasised western influences on art in Austria at this period; Frodl-Kraft, 'The Stained Glass' (as in n. 39), 398–403. The historical event linking Austria more obviously to the 'west' is the marriage of Albrecht III's nephew, Leopold IV, to Catherine of Burgundy in Dijon in September 1387, an event probably attended by Albrecht; see Lackner, *Hof und Herrschaft* (as in n. 8), 187–88.

51. Oberhaidacher-Herzig, 'Glasmalerei' (as in n. 20), cat. no. 181.

52. E. Frodl-Kraft, 'The Stained Glass' (as in n. 39), passim, providing a synthesis of her earlier work.

53. ibid., 391 92; Oberhaidacher Herzig, 'Glasmalerei' (as in n. 10), cat. no. 182. For a more detailed account, see E. Bacher, 'Die Glasgemälde in der Pfarrkirche St. Erhard in der Breitenau', in *Die Breitenau: Marktgemeinde am Fusse des Hochlantsch*, ed. G. Christian (Breitenau 1989), 116–19; the seated figure of St Erhard provides a good comparison to the Habsburg princes.

54. Oberhaidacher-Herzig, 'Glasmalerei' (as in n. 10), cat. no. 183.

55. Schmidt, 'Die Malerei' (as in n. 39), 469 (where a pre-1380 date is ruled out), 476–79.

56. F.-R. Erkens, 'Aspekte der Passauer Geschichte im 14. Jahrhundert: Das Bistum zwischen Habsburg, Wittelsbach und Böhmen und die kommunale Bewegung in Passau', *Ostbairische Grenzmarken*, 31 (1989), 61–85 (here 67–70). In 1393, Wenceslas was eventually forced to accept Albrecht's favoured candidate, Georg von Hohenlohe (who was to initiate the rebuilding of Passau Cathedral).

57. For these historical events — which have received little attention, not least as the source material leaves much room for interpretation — see the detailed analyses by J. Spěváček, *Václav IV. 1361–1419* (Prague 1986), 215–58, and A. Gerlich, *Habsburg - Luxemburg - Wittelsbach im Kampf um die deutsche Königskrone: Studien zur Vorgeschichte des Königtums Ruprechts von der Pfalz* (Wiesbaden 1960), 1–72. More recently, see J. K. Hoensch, *Die Luxemburger: Eine spätmittelalterliche Dynastie gesamteuropäischer Bedeutung 1308–1437* (Stuttgart 2000), esp. 206–11; Lackner, *Hof und Herrschaft* (as in n. 8), 28–29; and, very sceptical, E. Schubert, *Königsabsetzung: Eine Studie zum Werden der Reichsverfassung* (Göttingen 2005), 364–68, 427–28.

Paysage moralisé:
The Zderad Column in Brno and the Public Monument in the Later Middle Ages

ACHIM TIMMERMANN

This essay considers the so-called Zderad Column, a 12-m giant wayside cross on the outskirts of Brno, in its wider architectural, functional and perceptual context. Erected during the third quarter of the 15th century by masons working within the sphere of the Vienna Cathedral workshop, this elaborate structure was originally used as a so-called 'poor sinners' cross', marking the gallows nearby not as a place of terror, but of edification and redemption. In tandem with numerous other public monuments, such as market fountains or expiatory crosses, the Zderad Column also furnished a moralising gloss on the visible world, transcending Europe's late-medieval landscapes with exemplars of virtue and salvation.

IN the summer of 1091, the Přemyslid King Vratislav I (1061–92) besieged the city of Brno, hoping to oust his rebellious brother Konrád, who had taken refuge within the town walls. While searching for a place to pitch the war tents, the king's favorite minister, Zderad of Švábenice, suggested that Vratislav's son Břetislav camp at the edge of the River Svitava 'so that he may bathe often'. To the young prince and his supporters, this was an outrageous remark, because it brought back unpleasant memories of a campaign against the Saxons some years earlier, during which Břetislav had been captured by the enemy while bathing alone in a river. Hiding his anger, Břetislav asked Zderad for a meeting the following day. The unsuspecting minister arrived punctually, only to find the prince surrounded by his retainers. On Břetislav's command, Zderad was taken and brutally assassinated. Upon hearing of his beloved minister's atrocious end, Vratislav, struck with grief, ordered that Zderad be buried among the Přemyslid kings, and that a beautiful column be erected on the site of the murder.

This, in a nutshell, is the legend that gave Brno's Zderad Column (in Czech *Zderadův sloup*, in German *Zderadsäule*) its current name (Fig. 1).[1] Interesting though it may be to local antiquarians and folklorists, the legend does not stand up to historical scrutiny. The Zderad Column is clearly of Late Gothic rather than Romanesque design, and, as will be seen, its initial purpose was perhaps even more sinister than that suggested by the legend.

The present essay, the second in a three-part study exploring the significance of medieval and early-modern judicial monuments, comprises three concentric rings of enquiry.[2] The first reviews the difficult issue of style and dating, and corroborates previous attempts to ascribe the Zderad Column to craftsmen working within the

FIG. 1. Brno: the Zderad
Column, *c.* 1460–70
Achim Timmermann

ambit of the Vienna Cathedral workshop during the third quarter of the 15th century. The second is concerned with the monument's original function as a so-called 'poor sinners' cross', erected to mark the gallows nearby as a place not of terror, but of re-demption. The third — and widest — ring considers the Zderad Column within the larger pool of public monuments commissioned during the last two centuries of the Middle Ages, such as market fountains, and pilgrimage and expiatory crosses. While each type articulated a different religious or political discourse, it will be suggested that in their totality these monuments furnished a moralising gloss on the visible world, transcending it with exemplars of virtue, and promising salvation.

Located to the east of the city centre, near the Svitava Bridge (Zderadův most) on Křenová Street (Křenová ulice, which turns into Olomoucká, one of the main thoroughfares toward Olomouc), the Zderad Column is today completely absorbed into Brno's urban fabric. A glance at Joris Hoefnagel's late-16th-century engraving of Brno (Fig. 2) reproduced in the sixth volume of Braun and Hogenberg's famous *Civitatis orbis terrarum* (1618)[3] reveals, however, that the structure was initially located well outside the city walls, between the left bank of the River Svitava (in German *Zwittawa*) and the civic gallows, the *patibulum* first mentioned in a mid-14th-century law code known as the *Brno Book of Lay Assessors* (in German *Brünner Schöffenbuch*).[4] The column's physical structure has equally changed, particularly following an extensive restoration carried out between 1863 and 1865 under the supervision of Brno's neo-classicist architect Josef Arnold and Austria's Kaiserliche und Königliche Central-Commission zur Erforschung und Erhaltung der Baudenkmale (Imperial and Royal Central Commission for Research into and Conservation of Monuments). Among other things, this scheme necessitated a stone by stone disassembly, the addition of a more substantial base (which raised the overall height from just under 10 to 12.2 m), and the reconstruction of some architectural features, including the diagonal corner posts and cube-shaped finials of the openwork tier, as well as the waterspouts of the spire. These alterations notwithstanding, the current appearance of the column differs only in certain details from its pre-restoration state, as recorded in an engraving for Moriz Trapp's brief pamphlet on the monument, published in 1862 (Fig. 3).[5]

Entirely built from locally quarried encrinite limestone, and extrapolated from a square plan, the Zderad Column develops in four principal tiers. The first, comprising the socle, rises above the 19th-century base, and consists essentially of two cubes, of which the lower shows unadorned ashlar surfaces, while the upper is decorated with square tracery panels of vertical lancets and inscribed trefoil cusps. In the following tier, the architecture becomes diaphanous, featuring an outer, cage-like shell that rises over the socle corners, and a solid, octagonal core designed for the display of figural sculpture. While the former sports protruding, diagonal buttresses and a corona of triangular gablets with pinnacles and cubic finials, the latter exhibits engaged corner shafts, and, above eight corbelled supports, a sequence of now vacant statue niches. Further statuary would presumably have been housed by the subsequent and likewise octagonal storey, in which corner buttresses alternate with recessed fields surmounted by projecting triangular canopies. The elevation concludes in a stout spire embellished with openwork tracery, miniature waterspouts, and a terminating finial.

The structural alterations undertaken during the 19th century and the complete lack of imagery certainly render any attempt to date the monument on stylistic grounds difficult. The only other means of dating the structure more accurately consists of a series of masons' marks, discovered during the restoration and published by August Prokop in 1904;[6] to date, however, these marks have not been identified. In most accounts, the Zderad Column features as a monument of the second half of the 14th century or a later-14th-century work. The given reasons however are often insubstantial. For instance, in their monograph on Vienna's *Spinnerin am Kreuz*, Friedrich Dahm and Manfred Koller note a general resemblance between the column and the axial choir buttress of St Barbara in Kutná Hora, dating to *c.* 1390,[7] though in fact the structural and formal vocabularies deployed in both works are very different. A more promising line of inquiry was opened by Jan Sedlák, who in a footnote to an article published in 1971 proposed that the Zderad Column had been erected by a group of masons working on the choir of St James the Greater in Brno, which he believed dated to *c.* 1380–90.[8] Responding to a study published by Jaroslav Bureš the following year,[9] Sedlák subsequently revised his dating of St James's choir to 1456–73,

FIG. 2. Joris Hoefnagel, view of Brno, late 16th century, with the Zderad Column and gallows in the left foreground
Collection of the author

FIG. 3. Brno: the Zderad Column, as shown in an engraving of 1862
Achim Timmermann

furthermore suggesting Vienna's *Dombaumeister* Laurenz Spenning (d. 1478) as the likely architect.[10] In her recent monograph on Master Michael of Vienna, Elisabeth Hassmann tentatively concludes from Sedlák's observations that Spenning, while on assignment in Brno, could also have designed the Zderad Column.[11] She substantiates her argument by drawing attention to Spenning's use of tracery panels similar to those on the socle of the column, for instance in his drawing for the façade of Vienna's town hall (1455),[12] and to Spenning's previous experience with prestigious microarchitectural projects, in particular Hanns Puchsbaum's *Spinnerin am Kreuz* in Vienna (1451–52, Fig. 4), to which he had contributed as Puchsbaum's *Parlier*.[13]

Indeed, despite structural differences, both monuments tally in their deployment of a cage-like storey for the display of figural sculpture, and in their unprecedented use of microarchitectural theatrics. Hassmann's line of reasoning is commendable, even if Spenning's direct involvement in the construction of St James's choir is not unanimously accepted; Peter Kroupa, for instance, while reaffirming the architectural links between Brno's principal parish church and Viennese architecture of the third quarter of the 15th century, argues that during much of the 1450s the construction of St James's choir was overseen by one Hans Kurtz, the 'Meister zu Prunn', mentioned in third place (after Spenning and Jodokus Dotzinger) in the transactions of the Regensburg lodge conference of 1459.[14] Whether headed by Spenning or Kurtz, it seems that the workshop of St James

FIG. 4. Vienna: the *Spinnerin am Kreuz*, 1451–52
Achim Timmermann

159

was contracted for other architectural enterprises throughout Moravia, including the castle chapel at Lomnice (1460s), with its superb microarchitectural oriel, whose exterior panels of tracery lancets are identical to those on the socle of the Zderad Column.[15] In conclusion, the available evidence, though sketchy, suggests that the Zderad Column was erected during the third quarter of the 15th century (perhaps sometime between *c.* 1460 and 1470) by masons working on the choir of St James in Brno, and fully conversant with the architectural language pioneered by Puchsbaum, Spenning, and other members of the Vienna Cathedral lodge.

Like the *Spinnerin am Kreuz*, the *Bildseul beim gericht* in Niclas Meldemann's famous circular view of Vienna (1529),[16] the Zderad Column was originally located close to the civic gallows *extra muros*. This particular placement identifies both monuments as poor sinners' crosses or confessional crosses (in German *Armsünderkreuze* and *Beichtenmarter*), which were used as mental or visual rallying points during a condemned criminal's (that is a poor sinner's) last confession, or, as is shown in an illustration to the printed luxury edition of Emperor Maximilian's semi-autobiographical novel *Theuerdank* of 1517, even during the execution itself (Fig. 5 & Col. Pl. VIB in print edn).[17] First documented in the 1390s in the context of

FIG. 5. Execution of Fürwittig, with poor sinners' cross in the middle ground on the right, 1517 (*Abenteuer des Ritters Theuerdank* (as in n. 17))

the *ars moriendi* movement,[18] poor sinners' crosses became key instruments in the dispensation of late-medieval and early-modern criminal justice. This is suggested, among other things, by the frontispiece woodcut to the first edition of the *Constitutio Criminalis Carolina*, the most significant civil and criminal law code of the 16th century, ratified by the Diet of Regensburg in 1532 (Fig. 6).[19] The print shows an *arma Christi*-like line-up of a variety of torture and execution instruments, including a pillory and a blazing stake. The poor sinners' cross — here in the shape of an image-stele (or *Bildstock*) engraved with a Crucifixion scene — is visible at the back end of the so-called 'ravens' stone' or 'house of heads' (in German *Rabenstein* and *Kopfhäusel*), a circular, raised platform for beheadings and disembowelments accessible via a flight of stairs. The presence of the *Armsünderkreuz* brings to this otherwise terrifying pictogrammatic display of judicial power the possibility of mercy and redemption. In theory, at least, this particular arrangement ensured that the last thing the criminal saw in this life was the narcotic icon of Christ's ultimate act of salvation. Just which range of images the poor sinner would have beheld while kneeling in front of, or slowly trudging past, Brno's Zderad Column can only be conjectured. The narrow statue niches certainly imply a cycle of individual figures rather than narrative scenes, such as the Man of Sorrows, the Madonna of Mercy, St Leonard (the patron saint of prisoners), or the locally much-venerated St James the Greater.[20]

As demonstrated by the two artistic representations just discussed, and by extant monuments such as the gallows' cross (in German *Galgenkreuz*) at Zwettl (*c.* 1450, Fig. 7),[21] the majority of poor sinners' crosses were relatively modest structures in the form of a *Bildstock* or cross[22] that would certainly have furnished a salvific gloss on the performance of capital punishment, but whose visual appeal would otherwise have been limited. The ostentatious design of the Zderad Column, on the other hand, with its finery of delicate buttresses, baldachins and openwork tracery, suggests that in Brno the spectacle of judicial terror not only constituted a cathartic experience, but a sublime one as well; the even grander *Spinnerin am Kreuz* in Vienna must have structured a similarly uplifting viewer response. The aesthetic merits of public executions were also emphasised in contemporary legal and fictional texts. Witness for instance Heinrich Deichsler, who in his late-15th-century chronicle of the city of Nuremberg time and again speaks of the 'beauty' of repentant criminals, and praises the edifying speeches they delivered to the assembled crowds just before their violent ends.[23]

Though commissioned in considerable numbers for Europe's blood-stained execution sites, the Zderad Column and its *Bildstock*-shaped counterparts comprised but a single group among the many hundreds, if not thousands, of public monuments that were erected during the final two centuries of the Middle Ages. Providing focal points throughout the late-medieval city, or along the roads that radiated from it, such edifices, often simply called 'crosses', left a potent and characteristic signature on people's quotidien surroundings, and thus significantly contributed to shaping the very experience of everyday life.

Within town walls, microarchitectural fountains like Basel's 12-m *Fischmarkt-brunnen* of *c.* 1380 (now in the Historisches Museum, Fig. 8) identified the site where life-giving water could be drawn, and where, on market days, live fish were offered for sale (the fish were kept in custom-made baskets lowered into the fountain basin).[24] Many towns boasted not just one, but several such monuments. According to Jacques Lieur's *Livre enchaîné* of 1524–25, the city of Rouen possessed over forty fountains,

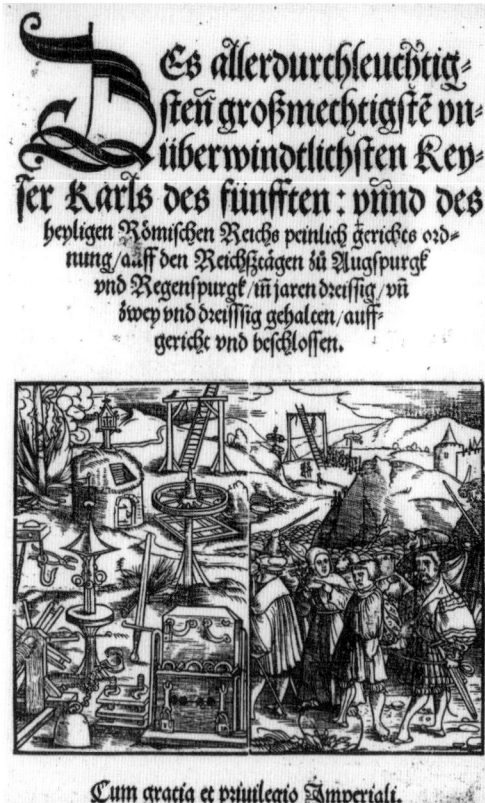

FIG. 6.   *Constitutio Criminalis Carolina*:
frontispiece, 1533

Achim Timmermann

FIG. 7.   Zwettl (Lower Austria): gallows
cross, *c.* 1450

Achim Timmermann

including the famous *Fontaine Croix-de-Pierre* in the Rue Saint-Hilaire and the *Fontaine de Sainte-Croix* in the Boucherie Saint-Ouen, both erected *c.* 1500 by the philanthropic Cardinal Georges d'Amboise.[25] In other cities, especially in the Holy Roman Empire, colossal statues of the legendary hero Roland made tangible a whole spectrum of market rights and other municipal privileges.[26] Bremen's Roland of 1404, which is crowned by a tall, polygonal baldachin, undoubtedly furnishes the most impressive example (Fig. 9).[27]

A related type of judicial monument was the pillory, which like the poor sinners' cross articulated, and perhaps also aestheticised, the discourse of corporeal punishment. Choreographic props to floggings and other forms of public humiliation, pillories were usually constructed on a city's main market square, and could assume the guise of delicate pinnacles or, as at Wrocław in 1492, of enormous tower monstrances (in German *Turmpranger*).[28] The appearance of Brno's own pillory — the *cippus* on the market square repeatedly mentioned in the *Brünner Schöffenbuch*[29] — is unknown, though it may be assumed that its elaboration matched that of the

FIG. 8. Basel: *Fischmarktbrunnen*, now in Basel, Historisches Museum, *c.* 1380

Historisches Museum, Basel

FIG. 9. Bremen: Roland, with the town hall in the background, 1404

Achim Timmermann

Zderad Column. A truly multi-purpose structure was the British market cross, which like the German Roland figures visualised a series of civic rights and liberties, but which (as Winchester's Buttercross of the early 15th century) could also double up as a pillory or preaching cross.[30] Other important urban spaces singled out by 'focal' monuments included parish cemeteries, where intricate lanterns of the dead — such as that of Maria Saal in Carinthia (1498) — illuminated ancestral burial grounds, while also marking the place where the living could seek asylum.[31] Like Nuremberg's Johannisfriedhof, some cemeteries were additionally accentuated by sequentially placed, *Bildstock*-shaped Stations of the Cross, an aid to substitute Holy Land pilgrimage introduced to Flanders and Germany during the final decades of the 15th century.[32]

Outside the protective ring of city walls, on the open roads traversing fields, forests and mountains, at crossroads, and on bridges thrown across streams and inlets, the range of public monuments was equally diverse. As seen in this essay, upon leaving Brno, Vienna and other towns with their own blood jurisdiction, a traveller would have come across the municipal *locus infamis*, the gallows with its adjacent poor sinners' cross. Further afield, he may have encountered boundary markers such as the 15th-century iron cross of Santa Maria in Lluçà (Catalonia), showing the Crucified amidst his Passion instruments,[33] as well as road shrines demarcating the routes of field- and weather-processions, as at Egglosheim in Franconia, where four processional wayside crosses (in German *Prozessionsbildstöcke*), all dating to *c.* 1500, have survived.[34] If the traveller were a pilgrim, he would look for specific shrines and crosses that served as guideposts to different monasteries, oratories and hostels, and in which he could deposit alms for the succour of those wayfarers who followed him. One such pilgrimage cross, dating to the 15th century and showing images of the Crucifixion and St James the Greater, still stands on the so-called Pont des Pèlerins at Saint-Chély-d'Aubrac (Aveyron), a station on the *Via Podiensis* to Santiago de Compostela.[35] Certainly the most common type of monument of which the traveller would have caught sight was the commemorative or memorial cross, which occasionally identified places of national historical significance, such as (in England) the famous Eleanor Crosses (*c.* 1291–94) or Nevill's Cross near Durham (after 1346),[36] but which more commonly marked the places of fatal accidents and murders. Of the few extant medieval accident crosses (in German *Unfallkreuze*) that on the Leine Bridge at Schloß Ricklingen near Hannover is particularly remarkable.[37] Designed as a disc-shaped cross, the monument pays tribute to Duke Albrecht of Saxony and Lüneburg who, while besieging the nearby castle in the spring of 1385, was hit by a catapult ball and mortally wounded. The cross not only shows the deceased amidst his heraldry, kneeling below a Crucifixion scene, but also displays the lethal projectile, which is secured to the disc with iron clamps. Of a similarly commemorative nature were so-called murder or penance crosses (in German *Mordkreuze* or *Sühnekreuze*), which convicted murderers were required to pay for in order to identify the sites of their crimes, and to atone for their sins.[38] One such cross was put up in 1436 just outside the town walls of Bremen, and marked the execution site of Johan Vasmer, a burgomaster who in 1430 had been wrongly convicted of treason and sentenced to death, but who was subsequently rehabilitated by the emperor.[39] Now on display in Bremen's Fockemuseum, the work shows the murder victim in ardent supplication below the Crucified, similar to the pictorial scheme of the Ricklingen accident cross (Fig. 10).

While erected to mark, reinforce and visualise a range of different topographies and trajectories (that is, political, legal, religious and commemorative), most medieval public monuments had one thing in common: they featured either Passion or hagiographical imagery, most commonly the Crucifixion, the Man of Sorrows, the *arma Christi*, or the agonies of a virtuous saint. In their totality, these structures projected countless images of holy torments into the quotidien environment of market squares, fields, vineyards and forests, investing these places with meanings that had little to do with their physical features. The late-medieval urban and rural environment, in other words, was suffused with the mortified bodies of Christ and

FIG. 10.   Bremen, Fockemuseum: murder
cross of Johann Vasmer, 1436
Achim Timmermann

his army of saints. They perpetually died their salvific deaths by the roadside, showing passers-by time and again their bleeding wounds, the instruments of their passion, snapshots of their last hours. As we have seen, the places that these images identified often resonated with memories — even sightings — of actual bodies, of poor sinners put to death, of knights killed in battle, and of ancestors displayed in the parish ossuary. As such, medieval public monuments transformed and transcended the mundane, furnishing an ethical gloss on the visible world, and promising ultimate delivery from the postlapsarian present. If 'landscape' is not just a given piece of geography, but, as Denis Cosgrove and others have shown, a powerful social and ideological construct,[40] then it can perhaps be argued that structures like the Zderad Column ultimately contributed to the making and shaping of moralised landscape, the *paysage moralisé*.

NOTES

1. For the legend, see J. N. Vogl, *Merkwürdigkeiten und Sagen aus der Umgegend Brünns* (Vienna 1842), 12–15. Previous discussions of the Zderad Column include J. W. Edler von Monse, *Uiber die ältesten Municipalrechte der königl. Stadt Brünn und dessen Bezirks; Nach einem Codex aus dem vierzehnten Jahrhundert* (Olomouc 1788), 110; C. D'Elvert, *Versuch einer Geschichte Brünn's* (Brno 1828), 25; E. Deutsch, *Führer durch Brünn und Umgebung: Zum Gebrauche für Finheimische und Fremde* (Brno 1865), 22; M. Trapp, *Die Zderad-Säule bei Brünn* (Brno 1862); K. Lind, 'Denksäulen', *Mitteilungen der K.K.*

Central-Commission zur Erforschung und Erhaltung der Baudenkmale, 16 (1876), liii–lviii (here lvi–lviii);
G. Trautenberger, *Die Chronik der Landeshauptstadt Brünn von der ältesten Zeit bis zum Jahre 1848*
(Brno 1897), 95–97; A. Prokop, *Die Markgrafschaft Mähren in kunstgeschichtlicher Beziehung*, 4 vols
(Vienna 1904), II, 597–98; J. Leisching, *Kunstgeschichte Mährens* (Brno 1933), 45; J. Sedlák, 'Zum Problem
der Datierung und des Stilcharakters des Presbyteriums der St. Jakob Pfarrkirche in Brünn', *Sborník prací
filozofické fakulty brnéské univerzity*, 14–15 (1971), 143–53 (here 149); F. Dahm and M. Koller, *Die Wiener
Spinnerin am Kreuz* (Vienna 1991), 68; *Umělecké památky Moravy a Sleszka*, 1 [A-I] (Prague 1994), 214;
E. Hassmann, *Meister Michael: Baumeister der Herzöge von Österreich* (Vienna/Cologne/Weimar 2002),
174–78; A. Timmermann, 'The Poor Sinners' Cross and the Pillory: late medieval microarchitecture and
liturgies of criminal punishment', *Umění*, 55 (2007), 362–73 (here 365).

2. Part I has appeared as 'Poor Sinners' Cross' (as in n. 1). Part 3 will examine the symbolic use of
punishment props — in particular pillories and mobile and stationary poor sinners' crosses — in the œuvre
of Pieter Bruegel and other 16th-century painters.

3. G. Braun and F. Hogenberg, *Civitatis orbis terrarum*, ed. R. A. Skelton, 6 vols (Cologne 1572–1617,
repr. Cleveland 1966).

4. E. F. Roesler, *Die Stadtrechte von Brünn aus dem XIII. und XIV. Jahrhundert*, Deutsche
Rechtsdenkmäler aus Böhmen und Mähren, II (Prague 1852, repr. Aalen 1963), fol. 19.

5. Trapp, *Zderad-Säule* (as in n. 1), frontispiece.

6. Prokop, *Markgrafschaft Mähren* (as in n. 1), II, 295, fig. 381.

7. Dahm and Koller, *Spinnerin am Kreuz* (as in n. 1), 68 n. 46.

8. Sedlák, 'Problem der Datierung' (as in n. 1), 149 n. 51.

9. J. Bureš, 'Der Meister des Preßburger Domes', *Acta Historiae Artium*, 18 (1972), 85–105.

10. J. Sedlák, 'Die Architektur in Mähren in der Zeit der Luxemburger', in *Die Parler und der Schöne Stil
1350–1400: Europäische Kunst unter den Luxemburgern*, ed. A. Legner, 5 vols (Cologne 1978–81), V, 123–36
(here 133, 136).

11. Hassmann, *Meister Michael* (as in n. 1), 176.

12. Vienna Academy no. 16836. See now J. J. Böker, *Architektur der Gotik: Bestandskatalog der
weltgrößten Sammlung an gotischen Baurissen (Legat Franz Jäger) im Kupferstichkabinett der Akademie der
bildenden Künste in Wien* (Vienna 2006), 305.

13. One could add Spenning's elaborate pillory for the Hoher Markt in Vienna (1455) and his likely
involvement in the furnishing of Steyr's town church (1450s) to this list. For Vienna's *Spinnerin*, see in
particular Dahm and Koller, *Spinnerin am Kreuz* (as in n. 1). See also A. Timmermann 'Altissimum ac
pretiosum: The Vienna Cathedral lodge and late medieval sacrament house design in East Central Europe',
Umění, 53 (2005), 539–50 (here 541–42); idem, 'Poor Sinners' Cross' (as in n. 1), 363–65.

14. P. Kroupa, 'Farní kostel sv. Jakuba Většího v Brně', in *Od gotiky k renesaci: Výtvarná kultura moravy
a slezska 1400–1500*, ed. K. Chamonikola, 3 vols (Brno 1999), II, 90–96 (here 94–96). See also K. Benešovská,
Architecture of the Gothic, Ten Centuries of Architecture, 2 (Prague 2001), 265. For Hans Kurtz, see also
T. Borovský, 'Kameníci, zedníci a malíři v Brně od poloviny 14. do třicátých let 16. století', in *Od gotiky k
renesaci: Výtvarná kultura moravy a slezska 1400–1500*, ed. K. Chamonikola, 3 vols (Brno 1999), II, 35–46
(here 38).

15. P. Kroupa, 'Hradní kaple v Lomnici', in Chamonikola ed., *Od gotiky k renesaci* (as in n. 14), II,
120–22. See also Benešovská, *Architecture of the Gothic* (as in n. 14), 266.

16. See Timmermann, 'Poor Sinners' Cross' (as in n. 1), fig. 5.

17. The woodcut, attributed to the Augsburg artist Leonard Beck, depicts the execution of Fürwittig, one of
the villains of the novel. See the facsimile edition *Die Abenteuer des Ritters Theuerdank* (Cologne 2003), with
an introduction by S. Füssel.

18. Timmermann, 'Poor Sinners' Cross' (as in n. 1), 362.

19. For the *Constitutio*, see for example the essays in *Strafrecht, Strafprozeß und Rezeption: Grundlagen,
Entwicklung und Wirkung der Constitutio Criminalis Carolina*, ed. P. Landau and F. C. Schroeder,
Juristische Abhandlungen, 19 (Frankfurt 1984).

20. Wratislaw Baron von Monse, writing in 1788, and the first to detect a possible symbiotic link
between the column and the adjacent gallows, hints at the former presence of 'representations of saints or the
suffering Saviour' ('Abbildungen der Heiligen oder des leidenden Heilands'); see Monse, *Municipalrechte* (as
in n. 1), 110.

21. *Dehio-Handbuch Niederösterreich nördlich der Donau*, ed. E. Benesch et al., Die Kunstdenkmäler
Österreichs (Vienna 1990), 1346.

22. See also the poor sinners' crosses at Murau (*c*. 1425–50) and Unterzeiring near Judenburg (16th century)
in Styria; at St. Stefan im Gailtal (1499), Millstadt (1520), and St. Veit an der Glan (early 16th century) in
Carinthia; at Oberweis (1499) in the Eiffel Mountains; and at Volkach (*c*. 1470) in Franconia.

23. See Timmermann, 'Poor Sinners' Cross' (as in n. 1), 364, with further references. See also Fürwittig's speech before the poor sinners' cross in Emperor Maximilian's *Theuerdank* (as in n. 17, and Fig. 5): 'Mir geschicht nach der gerechtigkeit/Danck got das mir der todt ist bereit/Dann ich hof dardurch die sünd mein/Zu püessen unnd im himel zu sein.' ('I am treated according to Justice, thank God that through my death I can atone for my sins and be in Heaven.').

24. See *The Historical Museum Basle: Guide to the Collections* (Basel 1994), 100 no. 142. For medieval fountains in the German-speaking world in general, see esp. A. Rautenberg, *Mittelalterliche Brunnen in Deutschland* (Freiburg im Breisgau 1965), 97–101, with a discussion of Basel's *Fischmarktbrunnen*.

25. See the fascimile edition *Le Livre Enchainé ou Livre des Fontaines de Rouen*, ed. V. Sanson, 2 vols (Rouen 1911), I, 36, with fig. 41, and II, 36–37, with fig. 45.

26. For an account of the development of these statues, see H. Rempel, *Die Rolandsstatuen: Herkunft und geschichtliche Wandlung* (Darmstadt 1989).

27. See K. Domanski and D. Friese, 'Roland und Karl der Große am Rathaus in Bremen: Legitimation einer städtischen Obersicht', in *Karl der Große als vielberufener Vorfahr: Sein Bild in der Kunst der Fürsten, Kirchen und Städte*, ed. L. E. Saurma-Jeltsch, Schriften des Historischen Museums Frankfurt am Main, 19.1994 (Sigmaringen 1994), 19–37.

28. For an extended discussion of microarchitectural pillories, including the work at Wrocław, see Timmermann, 'Poor Sinners' Cross' (as in n. 1), 365–69, with figs 8–10 and further literature.

29. Roesler, *Stadtrechte von Brünn* (as in n. 4), 189.

30. See A. Vallance, *Old Crosses and Lychgates* (London 1920).

31. See esp. F. Hula, *Die Totenleuchten und Bildstöcke Österreichs: Ein Einblick in ihren Ursprung, ihr Wesen und ihre stilistsche Entwicklung* (Vienna 1948), and M. Plault, *Les lanternes des morts: Inventaire, histoire et liturgie* (Poitiers 1988). For the 25-ft lantern at Maria Saal, see E. Skudnigg, *Bildstöcke und Totenleuchten in Kärnten*, Kärntner Heimatleben, 15 (Klagenfurt 1972), 275–78, with fig. 98.

32. See R. Zittlau, *Heiliggrabkapelle und Kreuzweg: Eine Bauaufgabe in Nürnberg um 1500* (Nuremberg 1992), with a discussion of Nuremberg's Stations, and further literature.

33. Now preserved in the Museu Episcopal in Vic. See *Museu Episcopal de Vic: Guide to the Collections*, ed. J. M. Trullén (Vic 2007), 313.

34. See J. Dünninger and B. Schemmel, *Bildstöcke und Martern in Franken* (Würzburg 1970), 168, with fig. 15.

35. See A. Timmermann, 'Wayside Shrines', in *Encyclopedia of Medieval Pilgrimage*, ed. R. Tekippe and K. Gower (Leiden forthcoming), with further literature. A separate study on the allegorical significance of pilgrimage crosses, based on a paper delivered at the 36th International Congress of Medieval Studies in Kalamazoo (2001), is in preparation.

36. For the Eleanor Crosses, which marked the route of Queen Eleanor of Castile's funeral cortège from Lincoln to London in 1290, see the essays in *Eleanor of Castile, 1290–1990: Essays to Commemorate the 700th Anniversary of Her Death*, ed. D. Parsons (Stamford 1991). For Nevill's Cross (destroyed), which glorified the Scottish defeat at the hands of an English army commanded by the Archbishop of York on 17 October 1346, see Vallance, *Old Crosses* (as in n. 30), 24–25.

37. See W. Müller and G. E. H. Baumann, *Kreuzsteine und Steinkreuze in Niedersachsen, Bremen und Hamburg*, Forschungen der Denkmalpflege in Niedersachsen, 5 (Hamburg 1988), 58–59, with further literature.

38. The post-medieval legend outlined at the beginning of this essay suggests that the Zderad Column was itself a murder cross.

39. See Müller and Baumann, *Kreuzsteine und Steinkreuze* (as in n. 37), 26, with further literature.

40. See D. Cosgrove, *Social Formation and Symbolic Landscape* (London 1984).

Karlstein Castle as a Theological Metaphor

MILADA STUDNIČKOVÁ

Karlstein, one of the most important foundations of Charles IV, is known as the depository of the imperial crown jewels and relics of Christ's Passion. The unique arrangement and decoration of the castle suggests that some of the architectural and artistic solutions employed may have been influenced by theological metaphors, a common feature of Charles's court culture. This paper aims to show that this is not only the case with the Holy Cross Chapel, which (it has been argued) embodies the concept of Heavenly Jerusalem, but also that there is an affinity between the staircase leading to the Holy Cross Chapel and the scala coeli *or Heavenly Ladder metaphor derived from the Book of Genesis. Like the Heavenly Ladder that appeared in Jacob's dream, St Wenceslas himself provided a spiritual path that Charles IV, his family, and his subjects could ascend, thereby attaining salvation. This study also offers a reinterpretation of the so-called relic scenes in the castle's chapel of Our Lady. It is argued that these are not depictions of specific historic events, but rather an* authentica *in pictorial form revealing the origin and authenticity of the relics. At the same time, the scenes are commemorative in nature, constituting a* memoria *of those depicted. In this context the portrait features of those depicted have an identificatory function.*

KARLSTEIN ranks among those foundations of Charles IV of Luxembourg, emperor of the Holy Roman Empire and the king of Bohemia, on the appearance and decoration of which the founder may be assumed to have had a great influence.[1] While considering the ideological concept of the castle, scholars have hitherto made little of the texts written by the sovereign himself or by those from his circle.

In his youth, Charles received a good education at the French royal court[2] and was introduced to the fundamental principles of scholastic theology. Pierre de Rosière, later Pope Clement VI (1342–52), an educated and exceptionally eloquent man, taught Charles the scriptures and played the intellectually most influential role in his early life. In his autobiography Charles described how, when listening to his mentor's preaching, he experienced such religious rapture that he asked himself: 'What is it about this man that causes so much grace to flow over me?'[3] Indeed, sources confirm that Charles IV strove to be regarded as a theologically educated man.[4] In his later writings, Charles employed biblical exegesis derived primarily from the writings of Augustine, Anselm of Canterbury, and Bernard of Clairvaux. He and his chancellery also drew on theological similes to illustrate contemporary phenomena; for instance, the text of the Golden Bull (the legal decree for the Holy Roman Empire issued in 1356) defines the role of the ruler and of the seven electors by means of such similes. The empire is, for example, compared with a building or a church; the electors illuminate the sacred empire as seven candelabrums 'in unitate spiritus septiformis'.[5] Expressing oneself by means of theological metaphors was a relatively common aspect of Charles IV's courtly culture. Furthermore, I believe that in many cases theological metaphors may have affected the actual appearance of individual works of art and architecture commissioned by the emperor.

Seen from the outside, Karlstein Castle, with the massive rising outlines of its three main structures (the palace and two rectangular towers), looks rather austere (Fig. 1), in complete contrast to its internal decoration.[6] Since we do not have the castle's foundation charter, it is impossible to establish beyond doubt whether this particular arrangement was associated with the documented function of Karlstein as a 'relic castle'.[7] Although it is not certain whether Karlstein had been intended as a storing place for the imperial insignia from the outset, from 1365 the castle provided a safekeep for the imperial crown jewels as well the extremely valuable relics of Christ's Passion, some of which were set directly into the sovereign's insignia.[8] Some sources and finds made during a survey of the castle indicate that prior to 1348 Karlstein was probably founded as a private residence of the sovereign, and only later adopted the function of a relic treasury.[9] Several elements, however, are neither very typical of nor functionally suitable for a purely residential castle.[10] Charles had been elected king of the Romans in 1346, but the imperial crown jewels were released to

FIG. 1.   Model of Karlstein Castle from the south-west according to D. Menclová
Klára Benešovská

him only in 1350 after protracted negotiations. For Charles IV, the acquisition, possession and public presentation of the imperial insignia were of exceptional importance, since they were perceived as the confirmation of his legitimacy as king of the Romans and were used to reinforce his power.[11]

In 1357, Charles, already Holy Roman Emperor, founded Karlstein's collegiate chapter, entrusting their members with the task of officiating at divine services in the two newly built chapels of the castle's Lesser Tower, one of which was consecrated to the Passion of Christ, the other, directly connected with the first, to the Virgin. The Karlstein chapter was commissioned to act as custodians of the relics of Christ's Passion, although the list of these mentioned in documents does not include those belonging to the imperial treasure, but a fragment of the True Cross, a nail, two thorns from the Crown of Thorns, and part of the sponge from which the crucified Christ drank vinegar; Charles had acquired these gradually and then deposited them in a newly made reliquary cross of the kingdom of Bohemia, which he had commissioned for this purpose.[12] It is believed that Charles's reliquary cross was provisionally stored in the Lesser Tower, in the small oratory adjacent to the chapel of Our Lady dedicated originally to the Passion of Christ but known since the 16th century as chapel of St Catherine. This arrangement lasted until the completion in 1365 of the larger chapel of the Passion of Christ and its Instruments in the Great Tower, now commonly known as the Holy Cross Chapel.[13]

The oldest and lowest section of the castle was the residential palace. Its second floor housed a large hall decorated with the now-lost mural of the genealogy of the Luxembourg dynasty in which — in keeping with biblical genealogy — Emperor Charles's origins were traced back to Noah.[14] According to an early-medieval legend, Noah — the only righteous man — had been the first inhabitant of a territory where Rome was later built.[15] According to the fifth homily from the text known as the *Moralitates*, largely attributed to Charles, 'Noah stands for Christ. For just as Noah planted out a vineyard after the deluge during the restoration of the world, thus Christ built the Church after the deluge of transgressions against the Old Testament. The vineyard is therefore the Church, which has yielded as many offshoots as there are chosen ones, from the righteous Abel to the last chosen one.'[16] Without any doubt, Charles felt himself to be chosen, since the genealogy substantiated his right to rule and constituted an expression of one of the graces divinely bestowed on him, that he should be heir to famous and God-fearing ancestors. Another event illustrating that Charles had indeed been chosen by God — the miracle of St Nicholas's finger, in which the sovereign was a direct participant — was depicted on the walls of the chapel of St Nicholas on the first floor of the palace.[17]

The second-floor hall of the palace used to lead to the Lesser Tower, the second floor of which housed the chapel of Our Lady. Fišer's assumption that this flat-ceilinged room, which originally took up the entire floor, was formerly a residential space,[18] runs somewhat contrary to the evidence of the original decoration of its window splays with their polished semiprecious stones; in other cases such decoration is reserved exclusively for sacral spaces. As has been noted, this chapel was consecrated to the Virgin, who was compared to a 'chamber of the word incarnate'; one of Charles's homilies, addressed to 'Our Mother of God', begins with the words: 'O Maria, cella verbi' ('O Mary, chamber of the word').[19] Comparisons of Mary's virginal body to a chamber, or to a royal hall receiving the Saviour, appear frequently in exegetic literature, with the Mother of God being also called *thalamus, aula Dei* or *aula regia*, *habitaculum*, and *verbi palatium*.[20] This Marian simile is evidently associated with some types of architecture used as the background to depictions of the Annunciation. At the same time, such renderings play on the dual meaning of the term *thalamus* as both a 'room' and a 'bedroom'. The question arises as to whether the seemingly unusual architectural solution (such as the rectangular windows with seats and the flat ceiling) of Karlstein's chapel of Our Lady might not be associated with the aforementioned Marian similes.

In fact, the theme of the Virgin as the main helper of mankind, who fights sin and vanquishes the devil, features in the painted decoration of the chapel of Our Lady, in the scenes from the Apocalypse, which represent the struggle waged by the earthly Church against the temptations of this world. The apocalyptic cycle ends with the image of the Women Clothed in the Sun, who is identified with Ecclesia and likened to the Virgin, and this motif is also emphasised in the eighth homily of Charles's *Moralitates*.[21] As we have seen, the chapel of Our Lady is connected with the oratory where the Bohemian reliquary cross was kept until 1365, and where the imperial treasure was probably also kept.[22]

The monumental painting on the south wall of the chapel of our Lady, which leads to the entrance into the oratory, may be associated directly with Charles's acquisition of the Passion relics (Fig. 2).[23] In my view, this representation cannot be regarded as depicting a historical event, that is the act of presenting the relics; it is rather a kind of pictorial *authentica*. Just as the text on a strip of parchment accompanying a relic specifies that relic's origin, thus confirming its authenticity, the Karlstein painting depicts those who had originally donated the relics to the emperor, subsequently set by him into the reliquary cross kept in the oratory, not those who had actually presented them to him. Seen in this light, we can say that the first scene depicts the French king, Jean le Bon (1350–64), the donor of the fragment of the True Cross and the two thorns from the Crown of Thorns, who issued the donation charter in May 1356,[24] and not the French dauphin Charles, who presented those relics to Charles IV at the imperial diet in Metz in 1356.[25] The portrait characteristics of the rulers

FIG. 2. Karlstein Castle: chapel of Our Lady, relic scenes

Alexander Paul

depicted in the relic scenes, widely discussed elsewhere, can therefore be justified from a functional standpoint, performing the role of heraldry as a form of identification.[26] The second scene probably shows the Byzantine emperor, John V Palaeologos (1341–76), who sent to Charles by a messenger, among other relics, part of Christ's sponge in 1359.[27] In both cases, these relics of the Passion had not previously been part of the imperial treasure. Charles IV's merits in acquiring them were thus perpetuated in a painting that, *inter alia*, urged the select number of pilgrims who came to worship the relics to pray for the salvation of the emperor's soul as well. The relic scenes have the character of *memoriae*, and, indeed, the beginnings of portraiture in the Middle Ages may be connected primarily with commemoration.[28]

The only way to Karlstein's principal shrine, the Holy Cross Chapel (Fig. 3), conceived as a vision of the Heavenly Jerusalem,[29] led through the chapel of Our

FIG. 3.   Karlstein Castle: the Holy Cross Chapel
Alexander Paul

Lady. The Virgin Mary was described as an intercessor for our salvation, and only though her was it possible to reach the Heavenly Kingdom.[30] The Holy Cross Chapel is on the second floor of the Great Tower, separated from the rest of the castle by a massive wall. The relics of Christ kept there — the 'material traces of the incarnation of the Divine Word'[31] — and the multitude of relics of patron saints set into the frames of the panel paintings that adorn the walls together represent an incursion of transcendence into the contemporary world, and offer some kind of possibility of experiencing the divine presence on earth. Ascending to the chapel, one had to go up a newel staircase, the walls of which were painted with scenes from the lives of St Wenceslas and St Ludmila, Charles's predecessors on the Bohemian throne, who played an important role in introducing Christianity into Bohemia. The narrative of the St Wenceslas cycle runs upwards on the outer wall of the staircase, while St Ludmila's runs in the opposite direction — downwards — on the awkwardly narrow surface of the twisting inner side of the staircase.

In many cultures the staircase has symbolised ascent to a higher level of being. In medieval theology the concept of a Heavenly Ladder was based on the metaphor of Jacob's dream from the Book of Genesis (XXVIII, 11–19).[32] According to the verse 17 — 'Quam terribilis est, inquit, locus iste! Non est hic aliud nisi domus Dei et porta caeli' ('"How terrible this place is!" he said. "This is none other than the house of God and the gateway to heaven"') — the point of contact of the Jacob's ladder with the earth designates a place of sanctity, and a church built on the site becomes a symbolic gateway to heaven. This idea is illustrated in a non-traditional way by the sculptural

FIG. 4.   The Ladder from St Benedict's *Regula* (Stuttgart, Landesbibliothek, Cod. hist. 2°415, fol. 87r, Zwiefalten, *c.* 1162)

Ústav dějin umění, Akademie věd České republiky, Prague

decoration of Bath Abbey, where ladders with the figures of angels are situated directly on the church towers of the west façade.[33] Exegetes saw in images of the ladder primarily an allegory of the ascent of the human soul towards God.[34] Jacob's ladder was interpreted as Christ's cross or a symbol of the universal Church, 'que ex parte militat in terris ex parte triumphat in coelis' ('which consists in part of the Church Militant on earth and in part of the Church Triumphant in heaven').[35] Moralising interpretation prevailed in monastic communities; the Ladder in St Benedict's *Regula*[36] (Fig. 4) and numerous commentaries on that work, according to which one ascended towards God on the steps of humility, good deeds and chastity, proved to be of particular importance for Western Christianity.[37] Acting in a spirit of Franciscan devotion, St Bonaventure, whose writings were disseminated at the royal court in Paris, developed an allegorical image featuring six steps of divine love, found, for instance, in the Psalter of Bonne of Luxembourg, sister of Emperor Charles IV (New York, The Metropolitan Museum of Art, inv. no. 1969, 69.86, fol. 315r).[38]

Seen in this light, the Karlstein staircase may be interpreted as a Heavenly Ladder or *scala coeli*.[39] St Wenceslas and St Ludmila rise towards the heavenly community thanks to their deeds: by likening themselves to Christ;[40] by obeying the ruling authority on earth, because 'regnare est servire Deo' ('to rule is to serve God')[41] (Fig.

FIG. 5. Karlstein Castle: Great Tower staircase, promotion of St Wenceslas to the dukedom of Bohemia

Vlado Bohdan

Fig. 6. Karlstein Castle: Great
Tower staircase, St Wenceslas
bakes hosts and takes them
to the church

Vlado Bohdan

5); and by dying martyrs' deaths. Moreover, the narrative of St Wenceslas's life
focuses in particular on acts of grace: giving alms, visiting prisoners, burying the
dead, praying for their souls, carrying timber from the forest to a poor widow, and
preparing Eucharistic gifts (with Wenceslas personally producing bread (Fig. 6) and
wine (Fig. 7) for the sacrament of the mass). The final scenes from the life of St
Wenceslas call to mind the Last Supper[42] and the conscious act of self-sacrifice
(Fig. 8).

Angels carrying scrolls with the text of the Marian antiphon 'Regina celi letare'
('Queen of heaven, rejoice!') appear in the highest zone, the vault of the staircase (Fig.
9), turning towards the face of God, which is painted on the vault above the landing,
immediately in front of the entrance to the chapel (Fig. 11); the face of God is usually
depicted at the end of the Heavenly Ladder. This antiphon seems to have had a similar
impact as the Marian prayer 'Vergine Madre, figlia del tuo figlio' ('Virgin mother,
daughter of your son') of St Bernard, which enables Dante to behold the face of God
at the very end of the *Divine Comedy* (Paradiso, XXXIII).[43] The end of the antiphon
'Regina celi', recited at the close of compline during the Easter period, could be
construed in similar vein: 'Rejoice, Queen of Heaven, because He whom you
merited to bear has risen from the dead, as He said. Intercede for us with God.' The
Assumption of the Virgin Mary into heaven (conveyed in her title *Regina celi*, 'Queen
of Heaven'), brought mortal Christians hope that they too would behold God and
eventually enter the Heavenly Kingdom. It also constituted a promise to Charles IV
and members of his wider family, who, engrossed in eternal prayer, are seen kneeling

FIG. 7. Karlstein Castle: Great
Tower staircase, St Wenceslas hoes
a vineyard and gathers grapes
Vlado Bohdan

at prie-dieus with books in their hands at the very top of the staircase, that they would behold the face of God. The family forms part of the scene depicted on the wall of the landing that faces the visitor at the top of the stairs, next to the entrance into the chapel (Fig. 10). The painting probably represents the translation of the Bohemian reliquary cross and the placing of a new relic into the cross on the day of the consecration of the chapel, in 1365. The relic held by Emperor Charles IV is probably an ampoule containing blood of St Wenceslas, subsequently set in the foot of the cross, to which the scene of the Wiping of St Wenceslas's Blood depicted on the wall of the staircase is related (Fig. 12 & Col. Pl. VIA in print edn).[44] As a result, this scene marks the culmination of the legend of St Wenceslas — with his blood becoming the key to Paradise[45] — as well as referring to the relics kept in the Holy Cross Chapel. Wenceslas thus becomes, metaphorically speaking, the Heavenly Staircase. In a similar vein, St Ladislas, the patron saint of Hungary, is called the *scala gentis Ungarorum* ('ladder of the Hungarian people') in the 14th century.[46] The text 'Sequentia de sancto Ladislao rege' ('Sequence of St Ladislas, King') is a variation on the sequence (sung or recited during mass, before the proclamation of the Gospel) relating to the Holy Cross. This particular theological metaphor finds its physical embodiment at Karlstein. At the same time, the patron saint of Bohemia has become the guardian of the relics of Christ, just as at the Sainte-Chapelle the relic of St Louis' head symbolically guarded the relics of the Passion kept in the *grande chasse*.[47]

The imperial relics were stored together with the relics of the kingdom of Bohemia in the Holy Cross Chapel. The idea of linking the Holy Roman Empire with the kingdom of Bohemia is emphasised visually by the imperial and Bohemian crowns offered by angels as sacrifice on the panels flanking that of the Crucifixion, placed

176

FIG. 8. Karlstein Castle: Great Tower staircase, St Wenceslas at a banquet on the eve of his murder

Vlado Bohdan

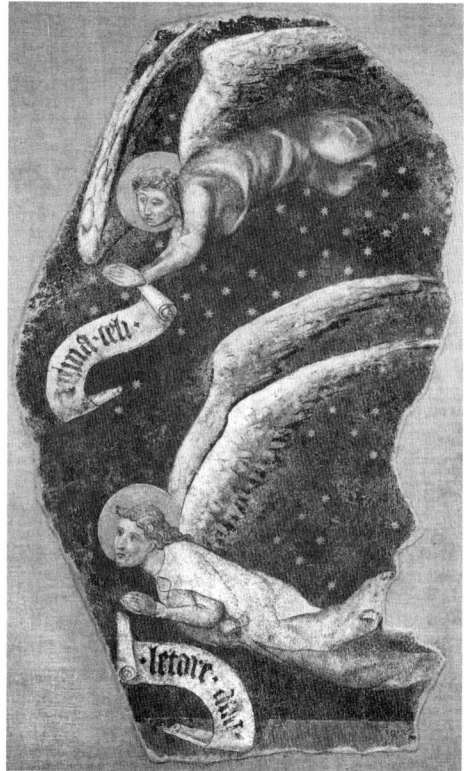

FIG. 9. Karlstein Castle: pair of angels holding scrolls with the text of 'Regina celi letare'. Mural transferred from the vault of the staircase in the Great Tower

Petr Zinke

high on the altar wall.[48] The iconography may be connected with the old imperial legend that goes back to the 10th century about the last peaceful emperor, who will deposit his insignia in Jerusalem at the end of time.[49]

The Holy Cross Chapel is also connected with the notion of *parousia*, or Second Coming. According to the *Libri Carolini* (a theological treatise in four books commissioned by Charlemagne that discusses the role of sacred images), paintings shall be consumed on the Day of Judgement, and saints shall rise from the dead, emerging from their relics (which, as mentioned above, were placed in the frames of the painted panels in the Holy Cross Chapel). During the Second Coming, Christ shall descend to the place where the *arma Christi* are deposited.[50] The Holy Cross Chapel in Karlstein's Great Tower was regarded as just such a place, and its staircase may therefore also be interpreted as a stairway along which Christ shall descend to earth at the end of time.[51]

Writing about Karlstein, Karl Möseneder discussed what he called the 'materialisation' of a theological concept.[52] I believe that this does not apply solely to

FIG. 10.   Karlstein Castle: Emperor Charles IV places the ampoule with the blood of St Wenceslas into the reliquary cross. Mural transferred from the facing wall of the landing before the Holy Cross Chapel in the Great Tower

Petr Zinke

FIG. 11.   Karlstein Castle: the face of God. Mural transferred from the vault above the landing before the Holy Cross Chapel in the Great Tower

Petr Zinke

FIG. 12. Karlstein Castle, Great Tower staircase: burying the body of St Wenceslas in a grave; wiping of the martyr's blood from the door of the church in Stará Boleslav
Vlado Bohdan

the Holy Cross Chapel, but also to other parts of the castle; the *scala coeli*, the staircase with scenes from the lives of Sts Wenceslas and Ludmila leading up to Karlstein's main shrine, is evidence of that. There are indications therefore that in interpreting monuments from the late Middle Ages, greater heed should be paid to contemporary theological thinking and the widespread incidence of scholastic exegesis.

NOTES

1. For Karlstein, see T. Durdík, I. Gottfried, M. Horynová and J. Úlovec, 'Výběrová bibliografie hradu Karlštejna', *Castellologica Bohemica*, 5 (1996), 363–70; J. Neuwirth, *Mittelalterliche Wandgemälde und Tafelbilder der Burg Karlstein* (Prague 1896); D. Menclová, 'Karlštejn a jeho ideový obsah', *Umění*, 5 (1957), 277–301; V. Dvořáková and D. Menclová, *Karlštejn* (Prague 1965); Z. Bouše and J. Myslivec, 'Sakrální prostory na Karlštejně', *Umění*, 19 (1971) 280–95; K. Möseneder, 'Lapides vivi. Über die Kreuzkapelle der Burg Karlstein', *Wiener Jahrbuch für Kunstgeschichte*, 34 (1981), 39–69; Z. Chudárek, 'Velká věž hradu Karlštejna', *Zprávy památkové péče*, 54 (1994), 67–72; F. Fišer, *Karlštejn* (Kostelní Vydří 1996); K. Stejskal, 'Die Wandzyklen des Kaisers Karls IV.', *Umění*, 46 (1998), 19–41; J. Fajt ed., *Magister Theodoricus, Court Painter to Emperor Charles IV: The Pictorial Decoration of the Shrines at Karlštejn Castle* (Prague 1998); H. Hlaváčková, 'Karlštejn', in *Středověká nástěnná malba ve středních Čechách*, ed. Z. Všetečková Průzkumy památek, 6 (1999), 39–63; J. Fajt ed., *Court Chapels of the High and Late Middle Ages and their Artistic Decoration* (Prague 2003).

2. J. Mezník, 'Berichte der französischen königlichen Rechnungen über den Aufenthalt des jungen Karl IV. in Frankreich', *Mediaevalia Bohemica*, 1 (1969), 291–95; K. Otavský, *Die Sankt Wenzelskrone im Prager Domschatz und die Frage der Kunstfassung am Hofe Kaiser Karls IV.* (Bern/Frankfurt/New York/Paris/

Vienna 1992); F. Šmahel, 'Monseigneur Charles de Bohême: Dětství a dospívání Karla IV. ve Francii', *Dějiny a současnost*, 27 (2005), 34–37; F. Šmahel, *Cesta Karla IV. do Francie 1377–1378* (Prague 2006), 27–28.

3. 'Quid est, quod tanta gracia michi infunditur ex homine isto?'. See *Karoli IV Imperatoris Romanorum Vita ab Eo Ipso Conscripta et Hystoria Nova de Sancto Wenceslao Martyre. Autobiography of Emperor Charles IV and his Legend of St. Wenceslas*, B. Nagy and F. Schaer ed. and trans. (Budapest/New York 2001), ch. III, 28–29.

4. 'Chronicon Benessi de Weitmil', in *Fontes rerum Bohemicarum* (as in n. 3), IV (1884), 459–548; U. Hergemöller, *Cogor adversum te: Drei Studien zum literarisch-theologischen Profil Karls IV. und seiner Kanzlei* (Warrendorf 1999), 254–55.

5. 'Tu quidem, Invidia, christianum imperium, a Deo ad instar sancte et individue Trinitatis fide, spe et caritate, virtutibus theologicis, roboratum, cuius fundamentum super christianissimo regno feliciter stabilitur, antiquo veneno, quod velut serpens in palmites imperiales et membra eius propinquiora impio scelere vomuisti, ut concussis columpnis totum edificium ruine subiceres, divisionem inter septem electores sacri imperii, per quos velut septem candelabra lucencia in unitate Spiritus septiformis sacrum illuminari debet imperium, multociens posuisti.' (http://www.koeblergerhard.de/Fontes/GoldeneBulleKarlsIV1356. htm, accessed February 2009). 'Thou, indeed, oh envy, hast, with impious wickedness, spued with the ancient poison against the Christian empire which is fortified by God, like to the holy and indivisible Trinity, with the theological virtues of faith, hope and charity; whose foundation is happily established above in the very kingdom of Christ. Thou hast done this like a serpent, against the branches of the empire and its nearer members; so that, the columns being shaken, thou mightest subject the whole edifice to ruin. Thou hast often spread discord among the seven electors of the holy empire, through whom, as through seven candlesticks throwing light in the unity of a septiform spirit, the holy empire ought to be illuminated.'; E. F. Henderson, *The Golden Bull of the Emperor Charles IV, 1356 AD*, Select Historical Documents of the Middle Ages (London/New York 1896, repr. New York 1965), pp. 220–261, here 221.

6. K. Benešovská, 'Architektura ve službách panovníka - základní architektonická koncepce Karlštejna a její inspirační zdroje', in *Schodištní cykly Velké věže hradu Karlštejna*, ed. Z. Všetečková, Průzkumy památek, 13 (2006), 96–105.

7. F. Kavka, 'The role and function of Karlštejn Castle as documented in records from the reign of Charles IV', in Fajt ed., *Magister Theodoricus* (as in n. 1), 16–28.

8. Koss introduced the idea of Karlstein as a castle built as an imperial treasury; R. Koss, *Archiv Koruny české, I: Dějiny* (Prague 1939), 61, 377.

9. See Kavka, 'Karlštejn Castle' (as in n. 7); and Z. Chudárek, 'Příspěvek k poznání stavebních dějin věží na hradě Karlštejně v době Karla IV.', in Všetečková ed., *Schodištní cykly* (as in n. 6), 106–38.

10. Benešovská, 'Architektura ve službách panovníka' (as in n. 6), 97.

11. For public display of the relics, see H. Kühne, *Ostensio reliquiarum: Untersuchungen über Entstehung, Ausbreitung, Gestalt und Funktion der Heiltumsweisungen im römisch-deutschen Regnum* (Berlin/New York 2000), 106–32.

12. J. F. Novák ed., *Acta Innocentis VI*, Monumenta Vaticana res gestas Bohemicas illustrantia, II (Prague 1907), 245, nos. 703 and 904. The cross, which was created in 1357 and depicted on the murals in Karlstein, is not preserved. In the 1370s, it was replaced by a new cross now in the tresury of St Vitus's Cathedral in Prague, inv. no. 25 (97); see K. Otavský, 'Goldenes Reliquienkreuz', in *Karl IV. Kaiser von Gottes Gnaden: Kunst und Represäntation des Hauses Luxemburg 1310–1437*, ed. J. Fajt (Munich/Berlin 2006), no. 24, 111–14.

13. Fišer, *Karlštejn* (as in n. 1), 15–17.

14. Copies of the Luxembourg genealogy are to be found in Cod. 8330 in the Österreichische Nationalbibliothek, Vienna (MS no. 8330), and in the Národní galerie, Prague (the Codex Heidelbergensis, Archiv, AA 2015). For the Vienna manuscript, see J. Neuwirth, *Der Bilderzyklus der Luxemburger Stammbaumes aus Karlstein* (Prague 1897); and P. R. Pokorný, 'Cod. 8330 Manuscript from Vienna', in *Court Chapels* (as in n. 1), 59–63. M. Bláhová locates the source of the concept in an unpublished Luxembourg genealogy of Jan de Klerk; M. Bláhová, 'Panovnické genealogie a jejich politická funkce ve středověku', *Sborník archivních prací*, 48 (1998), 11–47. See also J. Homolka, 'The pictorial decoration of the Lesser Tower of Karlštejn Castle', in Fajt ed., *Magister Theodoricus* (as in n. 1), 46–93; and H. Hlaváčková, 'Idea dobrého panovníka ve výzdobě Karlštejna', in Všetečková ed., *Schodištní cykly* (as in n. 6), 9–18, here 12.

15. A. Graf, *Roma nella memoria e nelle immaginazioni del medio evo* (Turin 1882), 72–108; K. Kubínová, *Imitatio Romae: Karel IV. a Řím* (Prague 2006), 85–87.

16. 'Noe designat Christum; nam sicut Noe in mundi reformatione plantavit vineam post diluvium, sic Christus plantavit ecclesiam post diluvium veteris legis transgressorum. Vinea igitur est ecclesia, quae tot palmites quot electos ab Abel iusto usque ad ultimum electum produxit'; K. Wotke' ed., 'Moralitates Caroli quarti imperatoris', *Zeitschrift des Vereines für die Geschichte Mährens und Schlesiens*, 1 (1897), 41–76 (here

65); Hergemöller, *Cogor adversum te* (as in n. 4), 293–312. The first to draw attention to this text was K. Stejskal; 'Die Rekonstruktion des Luxemburger Stammbaums auf Karlstein', *Umění*, 26 (1978), 535–62.

17. 'Johannis de Marignola Chronicon', in *Fontes rerum Bohemicarum* (as in n. 3), III (1882), 485–604. The event of the year 1354 is also described by Beneš Krabice of Weitmile; 'Chronicon Benessii de Weitmil', ibid., IV (1884), 459–548.

18. Fišer (*Karlštejn* (as in n. 1), 37) presumed that the rooms in the Lesser Tower were originally intended for the empress.

19. 'Moralitates Caroli' (as in n. 16), homily VIII.

20. For Maria as *thalamus*, see Augustinus Hipponensis, *Sermones* (sermo CCXCI), Patrologia Latina (PL), XXXVIII, col. 1319; Beda Venerabilis, *Homiliae* (XIII), PL, XCIV, col. 68; Rabanus Maurus, *Allegoriae*, PL, CXII, col. 1063; Anselmus Cantuarensis, *Hymni et psalterium de S. Maria*, PL, CLVIII, col. 1035; Bernardus Claraevallensis, *Tractatus ad laudem gloriosae V. matris*, PL, CLXXXII, col. 1143. For Maria as *aula Dei* or *aula regia*, see Ambrosius Mediolanensis, *Hymni*, PL, XVI, col. 1409; Bernardus Claraevallensis, *Sermones in Cantica*, PL, CLXXXIII, col. 920; and Adamus S. Victoris, *Sequentiae* (XIX), PL, CXCVI, col. 1483. For Maria as *habitaculum*, see *De corona virginis*, PL, XCVI, col. 293; Hugo de S. Victore, *Explanatio*, PL, CLXXV, col. 413; Bernardus Claraevallensis, *In assumptione*, PL, CLXXXIII, col. 428; and Amedens Lausannensis, *Homilia*, PL, CLXXXVIII, col. 1316. For Maria as *verbi palatium*, see *De corona virginis*, PL, XCVI, col. 1.

21. 'Moralitates Caroli' (as in n. 16), homily VIII.

22. Hypothesis proposed by Fišer, *Karlštejn* (as in n. 1), 60.

23. Möseneder ('Lapides vivi' (as in n. 1), 64) emphasised the similarities in the way in which relics were placed into reliquaries and presented at Karlstein, the Sainte-Chapelle, and the Sancta Sanctorum.

24. B. Mendl ed., *Regesta diplomatica nec non epistolaria Bohemiae et Moraviae*, VI/2 (Prague 1929), 194–95, no. 362.

25. J. Royt and H. Hlaváčková identified the first donor of the relics as Jean le Bon. See J. Royt, 'The dating and iconography of the so-called relic scenes in the Chapel of Our Lady at Karlštejn Castle', in *Court Chapels* (as in n. 1), 64–67; and Hlaváčková, 'Karlštejn' (as in n. 1), 48.

26. For the portraits of Charles IV, see H. Wammetsberger, 'Individuum und Typ in den Porträts Kaiser Karls IV.', *Wissenschaftliche Zeitschrift der Friedrich-Schiller-Universität Jena, Gesellschafts- und sprachwissenschaftliche Reihe*, 16 (1967), 79–93; R. Suckale, 'Die Porträts Kaiser Karls IV. als Bedeutungsträger', in *Das Porträt vor der Erfindung des Porträts*, ed. M. Büchsel and P. Schmidt (Mainz 2003), 191–203; and M. Bogade, *Kaiser Karl IV.: Ikonographie und Ikonologie* (Stuttgart 2005).

27. For the latest identification of the relic and the donor, see Otavský, 'Goldenes Reliquienkreuz' (as in n. 12), 113–14, n. 24.

28. M. Büchsel and P. Schmidt ed., *Das Porträt vor der Erfindung des Porträts* (Mainz 2003); P. Kurmann and B. Kurmann-Schwarz, 'Memoria und Porträt', in *Ars videndi: Professori Jaromír Homolka ad honorem*, ed. A. Mudra and M. Ottová (Prague 2006), 117–27.

29. Möseneder, 'Lapides vivi' (as in n. 1).

30. Hlaváčková, 'Idea' (as in n. 14), 14–15.

31. H. Hlaváčková, 'Středověký obraz v muzeu: Madona svatotomášská', *Bulletin Moravské galerie v Brně*, 50 (1994), 19–21.

32. Hlaváčková was the first to interpret the Karlstein staircase as Jacob's ladder; see Hlaváčková, 'Karlštejn' (as in n. 1), 63, and Hlaváčková, 'Idea' (as in n. 14), 15.

33. B. Cunliffe, *The City of Bath* (Gloucester 1990), 94; P. Dinzelbacher, *Himmel, Hölle, Heilige: Visionen und Kunst in Mittelalter* (Darmstadt 2002), 108–09.

34. For example, Philo de Alexandria, *De somniis*, ed. P. Savinel (Paris 1962), 133–56; Aurelius Augustinus, *Enarrationes in Psalmos* (CXIX.2, PL, XXXVII, col. 1597); and *De cataclysmo ad cathechumenos* (PL, XL, col. 698).

35. Rabanus Maurus, *De laudibus sanctae Crucis*, PL, CVII, cols 216, 282; Hugo de S. Victore(?), *Miscellanea*, PL, CLXXVII, col. 862; *De modo bene vivendi*, PL, CLXXXIV, col. 1276.

36. *Regula*, chap. vii: 'De humilitate'; PL, LXVI, col. 371.

37. Herrad of Hohenbourg, *Hortus deliciarum*, ed. R. Green (London 1979), 201. On the subject in general, see T. Eriksson, 'L'échelle de la perfection. Une nouvelle intérpretation murale de Chaldon', *Cahiers de Civilisation médiévale*, 7 (1964), 439–49; M. Smeyers, *Flemish Miniatures from the 8th to the mid-16th Century* (Leuven 1999), 73; W. Cahn, 'Ascending and descending from heaven: ladder themes in early medieval art', in *Santi e Demoni nell'alto medioevo occidentale secoli V–XI* (Spoleto 1989), 697–724; A. Eörsi, 'Haec scala significat ascensum virtutum. Remarks on the Iconography of Christ Mounting the Cross on a Ladder', *Arte Christiana*, 85 (1997), 151–66; M. Studničková, 'Sv. Václav jako *scala coeli*. K interpretaci nástěnných maleb schodiště Velké věže na hradě Karlštejně', in Všetečková ed., *Schodištní cykly* (as in n. 6), 71–73.

38. *Les Fastes du Gothique: le siècle de Charles V* (Paris 1981), 315–16; C. Heck, 'L'iconographie de l'ascension spirituelle et la dévotion de laïcs: le Trône de charité dans le Psautier de Bonne de Luxembourg et les Petites Heures du duc de Berry', *Revue de l'art*, 110 (1995), 9–22; M. Krieger, 'Der Psalter der Bonna de Luxembourg', in *King John of Luxembourg (1296–1346) and the Art of His Era*, ed. K. Benešovská (Prague 1998), 69–81.

39. Detailed argument may be found in Studničková, 'Sv. Václav jako *scala coeli*' (as in n. 37).

40. According to an ancient tradition, the *Scala Santa* leading to the Sancta Sanctorum was the staircase in Pontius Pilate's pretorium, which Jesus ascended after being beaten and scourged.

41. 'Et sic posset intelligi, quod dicit Augustinus: "Deo servire est regnare."'; 'Vita Karoli IV imperatoris' (as in n. 3), cap. XII.

42. According to M. Bartlová, 'Úvahy o vyobrazení svatováclavské legendy na schodišti Karlštejna', in *Schodištní cykly* (as in n. 6), 50–57.

43. Dante Alighieri, *La Commedia* (Pontedera 2006).

44. According to K. Kubínová, 'Panovnické postavy v závěru schodištních maleb', in *Schodištní cykly* (as in n. 6), 23–36.

45. 'tota paradisi clavis tuus sanguis est' ('your blood is the whole key of paradise'); Tertullian, *De anima*, ed. A. Reifferscheid and G. Wissowa (Vienna 1890), 55.

46. J. Török, 'Szent László liturgikus tisztelete', in *Athleta patriae*, ed. L. Mezey (Budapest 1980), 135–59, here 156; L. Mezey, *Deákság és Európa* (Budapest 1979), 141; E. Marosi, 'Der heilige Ladislaus als ungarischer Nationalheiliger. Bemerkungen zu seiner Ikonographie im 14.–15. Jahrhundert', *Acta Historiae Artium*, 33 (1987), 211–56, here 240.

47. K. Otavský, 'Reliquien im Besitz Kaiser Karls IV., ihre Verehrung und ihre Fassung', in *Court Chapels* (as in n. 1), 129–41.

48. J. Fajt and J. Royt, 'The Pictorial Decoration of the Great Tower at Karlštejn Castle. Ecclesia Triumphans', in Fajt ed., *Magister Theodoricus* (as in n. 1), 108–215, here 156 ff., fig. 135; 'Catalogue of the Panel Paintings in the Chapel of the Holy Cross', ibid., 296–503, here 466–67.

49. By Pseudo-Methodius and Adso de Montier-en-Der (Menasteriensis), *De ortu et tempore Antichristi*, ed. D. Verhelst (Turnhout 1976). See F. Kampers, *Die deutsche Kaisersage in Prophetie und Sage* (Munich 1896); E. Sackur, *Sibyllinische Texte und Forschungen: Pseudomethodius, Adso und die tiburtinische Sibylle* (Halle 1898); and B. Töpfer, *Das kommende Reich des Friedens: Zur Entwicklung chiliastischer Zukunfthoffnungen im Hochmittelalter* (Berlin 1964). See further V. Dvořáková, J. Krása, M. Merhautová and K. Stejskal, *Gothic Mural Painting in Bohemia 1300–1378* (London 1964), 57; H. Bredekamp, *Kunst als Medium sozialer Konflikte: Bilderkämpfe von der Spätantike bis zur Hussitenrevolution* (Frankfurt am Main 1975), 238.

50. Fajt and Royt, 'The Pictorial Decoration' (as in n. 48), 208.

51. See H. Sachs, E. Badstübner and H. Naumann, *Christliche Ikonographie in Stichworten* (Leipzig 1980), 342, s.v. 'Treppe'.

52. Möseneder, 'Lapides vivi' (as in n. 1), 62–63.

Vying for Supremacy:
The Cults of St Wenceslas and St Stanislas
in Early-Fourteenth-Century Cracow

AGNIESZKA ROŻNOWSKA-SADRAEI

Analysis of the cult of St Wenceslas in medieval Cracow has hitherto been distorted by the conviction that St Stanislas's spiritual hegemony was supreme and unbroken. This article argues that a study of art and architecture in early-14th-century Cracow — especially of the patronage of the Cracow Bishop Jan Muskata and of the iconography of municipal seals — leads to the conclusion that St Stanislas's status did not go unchallenged, indeed that St Wenceslas enjoyed a reputation on a par with, perhaps even superior to, that of the Polish pater patriae.

ST Wenceslas was the first patron of Cracow Cathedral, and it is not surprising that the city was one of the few places in medieval Poland where the cult of the patron saint of Bohemia enjoyed a considerable following. The rivalry between the cults of St Wenceslas and St Stanislas, the Polish *pater patriae*, was founded in national sentiment, and to a large extent the fortunes of St Wenceslas's cult in Cracow depended on the rapport between the governments of the two kingdoms at any given time, and the extent of the influence of Bohemian rulers in Poland. St Wenceslas was a royal saint from the Bohemian Přemyslid dynasty, killed in 935 by his elder brother Boleslav I (979–72). His relics were in time translated to the south apse of St Vitus's rotunda in Prague Castle, the construction of which Wenceslas had initiated himself.[1] The rise and success of the cult of St Wenceslas, canonised *causa orationis* by Bishop Dětmar at the end of the 10th century, was due to the patronage of Bohemian rulers, who transformed him into the *dux perpetuus* and patron saint of the nation.[2]

The origins of St Stanislas's cult could not be more different — yet it displays many parallels. A bishop of Cracow, St Stanislas was martyred by a Polish king, Boleslav the Bold, in 1079. His remains were translated to the cathedral, probably in the 11th century,[3] and elevated to the shrine in the centre of its crossing after his canonisation in 1253.[4] The martyr's cult prospered owing to the efforts of the Cracow episcopate, and in the late 13th and 14th centuries St Stanislas emerged as the guardian of Polish sovereignty, the patron saint whose intercession was believed to have brought the political unification of the kingdom after nearly two centuries of feudal disintegration.

Following St Stanislas's canonisation, his position as the principal patron saint of Poland remained uncontested, except during the twenty years after the Bohemian King Wenceslas II had ascended the Polish throne in 1300. The new king's political and liturgical strategies gave St Wenceslas pride of place over St Stanislas in Cracow for years to come.[5] The Dominicans seem to have compromised their old loyalty to

St Stanislas, for in 1296 and 1298 the Dominican Zdzisław, one of Wenceslas II's advisers, introduced the cult of St Wenceslas into the liturgy of his order.[6] But the most powerful figure in this shift of allegiances was Jan Muskata, Wenceslas II's new Bishop of Cracow (1295–1320). Evidence for the shift from St Stanislas to St Wenceslas may be found in two of Muskata's artistic enterprises: the design of the first Gothic cathedral choir on the Wawel, and the cathedral's oldest extant illuminated manuscript, the *Missale plenarium Cracoviense* (catalogued as KP3 in the Archiwa Katedry krakowskiej (Cracow Cathedral Archive)), which I believe to have been commissioned by Muskata.[7]

In c. 1300, Muskata began to rebuild Cracow Cathedral as the royal church, with the encouragement (or on the initiative) of King Wenceslas II. Nothing of his building survives above ground, but interpreting the latest excavations, Tomasz Węcławowicz has shown that this edifice, the first to be erected by the Přemyslids in Poland, was to boast a 'classic' French-inspired Gothic chevet, complete with an ambulatory and radiating chapels (Fig. 1).[8] This project never proceeded beyond the foundations and was aborted, probably shortly after 1305, in the wake of Wenceslas II's death.

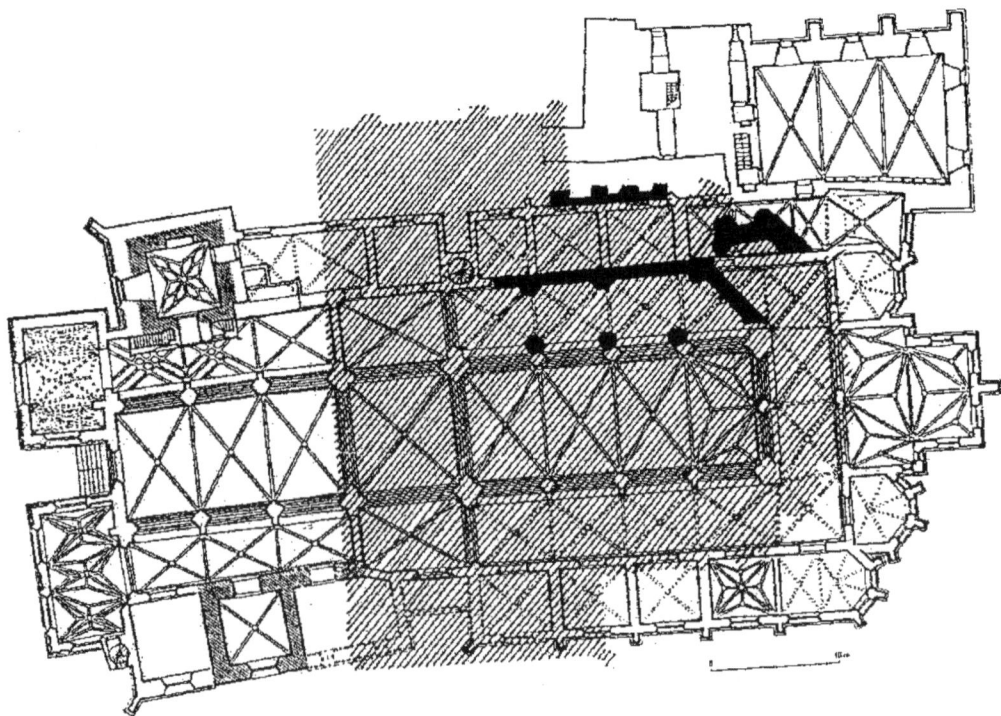

FIG. 1.   Cracow Cathedral: choir, the first Gothic phase (Muskata's choir), consisting of the polygonal chevet (hatched with foundation walls in black), superimposed on the ground-plan of the present, Late Gothic cathedral

Reconstruction by Tomasz Węcławowicz

However, its significance as a powerful symbol of Přemyslid rule is demonstrated by the fact that Muskata's successor, Bishop Nanker, an ardent advocate of all things Polish and a promoter of St Stanislas's cult, selected for his cathedral of 1320 an old-fashioned, flat-ended Cistercian choir instead of a grand chevet, despite the fact that such a chevet, by virtue of its association with the French monarchy, was better suited for a coronation church and the royal mausoleum. Muskata's design had envisaged the relics of St Wenceslas (probably buried in the eastern crypt of the old Romanesque cathedral) at the centre of the radiating-chapel system as if in the shape of a royal crown.[9] It seems to have been Nanker's intentions to counteract and eradicate this design, by planning his own cathedral church around the site of St Stanislas's shrine in the crossing (Fig. 2).

In Muskata's remodelled royal church, St Wenceslas, the first patron of the cathedral, who by then had been eclipsed by St Stanislas, would once again hold sway. Thus the cathedral's liturgy needed to be revised in favour of Bohemia, and service books whose decoration reflected the new allegiance were called for. I would like to suggest that the so-called Missal KP3 should be seen as one of the codices commissioned by Muskata for his new cathedral.

MISSAL KP3

MISSAL KP3 is a parchment codex conceived on a stately scale, with 265 folios.[10] Its decoration consists of twenty illuminated initials — four done in penwork, three

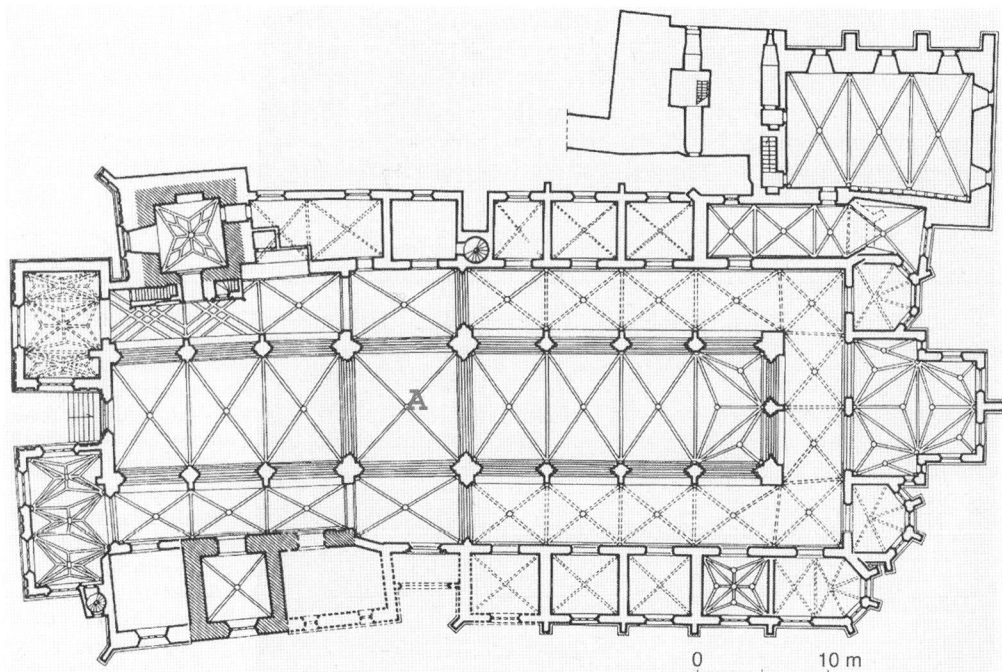

FIG. 2.   Cracow Cathedral: ground-plan of the Gothic structure. A — altar of St Stanislas
Agnieszka Rożnowska-Sadraei

so-called inhabited initials, and thirteen historiated initials — as well as rich marginal *drôleries*. It has hitherto been dated to post-1346 purely on stylistic grounds, in the absence of a colophon or any other identifying features, such as inscriptions or heraldry.[11] Although it is certain that it was created for use in the liturgy of Cracow Cathedral, since its initials form a cycle following the order of the liturgical calendar of the Cracow diocese,[12] some of its features make it unique amongst 14th-century Cracow manuscripts. Firstly, St Wenceslas holds a supreme position amongst the saints represented in the codex, while St Stanislas is shown without a pallium. This is unusual for the Wawel scriptorium and indicates that the manuscript may have been imported from one of the cosmopolitan monastic scriptoria of contemporary Bohemia. In addition, according to Janka Szendrei, the type of musical notation employed in the manuscript would indicate such a source: the missal employs gothicising neumes of the Metz-German type, but of a form that is strongly Bohemian in character.[13] This also tallies with the style of the illuminations, which are characterised by Italianate influences, but show inconsistencies in the modelling of draperies, facial features, hands and feet, and are notable for the prevalence of polished gold backgrounds that create the impression of a shallow picture space. Such a combination of stylistic and formal effects is in keeping with the character of early-14th-century Bohemian illumination.[14] Considering these factors, I would propose a revised analysis of the missal's style and — drawing attention to parallels with Bohemian codices created for Queen Elizabeth Richenza (known in Czech sources as Eliška Rejčka, the Polish princess who was the second wife of King Wenceslas II) — argue that it could have been illuminated as early as c. 1320.

My analysis focuses only on the illuminations of the first part of KP3, as I believe that the two initials in the sequentiary at the end of the codex, depicting the *Mater Dei de humilitate* (Madonna of Humility) on fol. 245v and the *Noli Me Tangere* on fol. 248r, are the product of a different hand and a later addition.[15] The creation of these two initials can be dated to post 1346, because the Madonna of Humility iconography made its first appearance in Central Europe in Bohemia around 1350, for instance in the panel of the Madonna of Vyšehrad dated to 1355 (now in Prague, Národní galerie).[16] The illuminator who painted the last two initials in KP3 strove to emulate the style of his gifted predecessor, but lacked his talent and dexterity. Given his awareness of Bohemian art of the second half of the 14th century, it is likely that the later illuminator worked in the Czech-inspired cultural milieu of Cracow under King Kazimir the Great (1333–70).

The most striking aspect of the main illuminator's hand is its effortless command of and extensive familiarity with the language of Italian illumination, its vocabulary and syntax, and its pictorial composition, figural motifs, and colour palette. For example, the ornamental, antique-looking foliage, the so-called Roman weed (*Cynaria scolymus*), often outlined in white and marked by tiny, white circles, was characteristic of early-14th-century Roman miniatures. Compare the scene of the Nativity on fol. 15v in KP3 (Fig. 3) with the illuminated initial on fol. 32r of the *Legenda Maior Sancti Francisci* (Rome, Biblioteca Nazionale, MS Vittorio Emanuele 411; Fig. 4).[17] Similarly Italianate is the distinctive motif of a golden bead hanging from, or entangled in, long whiskers, which appeared in Bolognese manuscripts as early as the 1280s. Its appearance in, for example, the initial with St Stanislas on fol. 180r in KP3 (Fig. 5) can be compared with the decoration on fol. 131r of the Ester e Assuero Bible (Turin, Biblioteca Nazionale, Ms. Lat. D II 3; Fig. 6).[18]

FIG. 3.   Missal KP3: Nativity, fol. 15v, *c.* 1320
Cracow, Archiwa Katedry krakowskiej

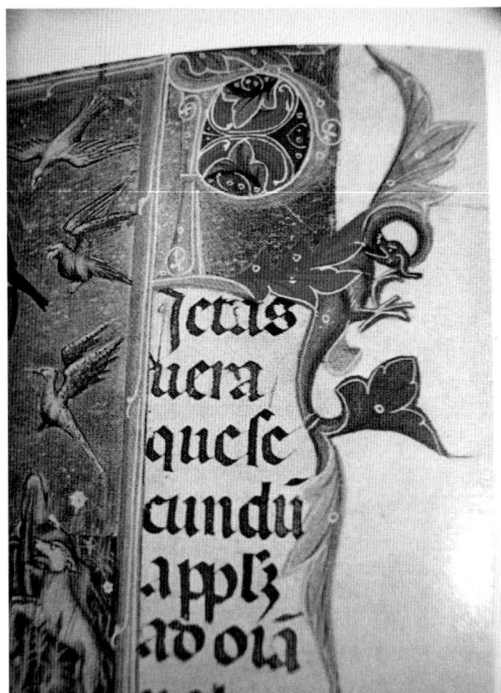

FIG. 4. *Legenda Maior Sancti Francisci*, fol. 32r, early 14th century (Rome, Biblioteca Nazionale, MS Vittorio Emanuele 411)

FIG. 5. Missal KP3: St Stanislas, fol. 180r

Cracow, Archiwa Katedry krakowskiej

FIG. 6.   Ester e Assuero Bible: fol. 131r, 1280s (Turin, Biblioteca Nazionale, Ms. Lat. D.II.3)

Italian influences become apparent in Bohemian art at the beginning of the 14th century, and the decoration of KP3 is dominated by features characteristic of contemporary Bohemian art with its calligraphic and schematised handling of facial features, hair and drapery.[19] The closest parallels for such a formal approach are found in liturgical codices produced from 1316 onwards for Queen Elizabeth Richenza.[20] The KP3 main illuminator's schematic rendition of facial features and modelling of hair with wavy strands clearly delineated by black contours find their closest parallels in the 1316 *Lectionarium officii* (Vienna, Österreichische Nationalbibliothek, Cod. 1772). Compare, for instance, Christ in the Resurrection scene on fol. 72r (Fig. 7) with St Wenceslas on fol. 202v in KP3 (Fig. 8 & Col. Pl. VB in print edn).[21] Furthermore the elegant poses and gestures, especially the elongated feet of King David on fol. 3v of KP3 (Fig. 9), are a product of the same artistic sensibility as those in the *Lectionarium* (see Fig. 7, for example).[22] In short, as far as the style of KP3 is concerned, it appears closer to that of Richenza's manuscripts than to that of the later Bohemian codices with which it has been compared, for example the Velislav Bible (Prague, Národní knihovna, XXIII C.124, dated to *c.* 1340),[23] or the *Liber Viaticus* of Jan of Středa of *c.* 1360 (Prague, Knihovna Národního muzea, XIII A.12).[24]

Crucial in uncovering the devotional and stylistic origins of the Cracow missal is the glaring contrast between its modest initials depicting the major Polish saints, St Stanislas (fol. 180v, Fig. 5) and St Adalbert (fol. 176v), with the sumptuous depiction of the patron saint of the Přemyslids, St Wenceslas (fol. 202v, Fig. 8 & Col. Pl. VB in print edn), included in the *Sanctorale* (or *Proprium de sanctis*). The two Polish bishop-martyrs are portrayed in an identical manner: seated on simple chest-thrones,

FIG. 7. Queen Elizabeth Richenza's *Lectionarium officii*: the Resurrection, fol. 72r, 1316 (Vienna, Österreichische Nationalbibliothek, Cod. 1772)

FIG. 8. Missal KP3: St Wenceslas, fol. 202v
Cracow, Archiwa Katedry krakowskiej

FIG. 9.   Missal KP3: King David, fol. 3v
Cracow, Archiwa Katedry krakowskiej

dressed in pontifical vestments, including mitre and liturgical gloves, and leaning on crosiers held in the left hand while blessing with the right. In contrast to these modest images St Wenceslas stands out, distinguished by size, lavish hues, and elaborated framing. The saint wears sumptuous armour with a flowing cape and ducal mitre. Standing in contrapposto, he leans on a lance held in his right hand while resting his left hand on a shield adorned with a black Bohemian eagle. Two angels, kneeling above the initial, hold a golden crown above the holy warrior's head. St Wenceslas is here shown as the *dux perpetuus*, the pious, wise and just ruler, and the royal patron and protector of Bohemia, as he was first characterised in the *vita* with the incipit 'Oriente iam sole', penned in 1250–60.[25] The saint was depicted as a holy prince wearing a mitre as early as the 11th century, for example on fol. 68r of the Coronation Gospel of Vratislav (the Vyšehrad Codex) of 1085.[26] In the 12th century, on Wenceslas I's denar of 1118–20, St Wenceslas was shown between angels, a hagiographic topos present in all his *vitae*,[27] and holding a silver shield with a black eagle, which was the oldest emblem of the Přemyslids.[28] The formula employed in KP3 adheres most strongly to the iconographic conventions for the representation of holy warriors established by Bohemian workshops at the beginning of the 14th century.[29] One parallel is the figure of St George on the reliquary offered in 1302 to the convent church of St George by its abbess, Kunegunda, who was a sister of King Wenceslas II. The Passional of Abbess Kunegunda (Prague, Národní knihovna, XIV A.17), dated to 1313–21 and left unfinished on her death, also employs the motif of crowning angels, this time in a representation of the enthroned abbess herself.[30]

St Wenceslas's iconographic supremacy in the KP3 missal shows that the codex was commissioned by a patron whose interests were closely bound up with Bohemia. It could be argued that it was created in the Cracow scriptorium in the second half of the 14th century, in the context of the high alliance of King Kazimir the Great and Emperor Charles IV, which was distinguished by a strong interest in Bohemian culture, its emulation and appropriation.[31] But it lay within the compass of bishops, not that of kings, to commission codices for their cathedrals — especially missals destined strictly for the use of priests as service books.[32] Muskata's successors to the Cracow *cathedra* were deeply devoted to St Stanislas, their commitment mirrored in their diocesan statutes. In 1320, Bishop Nanker ordered that the feast of the bishop-martyr's translation be celebrated in the whole of the diocese, and his statutes made no reference to St Wenceslas.[33] Jan Grot (1326–47) invoked St Stanislas as a special patron, and Piotr Wysz (1392–1412) as *patronus gloriosus*.[34] St Wenceslas returned to the cathedral in the 1330s–40s: together with St Stanislas he was represented kneeling by the cross in the now lost Crucifixion miniature from a Cracow Gospel of 1325–30,[35] and depicted as an enthroned prince on a choir vault boss completed some time before 1346. Yet St Stanislas was afforded pre-eminence in the decoration of the new Gothic church completed under Bishop Bodzanta in 1364, and the same bishop oversaw the elevation of the statue of the *pater patriae* to its superior location in the gable of the west front (Fig. 10). Thus, amongst the 14th-century bishops of Cracow, it is Muskata, protégé of King Wenceslas II and devotee of St Wenceslas, whose interests are best reflected in the iconography of Missal KP3.

In addition, the stylistic parallels outlined for KP3 acquire special significance in the light of Muskata's Bohemian and Italianate connections and his (not always legitimate) love of books. Contemporary records emphasised that the bishop's marauders in the Cracow diocese were under special instruction to deliver liturgical books from the cathedral in Sandomierz.[36] It is difficult to imagine that a prelate with such an extreme interest in books could have resisted collecting Italian manuscripts

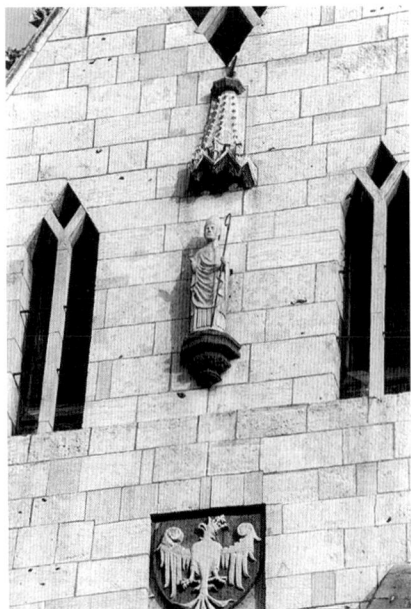

FIG. 10.   Cracow Cathedral: façade, statue of St Stanislas

Agnieszka Rożnowska-Sadraei

during his study years in Bologna, or while in the service of Cardinal Latino Frangipani in Rome.[37] The eventful, if taxing decade of Muskata's exile from Poland (between 1308 and 1318),[38] during which he travelled in Silesia, the kingdom of Bohemia, and Hungary (he spent some time in Olomouc and Bratislava),[39] provided more opportunities for him to explore his passion for manuscripts. We cannot exclude the possibility that, as the *amicus delicissimus*[40] of the late Wenceslas II and his honorary chaplain, he would have made the acquaintance of Elizabeth Richenza, the king's widow, who is known to have lived in Cracow for three years from 1300 to 1303.[41] It is therefore conceivable that Muskata, to celebrate his return to Cracow in 1318, commissioned Missal KP3 from one of the Bohemian scriptoria that worked for the queen and which he had visited during his exile, although this must remain speculative, as the hand of KP3's main illuminator cannot be detected in any of Richenza's manuscripts.

MUNICIPAL SEALS

CRACOW patricians were the other significant political force in early-14th-century Poland who chose St Wenceslas as their patron. Three municipal seals created between 1312 and 1320 are evocative manifestations of this allegiance.

The great council seal of *c.* 1312 awards St Wenceslas the heraldically more significant dexter position, while St Stanislas appears on the sinister. Two minor seals — the minor seal of the council and the seal of the Cracow *scabini* (jurists) — adopt the following iconographic hierarchy: the council, the most powerful municipal agency, accepted St Wenceslas as their representative, while the inferior body of the jurists adopted St Stanislas as the guarantor of their authority. The two minor seals have been dated to the years before Łokietek's coronation and most probably to 1314–20.[42]

The minor seal of the council depicts St Wenceslas as a nimbed knight in tunic and armour, with a long sword buckled at the belt (Fig. 11).[43] The saint stands erect, facing the viewer, his right hand holding a lance with a small banner attached, and his left a shield adorned with a cross.[44] The inscription, running on both sides of the figure, identifies him as 'S(ANCTVS) WENCESLAVS'. The displayed eagle is shown on the right, beneath the saint's hand, and a crown on his left. The legend, reading 'S(IGILLVM) MINVS CIVITATIS CRACOVIE', gives the rank of the seal and identifies the council as its owner.[45]

The seal of the jurists shows the frontal bust of St Stanislas against a diaper background (Fig. 12).[46] The saint is shown above a schematically outlined stretch of town wall with a gate opening (filled with a motif of four roses joined by their stems) in the centre. The jurists are named as the owners of the seal by the legend 'S(IGILLVM) SCABINOR(UM) CRACOVIE CIVITATIS'. The martyr's dress is in keeping with the already long-established formula — he wears pontifical vestments and a mitre — but there are elements in this design that had never appeared in conjunction with the image of St Stanislas: the saint's right hand, raised in benediction, points to a crown, and the crozier in his left hand to a displayed eagle. These symbols of Polish royal power are essential to explaining an allegory that one of St Stanislas's hagiographers, Wincenty of Kielcza, included in his *Vita maior Sancti Stanislai*.[47] This allegory was crucial in establishing St Stanislas as the champion of the Polish monarchy, as it foretold the restitution of the Polish state (symbolised by the eagle) through the intercession of the saintly bishop (depicted in pontifical dress), who administers the regalia (represented by the crown) kept safe in the capital city

FIG. 11.   The minor seal of Cracow Council
(1314–20)

Reconstruction after F. Piekosiński

FIG. 12.   Seal of the Cracow *scabini*
(1314–20) (Zakład Nauk Pomocniczych
Historii, Jagiellonian University, Cracow)

Agnieszka Rożnowska-Sadraei

of Cracow (signified by the stretch of town wall). The inclusion of the town wall demonstrates that the city was a necessary component in the process of political and spiritual restoration.[48] St Stanislas is thus represented here for the first time in art as the *pater patriae* whose intercession was essential for the process of restoration.

Polish historians have accepted that in keeping with the saint's status as the patron of Polish unification the design of the *scabini* seal should incorporate the figure of the holy bishop deploying the symbols of that revival. However, they have failed to explain satisfactorily the presence of the very same elements alongside St Wenceslas on the minor council seal. It has been suggested that the crown and eagle mirror here the political aspirations of the capital city of Cracow.[49] St Wenceslas, himself a ruler of the Přemyslid state, could easily have been adopted as the co-patron of a royal town such as Cracow. Yet we cannot fail to notice that instead of the black eagle a cross is shown on St Wenceslas's shield, suggesting his status not as a holy ruler but as an ideal *miles christianus*. Moreover, we should not ignore the fact that St Wenceslas was selected for the council's minor seal, which was used for documents of an economic or administrative nature.[50] This indicates that in the formation of the patricians' political identity a primary reason for the association with St Wenceslas was a desire for advancement through commercial success. In the minds of rich Cracow burghers St Stanislas represented the ambitions of the clergy and the ineffectiveness of the Piast princes in their effort to end the fragmentation of the Polish state, whereas St Wenceslas was a symbol of the economically advanced Bohemian kingdom, and his intercession was the key to their own version of a future unified Polish state.

An understanding of the loyalties of Cracow patricians in contrast to those of Łokietek and the Polish episcopate helps us to answer another question that Polish historians have struggled to explain, namely why St Stanislas was 'demoted' to the seal of the inferior body of the jurists.[51] A study of post-1312 Cracow municipal structures reveals that after Łokietek had abolished the hereditary office of *advocatus*, he became the head of the assessors presiding over the majority of the town's courts.[52] It is thus not surprising that the seal of the institution that in effect represented the authority of a prince striving for the restoration of the kingdom bore the image of the patron saint of that unification.[53] Łokietek had probably adopted the crowned eagle as his arms before the *scabini* seal was created, and the latter deliberately separates the crown and the eagle to bind them through the figure of St Stanislas, who acts as the keystone in the structure of the Polish kingdom.[54] The placing of the crown above the bishop's blessing hand alludes to Łokietek's imminent coronation and reinforces the martyr's status as the divinely appointed executive and guardian of royal power, a power that was Łokietek's life-long ambition.[55]

CONCLUSION

Analysis of St Wenceslas's cult in medieval Cracow has hitherto been distorted by the conviction of St Stanislas's omnipotent and unbroken spiritual supremacy. But a study of early-14th-century Cracow art and architecture leads to the conclusion that this status was not unchallenged, and that St Wenceslas enjoyed (for a time) a reputation on a par with, perhaps even superior to, that of the Polish *pater patriae*. We can also learn several important lessons. Firstly, we can see that patrons often made stylistic choices dictated by a political agenda, as we have seen when Muskata's 'Bohemian' cathedral chevet, with its focus on the relics of St Wenceslas, was superseded by Nanker's old-fashioned flat-ended choir in 1320, a dramatic and politically motivated stylistic U-turn. Secondly, more accurate dates can be proposed for objects such as Missal KP3 when their style and iconography are reconsidered in their historical context. Thirdly, the implications of the municipal seals show us that spiritual loyalties in saints' cults could be formed and changed by social factors, economic advantages, and political allegiances. The study of municipal sigillography in this period makes it evident that St Stanislas's supremacy had not yet been established, and that the success of the cult was not yet inextricably bound up with the sense of Polish national identity.

ACKNOWLEDGEMENTS

I would like to thank Prof. Paul Crossley and Dr Tomasz Węcławowicz for their help and advice with my research for this article. I am also grateful to Dr Zoë Opačić for inviting me to speak at the BAA conference in Prague, and to the BAA Council for funding my bursary scholarship.

NOTES

1. For the history of St Vitus's rotunda, see for instance L. Ormrod, 'The Wenceslas Chapel in St Vitus' Cathedral, Prague: the marriage of imperial iconography and Bohemian kingship' (unpublished Ph.D. thesis, Courtauld Institute of Art, University of London, 1997), I, 82–96.

2. For St Wenceslas's hagiography, see for instance E. Pražák ed., *Středověké legendy o českých světicích* (Prague 1998).

3. Historians' opinions are divided as to the date of the first translation of St Stanislas's relics from the church of St Michael, the site of his death, to Cracow Cathedral. Some believed it took place in 1088, and others date it to the 12th century. A study of sources and of the reconstruction of the second Romanesque cathedral shows that two translations may have occurred. See A. Rożnowska-Sadraei, 'Pater Patriae: the cult of St Stanislas and the art of the Polish kings (1200–1455)' (Ph.D. thesis, Courtauld Institute of Art, University of London, 1996), 30–37, now published as A. Rożnowska-Sadraei, *Pater Patriae: The Cult of St Stanislaus and the Patronage of Polish Kings 1200–1450* (Cracow 2008).

4. The ceremony was described by the 15th-century Polish historian Jan Długosz in his *Vita Sanctissimi Stanislai Cracoviensis Episcopi*, ed. A. Przezdziecki, in *Opera Omnia*, ed. I. Polkowski and Ż. Pauli, 14 vols (Cracow 1863–78), I (1887), 1–181, esp. 149.

5. E. Długopolski, *Władysław Łokietek na tle swoich czasów* (Wrocław 1951), 75–105; S. Gawlas, 'Człowiek uwikłany w wielkie procesy - przykład Muskaty', in *Człowiek w społeczeństwie średniowiecznym* (Warsaw 1977), 391–401; T. Pietras, *Krwawy wilk z pastorałem: biskup krakowski Jan zwany Muskata* (Warsaw 2001).

6. J. Długosz, *Liber beneficiorum dioecesis Cracoviensis*, ed. A. Przezdziecki, 3 vols (Cracow 1863–64), III, 452, as quoted in T. Węcławowicz, 'Bohemia Cracoviam muraverunt', *Umění*, 46/6 (1998), 410–19, esp. 417, n. 11.

7. I. Polkowski, *Katalog rękopisów kapitulnych katedry krakowskiej: Część pierwsza, Kodexa Rękopiśmienne 1–228* (Cracow 1884), 26.

8. T. Węcławowicz, *Krakowski kościół katedralny w wiekach średnich: Funkcje i możliwości interpretacji* (Cracow 2005), 47 63; see also idem, 'The Bohemian king, the Polish bishop, and their church: Wenceslas II's cathedral in Kraków (1295–1305)', in *The Year 1300 and the Creation of a New European Architecture*, ed. A. Gajewski and Z. Opačić (Turnhout 2007), 177–85.

9. Although St Wenceslas's body lay in Prague Cathedral, Cracow must have been in possession of some relics of the saint, to whom its cathedral was dedicated. We have no documents however specifying where the relics may have come from, or when they may have arrived in Cracow. The cathedral's dedication to St Wenceslas is mentioned in the 10th-century so-called *Codex Gertrudianus*, and it has been suggested that this refers to the dedication of the first Romanesque cathedral. See J. Rajman, 'Święta, relikwia i patrocinia w problematyce kultu świętych w Krakowie od końca X do połowy XIIIw.', in *Kraków w chrześcijańskiej Europie X-XIII w.*, Catalogue of the Exhibition in the Historical Museum of the City of Kraków, 5 June–12 November 2006 (Cracow 2006), 127; idem, *Średniowieczne patrocinia krakowskie* (Cracow 2002), 115. The cathedral inventory of 1110 describes its treasury as *aerarium sancti Wenceslai*; *Monumenta Poloniae Historica*, 6 vols (Lwów/Cracow 1864–93), I, 377.

10. After trimming it measures 383 by 296 mm; see B. Miodońska, *Małopolskie malarstwo książkowe 1320–1540* (Warsaw 1993), 112, 197.

11. Miodońska, *Małopolskie malarstwo* (as in n. 10), 112, 197; idem, 'Malarstwo miniaturowe', in *Sztuka w Krakowie w latach 1350–1550* (Cracow 1964), 91–121; *Katalog Zabytków Sztuki w Polsce*, IV, ed. J. Szablowski (Warsaw 1965), 132; R. Knapiński, 'Ikonografia Świętych polskich około roku 1400', in *Sztuka około 1400* (Warsaw 1996), 189–207, esp. 196.

12. Miodońska, *Małopolskie malarstwo* (as in n. 10), 112, 197.

13. J. Szendrei, 'Staff notation of Gregorian Chant in Polish sources from the twelfth to the sixteenth century', in *Notae musicae artis*, ed. E. Witkowska-Zaremba (Cracow 2001), 211–24, esp. 215. I would like to thank Dr Jakub Kubieniec from the Institute of Musicology of the Jagiellonian University for bringing this article to my attention.

14. A. Karłowska-Kamzowa, *Malarstwo gotyckie Europy środkowowschodniej. Zagadnienie odrębności regionu* (Warsaw/Poznań 1972), 21–28.

15. Illustrated sequentiaries are rare; see J. F. Hamburger, *St John the Divine: The Deified Evangelist in Medieval Art and Theology* (Berkeley 2002), 105.

16. Miodońska, *Małopolskie malarstwo* (as in n. 10), 112; J. Royt, *Středověké malířství v Čechách* (Prague 2002), 55.

17. M. Salmi, *Italian Miniatures* (London 1957), pls XIIIb, XIVb.

18. For images, see *La Miniatura italiana in età romanica e gotica* (Florence 1979).

19. A. Merhautová-Livorová, 'A short survey of mural painting', in *Gothic Mural Painting in Bohemia and Moravia 1300–1378*, ed. V. Dvořáková, J. Krása, A. Merhautová and K. Stejskal (London 1964), 25–40, esp. 30.

20. They married in 1303. For a study of Richenza's manuscripts, see J. Květ, *Iluminované rukopisy královny Rejčky: příspěvek k dějinám české knižní malby ve století XIV.* (Prague 1931).

21. For Richenza's codices, see A. Fingernagel and M. Roland ed., *Mitteleuropäische Schulen I (c.1250–1350)*, Die illuminierten Handschriften und Inkunabeln der Österreichischen Nationalbibliothek, X (Vienna 1997), 225–52.

22. ibid., 236–40.

23. K. Stejskal ed., *Velislai Biblia picta* (Prague 1970).

24. P. Brodský, *Katalog iluminovaných rukopisů Knihovny Národniho muzea v Praze* (Prague 2000), 158–63. R. Suckale and J. Fajt, 'The circle of Charles IV', in *Prague: The Crown of Bohemia 1347–1437*, ed. B. Drake Boehm and J. Fajt (New York 2005), 35–45, esp. 41–42.

25. The text of the *vita* is translated and published as the 'Legend of St Wenceslas' by M. Kantor, *The Origins of Christianity in Bohemia: Sources and Commentary* (Evanston IL 1990), 215–44.

26. Now in the collection of Prague, Národní knihovna, XIV A.13; see J. Cibulka, 'Obraz svatého Václava', *Umění*, 3 (1930), 157–86, here 163.

27. For the denar, see ibid., 166–67.

28. Mentioned for the first time *c.* 1180; see W. Kliś, 'Czy istnieje zależność przedstawień krakowskich św. Wacława od ikonografii czeskiej?', in *Lapides Viventes: Zaginiony Kraków wieków średnich* (Cracow 2005), 193–208, esp. 196–97.

29. For the relationship between Cracovian depictions of St Wenceslas and Bohemian iconography, see ibid., 194.

30. In her Passional Kunegunda herself is shown being crowned by two angels (fol. 1v). The reliquary of St George is today kept in the St Vitus treasury, Prague Cathedral. See Miodońska, *Małopolskie malarstwo* (as in n. 10), 112; K. Benešovská, 'The abbess with the crown', in *The History of the Prague Castle* (Prague 2003), 150–58.

31. P. Crossley, 'Bohemia Sacra and Polonia Sacra. Liturgy and history in Prague and Cracow Cathedrals', *Folia Historiae Artium*, 7 (2001), 49–69; idem, '"Ara Patriae": St. Stanislaus, the Jagiellonians and the coronation ordinal for Cracow Cathedral', in *Künstlerische Wechselwirkungen in Mitteleuropa*, ed. J. Fajt and M. Hörsch (Ostfildern 2005), 103–23.

32. Miodońska, *Małopolskie malarstwo* (as in n. 10), 34; C. de Hammel, *A History of Illuminated Manuscripts* (London 1994), 202–03.

33. J. Fijałek, *Najstarsze statuty synodalne krakowskie biskupa Nankera z 2 października 1320r* (Cracow 1915), 24; J. Kopeć, 'Św. Stanisław, biskup krakowski, *Pater Patriae*, w tekstach liturgii średniowiecznej', in *Święty Stanisław w życiu kościoła w Polsce* (Cracow 2003), 183–202, esp. 189.

34. See Wysz's statutes in A. Z. Helcel ed., *Starodawne prawa polskiego pomniki*, 12 vols (Warsaw/Cracow 1856–1921), IV (1875), 58, 120.

35. Formerly Biblioteka Narodowa, Warsaw, MS lat. Q, I, fol. 73. See Miodońska, *Małopolskie malarstwo* (as in n. 10), 110.

36. E. Długopolski, *Władysław Łokietek na tle swoich czasów* (Wrocław 1951), 81.

37. Muskata enrolled at Bologna University in 1278, and his presence is recorded again in Wrocław in 1282. For Muskata's Italian connections, see Długopolski, *Władysław Łokietek* (as in n. 36), 75–76; K. Kuźmak, 'Frangipani', in *Encyklopedia Katolicka* (Lublin 1973 onwards), V (1989), 674.

38. Długopolski, *Władysław Łokietek* (as in n. 36), 79.

39. ibid., 99–105.

40. *Kodeks dyplomatyczny katedry krakowskiej św. Wacława*, ed. F. Piekosiński, 2 vols (Cracow 1874, 1883), I, 137, no. 101; Długopolski, *Władysław Łokietek* (as in n. 36), 78; Gawlas, *Człowiek uwikłany* (as in n. 5), 398.

41. K. Benešovská, 'Das Zisterzienserinnenkloster von Altbrunn und die Persönlichkeit seiner Stifterin', in *Cystersi w Kulturze Średniowiecznej Europy*, ed. J. Strzelczyk (Poznań 1992), 83–100, esp. 84.

42. Z. Piech, 'Święty Stanisław szafarzem korony Królestwa Polskiego. Ze studiów nad średniowieczną sfragistyką miasta Krakowa', in *Rocznik Krakowski*, 57 (1991), 5–16, esp. 14–15.

43. 50 mm in diameter.

44. A. Chmiel, 'Pieczęcie miasta Krakowa, Kazimierza, Kleparza i jurydyk krakowskich do końca XVIII wieku', *Rocznik Krakowski*, 9 (1909), 79–99; Kliś, 'Czy istnieje zależność' (as in n. 28), 199–200.

45. Piech, 'Święty Stanisław' (as in n. 42), 6.

46. 53 mm in diameter, attached to a document of 1382 (in the Cistercian monastery of Mogiła); see M. Gumowski, *Najstarsze pieczęcie miast polskich XIII i XIVw.* (Toruń 1960), 123.

47. *Vita Sancti Stanislai Cracoviensis Episcopi (Vita maior)*, ed. W. Kętrzyński, in *Monumenta Poloniae Historica* (as in n. 9), IV (1884), 319–438.

48. The crown and eagle were first employed as the 'signs of victory' (*vitricia signa*) on the majestic seal of Przemysł II. The inscription reads: '*REDDIDIT IPSE P[OTENS V]ICTRICIA SIGNA POLONIS*'; see Piech, 'Święty Stanisław' (as in n. 42), 12–13.

49. Piech, 'Święty Stanisław' (as in n. 42), 13.

50. See M. Koczerska, *Zbigniew Oleśnicki i kościół krakowski w czasach jego pontyfikatu* (Warsaw 2004), 162.

51. B. Wyrozumska, 'Sądownictwo miejskie w dawnym Krakowie', *Rocznik Krakowski*, 67 (2001), 5–11, esp. 5, 7–8; Z. Noga, *Krakowska Rada miejska w XVI wieku: Studium o elicie władzy* (Cracow 2003), 38.

52. We can surmise that Łokietek held this office because his chancery took over the income of the *advocatus*; see J. Wyrozumski, *Dzieje Krakowa, I: Kraków do schyłku wieków średnich* (Cracow 1992), 137.

53. Piech ('Święty Stanisław' (as in n. 42), 13) suggested that the royal chancery influenced the design of the seal, but failed to explain the full implications of this observation.

54. Piech, 'Święty Stanisław' (as in n. 42), 12–13.

55. St Stanislas, as the patron of all Polish prelates, would have been perceived as the superior executor of God's command, as is made manifest in the Polish coronation ordinal. In the coronation allocution the presiding archbishop, while placing the crown on the king's head, announces that divine will entrusts the church and the kingdom to the anointed monarch through the act of blessing performed by the priest: '. . . tu quoque in exterioribus verus Dei cultor strenuusque contra omnes adversitates ecclesiae Christi defensor regnique tibi a Deo dati et per offitium nostrae benedictionis . . .' (' . . . in external matters you [will be] a true worshipper of God, and an active defender of the church of Christ against all adversities, and of the kingdom given to you by God and through the service of our blessing . . .'). See W. Sawicki, 'Rytuał sakry — koronacji jako źródło prawa i ustroju państw średniowiecznej Europy', *Archiwa Biblioteki i Muzea Kościelne*, 24 (1972), 279–93. This ordinal was used in the coronation of Wladislas Warneńczyk in 1434, but all the allocutions and blessings are identical with the 10th-century German ordinal, which was probably used at the coronation of Boleslav the Bold in 1025, and we can surmise that they were used in Polish coronations throughout the Middle Ages.

Arbor vitae and Corpus Christi:
An Example of Chasuble Iconography
from Late-Medieval Central Europe
in the Context of the Mass

EVELIN WETTER

From the middle of the 14th century, a specific chasuble iconography emerged in Central Europe: the Eucharistic interpretation of the Holy Cross as the Tree of Life, with a beautifully drawn body of the crucified Christ and Mary Magdalene imploringly embracing the foot of the cross. Firstly, this article attempts to draw together the various pieces of evidence for this iconography in museums and the original circumstances of their transmission. Some of the earliest examples appear to have been made in Bohemia. Secondly, therefore, these images will be interpreted in connection with contemporary local hymns and prayers. A key to understanding this iconography and its stylistic transformation into the so-called Beautiful Style may be an edition and commentary on the writings of St Bridget of Sweden that rapidly found a receptive readership in the spiritual environment of late-medieval Bohemia; here adoration of the beautifully rendered Christ was always associated with adoration of the host, the Corpus Christi. *Reading the influential* Rationale divinorum officiorum *of Durandus, bishop of Mende, this chasuble iconography further seems to play an important role in a visual spectacle that takes place during the celebration of the Eucharist. The theological concept of the crucified Christ as* Corpus Christi *was expressed in different media and could be thus perceived through various senses. Within this conceptual, semiotic framework, and judging by the quality of its signs, the iconography described here has to be understood as an integral part of the entire liturgy.*

IN her analysis of the embroidery on the chasuble in Rokycany, Leonie von Wilckens pointed out the existence of a distinctively Bohemian chasuble iconography that developed alongside a strong devotion to the Virgin Mary.[1] These concomitant developments were founded in both religious practice and political circumstances, as is evident from the accumulation of images in various iconographic forms honouring the Virgin considered in conjunction with the hymns found in contemporary sources and sung in the new liturgical foundations of Charles IV.[2] It is therefore not surprising that similar iconographic programmes appear on the copes that were the overgarments of the *cantores* who sang these hymns.[3] The siting of Marian-centred iconography on liturgical vestments in this context was not so much intended to denote the *cantores* as an embodiment of the heavenly choirs, but to stand for a more general *laudatio* to the Virgin; the impression made by the liturgy was enhanced by the plurality of senses through which it was perceived, in this case sight and hearing.

In the Middle Ages, the iconography of liturgical vestments was strategically integrated into a wider system determined by various traditions of theological thought and adapted to liturgical frameworks. It is barely possible for us today to comprehend the system in its entirety, let alone describe the *modi operandi* of its various parts. One problem is that the appearance of most objects available as primary sources has been corrupted by various factors, including whether they are considered from their manufacture to be works of art or craft products. One also needs to consider the confessional traditions in the context of which liturgical vestments have survived. Analysis of a specific iconography of a liturgical vestment in the context of the mass should therefore only be undertaken with a carefully nuanced understanding of the sources; secondary sources describing the use of a specific vestment in specific liturgical contexts are rather rare. The only way out of this impasse is perhaps a series of case studies taken from a broad range of objects, but concentrating on one type of iconography.

From a survey of the extant material and the diverse circumstances in which objects survive[4] there emerges a further type of chasuble iconography that may have its roots in Central European religious life. This iconography centres on the simultaneous interpretation of the Holy Cross as the *Arbor vitae* and of the crucified Christ as the *Corpus Christi*, the Eucharistic host. In this article I would first like to set out the Bohemian chasubles proposed as prototypes for this iconography, and to discuss how they developed in relation to manufacturing methods found within the corpus of chasuble orphreys. The evident success of the *Arbor vitae-Corpus Christi* iconography encourages us to explore its theological and liturgical basis. By looking at an embroidery not only as an image, but as an orphrey on a vestment intended for a specific liturgical function and integrated into a religious spectacle that adopts various strategems, we are able to achieve a broader understanding founded in the semiotics of this nexus of signs.

CHASUBLE CROSSES WITH EUCHARISTIC *ARBOR VITAE* ICONOGRAPHY

AN initial systematic (albeit not exhaustive) survey of the extant material reveals the following picture. The oldest embroidery with a Eucharistic *Arbor vitae* iconography, featuring the Virgin and St John, seems to be an orphrey on the chasuble from Břevnov Monastery near Prague (*c.* 1380, Fig. 1).[5] A Y-shaped shaped *praetexta*, it shows in its centre the crucified Christ, the blood of whose side wound is collected by an angel, whilst another heavenly creature holds a censor. The Virgin, fainting with grief and supported by St John, stands beneath the cross alongside another woman; Mary Magdalene embraces the cross imploringly in the background. The ends of the arms of the cross show Mark, Matthew and Luke seated, each facing the creature described in the Apocalypse and traditionally taken as the symbol of that Evangelist; these are the witnesses of Christ's life and Passion. The cross itself is depicted as an *Astkreuz*, reflecting the wood's origin in the Tree of Life from the Garden of Eden.[6] The embroidery was applied to the red velvet of the present chasuble only in the 17th century.[7]

Chasubles with this kind of iconography are comparatively well preserved in Central Europe, and their *pretextae* are further testimony to a type of cross also found on altarpieces and in metalwork.[8] Among extant orphreys one should note the

F<small>IG</small>. 1.   Chasuble from Břevnov: the orphrey, Prague, *c.* 1380, with later changes
(Benediktinské Arciopactví sv. Vojtěcha a sv. Markéty v Praze-Břevnov, 52.901)
Uměleckoprůmyslové muzeum v Praze

pearl-embroidered cross in St. Marienstern (Upper Lusatia), which was reformed after 1710 (Fig. 2 & Col. Pl. VIIʙ in print edn).[9] With its leaves blossoming from the trunk the Marienstern cross symbolises the *Arbor vitae* even more vividly than other examples, and hence the triumph over death through the sacrifice of Christ. Other objects making the same allusion draw on the *Physiologos*, for example the Pelican in her Piety, as seen on the chasubles of Görlitz (Fig. 5 & Col. Pl. VIIA in print edn) and Brno,[10] or the eagle used as a symbol of the Lord's Ascension, seen on a chasuble in the Victoria & Albert Museum in London.[11] All of these chasubles were produced in the 17th or 18th centuries. Their provenance, present location, and the specific way in which they were cut indicate that this iconography was transmitted through the Catholic circles; only the Görlitz chasuble comes from a Lutheran context (a parish church).

As far as embroidered orphreys alone are concerned, there exists a larger group of items from the early 15th century with iconographically appropriate depictions of the prophets on the arms of the cross. To this group belong two Crucifixions, one in Detroit (Fig. 3), the other in Regensburg,[12] both attached to later chasubles;[13] a fragment in the Magyar Nemzeti Múzeum (Hungarian National Museum) in Budapest;[14] and an orphrey still applied to a medieval chasuble in the treasury of Brandenburg Cathedral (Fig. 8).[15]

FIG. 2. Chasuble in St. Marienstern (Upper Lusatia): the orphrey Bohemia(?), end of the 14th century, with later changes (St. Marienstern, Zisterzienserinnenabtei)

János Steckovics, Halle

Another example in the Hungarian National Museum, which was attached to a blue chasuble in the 17th century, shows an iconographical variant of the *Arbor vitae* cross in the form of the *Crux florida*, that is a blossoming cross, sprouting out leaves and sometimes also flowers.[16] Similar to this example are a cross in the textile treasury in Braşov (Transylvania),[17] and another in the collection of the Abegg-Stiftung in Riggisberg (Switzerland, Fig. 4 & Col. Pl. VIIc in print edn).[18] Both these orphreys present an intensified image of the *Arbor vitae* iconography with acanthus-like leaves spreading vividly over golden backgrounds. Although the provenance and therefore also the manufacture of all of these items can be located in Central Europe, they differ in technique, suggesting that they are the products of different workshops. It would seem that an iconographical canon for chasuble orphreys had become established by this time.

A comparison between the Břevnov and Görlitz orphreys (Fig. 1 with Fig. 5 & Col. Pl. VIIa in print edn) shows that this iconography was not only informed by the

FIG. 3. Orphrey, German, early 15th century (The Detroit Institute of Arts, Founders Society Purchase with funds from Mr and Mrs Leslie H. Green)

The Detroit Institute of Arts

FIG. 4. Orphrey, eastern Central Europe, second quarter of the 15th century (Riggisberg, Abegg-Stiftung)

Abegg-Stiftung, CH 3132 Riggisberg (Christoph von Viràg)

FIG. 5.   Chasuble from St Peter's Church in Görlitz:
the orphrey Prague, *c.* 1380 (Görlitz, Kunst- und
Kulturhistorisches Museum)
Friedemann Raatz, Leipzig

donor's wishes or even the designer's inventiveness, but was also the result of certain workshop practices. Although the legs of Christ on the Břevnov piece appear to be a little stiff, the shape of his body and even the drapery of his loin cloth seem to be identical to those seen in the Görlitz ensemble. We may therefore assume that they share the same model (or even pattern); the crucified Christ on the Detroit chasuble (Fig. 3) can also be traced back to the same model.

The same observation can be made regarding the figure of Mary Magdalene, who is shown kneeling on the ground and embracing the cross. Always seen in three-quarter or full profile, she is part of a canonical scene that was ultimately re-used in other forms, such as the Magdalene praying by herself on the embroidery in the Abegg-Stiftung (Fig. 4 & Col. Pl. VIIc in print edn), where there was clearly a strong desire to give prominence to the figure of the Magdalene. Since we do not find an identical shape in any of the extant examples, the common practice of copying by way of tracing can be excluded here.[19] One should also consider the earlier iconographic tradition of this motif. The first surviving representation of Mary Magdalene in Central European painting is in the Kaufmann Crucifixion in the Berlin Gemäldegalerie. The figure of her here is an adaptation of a pictorial invention by Giotto in the Arena Chapel, where her tears drop onto Christ's feet.[20] A characteristic of the northern European version of Giotto's iconography is her white veil, which is pushed far back in recognition of the moving nature of the event depicted. Although this detail is found more rarely in Bohemian panel painting than in Austrian,[21] it belongs to the same pictorial tradition, as is shown by the iconography of liturgical vestments from Bohemia discussed here and the objects clearly influenced by them (Figs 1, 3–5, 8, & Col. Pls VIIA, c in print edn).

The issue of invention falls outside the scope of this article; instead I will next focus on the circumstances that led to the creation of this iconography in the late 14th and early 15th centuries.

IMAGES OF THE PASSION AND THE EUCHARIST IN HYMNS, PRAYERS AND VISION LITERATURE

SOME details of the Crucifixion iconography discussed above may be related to contemporary hymns and prayers. Christian of Lilienfeld, a follower of Konrad of Hainburg, wrote the following verses in his 'De sancta cruce': 'Ave semper florida, O crux pretiosa, / Tua virtus vivida Atque gratiosa . . . Ave restitutio, O crux, sanitatis / Que evacuatio Es infirmitatis . . . Ave, meum gaudium, O crux, dulce lignum, / Ornata per filium Virginis benignum . . .' ('Hail, oh ever-flowering and precious cross, / yours is the power of life and grace . . . Hail, oh cross, who restore us to health and free us from sickness . . . Hail my joy, oh cross, sweet wood, / beautified by the fruitful son of the Virgin . . .').[22] Just as the well-known hymn 'Ave vivens hostia'[23] praises the real presence of Christ in the Eucharist, a Bohemian manuscript also contains the line: 'Corpus, quod penderat, / In cruce dum aruerat, Nunc stat in altari / Deitate parili / Debet adorari, / Singultibus ac vocibus Prae omnibus laudari' (perhaps 'The body that hung on the cross until it had withered now stands on the altar, like unto God. It should be adored with weeping and praised with prayers(?) above all other things').[24] The same mystical identification of the host with the real presence is found throughout the hymns by the influential Prague archbishop, Jan of Jenstein (d. 1400): 'O sacrata hostia, panis angelorum . . . Caro Christi mystica, salus miserorum' ('Oh consecrated host, bread of angels . . . mystical flesh of Christ, salvation of the wretched').[25] That thought is expressed pictorially on a small parchment sheet of *c.* 1390, where a Man of Sorrows with his blood dripping into a chalice is represented together with the host.[26] A kneeling monk with an inscription roll pleads 'Misere(re) mei s(an)c(t)us s(an)c(t)or(um) [?]' ('Have pity on me, holy of holies'). As an expression of private devotion to the *Corpus Christi*, the parchment could have been used as it is preserved, as a single devotional image.

In this context an examination of the closely related vision literature and prayers ascribed to St Bridget of Sweden (1303–73), which were influential in the whole of late-medieval Europe, may also be helpful.[27] Firstly, there is Bridget's vision of Christ's birth — set in a cave with the Child placed on the ground, surrounded by golden rays and adored by the kneeling Virgin — which was expressed in the now familiar iconographic form immediately after it was penned.[28] In addition to the vision of Christ's birth, there is also the 'Revelation concerning Christ's Suffering and Death'.[29] Against the religio-historical background of the so-called *devotio moderna*,[30] it seems only logical that St Bridget's writings were soon edited and discussed in Bohemia.[31] The verses on the Passion (often wrongly attributed to St Bridget) that follow the text of her *Revelationes*,[32] allude to those bittersweet lamentations that — in the iconographic context of chasuble embroideries discussed here — could have been uttered by the Virgin and especially by Mary Magdalene.[33] Exclamations honouring the holy body such as 'O, dobrý Ježíši, světlosti věčná, Chlebe věčného života!' ('Oh, good Jesus, eternal light, bread of eternal life'),[34] explore not only the real presence in the host, but also the beauty of the crucified Christ ('O, najkrasší, milý Ihesu Criste!', 'Oh, you most beautiful, dear Jesus Christ!').[35] Here Passion piety is manifested in Eucharistic piety.[36]

Furthermore, the beauty of Christ's body mentioned explicitly in writings on the Passion of Christ provides an explanation for the appearance of the beautiful, sensitively drawn body of Christ on (for instance) the Görlitz chasuble (Fig. 5 & Col. Pl. VIIA in print edn). The smooth linearity of his loin-cloth may result from the skills of the draftsman and embroiderer, though it should not be explained away entirely as a manifestation of the prevalent stylistic idiom known as the Beautiful Style.[37] If the connotations of the real presence and beauty of the *Corpus Christi* are intentional, this may reflect rather theological (or at least religio-historical) concerns, as is also found in other media.[38]

A similar phenomenon is evident in representations of the Pietà of this period, which are based on comparable theological concepts. The Magdeburg Pietà, for example, was even commissioned for an altar dedicated to the *Corpus Christi*.[39] A direct parallel to the beautiful crucified Christ adored by Mary Magdalene, and to the Eucharistic Man of Sorrows, is found in the Crucifixion miniature of the Hasenburg Missal (1409–10) in Vienna's Österreichische Nationalbibliothek (Cod. 1844, fol. 149v, Fig. 6), as well as in a wall-painting of the today Lutheran parish church in Sibiu (Translyvania). Here the Man of Sorrows appears behind a grill, an evocation of the host in a sacrament house. An allusion to the Crucified as the host is also given by the angels in the Riggisberg Crucifixion (Fig. 4 & Col. Pl. VIIc in print edn), who

FIG. 6.   Missal of Sbinko of Hasenburg: fol. 149v, Crucifixion miniature, Prague, 1409–10 (Vienna, Österreichische Nationalbibliothek, Cod. 1844)
ÖNB Vienna

bring to mind the presenting, adoring or ascending angels that feature in the pictorial programmes of monstrances.

CHASUBLE ICONOGRAPHY AND THE *MISE EN SCÈNE* OF THE *MYSTERIUM FIDEI*

AT this point we should also consider the original function of the chasuble, the priestly garment worn during the celebration of the Eucharist, that has often been interpreted allegorically by the church fathers and other liturgists. Anton von Euw, and the Jesuit Joseph Braun before him, clearly defined two possible mystical interpretations of liturgical garments: a moral one (in which the garments are associated with the priest's qualities and virtues), and a typological one (which focuses on Christ, the great sacrificing priest, as whose image and representative the celebrant would have been seen).[40] This interpretation of the chasuble as the garment of the priest, and therefore of Christ's representative during celebration of the Eucharist, can be traced in various textual sources, and is typical of the dogma expounded in relation to Christ. It is astonishing that the Lord's sufferings and his sacrifice on the cross are not the focus of attention in these interpretations; only William Durandus, bishop of Mende (1230/31–96), viewed the garments as representations of the dogma of the Saviour's suffering, perhaps in an attempt to initiate believers further into the meaning of the holy mass.[41]

With its sumptuous illustration, realised over generations, the translation of Durandus's *Rationale divinorum officiorum* from Latin into German, begun in 1385 by the Habsburg Duke Albrecht III, almost appears to have been undertaken in competition with the translation and illumination of King Wenceslas IV's German Bible (Vienna, Österreichische Nationalbibliothek, Cod. 2759–64; the translation was commissioned by the Prague burgher Martin Rotlev *c.* 1375–80, while the illuminations are usually dated to 1390–95 or the late 1390s). The *Rationale Durandi* may be seen as a manual of liturgy and its allegorical explanation.[42] In the third book the chasuble is interpreted in a moralising and allegorical manner. Worn by the priest, it symbolises the right kind of love: the love of God and of justice.[43] This moralising tendency is reflected in late-medieval prayers said during the robing of the priest.[44] Although liturgical vestments have even been understood as defensive armour — for instance by the Brandenburg canon and *magister scholarum* John Cassel, who began his collected writings of 1413/14 with 'Put on the whole armour of God, that ye may be able to stand against the wiles of the devil' (Eph. VI, 11)[45] — the iconographic programmes on extant chasubles and other liturgical vestments could hardly be interpreted in this way.

In the passage 'Super uerbum mysterium fidei' Durandus focuses on comprehending the mystery of faith through the eye and the ear, as well as through taste.[46] This is reflected in the various constituents of the liturgy of the mass, whose combined effects are appreciated by a range of senses. Durandus's discussion of the dimensions of a medieval sanctuary and its decoration (under the heading 'Ornamenta'),[47] as well as of the broad spectrum of iconography representing the Eucharist, reveals an increasing emphasis on the significance of the Eucharist. Durandus himself realises this, when he writes: 'propter quod in plerisque sacramentariis, inter prefationem et canonem, ymago crucifixi depingitur, ut non solum intellectus littere, uerum etiam aspectus picture, memoriam dominice passionis inspiret' ('On account of this, in many sacramentaries, an image of the Crucifixion is painted between the preface and the canon, so that not only the understanding of the words, but also the appreciation of the picture should inspire the commemoration of the Passion of our Lord').[48] In a system of signs at the centre of which are the sacrament of the Eucharist and appropriate *decorum*, perception through the senses, including that of sight, plays a significant role.[49] It follows that the iconography discussed above, of the crucified Christ (or the *Corpus Christi*) represented together with an *Arbor vitae* cross (symbolising the triumph over death through the sacrifice of God's son), should be located at the centre of this complex system. In this context, the import of a chasuble's pictorial content has to be deduced from a specific function, rather than from a general allegorical reading of its meaning. A later visualisation of Durandus's semiotic concept of a *mise en scène* of the *mysterium fidei* is found in the iconography of the Mass of St Gregory.[50] In its accumulation of pictorial strategies by which the vision (with its concomitant acceptance of the real presence) is represented, the Mass of St Gregory reflects the multi-sensory staging of the mass and the way in which, following Durandus, it affects all the senses (Fig. 7). We have to site the roots of Eucharistic *Arbor vitae* iconography on liturgical vestments within this liturgical performance.

A methodological problem that affects study of the iconographic programmes and allegorical interpretations of vestments in the context of the mass is the fragmentary nature both of the objects in the preserved corpus and of the sources that contextualise the specific functions of these garments; these include codices that contain instructions (such as *missalia*, *pontificalia* and general *ordinaria*),[51] and also inventories (which in some cases provide evidence for the functions of certain items). We are fortunate in having the textile treasury at Brandenburg Cathedral, where a red chasuble with an embroidered cross depicting the *Arbor vitae* (Fig. 8) has been preserved and can be considered in the light of evidence from local inventories within a context where many vestments have survived. Whereas all the original chasubles to which all the orphreys discussed here originally belonged have not survived, the Brandenburg chasuble, made from re-used red velvet, is largely original, dating from the early 15th century. It was undoubtedly worn during mass when the liturgical colour red was required,[52] but we can further assume that it would have been used during the Good Friday liturgy, as described in the Brandenburg missal, dated 1421.[53] Although closely connected to the sacrifice of Christ, this liturgy does not include celebration of the Eucharist. However, a manuscript offers a lively picture of how this iconography may have constituted an integral part of the performative liturgical act.

According to the manuscript, in the Staatsbibliothek in Berlin, the main service in the morning opened with a procession of the celebrant and his assistants, all clothed in black, into the undecorated cathedral. During the sermon on the Passion two small *vela* (veils), hanging on the main altar, were removed to recall the division of Christ's undergarment; after intercessions two priests in red chasubles sang the *improperia* (reproaches) and were answered by other singers and the choir. In the meantime, the sacristan spread carpets on the spot where the cross would be venerated. Three deacons, barefoot and in black chasubles, then carried in the cross, which was veiled with a red chasuble. While 'Hagios ho theos' or 'Sanctus deus' ('Holy is God') was sung, the red chasuble was removed; 'Ecce lignum crucis' ('Behold the wood of the cross') was then sung by the two priests and the provost. After the provost had positioned the cross on its prescribed place, everyone, including the congregation, approached the cross to venerate it by prostrating themselves before it and kissing it, while the choir sang hymns such as 'Crux fidelis'.[54]

FIG. 7. Mass of St Gregory on the altarpiece of the Corpus Christi Fraternity, ascribed to
Henning van der Heide and Wilm Dedeke, 1495–97 (Lübeck, St. Annen-Museum)

Museen für Kunst und Kulturgeschichte der Hansestadt Lübeck

FIG. 8. Chasuble in Brandenburg
Cathedral, *c.* 1415–30 (Brandenburg,
Dommuseum)

Hans Uwe Salge, Brandenburg

The veiling of the cross, perhaps with the chasuble illustrated here, belongs to a
tradition dominated by the thinking of Durandus on the concealing and therefore
transformative qualities of *vela*. These imply 'the conscious guidance from the visible
to the invisible' ('die bewußte Führung vom Sichtbaren zum Unsichtbaren'),[55] the *mise
en scène* of the *mysterium fidei*.[56] The latter may be said to be the function of Lenten
hangings, and may also explain the iconography of the Brandenburg chasuble. On
the one hand, the crowned King David above represents an ancestor of Mary and
therefore also of Christ, connecting the Old and the New Testament typologically.
On the other hand, Jonah and Jesse on the arms of the cross, identifiable by their
appearance and by the traces of inscriptions bearing their names, foretold with their
prophecies Christ's suffering as well as his triumph over death through sacrifice, as
shown by the branch-shaped cross — that is, the *Arbor vitae*.

CONCLUSION

TO summarise the various arguments regarding the interpretation of chasuble iconography presented here, bearing in mind the caveats of the objects' state of preservation
and the paucity of sources, the following points might be stressed. Firstly, it seems
very important to take into account the possibility of changes made to the extant
material subsequent to its manufacture. Of the items discussed here, only the
Brandenburg chasuble has kept its original appearance; all other objects are strictly
speaking constructions of the last four centuries, either belonging to Protestant
parishes, Catholic churches, or museum collections. Secondly, an interpretation of the
Arbor vitae iconography based on an allegorical writings about the various vestments
by Durandus and others is rather difficult, especially because of their moralising
tendency. When combined with the figure of the lamenting Magdalene, the *Arbor*

vitae can be said to constitute a general *memoria passionis*, and the beautiful figure of Christ to be a manifestation of Eucharistic piety.[57] Worn by the celebrant and therefore located right at the heart of the celebration of the Eucharist, the chasuble with *Arbor vitae* iconography has to be considered — in all its ramifications — as an integral and semiotic part of the staging of the liturgy.

NOTES

1. Rokycany, Řimskokatolická farnost (Roman Catholic parish, ZPČG 214, VO 661/2000). L. v. Wilckens, 'Ein Kaselkreuz in Rokycany. Hinweise zur böhmischen Marienverehrung unter Karl IV. und den ersten Prager Erzbischöfen', *Anzeiger des Germanischen Nationalmuseums* (1964), 33–51. On the style and dating, see B. Drake Boehm and J. Fajt ed., *Prague, the Crown of Bohemia, 1347–1437*, exhibition catalogue (New Haven/London 2005), 173, cat. no. 40 (entry by R. Suckale and J. Fajt).

2. See, for instance, *Conradus Gemnicensis: Konrads von Haimburg und seiner Nachahmer, Alberts von Prag und Ulrichs von Wessobrun Reimgebete und Leselieder*, ed. G. M. Dreves, Analecta Hymnica Medii Aevi, III (Leipzig 1888, reprinted New York/London 1961), 21–44, nos. 1–11. For considerations of panel painting, see also R. Suckale, 'Die Glatzer Madonnentafel des Prager Erzbischofs Ernst als gemalter Marienhymnus. Zur Frühzeit der böhmischen Tafelmalerei mit einem Beitrag zur Einordnung der Kaufmannschen Kreuzigung', *Wiener Jahrbuch für Kunstgeschichte*, 46/47 (1993/94), 737–56; and J. Royt, 'Die ikonologische Interpretation der Glatzer Madonnentafel', *Umění*, 46 (1998), 51–60.

3. E. Wetter, *Böhmische Bildstickerei um 1400: Die Stiftungen in Trient, Brandenburg und Danzig* (Berlin 2001), 69–73 and 100–01.

4. Apart from some objects that came into museum collections through the art market in the 19th and 20th centuries, which are not part of the discussion here, there are the great treasuries of later Lutheran churches; see W. Mannowsky, *Der Danziger Paramentenschatz: Kirchliche Gewänder und Stickereien der Danziger Marienkirche*, 5 vols (Berlin/Leipzig 1931–38); *Liturgische Gewänder und andere Paramente im Dom zu Brandenburg*, ed. H. Reihlen (Brandenburg/Riggisberg 2005); and E. Wetter, 'Der Kronstädter Paramentenschatz. Altkirchliche Messgewänder in nachreformatorischer Nutzung. Mit einer Bestandsaufnahme in Zusammenarbeit mit Jana Knejfl-Fajt', *Acta Historiae Artium*, 45 (2004), 257–315. A survey of the textile treasures of Halberstadt Cathedral is to be published by Barbara Pregla; until then, see J. Flemming, E. Lehmann and E. Schubert, *Dom und Domschatz zu Halberstadt* (Vienna/Cologne 1972); and *Kostbarkeiten aus dem Domschatz zu Halberstadt* (Halle 2001). On the Stralsund treasure, see J. v. Fircks, *Liturgische Gewänder des Mittelalters aus St. Nikolai in Stralsund* (Riggisberg 2008). See further L. v. Wilckens, *Die mittelalterlichen Textilien: Katalog der Sammlung im Herzog Anton Ulrich Museum, erweitert um Textilanalysen von Eva Jordan Fahrbach* (Braunschweig 1994); A. Branting and A. Lindblom, *Medeltida vävnader och Broderier i Sverige*, 2 vols (Uppsala/Stockholm 1928); and A. Geijer, *Textile Treasures of Uppsala Cathedral from Eight Centuries* (Stockholm/Göteborg/Uppsala 1964).

5. Prague, Benediktinské Arciopactví sv. Vojtěcha a sv. Markéty v Praze Břevnov (Benedictine archabbey of Sts Adalbert and Margaret in Prague, Brevnov), inv. no. 52.901. This is the only extant rear of a chasuble (106 cm x 60 cm). On the front side there was once the embroidered *clypeus* (c. 1500) of a cope, which was removed during restoration (1964–71). For further references, see J. Fajt, M. Hörsch and A. Langer ed., *Karl IV. Kaiser von Gottes Gnaden: Kunst und Repräsentation des Hauses Luxemburg 1310–1347* (Munich 2006), 134–35, cat. no. 37 (entry by E. Wetter); the measurements recorded there are unfortunately incorrect. A predecessor to this iconography, still without Mary Magdalene, can be found in *opus anglicanum* in the chasuble from the Melk, today Vienna, Österreichisches Museum für angewandte Kunst (inv. No. T 8724–1–1935); see A. G. I. Christie, *English Medieval Embroidery* (Oxford 1938), 130–33.

6. For an account of the whole tradition, see G. Schiller, *Ikonographie der christlichen Kunst*, 5 vols (Gütersloh 1966–91), II (1968), 145, and P. Binski, *Becket's Crown: Art and Imagination in Gothic England 1170–1300* (New Haven/London 2004), 209–18.

7. To fit the smaller measurements of the garment the embroidery had to be shortened. This necessitated replacing the separately worked figures beneath the cross. As a result, the gilded silver sheets with garnets and pearls forming the haloes and the embroidered *titulus* also had to be replaced. The nimbus of the woman on the left today has a pure linen ground with traces of stitching from the former pearl embroidery; the nimbus of Mary Magdalene was covered with gold thread at a later date. The haloes mark the original position of the group. There is also a 5-mm-wide leather strip covered with gold thread under the later green silk weaving. On the development of chasuble forms, see J. Braun, *Die liturgische Gewandung in Occident und Orient nach Ursprung und Entwicklung, Verwendung und Symbolik* (Freiburg im Breisgau 1907),

184–97; and K. Stolleis, *Messgewänder aus deutschen Kirchenschätzen vom Mittelalter bis zur Gegenwart: Geschichte, Form und Material* (Regensburg 2001).

8. For instance, the upper part of the Holy Cross retable in the Cistercian church at Bad Doberan; see A. Laabs, *Malerei und Plastik im Zisterzienserorden* (Petersberg 2000), 62–74. An example of metalwork is the gold reliquary cross from Çisnadie, now in the Museul Brukenthal, Sibiu (inv. no. T 29/4749); see I. Takács, Zs. Jékely, Sz. Papp and G. Poszler ed., *Sigismundus, Rex et Imperator: Kunst und Kultur zur Zeit Sigismunds von Luxemburg 1387–1437*, exhibition catalogue (Budapest 2006), 644–46, cat. no. 7.90 (entry by E. Wetter).

9. J. Oexle, M. Bauer and M. Winzeler ed., *Zeit und Ewigkeit: 128 Tage in St. Marienstern*, exhibition catalogue (Halle an der Saale 1998), 186–87, cat. no. 2.127 (entry by E. Wetter).

10. The chasuble from St Peter and Paul in Brno is today in the Moravská galerie there (inv. no. 27 414); see Drake Boehm and Fajt ed., *The Crown of Bohemia* (as in n. 1), 277–79, cat. no. 119 (entry by P. Barnet, with references to previous literature). The chasuble from Görlitz is today in the Kunst- und Kulturhistorisches Museum there (inv. no. 14–61); see A. Kutal, 'Česká kazule ve Zhořelci', *Časopis společnosti přátel starožitností*, 60 (1952), 163–72.

11. Victoria & Albert Museum (inv. no. 1375–1864). The chasuble was acquired in 1864 from Franz Bock; see Wetter, *Böhmische Bildstickerei* (as in n. 3), passim, and esp. 118–19; and P. Johnstone, *High Fashion in the Church: The Place of Church Vestments in the History of Art from the Ninth to the Nineteenth Century* (Leeds 2002), 57.

12. Detroit, Institute of Arts (inv. no. 46.1); see P. Barnet, *Clothed in Majesty: European Ecclesiastical Textiles from the Detroit Institute of Arts* (Detroit 1991), 18–19, cat. no. 4.

13. A. Hubel, *Der Regensburger Domschatz* (Munich/Zurich 1976), 244–45, cat. no. 117.

14. Budapest, Magyar Nemzeti Múzeum (inv. no. 53.164); see Takács et al. ed., *Sigismundus* (as in n. 8), 635, cat. no. 7.78 (entry by E. Wetter).

15. Dommuseum (inv. no. C 10); see *Liturgische Gewänder* (as in n. 4), 200–03, cat. no. 14 (entry by C.-M. Jeitner and E. Wetter).

16. Budapest, Magyar Nemzeti Múzeum (inv. no. 53.143); see Takács et al. ed., *Sigismundus* (as in n. 8), 634–35, cat. no. 7.77 (entry by E. Wetter and E. Sipos). See also Schiller, *Ikonographie* (as in n. 6), II, 147.

17. Evangelische Honterusgemeinde (inv. no. 342); see Wetter, 'Der Kronstädter Paramentenschatz' (as in n. 4), 272–73 and 306, cat. no. 12.

18. Riggisberg, Abegg-Stiftung (inv. no. 5); unpublished.

19. See Wetter, *Böhmische Bildstickerei* (as in n. 3), 84 and 95–98; and D. Buran ed., *Gotika: Dejiny slovenského výtvarného umenia*, exhibition catalogue (Bratislava 2003), 807–08, cat. no. 7.6–7.7 (entry by E. Wetter).

20. G. Schmidt, *Malerei der Gotik: Fixpunkte und Ausblicke*, 2 vols (Graz 2005), I, 228–58, esp. 234–35.

21. ibid., 242–47.

22. Munich, Bayerische Staatsbibliothek, Cod. SS. Uldarici et Afrae (Clm. Monac. 4423), fol. 133v, cited after Dreves ed., *Conradus Gemnicensis* (as in n. 2), 174–75. Here the verses are still ascribed to Uldaricus Wessofontanus; see J. Schaber, 'Stöckl, Ulrich', in *Biographisch-Bibliographisches Kirchenlexikon*, ed. F. W. and T. Bautz, 28 vols (Hamm, Herzberg and Nordhausen 1975–2007), X (Nordhausen 1995), cols 1514–16.

23. F. V. Spechtler, 'Ave vivens hostia' (deutsch), in *Die deutsche Literatur des Mittelalters: Verfasserlexikon*, ed. K. Ruh, 2nd edn, 10 vols (Berlin 1977–99), I, cols 571–72.

24. G. M. Dreves ed., *Cantiones Bohemicae: Leiche, Lieder und Rufe des 13., 14. und 15. Jahrhunderts nach Handschriften aus Prag, Jistebnicz, Wittingau, Hohenfurt und Tegernsee*, Analecta Hymnica Medii Aevi, I (Leipzig 1886), 87–98, no. 61.

25. G. M. Dreves ed., *Hymnographi latini: Lateinische Hymnendichter des Mittelalters* (Leipzig 1905), 450 (no. 424) and 431 (no. 401, 'De corpore Christi'). See also M. Luchterhandt, 'Johann II. von Jenstein', in Bantz ed., *Biographisches-Bibliographisches Kirchenlexikon* (as in n. 22), III (1992), cols 159–60.

26. New York, collection of Jonathan J. G. Alexander; published in Fajt et al. ed., *Karl IV. Kaiser von Gottes Gnaden* (as in n. 5), 563–64, cat. no. 202 (entry by B. Drake Boehm).

27. See B. Morris and V. O'Mara, *The Translation of the Works of St. Birgitta of Sweden into Medieval European Vernaculars* (Turnhout 2000).

28. B.-A. Kéry, 'Über die Veränderung der ikonographischen Typen der Geburt Christi in der österreichischen Buchmalerei der internationalen Gotik', in *Internationale Gotik in Mitteleuropa*, ed. G. Pochat and B. Wagner (Graz 1990), 103–13.

29. See, for example, U. Montag, *Das Werk der heiligen Birgitta von Schweden in oberdeutscher Überlieferung: Texte und Untersuchungen* (Munich 1978), 202–11, here 206–08.

30. J. Gierke-Schreiber, 'Die böhmische Devotio moderna', in *Bohemia sacra: Das Christentum in Böhmen 973–1973* (Düsseldorf 1972), 81–91.

31. Thanks to the dissertation by Pavlína Rychterová the history and editions of St Bridget's writings in Bohemia are now easier to follow; see P. Rychterová, *Die Offenbarungen der heiligen Birgitta von Schweden: Eine Untersuchung zur alttschechischen Übersetzung des Thomas von Štítné (um 1330-um 1409)* (Cologne/Weimar/Vienna 2004).

32. Montag, *Das Werk der heiligen Birgitta* (as in n. 29), 25–26; Rychterová, *Die Offenbarungen der heiligen Birgitta* (as in n. 31), 103–10.

33. For the Czech quotations, see Rychterová, *Die Offenbarungen der heiligen Birgitta* (as in n. 31), 103–04, n. 86.

34. ibid., 104, n. 86.

35. ibid., 103, n. 86.

36. Two further groups of chasubles with crosses — one Swedish and one emanating from the monastery of St Bridget in Gdańsk (founded in 1396) — also point to the close connection of this iconography with a Brigittine tradition; see M. Želewska, 'Hafty Gdańskich Brygidek', *Gdańskie Studia muzealne*, 3 (1981), 9–24; Geijer, *Textile Treasures of Uppsala Cathedral* (as in n. 4), 33 (cat. no. 15) and 35 (cat. no. 19).

37. See G. Schmidt, 'The Beautiful Style', in Drake Boehm and Fajt ed., *The Crown of Bohemia* (as in n. 1), 105–11; and G. Pochat and B. Wagner ed., *Internationale Gotik in Mitteleuropa*, Kunsthistorisches Jahrbuch, XXIV (Graz 1990).

38. See also R. Suckale, 'Die Sternberger Schöne Madonna', in *Die Parler und der Schöne Stil 1350–1450: Europäische Kunst unter den Luxemburgern*, ed. Anton Legner, 5 vols (Cologne 1978–81), V, 117–22.

39. M. Deiters, *Kunst im Erzstift Magdeburg: Studien zur Rekonstruktion eines verlorenen Zentrums* (Berlin 2006), 71–74.

40. Braun, *Die liturgische Gewandung* (as in n. 7), 701: '. . . wonach die verschiedenen Bestandteile der liturgischen Kleidung entweder *moralisch* auf die dem Priester nötigen Eigenschaften und Tugenden hinweisen, oder *typisch* auf Christus, den großen Opferpriester, dessen Abbild und Vertreter der zelebrierende Priester ist. Man kann diese letzere Symbolik passend die *dogmatische* nennen, wie sie an das erinnern soll, was der Glaube von Christus lehrt.' ('. . . [whereby] the different constituent parts of liturgical dress can be understood from a *moral* point of view, as indicating those qualities and virtues that are necessary for a priest, or from a *typological* one, indicating Christ the great sacrificing priest, whose image and representative the celebrant priest is. One can appropriately denote this second approach to the symbolism as a *dogmatic* one, in that it is a reminder of what belief in Christ teaches.') See also A. v. Euw, 'Liturgische Handschriften, Gewänder und Geräte', in *Ornamenta Ecclesiae: Kunst und Künstler der Romanik*, ed. A. Legner, exhibition catalogue, 3 vols (Cologne 1985), I, 385–414, esp. 396–402.

41. Braun, *Die liturgische Gewandung* (as in n. 7), 705.

42. Vienna, Österreichische Nationalbibliothek, Cod. 2765; see A. Fingernagel, 'Die Wiener Hofilluminatorenwerkstatt. Prachthandschriften der frühen Habsburger', in *Kunst als Herrschaftsinstrument unter den Luxemburgern: Böhmen und das Heilige Römische Reich im europäischen Kontext*, ed. J. Fajt and A. Langer (Munich/Berlin forthcoming). For the translation, see G. H. Buijssen, *Durandus's Rationale in spätmittelhochdeutscher Übersetzung*, 5 vols (Assen 1974–83).

43. *Guillelmi Duranti Rationale Divinorum Officiorum*, ed. A. Davril and T. M. Thibodeau, 4 vols, Corpus Christianorum, Continuatio Mediaevalis, CXL (Turnhout 1995), III, vii, §§ 1–5 (pp. 195–96). See also Buijssen, *Durandus's Rationale* (as in n. 42), I, 207–10.

44. See also Braun, *Die liturgische Gewandung* (as in n. 7), 718, who underlines this further: 'Allein die Kasel erscheint in den Ankleidegebeten keineswegs ausschließlich als Sinnbild der Liebe wie bei den Liturgikern, sondern auch als Symbol der priesterlichen Gerechtigkeit und Heiligkeit, als Abbild der Gnade des heiligen Geistes, welche der Priester beim Anlegen des Meßgewandes auf sich herabflehte, ja sogar vereinzelt als Panzer des Glaubens und als Helm der Hoffnung.' ('In robing prayers only the chasuble seems in no way to be exclusively a symbol of love, as is found among liturgists, but also a symbol of priestly righteousness and holiness, an image of the grace of the Holy Spirit that the priest brings upon himself while donning his mass vestmests, and even on occasion the armour of faith or the helmet of hope.')

45. Berlin, Staatsbibliothek, Ms. theol. lat. fol. 47, Sammelbuch des Johannes Cassel, fols 253r–263v, here 253r. See also E. Lecheler and E. Wetter, 'Der Paramentenbestand des Domes im Verhältnis zu den Brandenburger Ordinarien des 15. Jahrhunderts', in *Heilige Gewänder - Textile Kunstwerke: Die Gewänder des Doms zu Brandenburg im mittelalterlichen und lutherischen Gottesdienst*, ed. H. Reihlen (Regensburg 2005) 26–41, esp. 26.

46. *Guillelmi Duranti Rationale* (as in n. 43), IV, xlii, § 32 (p. 480).

47. ibid., I, iii, §§ 23–50 (pp. 42–51).

48. ibid., IV, xxxv, § 10 (p. 416).

49. K. Faupel-Drevs, *Vom rechten Gebrauch der Bilder im liturgischen Raum: Mittelalterliche Funktionsbestimmungen bildender Kunst im Rationale Divinorum Officiorum des Durandus von Mende*

(*1230/1–1296*), Studies in the History of Christian Thought, LXXXIX (Leiden/Boston/Cologne 1995), 161–77.

50. See E. Meier, *Die Gregorsmesse: Funktionen eines spätmittelalterlichen Bildtypus* (Cologne/Weimar/ Vienna 2005), 97. See also T. Lentes, 'Verum Corpus und Vera Imago. Kalkulierte Bildbeziehungen in der Gregorsmesse', in *Das Bild der Erscheinung: Die Gregorsmesse im Mittelalter*, ed. A. Gormans and T. Lentes (Berlin 2007), 12–33, esp. 30–33; C. Gärtner, 'Die 'Gregorsmesse' als Bestätigung der Transsubstantiationslehre? Zur Theologie eines Bildsujets', ibid., 124–53; and S. Wegmann, 'Passionsandacht und Messerklärung. Die Verwendung der 'Visio Gregorii' im Buch', ibid., 402–46.

51. On the state of research, see F. Kohlschein and P. Wünsche ed., *Heiliger Raum: Architektur, Kunst und Liturgie in mittelalterlichen Kathedralen und Stiftskirchen* (Münster 1998); A. Odenthal, *Die ORDINATIO CULTIS DIVINI ET CAEREMONIARUM des Halberstädter Domes von 1591: Untersuchungen zur Liturgie eines gemischtkonfessionellen Domkapitels nach der Einführung der Reformation* (Münster 2005).

52. Reihlen ed., *Liturgische Gewänder* (as in n. 4), 200–03, cat. no. 14 (entry by C.-M. Jeitner and E. Wetter).

53. See R. Kroos and F. Kobler, 'Farbe, liturgisch', in *Reallexikon der deutschen Kunstgeschichte*, currently 9 vols (Munich 1937–2003), VII (1981), cols 54–90, esp. 83–86.

54. Berlin, Staatsbibliothek, Ms. theol. lat. 299, fol. 67v–68v; see E. Wetter, 'Zur Funktion der liturgischen Gewänder im Brandenburger Dom anhand der Ordinarien des 15. Jahrhunderts', in *1050 Jahre Domstift Brandenburg: Beiträge zur Geschichte und Kultur* (Brandenburg 1998), 90–97, esp. 93; and E. Lecheler, 'Gottesdienst im mittelalterlichen Brandenburger Dom', in Reihlen ed., *Heilige Gewänder* (as in n. 45), 11–25, esp. 19–20.

55. Faupel-Drevs, *Vom rechten Gebrauch der Bilder* (as in n. 49), 313.

56. ibid., 312–15.

57. B. Neunheuser, *Eucharistie in Mittelalter und Neuzeit* (Freiburg/Basel/Vienna 1963), 11–51; M. Rubin, *Corpus Christi: The Eucharist in Late Medieval Culture* (Cambridge 1991); J. Nowiński, *Ars Eucharistica: Idee, miejsca i formy towarzyszące przechowywaniu eucharistii w sztuce wczesnochrześcijańskiej i średniowiecznej* (Warsaw 2000); E. Wipfler, *"Corpus Christi" in Liturgie und Kunst der Zisterzienser im Mittelalter* (Münster 2003). On sacrament houses and visualising the Eucharist, see A. Timmermann, 'Designing a house for the body of Christ: the beginnings of eucharistic architecture in western and northern Europe, c. 1300', *Arte medievale*, 4 (2005), 119–29.

Some Remarks on the Aristocratic Patronage of Franciscan Observants in Jagiellonian Bohemia

JAN CHLÍBEC

At the beginning of the 1450s, after the gruelling decades of the Hussite Wars, the mission of John Capistran in Moravia and Bohemia had a considerable impact. Capistran's goal was expressly political: eradication of the lingering Hussite ideology and the return of the nation to the fold of the Catholic Church. During the short period of his mission, Capistran managed to invigorate the order of the Franciscan Observants, as is evident from the growth in the number of their monasteries. This building activity was supported by Bohemian Catholic aristocracy, who saw it as an opportunity to fulfil their political ambitions. A typical architectural feature of many Franciscan monasteries at the end of the 15th and the beginning of the 16th centuries was the diamond vault, which stood in contrast to the otherwise austere elevations and exteriors of monastic buildings. There were also rich libraries, wonderful wall-paintings on new themes, and superb tomb sculpture. The aristocracy would have felt that assuming the role of patron within the context of these new artistic trends enhanced their prestige. Among the Observants' monasteries in the province of Bohemia, two enjoyed special status: the monastery in Kadaň in north-west Bohemia, with its church consecrated to the Fourteen Holy Assistants, and that in Bechyně in southern Bohemia, with the church of the Assumption of Our Lady. Both were important cultural centres filled with major works of Late Gothic art commissioned by the founders.

PASSING through Prague in 1591, Fynes Moryson, an English student of law, made some unflattering comments about the architecture of the Bohemian capital. He wrote: 'Prague consists of three towns, each of which is walled, yet it does not seem well fortified. The streets are filthy. There are a few large squares, and some buildings made of brick; most, however, are of wood and clay, built with little charm or skill. The walls are made of whole tree trunks, which look as if they have just been dragged out of the forest. In many places on both sides, one can still see traces of the bark.'[1] I am convinced that, if this gentleman had had the opportunity to visit one of the Bohemian monasteries of the Franciscan Observants' order built in the Jagiellonian period (1471–1526), he would have discovered a beautiful jewel within austere walls and been compelled to write about these structures in glowing terms.

In the wake of the devastating Hussite Wars (1419–34), the religious and political situations in Bohemia were still in a state of chaos. Essentially, two religious groups co-existed there: the Utraquists, who had benefited from the Hussite revolution, and the Catholics.[2] Although the Catholics made up roughly less than a quarter of the population, they strove to regain the political and economic positions they had enjoyed in the Luxembourg era.

The mission of John Capistran (1385–1456), at the beginning of the 1450s, had a considerable impact on the Bohemian political and religious milieu. He was active in 1451–52 in Moravia and outlying areas of Bohemia (for example, in Český Krumlov, Cheb, Most, and according to Václav Hájek of Libočany also in Kadaň), where he preached under the patronage of Pope Nicholas V and Cardinal Piccolomini (later Pope Pius II). Their goal was expressly political: they aimed to eradicate the lingering Hussite ideology and bring the nation back into the fold of the Catholic Church. In the short period that he was active there, Capistran managed to invigorate the order of the Franciscan Observants, as is evidenced by the increased number of their monasteries. This building activity was supported by Bohemian Catholic aristocrats, who saw it as a chance to implement their ambitions for power. They felt that assuming the role of patrons of the new artistic trends manifest in the architecture and interior decoration of the Franciscan monasteries would enhance their prestige. A typical architectural feature of many Franciscan monasteries at the end of the 15th and beginning of the 16th centuries was the diamond vault, which contrasted with the austerity of the monastery buildings. There were also rich libraries (in Bechyně, for example). The monastery churches (Olomouc, Plzeň, Kadaň, Bechyně) were decorated with wonderful wall-paintings on new themes and superb tomb sculpture (Horažďovice, Bechyně, Kadaň). All this indicates that the Franciscan milieu was open to new cultural influences. It was with good reason, therefore, that the Utraquists attacked the Franciscans for betraying the order's original principles of poverty. The eminent Utraquist ideologue Václav Koranda criticised this state of affairs: 'St Francis went barefoot and gathered his meagre fare with his own thin hands: they live in princely monasteries and serve feasts.'[3]

The arrival of John Capistran in Bohemia sparked an intense debate about images, which was prefigured in the Hussite period. Capistran was a fanatical promoter of the cult of the main organiser and reformer of the Franciscan Observants, Bernardino of Siena (d. 1444), who was canonised in 1450, thanks to Capistran's intercession. There was a brisk trade in images of St Bernardino throughout Europe. In Utraquist Prague, however, the cult of his image was vigorously suppressed; one finds depictions of this saint and of his promoter in Bohemian art, but only that produced in Catholic areas. For example St Bernardino appears on the painted frame of the Krumlov Madonna (c. 1450; Hluboká nad Vltavou, Alšova jihočeská galerie), while the wall-painting from the Minorite monastery church in Jindřichův Hradec depicts Capistran preaching. A unique depiction of Capistran alongside St Bernadino was recently uncovered in the Franciscan Observant church in Olomouc. It depicts a historical scene of the defence of Belgrade against the Turks in 1456. John preached before this battle, in which the Turks were defeated (Fig. 1).[4]

In Bohemia and Moravia Capistran's activities were a frequent target of artistic invectives and burlesque allegories. He was depicted hanging by his feet from a tree (sometimes in the company of women and devils) and probably falling into the arms of beautiful women. The comical counterpoint of the dry Franciscan in the company of sensual lewd women provided a welcome artistic revenge for Capistran's constant fanatical attacks on Utraquist Bohemia.[5] Likewise, in the 1460s in Prague and other towns one saw paintings of trees in which naked young women grew instead of fruit. When they were 'ripe', the women fell onto the cloaks that the pope, cardinals, bishops, monks and priests had spread under the trees.[6] These paintings, which

216

FIG. 1.   Olomouc, church of the Franciscan
Observants, presbytery: *The Defence of Belgrade
against the Turks, c.* 1468
Jan Chlíbec

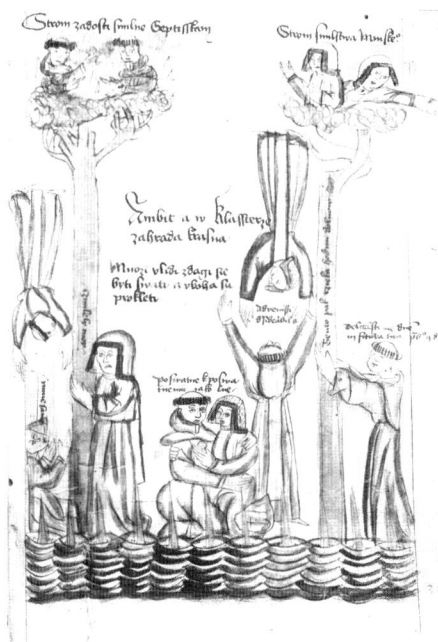

FIG. 2.   Manuscript illumination depicting trees
of fornication, fol. 35r, 1462–65 (Göttingen,
Niedersächsische Staats- und
Universitätsbibliothek, MS theol. 182)
Karel Stejskal

217

burghers probably also had painted on the façades of their houses, performed a specific 'dialogue' with passers-by. This was a popular form of anti-Catholic propaganda, and it appeared in many variations, such as the illumination in the Codex of Göttingen (Göttingen, Niedersächsische Staats- und Universitätsbibliothek, MS theol. 182), which presents two trees of fornication: from one a nun is falling down into the arms of a monk, from another a monk into the arms of a nun (Fig. 2).

Despite the animosity between Capistran and his supporters and the Utraquists, Capistran deliberately and programmatically drew on the ideas of moderate Utraquists, especially those aspects concerning the function of artworks in a sacred milieu. Capistran's rhetorical question, quite in accordance with St Bernardino of Siena — 'Did you always venerate the body of the Lord in church and did you not run straight to the images, venerating them without even praying to Him?'[7] — appears in various versions in the texts of eminent Utraquist ideologues. In this way, the Franciscan Observants were aiming to impress a population that had grown up with Hussite traditions and their concept of life in poverty and simplicity. The Utraquist leaders were, of course, well aware of this danger and thus constantly pointed out the order's betrayal of its original principles, as mentioned above. From the outset, the Franciscan order had a very ambivalent attitude towards art, restricted by the order's traditional requirement of simplicity and poverty. For this reason, the Franciscan general chapter meeting of 1260 held in Narbonne rejected any kind of decorative paintwork or architectural detailing. Architecture was to be simple. Church windows were not supposed to have historical scenes or similar depictions.[8] Likewise, in the late 15th century, there were calls in the chapters of the Observants to restrict the development of manuscript illumination. For example at the meeting of the chapter in Wrocław in 1495, decorative initials were forbidden, as was the use gold and silver. Illuminators were not supposed to embellish manuscripts with ambiguous motifs, animals (such as monkeys, and also birds, including peacocks), or secular scenes. This was, of course, difficult to put into practice, as some monasteries did not respect these regulations.[9]

As far as the decoration of the monasteries was concerned, friars tended to be passive, because the order's rules rejected property and promoted a simple life. In some cases, they may have provided intellectual inspiration for potential patrons; they did not, however, commission work themselves, and therefore had little influence on the decoration of the various spaces within the monastery. By contrast, secular founders and their relatives used their privileged status as an opportunity to have themselves commemorated within the walls of their monasteries. They invested large sums in their foundations, and also in the establishment of family burial sites in monastic churches.

As for architecture, many of the monasteries of the Franciscan Observants in Central Europe from the end of the 15th and the beginning of the 16th centuries had diamond vaults. This type of vault, which originated in the Meissen workshop of Arnold von Westfalen, became popular soon after its invention.[10] Under the influence of the Saxon aristocracy, it spread first to the monasteries of the Franciscan Saxon province, and subsequently to the provinces of Bohemia and Poland. It is not clear to what extent the friars themselves influenced the decision to construct this type of vault in their monasteries, or whether the vaults had some sort of theological interpretation. Although they are a striking and frequent feature of Franciscan interiors and in that sense something of an architectural trademark, thus far no written evidence has emerged to explain their choice or the vault's symbolic significance.

Among the monasteries of the Franciscan Observants' Bohemian province, two enjoyed a special status: the monastery of Kadaň with its church consecrated to the Fourteen Holy Assistants, in north-west Bohemia; and Bechyně with its church of the Assumption of Our Lady, in southern Bohemia. Both were important cultural centres where their founders amassed major works of Late Gothic art, and both can be deemed to have inspired the spread of diamond vaults over the territory of Bohemia (Fig. 3). Since the subject of diamond vaults has been covered extensively by Zoë Opačić recently, the focus here will be on key works of art decorating the churches.

The monastery of Kadaň was founded in 1473 outside the walls of the city (*extra muros*), like all the other foundations of the order (Fig. 4). It was not owned by the order, as this was against its own rules. Instead, the owners were initially King Vladislav Jagiełło and the burghers of Kadaň. In 1481, the king transferred the founder's rights to Jan Hasištejnský of Lobkovice, a diplomat and eminent nobleman of his day. He was the actual builder of the monastery, as is implied by the inscription on his tomb, which refers to him as the 'primus fundator huius monasterii' ('the first founder of this monastery'). Following his wishes, secular rooms and a private chapel serving the needs of his family were constructed in the monastic complex.[11]

FIG. 3.   Kadaň, monastery of the Franciscan Observants: diamond vaults in the hall
Klára Benešovská

FIG. 4.   Kadaň, monastery
of the Franciscan
Observants, 1494–1506
Lukáš Gavenda

A lengthy investigation and restoration of the rooms of the Kadaň Monastery is currently under way, and this work may yield new discoveries and a greater understanding of the semantic context of the monument's decoration. One such that has been gradually uncovered in the church's presbytery is the Crucifixion with Sts Barbara, Catherine and the Virgin Mary, members of the Lobkovice family, and the family castle (Hasištejn) in the background (dated *c.* 1520).

One of the most remarkable monuments in the Kadaň Monastery church is the tomb of Jan Hasištejnský of Lobkovice (d. 1517), which belongs in the category of cadaver or transi tombs (Fig. 5). What was the inspiration behind this type of tomb? The poem 'Man's Discourse with Death', by an anonymous Hussite poet of the 15th century, is permeated by a horror of the plague. In the poem, face to face with a personification of Death, the man says: 'Oh, how unfortunate was the day / when I, wretched, was born. / May the night also be cursed / when my mother conceived me. / [. . .] If only I had vanished in my mother's belly / before I saw the light of the world. / Why did she not kill me there / and make a grave of her belly?'[12] The macabre imagination of these sentiments, which seems surrealist to us, was inspired by a terror of the plague, which was mercilessly mowing down the population of medieval Europe in successive waves. In the plague, death manifested itself in all its horror, it became a part of everyday life. Fear of death, often transformed into a morbid obsession, permeated various artistic spheres directly or indirectly. It had the greatest impact on tomb sculpture and especially on the distinctive type known as the transi tomb, which first appeared in the second half of the 14th century. Transi tombs were also inspired by literary sources, such as the legend of the Three Living and the Three Dead, which is of Arabian origin but frequently found in European manuscripts going back to the 13th century.

As a representation of the decaying human body, the transi appeared after the first waves of the plague in the last decades of the 14th century. With its invention the idealised portrait of the deceased, prevalent until then, was replaced by a depiction of

FIG. 5.   Kadaň, monastery of the Franciscan Observants: tomb of Jan Hasištejnský of Lobkowicz (d. 1517), detail
Jan Chlíbec

FIG. 6.   Kadaň, monastery of the Franciscan Observants: tomb of Jan Hasištejnský of Lobkowicz
Jan Chlíbec

the deceased's body in a whole range of states after death, from being wrapped in a shroud (found mainly in northern France, Burgundy, England and The Netherlands), to the dried-out, bony body (in England), and the skeleton or rotting corpse crawling with snakes, worms and frogs (in Germany, Austria and Bohemia).

Gradually, the composition of the tombs also developed, from the simplest type, in which the representation of the deceased constituted the only element apart from the tomb, to the type such as the tomb of Bishop Bernhard of Polheim (d. 1504) in Wels (Upper Austria) that included a relief of the Crucifixion or Resurrection of Christ (emphasising faith in salvation), to the most interesting, two-storey type. This last type was particularly common in English funerary sculpture, and it was later taken up on the Continent. Its form was based on the contrast between two images of the deceased: the transi — the supine, dead body — in the lower section, and the effigy of the deceased with eyes open, usually in prayer, dressed in clothes befitting his status and office in the upper section. With the creation of this type of tomb, the medieval tomb effigies became more individual. According to Kantorowicz, dual representations of the deceased in the tombs of kings and high church dignitaries had two symbolic functions: the upper section, the living figure, represented eternity and the continuity of the office of the deceased; the lower section, the transi, represented the transient nature of the individual.[13] The transi, the déclassé, humiliated human body in a state of decay, was an expression of repentance, a strange kind of self-flagellation. Through artistic extremes it negated human pride, symbolised humility, and strove to be a means of salvation for the soul of the deceased.

The tomb of Jan Hasištejnský of Lobkovice, a work from the second decade of the 16th century conveying the fleeting nature of the human body in all its extremes, is the only signed work of Ulrich Creutz, a sculptor who was probably in Jan's service for some time (Figs 5, 6). The choice of this type of tomb was an expression of humility, for there was an established tradition in the Hasištejnský family, closely connected with their support of the order of the Franciscan Observants.[14] The marble relief depicts the dead body as a skeleton, partially covered in skin and a twisting strip of cloth. The massive skull rests on a shaped stone, which also symbolises repentance and humility. Two snakes wind around the body. Frogs, lizards and a snake — traditional symbols of transience typical of this type of tomb — are scattered around the bottom edge. The work was most likely part of a semantic unit that included the larger-than-life marble relief of the aristocrat in full majesty holding the family pennant in his hand. The relief bears no inscription, only the date 1516, and is incorporated in the wall of the presbytery, on the main axis of the church and behind the altar. The fact that it was placed in such an important location suggests that Jan is represented as the founder of the monastery church. Observed together the two commemorative works constitute a loose version of the classic, two-storey transi tomb.

The Hasištejnský relief is also important because its 'realistic' individualised features make it the first portrait in Bohemian Late Gothic tomb sculpture. It does not merely present a type, as had been common in Bohemian sepulchral sculpture until that point (Fig. 7 & Col. Pl. IIA in print edn). It is interesting to mention in this context Jan's trip to the Holy Land via Venice in 1493. One has to wonder whether his three-week stay in the city of the lagoons may have had an impact on the decoration of the Kadaň Monastery. Using his notes, Jan wrote a travel book in 1505, a fascinating piece of art-historical topography. His detailed description of the terracotta group *The Lamentation*, made by Guido Mazzoni in 1485–89, serves as a crucial source for the reconstruction of this sculptural work, which survives today in a fragmentary state (originally in S. Antonio di Castello in Venice, now in the Museo Civico in Padua, Fig. 8).[15] In my opinion, the unflattering, realistic depiction of Jan's wrinkled face (a realism so strong that it created a mistaken impression that his eyes

FIG. 7.   Kadaň, monastery of the Franciscan
Observants: presbytery wall relief of Jan
Hasištejnský of Lobkowicz, 1516
Jan Chlíbec

FIG. 8.   Guido Mazzoni,
The Lamentation, 1485–89
(Museo Civico, Padova)
Collection of the author

are made of glass),[16] which is essentially the first Renaissance portrait in
Bohemian sculpture of the Jagiellonian period, was influenced by Jan's recollections
of Mazzoni's expressive group. Mazzoni, who was from Modena, often incorporated
crypto-portraits of donors in his Lamentation sculptures. These portraits were based
on casts of their faces, made while they were still alive; the realistic stone portrait of
Jan Hasištejnský is similar. He may have seen other examples of distinct, individual
sculptural portraits in Venice, although he did not mention them specifically. These
could have also included works from the circle of Antonio Rizzo, such as the marble

FIG. 9.   Bechyně, monastery of the Franciscan Observants: nave of the church
with diamond vaults, 1491–1513

Klára Benešovská

bust of Lorenzo Giustiniani, from around 1460, located in the Venetian church of S. Pietro di Castello. In terms of its composition, however, the Hasištejnský relief belongs to the tradition of German tomb sculpture, and there are similarly no signs of Jan's experiences in Venice in the rest of the decoration of the Kadaň Monastery and church.

The monastery at Bechyně was another important centre of the order of the Franciscan Observants. It was re-founded in 1490 under the patronage of Zdeslav of Šternberk, lord of Bechyně (Fig. 9). In 1492, the monastic church, dedicated to the Assumption of the Virgin, was consecrated by Jan Filipec, bishop of Oradea (originally part of Hungary, now in Romania), and the diplomat and chancellor of Matthias Corvinus (1443–90). This highly educated man, who relinquished all his church privileges at the end of his life and joined the Discalced Franciscans in Wrocław, visited Bechyně several times and was deeply fond of it. Alongside the noble families of Šternberk and Švamberk, Jan was one of the greatest benefactors of the monastery and he bequeathed many valuable jewels to its church.[17] As a result of the re-foundation, the 14th-century church and monastery were extensively renovated. The strikingly bright double-aisle church was vaulted with diamond vaults before 1500, and other parts of the monastery were later vaulted in the same way. The renovation of the entire structure was completed under Zdeslav's brother Ladislav. It is assumed that this work was executed by a group of builders from the Meissen/Saxony region who were responsible for the diffusion of diamond vaults throughout the region of southern Bohemia.

In the presbytery of Bechyně's church is the tomb relief of the benefactor of the monastery, Chancellor Ladislav of Šternberk (d. 1521, Fig. 10). Šternberk's presence at Bechyně is part of a trend whereby militant Catholic aristocracy in Bohemia chose Franciscan Observants' churches for their family mausoleums. The creation of ostentatious tomb monuments and the holding of pompous funeral ceremonies in the churches of this order were unsurprisingly criticised by the Utraquists. They accused the Observants of greed, pride, and betrayal of the original principles of the order.

The artistic contribution of sepulchral sculpture in Bohemia of the Jagiellonian period lies in the fact that this branch of sculpture helped to shape the portrait genre that gradually liberated itself from the medieval, normative type. One of the main sources of inspiration for the creation of individual portraits in Bohemian sculpture of the Late Gothic and Early Renaissance periods was Passau tomb sculpture. Works from the Danubian Basin, in particular from Passau, were sometimes imported ready made to Bohemia (such as the tombstone of Abbot Christoph Knoll (d. 1542) at the Cistercian church of Vyšší Brod, executed before 1521 by Jörg Gartner; and the tombstone of Půta Švihovský, discussed below). Sometimes marble imported from the Salzburg/Bavaria region was sculpted in Bohemia.[18]

The tomb of Ladislav of Šternberk belongs to a coherent group that consists of three figural tombs from churches of the Franciscan Observants: the tombstone of Půta Švihovský (d. 1504) from Horažďovice; Ladislav's tombstone; and the latter's weaker derivative, the tombstone of Kryštof of Švamberk (d. 1534), also from Bechyně (Kryštof gained the whole town Bechyně in 1530). Another abortive variation of Ladislav's tomb is that of Jan Kunáš of Machovice from the first third of the 16th century, in the Dominican church in České Budějovice. The composition and sculptural treatment of the Bechyně works were based on Půta's tombstone, which has all the hallmarks of Passau provenance, including the delicate combination of

FIG. 10. Bechyně, monastery of the Franciscan Observants: tombstone of Ladislav of Šternberk (d. 1521), detail
Jiří Roháček

FIG. 11. Horažďovice: tombstone of Půta Švihovský (d. 1504), detail
Jan Chlíbec

red and white marble (Fig. 11).[19] In this group of sculptures, Ladislav's tomb was innovative, in that the figure stands in a clearly delimited space, unlike earlier supine figures of the medieval tradition. The artistic concept belongs therefore to the world of the Renaissance. Another indication of the Renaissance is the fact that Ladislav's face was portrayed realistically. When one compares Ladislav's likeness in his manuscripts, where he was depicted as a benefactor, with his likeness on the tomb panel, it is clear that the tomb portrait is eminently realistic (including the depiction of his pupils, wrinkles, and veined hands).

At first, I was convinced that the sculpture was the work of an anonymous sculptor from the Danubian region working in Bohemia under the supervision of the art-loving chancellor;[20] because the face constitutes a true portrait, I also assumed that the tomb was made when Ladislav was still alive. I was wrong. I later found an archive document in the Státní oblastní archiv v Třeboni (Třeboň State Archive) that indicated that the sculptor was an anonymous stone mason, working in a large workshop near Kunžak in southern Bohemia, who signed a contract to make Ladislav's tombstone a year after his death, in 1522. The relief of Ladislav of Šternberk demonstrates that this workshop from southern Bohemia created tombstones that rivalled in quality those produced in the specialised ateliers of the Austro-German part of the Danube region. Today only a very small number of medieval and Renaissance works survives in the monastery's church; many were destroyed by the Protestant army in 1619, at the outset of the Thirty Years' War. The hatred of the protestant soldiers turned them against the tombs of the Catholic noblemen.[21]

NOTES

1. F. Moryson and J. Taylor, *Cesta do Čech* (Prague 1977), 30.

2. Utraquism is the Hussite doctrine that both the laity and the clergy should receive communion in the form of both bread and wine ('sub utraque specie').

3. Quoted in J. Truhlář, 'O životě a spisech známých i domnělých bosáka Jana Vodňanského', *Časopis muzea Království českého*, 58 (1884), 524–47, here 529.

4. M. Togner, 'Objev pozdně gotických nástěnných maleb v Olomouci', *Umění*, 32 (1984), 252; I. Hlobil, 'Bernardinské symboly Jména Ježíš v českých zemích šířené Janem Kapistránem', *Umění*, 44 (1996) 223–34, here 226–27.

5. *Acta Sanctorum Octobris* (Brussels 1861). Jan Christophorus de Varisio, 'Vita S. Joannis a Capistrano', 500–01: 'Sed quod non potuerunt ei facere, fecerunt ejus imagini. Ipsum namque suspensum per pedes, quandoque cum mulieribus, quandoque cum diabolis publice depinxerunt. Ultra haec cantilenas derisorias de ipso cantabant sacerdotes eorum, ipsum fore antichristum, seductorem et diabolum incarnatum, in ambonibus praedicabant.' ('But what they were unable to do to him they did to his image. For they painted him in public suspended by his feet, sometimes with women, sometimes with devils. Beyond this, their priests sang pejorative songs about him, and preached in the pulpits that he was the Antichrist, a seducer, and the devil incarnate.')

6. Peter Eschenloer, the town notary of Wrocław, wrote: 'Vil ander schendliche Gemäle lissen die Bürger zu Prage und in andern ketzerischen Stäten in iren Heusern dem Jirsik und Rokyczan zu Libe, malen, nämlich einen Baum, dorauf nakete schöne Frawen wuchsen und reif abfilen, und unter dem Baume stunde gemalet der Babst, Cardinäle, Bischofe, Prälaten, Münche, Pfaffen, und ufhilden ire grosse Mentel und Kappen, und fingen dorein die Frawen, die vom Baume filen. Vil andere Gemäle und Gesenge kamen auf zu diser Zeit zu Prage wider die Ere und Wirdikeit der h. Röm. Kirchen, dass auch die Behem, besondern Rokyczan und Jirsik, ob sie sonst gut weren gewest, dorumbe Ketzer, und vermaledeiete Leute billig sein sollen.' ('The citizens in Prague and in other heretical cities had many other shameful paintings painted in their houses, to the delight of Jirsik and Rokyczana, more specifically trees with beautiful naked women growing on them and falling off when ripe, with the pope, cardinals, bishops, prelates, monks and clerics standing under them, holding up their large cloaks and hoods and catching the women who fell from the trees in them. Many other pictures and songs surfaced at this time in Prague besmirching the honour and dignity of the holy Roman church, such that Bohemians, and in particular Jirsik and Rokyczana, even if they were otherwise good, should rightly be seen as heretics and cursed people as a result.') *P. Eschenloer's, Stadtschreibers zu Breslau, Geschichten der Stadt Breslau, oder Denkwürdigkeiten seiner Zeit vom Jahre 1440 bis 1479*, ed. J. G. Kunisch, 2 vols (Wrocław 1827–28), I, 259–60. Capistran's 'caricatures' in Kroměříž, painted by Utraquist priests, are mentioned by F. Valouch, *Životopis sv. Jana Kapistrána* (Brno 1858), 236.

7. '... Item cum non exhibuisti reverenciam sacramento corporis cristi In ecclesia currebas ad ymagines et corpus cristi non adorabas ...'; quoted in E. Jacob, *Johannes von Capistrano*, 2 vols (the second in three parts), (Wrocław 1903–11), II/iii, 126. In 1424, Bernardino said: 'Go to a high altar when you enter a church, and adore it, rather than stand before painted images. First give due reverence to the body of Christ, then show your devotion to the other figures which represent to you other devout saints'; quoted in S. Bernardino da Siena, *Le Prediche Volgari*, ed. C. Canarrozzi, 2 vols (Pistoia 1934), I, 212.

8. *Archivum Franciscanum Historicum*, XXIV (Quaracchi 1941), 48–51.

9. Quoted in P. Hlaváček, *Čeští františkáni na přelomu středověku a novověku* (Prague 2005), 98.

10. M. and O. Rada, *Kniha o sklípkových klenbách* (Prague 1998); Z. Opačić, *Diamond Vaults: Innovation and Geometry in Medieval Architecture* (London 2005).

11. On Kadaň Monastery, see, for example, Hlaváček, *Čeští františkáni* (as in n. 9), 113–17.

12. 'Ó, nešťastný jest ten den, / v němž jsem já bídný narozen. / I ta noc buď zlořečená, / v níž jest mne matka má počala. / [...] Kéž jsem v bříše matky zmizal, / než jsem světlo světa poznal. / Proč mne tam neumořila / a v bříše hrobu neudělala.', quoted from 'Rozmlouvání člověka se smrtí', in *Veršované skladby doby husitské*, ed. F. Svejkovský (Prague 1963), 83.

13. E. Kantorowicz, *The King's Two Bodies* (Princeton 1957). On the morphology of transi tombs, see K. Cohen, *Metamorphosis of a Death Symbol: The Transi Tomb in the Late Middle Ages and the Renaissance*, California Studies in the History of Art, XV (Berkeley/Los Angeles/London 1973), and S. Oosterwijk, 'Food for worms — food for thought. The appearance and interpretation of the "verminous" cadaver in Britain and Europe', *Church Monuments*, 20 (2005), 40–80, 133–40.

14. For a further discussion of this monument, see J. Chlíbec, 'Náhrobek Jana Hasištejnského z Lobkovic a místo pozdně gotické sepulkrální plastiky ve františkánských klášterních kostelech', *Umění*, 44 (1996), 235–44.

15. J. Chlíbec, 'A description of Guido Mazzoni's *Lamentation* in Venice by a Bohemian traveller in 1493', *The Burlington Magazine*, 146/1186 (2002), 19–21.

16. P. Hlaváček, *Kadaň mezi středověkem a novověkem* (Ústí nad Labem 2005), 126.

17. J. Labe Turnovský, *Historie o třích svatých obrazích, totiž Ukřižovaného Pána Ježíše a dvojnásobného Panny Marie, Matky bolestné, kteří v chrámu Páně bechyňském ctihodných páteřův františkánův k pobožnosti veřejně jsou vystaveny* (Prague 1746), 47–52, 54–55, 80. Filipec (d. 1509) was buried in the church of the Discalced Franciscans' monastery in Uherské Hradišti in southern Moravia, which he also founded. The effigy on his tomb (of *c.* 1510) shows him wearing bishop's vestments over a Franciscan habit and sandals, and thereby symbolically as a member of the Franciscan order. According to Turnovský (51), Jan's great supporter King Vladislav Jagiełło visited the tomb in 1511 to show his respects.

18. J. Chlíbec, 'Die Grabmäler der Passauer Werkstätten in Böhmen', *Das Münster*, 55 (2002), 319–28; J. Chlíbec, 'Poznámky k figurálnímu sepulkrálnímu sochařství jagellonské doby', *Epigraphica & Sepulcralia*, 1 (2005), 79–101.

19. J. Chlíbec, 'Náhrobek Půty Švihovského a jeho symbolika v kontextu pozdně gotické náhrobní plastiky', *Umění*, 31 (1983), 27–33.

20. Chlíbec, 'Die Grabmäler' (as in n. 18), 326. P. Kalina ('The Bechyně Crucifix and its place in the development of Central European art at the beginning of the 16th century', *Umění*, 44 (1996), 245–56) suggests that the sculptor of Ladislav's head was an anonymous master of Salzburg, and that Ladislav's body was completed by his assistants.

21. 'Monasterium fuit totaliter spoliatum ac devastatum, Ecclesia profanata, devastata, altaria diruta, imagines conculcatae, supellex sanè pretiosissima, tum ab Illustriss. Fundatoribus de Sternberg, tum à Dominis de Swamberg, aliísque liberalissimè donata, direpta ac distracta fuit: nec sepulchris parsum, ob tumbas Magnatum, quorum binae perhibentur fuisse argent[e]ae, aliae cupreae, aeneae, stanneae, ità ut Ecclesia versa sit in morticinium, nihil intactum, nihil, quòd rabiem exsaturare potuisset, quod malum, quantùm Deo displicuerit, multa miracula testantur.' ('The monastery was totally despoiled and devastated, the church was profaned and devastated, the altars ruined, the images trampled on, and the extremely precious furnishings — including those of our most illustrious founders the Šternberks, as well as of the Švamberk lords and of others, most generously donated — were torn apart and destroyed. Nor were the tombs spared, even the coffins of the magnates (of which two are said to have been made of silver, others of copper, bronze and tin), such that the church became a corpse with nothing left — nothing! — that might sate their anger; and many miracles bear witness to this evil, as far as it will have displeased God.'); quoted in Labe Turnovský, *Historie* (as in n. 17), 96.

Josef Mocker and Prague's Medieval Landscape (1872–1899)

TAŤÁNA PETRASOVÁ

The reconstructions that architect Josef Mocker (1835–99) carried out between 1872 and 1899 in Prague have greatly shaped our understanding of what the medieval city was like. Mocker became the most important representative of the Czech Gothic Revival thanks of his position as master builder of Prague Cathedral. Apart from his work at the cathedral, he dealt with about fifteen other Prague buildings, among them eleven secular buildings or rooms that were preserved for posterity by being reconstructed, or by being recorded before being demolished during the modernisation of Prague and the improvement of sanitary conditions in the city. The less well-known part of Mocker's work relates to five secular buildings in Prague and includes the Vladislav Hall in Prague Castle. In 1863–64, Mocker studied in Vienna with the Austrian architect Friedrich Schmidt, of whose principles he became aware while preparing (1866) and then leading the reconstruction of Karlstein Castle (from 1887).

THE regothicisation of Prague's medieval monuments in the last quarter of the 19th century was influenced by the architect Josef Mocker (1835–99) to such an extent that his work has overshadowed the earlier Gothic Revival of the 1850s and 1860s as well as other repairs undertaken in the city in his day. The principal reason for this is that his regothicisation became part of official thinking on monument conservation in the Austro-Hungarian empire, as formulated from 1856 in legal and professional terms by the Kaiserliche und Königliche Central-Commission für Erforschung und Erhaltung der Denkmäle (Imperial and Royal Central Commission for the Research and Conservation of Monuments). Aesthetic standards were determined by the course on medieval architecture at the Akademie der bildenden Künste (Academy of Fine Arts) in Vienna, which was established in 1859 with the arrival in Vienna of Friedrich Schmidt (1825–91). Mocker studied with Schmidt in 1863–64, and in 1866–69 he began his career with repairs to the south tower of St Stephen's Cathedral in Vienna. Part of Schmidt's educational method was to take his students on research trips to Lower Austria, Bohemia and the Spiš region (then part of Upper Hungary), the results of which were published as a set of architectural drawings with the title *Wiener Bauhütte*. During his time as a student with Schmidt, Mocker worked on his first Prague building, the Vladislav Hall (Vladislavský sál) in Prague Castle, which he surveyed and documented while on his scholarship trip to Bohemia in 1864.[1]

Another reason for Mocker's exalted status is that he was the master builder (*Dombaumeister*) of St Vitus's Cathedral in Prague, a post he held from February 1872 until his death in January 1899. He obtained this position on the recommendation of Count Franz Thun-Hohenstein (1804–70), in whose architectural office in

Děčín Mocker started working in 1869. This conservative Bohemian politician led the Ministry of Education's Department of Art from 1850, and together with his brother Leo Thun-Hohenstein, at that time the Minister of Education, he determined the direction of artistic development in the Habsburg monarchy. Franz Thun-Hohenstein is also connected with the first undertaking in Prague to protect a Gothic monument — a petition against the demolition of the south wing of the Old Town Hall (Staroměstská radnice) in 1841 — as well as with the establishment of the association that from 1861 organised the reconstruction and completion of Prague Cathedral.

Mocker's regothicisation projects in Prague originated mainly in directives from the city council, which funded repairs and initiated demolitions with the aims of reviving the construction industry, improving sanitary conditions, and beautifying the city. Further projects were commissions from the Jednota pro dostavění hlavního chrámu sv. Víta (Union for the Completion of the Metropolitan Cathedral of St Vitus), the chapters of Vyšehrad and St Vitus, and the government (zemské místodržitelství, the highest administrative authority of Bohemia). Following the victory of the Bohemian national party in municipal elections in 1861 and the exclusively Czech presence in the City Hall in the 1880s, a series of regothicisation projects were initiated that were underpinned by efforts to demonstrate the independence, viability and tradition of Bohemian culture.

The response to Mocker's reconstruction projects exponentially increased his standing in the Spolek architektů a inženýrů (Engineers' and Architects' Association) from 1872, with a concomitant increase in his presence in the association's journal and his participation in association exhibitions. As an ordinary member with extraordinary prestige, he sat from the beginning on a number of commissions that aimed to reconcile contemporary building developments with the needs of historical monuments (the expansion of the city in 1873, memorandum on towers in 1874, the regulation of inner Prague in 1889).

The following summary of Gothic buildings associated with Mocker's work in Prague is divided into three parts.

1) The Gothic Revival, including the restoration work on and new additions to Prague Cathedral, 1872–99; the church of St Peter 'Na Poříčí' and its bell tower, 1875–78; St Stephen's, 1874–79; the Powder Tower (Prašná brána), 1875–89; the bell tower of Sts Henry and Kunegunda (the so-called Henry Tower (Jindřišská věž)), 1879; the Malá Strana Bridge Tower (Malostranská mostecká věž), 1879–83; the oriel of the chapel at the Carolinum (Charles University), 1879–81; the Old New Synagogue (Staronová synagoga), 1884; the oriel of the Old Town Hall, 1880–88; the dean's church of Sts Peter and Paul at Vyšehrad, 1885–96; and St Apollinaris's, 1895–96).

2) The documentation of buildings slated for demolition, threatened sacred monuments, and archaeological findings. In the Old Town they included the following: the Church of the Holy Cross the Greater; house on plot no. 460/I with St Michael's chapel; St Ludmila's chapel in the Týn Church; and the Agnes Convent (Anežský klášter). In the New Town: the churches of St Lazarus and St Bartholomew. In Smíchov: the church of Sts Phillip and James.

3) The documentation of medieval houses. In the Old Town: the house on plot no. 144/I. In the New Town: the houses on plots nos. 22/II and 832/II, as well as the house in Hybernská Street (Hybernská ulice).

MOCKER AND THE GOTHIC REVIVAL

MOCKER'S most prestigious commission, which he won right at the outset of his career, was the restoration and completion of Prague Cathedral. He took up the post of master builder of the cathedral in 1872, at a time when reconstruction of the choir, led since 1861 by Josef Kranner (1801–71), had come to an end and preparations were under way for the technically challenging repairs to the south façade and portal, the transept, and the main tower, which had been damaged by fire in 1541.[2] Construction of the Gothic south façade had begun in accordance with a plan determined by the form of the Wenceslas Chapel (c. 1358; the chapel was consecrated in 1366). In 1370–71, the south portal was decorated with mosaic, and the south tower was built between 1392 and 1396 following the design of Peter Parler (d. 1399). The tracery and vaulting of the Hasenberg Chapel, chapter library, and archives are the work of Parler's sons, who adopted their father's architectural style in the choir and in the St Wenceslas Chapel. Above the string-course of the ground floor, the tower's design is the work of Johann Parler (in the early phase) and of his successor Petrlík (in the later stages).[3] Construction of the cathedral was suspended in 1419 with the outbreak of the Hussite Wars. New structures gradually encroached on the south tower's exterior in the 16th and 17th centuries: from the east the chapel of the Holy Trinity, erected in the south transept, and from the west side the complex of the provost's residence with the chapel of St Maurice. Equally complicated was the situation inside the tower. Four massive corner buttresses rise up above the foundations shoring up the Hasenberg Chapel on ground level. From a structural point of view the chapel was a daring if not precarious design: its north and east sides consisted of an open arcade leading into the nave (both walled up after the fire in 1541), the south wall was dominated (and weakened) by a large window, while the west wall incorporates a spiral staircase (leading to the level above the star vault of the Hasenberg Chapel) and a short gallery (leading to the archives situated above the chapter library), both wedged between the two western buttresses of the tower. The only stone vaulting in the tower was in the Hasenberg Chapel; its star vault had a circular aperture (oculus) in its centre that looked into the space above the chapel. Further levels of the tower were divided up by the wooden trusses of the bell tower, with the remains of wooden-beam structures between them (as was recorded in a Baroque plan of c. 1730). The intention for the tower was that the Renaissance extension with a gallery and the bell ringers' quarters, topped with a classicising roof, be replaced in the course of Mocker's reconstruction with a polygonal storey terminating in a spire with tracery.

Mocker based his approach to the structural repair of the large tower (Fig. 1) on the findings of one commission (consisting of local experts and architects) formed in 1879 to assess the tower's foundations, and another commission (consisting of Friedrich Schmidt and the architect and entrepreneur Josef Hlávka) formed in 1883 to assess the state of the north-east corner buttresses.[4] Reconstruction of the tower started in 1879 with the reinforcement of the foundations, and in 1880 Parler's large window in the south wall of the Hasenberg Chapel was walled up; a new, narrower window was installed in 1886 (Fig. 2), but the original jambs were preserved. The facing of the wall is a result of Mocker's repairs, but some details, such as the completion of the missing string-course, attest to earlier interventions. He introduced a new entrance on the ground floor of the south wall providing direct external access to the tower. The entrance had been opened up in 1881; the portal was constructed in 1886, and the door itself, by Kamil Hilbert, dates from 1906.

FIG. 1. Prague Cathedral: the great tower (1366–1418), restoration by Josef Mocker (1879–99)
Ústav dějin umění, Akademie věd České republiky, Prague (Josef Sudek)

In 1881, Mocker was commissioned to demolish and rebuild the west wall of the chapter library, which was re-erected after the fire in 1541. Also at this time, the provisional vaults above the chapter library and the chapter archive from the period after 1541 were removed. New vaulting over the two rooms was constructed by Hilbert after Mocker's death. In the years 1883–84, the south window illuminating both storeys of the chapter treasury (that is, the library and the archive) was removed, and a window was created on the west side at the same time. In 1886, the structurally weakest north-west corner buttresses of the tower were massively reinforced, and in the following year repairs began on the north-east corner buttresses. During repairs in 1888, Mocker made one of the most important discoveries in the history of the cathedral: he uncovered the west front of the Wenceslas Chapel, that is a portal with a relief of Christ's face (*Vera icon*) in its gable and three buttresses (two flanking the portal and another at the north-west corner), obscured by the presence of the Trinity Chapel. This discovery fundamentally changed the previous interpretation of the

FIG. 2.   Prague Cathedral: south window of the great tower (before 1395), restoration by Josef Mocker (1880)

Ústav dějin umění, Akademie věd České republiky, Prague (Jiří Hampl)

FIG. 3.   Prague, New Town: St Stephen's (1351–1401), restoration by Josef Mocker (1874–79)

Ústav dějin umění, Akademie věd České republiky, Prague (Tomáš Vojta)

history of the chapel, as published by the historians August W. Ambros, Václav V. Tomek or Bernard Grueber. For the Central-Commission in Vienna, the finding corroborated the hypotheses proposed in older literature that the Wenceslas Chapel had once been an independent structure, and that the account of its 1366 consecration in the chronicle of Beneš of Weitmile related only to the structure in the south portal. It was therefore requested of Mocker that the shape of the new buttresses indicate that the origins of the chapel predate the first phase of the construction of the Gothic structure under Matthias of Arras (1344–52). Mocker rejected this austere form for aesthetic reasons, and insisted on implementing a corner buttress with a canopy.

After Mocker's death, Kamil Hilbert continued the exterior alterations project as part of his reconstruction of the Wenceslas Chapel (1908–11). In 1896, the last remnant of Parler's design for the ground floor of the tower was removed: the spiral staircase of the Hasenberg Chapel was torn down, from whose rich decoration only the heraldic shields were preserved. At that time or during the previous masonry work on the west wall, the gallery providing access from the staircase to the chapter archives was also removed. According to contemporary records, casts were made from fourteen fragments of corbel masks that are unaccounted for today. The only known record of the original appearance of the staircase and gallery remains the details of corbels and heraldic shields published by Antonín Podlaha in 1906.[5] In the 1890s, the exterior of the tower's upper storeys was repaired. From this period date four tabernacles placed against the corner buttresses at gallery level (1894), as well as the reconstruction of the triforium, and a window with blind tracery (originally partially open) above it in the east wall of the tower (1897–98).

Mocker's interventions on the south portal began in 1889 with the dismantling of the mosaic — which for preservation purposes he proposed to place inside the cathedral — together with repairs to the vaulting of the porch and of the portal's three arches. In 1891, fifteen new canopies were installed, seven on either side of the portal and one centrally placed on a pillar. Of Mocker's intended regothicising restoration of sculptural decoration, only the preliminary sketches are preserved.

The common thread of Mocker's reconstructions of urban architecture was to be the restoration of towers. His first commission came in July 1874, when he was asked by the city council to submit a proposal for the detached bell tower of Sts Henry and Kunegunda's in the New Town. The bell tower had once belonged to the cemetery of the church. Its origins can be dated, in light of the clock chimes, to the year 1577. Reconstruction of the bell tower (1874–80) included the walling up the original staircase in the south-west corner of the tower, the repair of the decorative portal archivolt, and of the corbels in the corners of the gallery, and the changing of the roof beams that had been installed during the repairs in 1808. In this reconstruction the style of the work as executed does not relate to Mocker's dating of the tower, which the architect placed in the 1490s, based on analogies with two other monuments he helped to regothicise (the churches of St Peter 'Na Poříčí' and of St Stephen (in the New Town)), and through comparison of stonemasons' marks.[6]

The tower of St Stephen's was another New Town tower regothicised by Mocker on which reconstruction had begun previously (Fig. 3). A parish church administered by the Knights Hospitaller and built between 1351 and 1401, this Gothic basilica, consisting of a nave, side aisles, and a polygonal presbytery, has a west tower placed over the west bay of the nave. Mocker's renovations in 1874–79 included the addition of new tracery to all windows, and he also had a new window cut on the third storey of the tower. The main feature of the tower's reconstruction was a new pyramidal roof with corner turrets; the extensions of the Kornel Chapel (1686) and the Branberger Chapel (1736) remained preserved.

The reconstruction of roofs was the main intervention in most neo-Gothic renovations, and was associated with efforts to return buildings to their 'original' appearance, lost when roofs were replaced, mostly in the Baroque period. Mocker, together with the architects Josef Schulz (1840–1917), Josef Zítek (1832–1909), Achille Wolf (1834 or 1832–1891) and Augustin Víšek (1840–?), began to advocate that part of any reconstruction should be the documentation of the existing state, including damaged details. It is significant that the text, addressed by the five to the Prague city council in 1875, entered into general consciousness as a memorandum about the repair of Prague towers.[7] The text is sometimes mistakenly connected with Mocker's repair methods, but it refers in fact to ongoing or planned repairs to the tower of St Henry (1874, by an unknown builder), the Old Town Bridge Tower (Staroměstská mostecká věž) (1874–78, stone repairs under the supervision of the builder Jan Bělský and official city builders Franz Havel, Arnošt Jenšovský and A. Tatoun), and the Malá Strana Bridge Tower (around 1875, Mocker's plans date from 1879–83). Claims made by the five Bohemian architects about the exceptional qualities of Prague towers refer to Viollet-le-Duc's *Dictionnaire raisonné de l'architecture française*, in which the author cites the Old Town Bridge Tower as a most beautiful example of an urban tower with a defensive external gallery.[8]

In 1875, the city council asked Mocker to submit a proposal and a budget for the reconstruction of the church of St Peter 'Na Poříčí'. This is an important city church, whose origins in the middle of the 12th century were connected with the settlement of German merchants in Poříčí (now part of the New Town). It was purchased in 1233 by the widow of Přemysl Otakar I, Queen Constanca, so that she could donate it to the hospital of St Francis in 1235. As the property of the Knights Hospitaller the Romanesque two-tower basilica with a western gallery was extended *c.* 1382 into a double-aisled Gothic church, to which a new presbytery and a south aisle were added *c.* 1398. In 1598, a free-standing low bell tower was erected, marking the entrance into the cemetery. After a fire in 1653, the church acquired its Baroque appearance.

Mocker probably reconstructed the church in two stages. Firstly (in 1875–78), he focused on securing the walls and replacing the building's weathered socle; he rebuilt five pilasters on the north side and one on the south side, partly using old materials, and removed the Baroque portal, gable and cornice. Not only was the replacement of the roof intended to solve technical problems (in this case the draining of water between the nave and the south aisle), it also addressed the aesthetic requirements associated with renewing the silhouette of the Gothic roof. The reconstruction removed the Baroque plaster from the Gothic exterior walls and stylistically united the interior with neo-Gothic polychromy, which deliberately covered up fragments of wall-paintings found in the south aisle and near the organ loft. The contemporary view on polychromy is apparent in the differentiation by colour of structural elements, including arches, corbels, bosses and ashlars. This polychromy was removed in some of the subsequent reconstructions of the 20th century; similarly, the neo-Gothic furnishings designed for the church have not been preserved. By contrast, some of the Baroque furnishings remained, consisting even after reconstruction was

FIG. 4.   Prague, Old Town: sections of the Powder Tower (1475–80s),
restoration by Josef Mocker (1875–89)

Ústav dějin umění, Akademie věd České republiky, Prague (Zdeněk Matyásko)

completed in 1884 of eleven altars, a pulpit, and an organ.[9] The city council commissioned heraldry standing for Bohemia and Prague's New Town to be placed on the sides of the main portal; it evidently wished to have a visual reminder of the Czech impact on the history of Prague.[10]

Elements of the Late Gothic, from which the most interesting details are the corbels with angels in the south aisle, were left intact, despite the critical contemporary attitude towards this phase of Gothic architecture. This attitude is clearly demonstrated in the reconstruction of the Powder Tower in 1875–89 (Figs 4, 5). A tower with a gate, known as Horská, stood on this site no later than 1310. After 1383, during the reign of Wenceslas IV, it was connected with the neighbouring residence of the Bohemian kings (situated on the site of today's Municipal House (Obecní dům)). Building of the Late Gothic tower was led by Matthias Rejsek from 1475 to the mid-1480s, when work ceased after the relocation of the royal court to Prague Castle in 1485.[11] Mocker considered this grand structure, which served mainly for the collection of customs duties — defence of the city was provided by the New Town walls — as being parallel to the Old Town Bridge Tower.[12] The hierarchy of sculptural decoration began on the ground floor with a portrait bust of Master Matthias Rejsek, continued on the first storey with figures of monarchs (apparently Charles IV and Wenceslas IV on the façade facing the Old Town, and perhaps Vladislav II and George of Poděbrady on the New Town side of the tower), and

FIG. 5.   Josef Mocker, canopy of the Powder Tower (1880s)

Ústav dějin umění, Akademie věd České republiky, Prague (Zdeněk Matyásko) culminated with the figures of the nation's patron saints.[13] In his own words, the task given to Mocker by the city council was not simply to repair but to complete the Powder Tower, according to the 'accepted forms'. His regothicisation, however, was based on the forms of the Old Town Bridge Tower, and in its shape the blind tracery extending from corbels over the first and second storeys became a paraphrase of the arched 'trefoil' of Parler's tower. Mocker's unmistakeable stylistic signature is the gallery with corner turrets and a tall pyramidal roof. The interiors, with reconstructed star vaulting resting on figural corbels and newly built fireplaces, are rare examples of secular neo-Gothic designs in Mocker's work. This commission was a major opportunity for sculptors of the time, who created not only the sculptural details for the two chambers, but also the figures of kings with heraldic emblems, saints, Christ, the Virgin, angels, and the emblems of the royal cities in the time of Vladislav II (1471–1516) for both façades. In his *Katechismus der Denkmalpflege* Max Dvořák cited the Powder Tower as an example of the 'Zerstörung alter Denkmäler auf falscher Verschönerungssucht' ('destruction of ancient monuments in a false quest for beautification'). He viewed not only Mocker's reconstruction but also the massive building of the Municipal House as a serious encroachment into the historic fabric of the past.[14]

In its final phase, the reconstruction of the Powder Tower provoked strong objections among conservators on the Central-Commission. Hermann Bergmann, known for his repairs to the now destroyed east wing of the Old Town Hall (in 1847–48), lodged a protest against the plan to complete the Powder Tower in his 1884 report on Mocker's reconstructions in Bohemia,[15] and the Central-Commission advised Mocker that it disagreed with his plan. This, however, did not mean an official deviation from the view that a well-documented monument could be either completed or demolished during reconstruction.

In the same period, Mocker led the repair of the Old New Synagogue (Fig. 6). The oldest preserved building of Prague's Jewish Quarter (known as Josefov), from the late 1270s, it is an important example of Early Gothic in Bohemia, with a quality of detail that is comparable to that of the nearby Agnes Convent, which was constructed around the same time by the same team of royal builders. The building lies on the floodplain, and cracks were threatening its structural soundness. For this reason, Mocker tore down the east gable and rebuilt it in brick. In the interior he added the mouldings and part of the tracery of the Gothic rose windows that were set into the new gable. He repaired the vaulting and its corbels and bosses. During the removal of the wooden lectern by the old *aron kodesh* where the Torah scrolls were stored, Mocker discovered the remains of a lower part of polychromed stone *aron kodesh* and reconstructed it. Although he changed some details at the synagogue (adding the new roof beams and the new west gable of the south porch, for example), the building retained its Renaissance and Baroque extensions (west vestibule, women's gallery, Baroque portal).

The last commission Mocker received from the Prague city council was the repair of the oriel window of the Old Town Hall in 1883–87 and of the Astronomical Clock (Orloj) in 1890. Mocker continued the reconstruction, which had begun in 1881, and renovated mainly the interior, in co-operation with the painter František Sequens (1836–96, one of Mocker's longstanding collaborators) and the builder and stonemason Augustin Víšek. Mocker can be credited with the survey of the fabric completed before the repairs; this led to the restoration of inscriptions and crests of guilds and Prague burghers in the chapel's interior, which Sequens incorporated into the renovated polychromy. The main task for Mocker was to equip the regothicised

FIG. 6.   Prague, Old Town (Josefov): Old New Synagogue (1370s), restoration by Josef Mocker (1884)

Ústav dějin umění, Akademie věd České republiky, Prague (Daniela Vokounová)

interior with a neo-Gothic altar, stained-glass windows, and a set of liturgical objects (a lamp, candlesticks, and a crucifix).

Almost simultaneously, Mocker repaired, at the request of the Ministry of Culture and Education in Vienna, the oriel window of the nearby Carolinum (Fig. 7). The oriel of the chapel of Sts Cosmas and Damian was part of the university masters' residence, founded by royal mint master Jan Rotlev in 1383. Mocker removed the entire oriel right down to the window parapets and reinforced the foundations, though, because the level of the street had been raised, he did not reconstruct the base of the pillar that bears the weight of the oriel. He then reassembled the oriel, added canopies, tracery cusps functioning as supports, tracery on the windows, and a roof. Despite this, original details of the structure were kept in place, such as the damaged medieval consols. In the interior Mocker discovered remains of Gothic gilding and polychromy from the time of Charles IV and figurative murals from the 16th century.[16]

Mocker's last Prague reconstructions were completed in the 1890s, and they were commissioned by the chapters of Vyšehrad and Prague Cathedral. The former entrusted him with the reconstruction of the medieval church of Sts Peter and Paul at Vyšehrad, the project for which preparations had already begun in the 1870s and which was completed after Mocker's death by his pupil and colleague František Mikš (1852–1924). The latter commissioned him with the regothicisation of St Apollinaris's in Prague's New Town (1893–98), which additionally addressed structural problems that had surfaced by 1890. The rebuilding of Vyšehrad's Romanesque basilica (whose original form is still debated) was begun prior to 1330 under Queen Elizabeth Přemyslovna; after 1369 the church received a presbytery and a side chapel, which

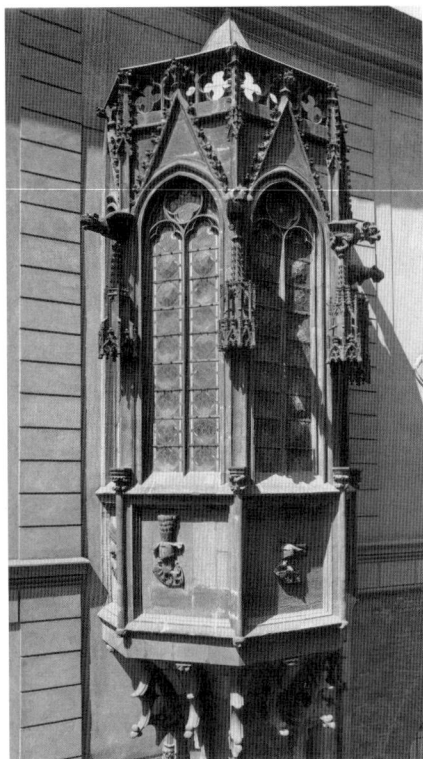

FIG. 7. Prague, Old Town: Carolinum, chapel oriel (after 1383), restoration by Josef Mocker (1879–81)

Ústav dějin umění, Akademie věd České republiky, Prague (Prokop Paul)

were linked with the building's transformation into a Gothic church.[17] Mocker's reconstruction began with a rebuilding of the presbytery for the chapter prior Václav Štulc in 1880; in 1885–87, in an amended version of the plans, the sacristy was enlarged, together with the treasury above it. From 1893, the south aisle was reconstructed, and from the following year the north aisle. In 1895, Mocker put forward a plan for the demolition of the Baroque façade. In 1900–03, František Mikš carried out the changes to the façade according to plans he had made himself. Mocker designed the main altar, the altars in the side chapel, and liturgical objects.[18]

The single-nave church of St Apollinaris, with a three-bay presbytery and a south-western tower, was built *c.* 1360, after the foundation of the New Town, and until 1420 it belonged to the chapter of Prague Cathedral. Its location on a promontory above the Nusle Valley probably contributed to its structural problems. In the course of his work, Mocker removed the Gothic pulpit, the original western gable, and fragments of the sedilia, which were destroyed in the course of inserting of a new portal in the presbytery, to which Mocker also added a new sacristy. He renewed window tracery throughout the entire church. During repairs, he discovered the original polychromy of the vaulting ribs and bosses as well as murals. This last recorded reconstruction by Mocker achieved little public acceptance, even in the time of its execution, and it is generally true that the reconstructions carried out in the 1890s in particular contributed to the subsequent strong condemnation of Mocker's entire body of work.

THE RECORDING OF RELIGIOUS BUILDINGS

IN his reconstructions Mocker always tried to maintain a certain independence from a building's historical status. He was governed by his understanding of what Gothic style was and also by the notion that regothicisation was a creative process with its own artistic values. In his writing on reconstruction, he frequently expressed his aim to endow the buildings he worked on with a richer articulation, but in his role as a conservator for the Central-Commission in Vienna, he accomplished the task of documenting deteriorating monuments well, by the standards of his time. Although there is no abundance of detail in a number of his published plans, Mocker's illustrations are used to this day as the only evidence for the state of the buildings he recorded prior to their restoration or demolition. It is often hard to determine beyond doubt whether a drawing was made in preparation before a modification of details took place, or was merely destined for a sample book, to be used elsewhere. For example, the heads of kings in the oriel window of the Old Town Hall were used as details on the west façade of St Vitus's Cathedral; models for gargoyles on the cathedral were re-used in the reconstruction of the cathedral of St Barbara in Kutná Hora; and Mocker wanted to use some of the reconstructed details of the Old Town Bridge Tower in further reconstructions. Unlike the texts of the earlier Gothic revivalist Bernard Grueber (1807–1882) or his contemporary Josef Schulz, Mocker's articles do not have ambitions to be historical studies or theoretical treatises. They are descriptions complemented by brief historical introductions, based mostly on Tomek's well-known *Dějepis* ('History'),[19] but they do not refrain from making analogies with his other projects.

When Mocker, having been one of a group of correspondents, came in 1882 to work among the monument conservationists of the Central-Commission for Prague (he was responsible for the centre of the city while Moric Lüssner was in charge of its suburbs), it meant not only that Mocker had to file regular reports on ongoing reconstructions, but also that he had to focus on and evaluate buildings destined for demolition. For the most part this meant medieval chapels and churches occupying city land earmarked for public buildings, and in one case monuments in the Josefov area. This slum area (roughly between the Clementinum, the Old Town Square and the Agnes Convent) had developed as a Jewish ghetto in the 15th century and was slated for clearance. The plan to 'sanitise' Josefov was branded in 1896 as a 'triumphant beast' that allowed Philistines and speculators to destroy hundreds of houses of the medieval town and replace them with unexceptional apartment buildings. Some ten years earlier, the project had not yet been branded as cultural barbarism, and Mocker contributed comments to the Central-Commission debate as to whether new streets should run through the old Jewish cemetery. His argument, that a new street could pass through the cemetery because it is not the oldest site of its kind in Prague and dates only from the 15th century, does not sound very professional from the modern point of view regarding the protection of monuments. Mocker, however, pragmatically conceded that the votes against this unnecessary infringement upon the integrity of the cemetery should prevail.

Also connected with the plight of the Jewish quarter, which in the 1880s suffered from a high density of buildings, flooding, and substandard sanitary conditions, was the demolition of the church of the Holy Cross the Greater, situated on the border of the area designated for slum clearance. The church was pulled down before the start of mass demolition in 1896–97, having stood on land for which the city council had initially issued a permit allowing it to be parcelled up; this effectively meant that the council agreed to the church's demolition.[20] The council then asked the architect for his expert opinion, and on that basis in 1889 it purchased the church, which had not served its original purpose since 1782. The project for a school intended to be built on the site of the church, however, was not approved until 1892, and the new building was granted final approval the following year.

The church of the Holy Cross the Greater with a Cyriac monastery (today Dušní Street (Dušní ulice), plot no. 886/I in the Old Town) was founded by King Přemysl Otakar II in 1256 to commemorate the victory over Prussia, and it later passed into the administration of the Cyriacs. The order twice abandoned the monastery, and when they returned in 1628 they rebuilt both the church and the monastery. The church had a nave and side aisles, each three bays long, and a presbytery of the same length. Mocker noted that the buttresses of the presbytery as well as the vaulting with Gothic bosses were in good condition. The side aisles were divided into several storeys for residential purposes (after 1782). The entrance into this residence was in the nave. Adjoining the south side aisle was an extension, which Mocker believed to be the former cloister of the monastery; on the east side it led to a bell tower whose upper storeys dated from the 17th century. According to Mocker's assessment, it was of historical and architectural value.

In 1884, Mocker addressed a similar problem in the case of St Bartholomew's, built on the site of the city poorhouse (today Vyšehradská Street (Vyšehradská ulice) and Na Slupi Street (Ulice Na Slupi), plot no. 427/II in the New Town). The city authorities wanted to build a school for the poor on the site and decided to demolish the medieval church founded together with a convent, according to the early-14th-century Zbraslav chronicle, by Queen Elizabeth Přemyslovna. The queen's grandson, Wenceslas IV, had patronal rights over the whole foundation. According to Mocker's plans, the structure showed traces of several phases of construction: a polygonal presbytery of two bays vaulted with an eight-part vault adjoins at an angle a nave of equal length. The north aisle was built at the same time as the nave, while the south, somewhat higher aisle of three bays was the last to be built. Mocker stated only one single firm date from the building's history — the year 1505, when he supposed that the nave and north aisle were added to the presbytery.

A third church about which Mocker filed a report, in connection with the planned demolition of neighbouring houses, was the church of St Lazarus, now where Lazarská Street (Lazarská ulice), and Spálená Street (Spálená ulice) and Charles Square (Karlovo náměstí) meet, plot no. 6/II in the New Town. The demolition did not take place until 1900. Mocker knew the structure as part of a hospital, whose cemetery served as a burial ground for victims of the plague of 1282, and which later served as the chapel of the New Town butchers. The church consisted of a one-bay-long nave with a quadripartite vault and a presbytery also of one bay. The tympanum of the portal depicting the Baptism of Lazarus was at that time already in the collection of the Národní muzeum (National Museum) in Prague. Three corbels remained *in situ*, and Mocker sketched them, together with the mouldings of the vault ribs and a boss.

As for medieval chapels in the Old Town, Mocker also published drawings of St Michael's chapel at the house on plot no. 460/I, which was deconsecrated in the 1780s. It was later used for residential and other purposes, and since it occupied the interior of a courtyard, it was destined for demolition in the Prague slum-clearance programme. Although Mocker's structural documentation was schematic, thanks to his co-operation with the painter František Sequens it was augmented by the transfer of an early-15th-century mural to the Muzeum hlavního města Prahy (Prague Municipal Museum).[21]

In 1889, Mocker made a report regarding the demolition of the small Romanesque church of Sts Phillip and James on Újezd (now Prague-Smíchov). Mocker's plans of the church are not preserved, so we only know from the description that it had an apse and that its exterior walls were articulated with lesenes. In the interior, the report mentions columns and bases, window jambs, and fragments of Gothic vault ribs. The church interior was decorated with murals, from whose Romanesque phase figures of two bishops have survived; from the same or a later period are the figure of St Christopher and an inscription '*Torum anime*'.

In 1889, the city council began making preparations for repairs to the Týn Church, intending to replace the roof from the 1820s, to supplement the missing window tracery, and to replace the Baroque vault in the nave. At the beginning of archaeological excavations on the south side, Mocker discovered a crypt of the so-called chapel of St Ludmila behind the presbytery of the Týn Church, which he dated, in accordance with the opinion of the Central-Commission, to the beginning of the 14th century. According to the preserved ground-plan, the so-called chapel of St Ludmila was a part of an old church that consisted of a nave of two bays, an equally long presbytery with a crypt, and a two-tower façade. On the basis of a preserved set of eight capitals, modern scholarship dates the building to the period of the so-called Přemyslid Gothic of the second half of the 13th century, but there are no suggestions as to the appearance of the structure or who the patron may have been.[22]

THE RECORDING OF SECULAR BUILDINGS

AN unusual group of buildings associated with Mocker's conservation work is represented by burgher houses, which impressed him with their vaulting. Unlike similar buildings in the southern Bohemian town of Třeboň, Mocker probably did not publish the drawings himself.[23] The first such building he documented, on a visit to Bohemia in 1866, was a house with a star vault from around 1500 in Prague's Old Town (plot no. 144/I, at 1, Lesser Square (Malé náměstí)); it cannot be ruled out that Mocker wanted to use the type of vault seen there in a design for the neo-Gothic reconstruction of the house on plot no. 22/II (at no. 9, Jungmannova). The house, originally medieval, underwent alterations in the Renaissance and early Baroque periods, and was reconstructed in 1862–63 and again in 1866, probably following Mocker's design. Plans of a Renaissance house from the second half of the 16th century, on plot no. 832/II (at 19, Wenceslas Square (Václavské náměstí) and 1, Jindřišská, street (Jindřišská ulice)), were drawn by Mocker before 1895 to document its state before the house was demolished to make way for a new building by Friedrich Ohmann for the Assicurazioni generali insurance company.

In the same period that Mocker was making his first drawings of Prague burgher houses, he also focused his attention on Karlstein Castle, the most discussed among his reconstructions after St Vitus's Cathedral. During the Karlstein project, of course, his role was defined by the authority he had as the principal planner of the reconstruction proposed by Friedrich Schmidt. The Central-Commission had warned the Bohemian government about the deteriorating condition of the castle in 1858, to no avail. Only after publication of an article by Franz Bock in 1863 did the Bohemian government draw up a cost estimate and ask three experts — Bernard Grueber, Wilhelm A. Ambros and Friedrich Schmidt — for a report.[24] In the report of 1864,

TAŤÁNA PETRASOVÁ

Schmidt expressed the opinion that — in addition to the need for a thorough survey to be conducted — the shape of the roof was of the greatest importance for this castle, whose exterior profile is silhouetted against the sky. In his written proposal of 1864, therefore, it seemed to him necessary to increase the height of individual parts of buildings with masonry, while reducing others to their original height.[25] Ambros proposed a thorough reconstruction in the manner of Wartburg Castle in Germany. Schmidt secured funds for the project based on the survey by Mocker and J. W. Wächter, and extant murals were documented by the Austrian Nazarene School painter Franz Jobst (1840–90). The first project proposal by Schmidt was completed in 1870, but due to lack of funding work did not begin until 1887 and was based on a later variant (of 1882–83) of Friedrich Schmidt's proposal. Further alterations to the project were made based on the reconstruction drawn by the project leader Jan Střelba, for whom Mocker acted as liaison with Schmidt.[26]

The castle, founded in 1348 by Emperor Charles IV, stands on four stone terraces, the lowest of which, hewn at the end of the 15th century, formed the foundation for the settlement below the castle. Through the second gate one enters into the burgrave's courtyard, which is defended by a dry moat. The third gate leads to a courtyard with the imperial palace, which was designated for courtiers, the emperor, his wife, and her ladies-in-waiting. All three storeys were connected on the east side by a tower, sometimes called the St Nicholas Tower (Mikulášská věž). From its second storey, designated for the emperor, a wooden bridge led to the first storey of the Lesser Tower with the chapels of Our Lady and St Catherine (originally dedicated to the Passion of Christ), the latter serving as the emperor's private oratory. Through the sacristy behind the chapel of Our Lady one entered a wooden corridor leading to the Great Tower. Despite the different functions of each storey, the tower provided its occupant with complete privacy, because the storeys were connected by a separate staircase decorated with murals from the legends of Sts Wenceslas and Ludmila. The castle underwent adaptations in the 15th century (gradual expansion of the burgrave's palace, removal of the timber partition walls from the top storey and of a gallery in the imperial palace, removal of a wall in the chapel of Our Lady), which, together with subsequent alterations of the castle gates, were radically changed by Schmidt's reconstruction.

Schmidt's project underwent the most radical changes on the basis of 1887 findings relating to repairs to the loft of the Lesser Tower, when Střelba determined that the stone masonry did not originally continue above the cornice (now removed) under the parapet. After this, Schmidt completed the Lesser Tower's roof with an enclosed wooden gallery passage with trap doors in the floor. Without any support from the findings, Schmidt modified the roof of the Great Tower. His renovation of the timber partitions and of a series of oriel windows in the imperial palace was, however, based on discoveries made in 1888. Mocker submitted two reports on the progress of work before Schmidt's death.

From these reports, it is clear that in the period 1887–91 the following repairs took place at the castle: in the imperial palace (with the chapels of St Nicholas and St Wenceslas in the St Nicholas Tower) and in the canons' house, the roof and the third storey were removed; the west wall of the palace was demolished, as was the east wall of the St Nicholas Tower in part; new masonry work was done on five pillars on the ground floor of the palace; the outdoor staircase leading to the first storey was taken down; and the floor-plans were altered. A big transformation to the south exterior wall of the imperial palace occurred with the replacement and repair of the windows. In the chapel of Our Lady in the Lesser Tower, the partition wall between the chapel and the sacristy, torn down during the Renaissance period, was restored. Mocker reported on the dismantling of the altar (moved during Renaissance alterations) in connection with the discovery of the seal of Archbishop Arnošt of Pardubice, the so-called *sigillum secretum* of the chancellor, the seal of Bishop Jan of Středa, and the seals of Theodor Janovic, bishop of Olomouc.[27] A new indoor corridor connecting the chapel of Our Lady with the Great Tower was built, because the original portal leading from the Lesser to the Great Tower was discovered while the plaster was being removed. The most difficult repairs in the Great Tower (which houses the chapel of the Holy Cross) were to the staircase and the interior vaulting. Almost all of the window jambs were replaced. General modifications were made to the ground floor of the Great Tower, which was converted in the 16th century to a prison, and fireplaces on the first and second storeys were disassembled and rebuilt.[28]

According to plans prepared by Mocker in 1892–98 (after Schmidt had died), further building modifications were made to the west wall of the palace (arch and windows added in 1893), to the first and second castle gates (1894), and to the interior (1897–98, altars for a chapel in the imperial palace and the chapel of Our Lady in the Lesser Tower).

From the early 1890s, journalists began, even during official occasions such as the large National Jubilee Exhibition in Prague in 1891, to rail against Mocker's monopoly and the problems arising from it. Mocker was branded as 'almost the only one who determines the direction and nature of work on Gothic architecture in Bohemia today'.[29] Mocker was indeed in a privileged position to influence the direction of conservation, which meant, thanks to Schmidt's demand that surveys be made prior to (often devastating) reconstruction, that his thinking held sway for a long time as the modern and indisputable approach. Although Mocker's documentation is from a present-day perspective too general, it still has validity akin to old photographs — it records the building's former state, though is not legible in all its details. Mocker supplemented his documentation with records of inscriptions and extraordinary findings, and even sketches of murals, which he had copied.

Of greater value as documents are Mocker's building plans, which were created as part of his regothicisation projects. Only after Mocker's death did people begin to openly question the principle that a well-surveyed public monument can be utilised according to exigency. From 1904, debates about monument conservation spread to cultural periodicals and even newspapers, initially in the context of efforts to halt the completion of the great tower of Prague Cathedral. The sharpest attacks at that time against Mocker's purist approach, along with all its predecessors and successors, were, of course, published only under initials. Cited as cautionary examples were, first and foremost, the plan for the completion of the Gothic tower of Prague Cathedral, as well as the plans for Karlstein Castle, the Powder Tower and Vyšehrad, but also the reconstruction of monuments in Kutná Hora, Vysoké Mýto, Plzeň and Polička. Czech art historians blamed these failures on Vienna's autocratic Central-Commission and its maintenance of obsolete practices that had stood at the forefront of monument protection half a century earlier.

NOTES

1. *Wiener Bauhütte: Stipendium-Reise* (Vienna 1865), survey with longitudinal section and floor-plan of the Vladislav Hall undertaken in co-operation with August Prokop, Ferenz Schulcz and Franz Segenschmidt, fellow students from Schmidt's class.

2. 'Die fortschreitenden Restaurations-Arbeiten am St. Veit-Dome in Prag', *Mittheilungen der k. k. Central-Commission zur Erforschung und Erhaltung der Kunst- und Historischen Denkmale*, new series, 16 (1890), 204–05.

3. K. Benešovská, 'La haute tour de la cathédrale Saint-Guy dans ses rapports avec la façade sud', *Umění*, 49 (2001), 271–89. See also the article by Tim Juckes in this volume.

4. T. Petrasová, 'Die unvollendete puristische Instandsetzung des hohen Turms der St.-Veits-Katedrale zu Prag (1879–1911): Quelle der Erkenntnis und Ursprung von Irrtümern', *Umění*, 49 (2001), 305–20.

5. A. Podlaha and K. Hilbert, *Metropolitní chrám sv. Víta v Praze: Soupis památek historických a uměleckých* (Prague 1906), 74–93, 126–27, 129.

6. J. Mocker, 'Zvonice u chrámu sv. Jindřicha v Praze', *Zprávy Spolku architektů a inženýrů*, 15 (1880), 37–39.

7. On the restoration of Prague towers, see *Světozor*, 9/8 (19 February 1875), 95.

8. E. Viollet-le-Duc, *Dictionnaire raisonné de l'architecture française du XIe au XVIe siècle*, 10 vols (Paris 1858–68), V, 116–17, s.v. *échauguette*: 'La belle porte qui, à Prague en Bohême, defend l'entrée du vieux pont jeté sur la Moldau, du côté de la ville basse, est munie, sur les quatre angles, de charmantes échauguettes . . .'

9. F. J. Lehner, 'Kostel sv. Petra na Poříčí v Praze', *Method*, 10 (1884), 64–69, 80–89.

10. J. Mocker, 'Chrám sv. Petra na Poříčí v Praze', *Zprávy Spolku architektů a inženýrů*, 14 (1879), 29–30.

11. W. W. Tomek ('Zprávy dějepisné', in W. W. Tomek and J. Mocker, *Prašná věž v Praze. Das Pulverthurm. Le tour de poudre* (Prague 1889), 1–3) cites *Staří letopisowé česstj od roku 1378 do 1527, čili pokračowanj w kronikách Pribjka Pulkawy a Benesse z Hořowic, z rukopisů starých wydané* (Prague 1829, 249–50), from which he concludes that the tower was still being worked on in 1493. J. Petráň ('Stavovské království a jeho kultura v Čechách', *Pozdněgotické umění v Čechách (1471–1526)* (Prague 1985), 14–72, 67–68) calls attention to the fact that in the 1480s the city councils of the Old Town and New Town focused their attention on meeting the needs of the citizens, owing to a lack of funds: the construction of representative buildings was stopped, and city waterworks were built. J. Homolka ('Sochařství', ibid., 170–254, here 218) proposes a completion date of 1483, when a commotion broke out in the city caused by dissent between the municipality and the king. J. Vítovský ('Rejsek z Prostějova', in P. Vlček ed., *Encyklopedie architektů, stavitelů, zedniků a kameníků v Čechách* (Prague 2004), 543), thinks that the tower was completed in 1489, but only with a temporary roof.

12. J. Mocker, 'Popis Prašné věže', in Tomek and Mocker, *Prašná věž* (as in n. 11), 3–5.

13. Homolka, 'Sochařství' (as in n. 11), 217–18.

14. M. Dvořák, *Katechismus der Denkmalpflege* (Vienna 1918), 17–20, ills 66–67.

15. 'VIII. Bericht der k. k. Central-Commission für Erforschung und Erhaltung der Kunst- und historischen Denkmale über ihre Thätigkeit im Jahre 1882', *Mittheilungen der k. k. Central-Commission zur Erforschung und Unterhaltung der Kunst- und Historischen Denkmale*, new series, 9 (1883), i–xxii, here xix.

16. J. Mocker, 'Arkýř kaple universitní Karlo-Ferdinandské v Praze', *Zprávy Spolku architektů a inženýrů*, 16 (1881), 85.

17. H. Soukupová, 'K problematice Vyšehradu', *Průzkumy památek*, 12/2 (2005), 3–54.

18. 'Kollegiáltní chrám Vyšehradský', *Zlatá Praha*, 13/42 (28 August 1896), 500, 501, 504.

19. W. W. Tomek, *Dějepis města Prahy*, 12 vols (Prague 1855–1901).

20. On the demolition of the church of the Holy Cross the Greater, see *Mittheilungen der k. k. Central-Commission zur Erforschung und Unterhaltung der Kunst- und Historischen Denkmale*, new series, 15 (1889), 127–28: 'Das Mauerwerk der Kirche und des Thurmes ist in gutem Zustande und zeigt keinerlei Risse oder Sprünge, auch die Gewölbe sind gut gehalten. Der Kirche kann weder historischer noch künstlerischer Werth abgesprochen werden.' ('The stonework of the church and the tower are in good condition and shows no evidence of cracks or splits; the vaults are also well preserved. The church's historical and artistic worth cannot be disputed.'). See also D. Líbal, 'Architektura', in E. Poche ed., *Praha středověká* (Prague 1983), 187.

21. B. M., 'Kaplička starožitná v domě čp. 460 v Starém městě pražském', *Památky archeologické*, 13 (1885–86), cols 43–44.

22. Homolka, 'Hlavice přípory z býv. kaple sv. Ludmily u kostela p. Marie před Týnem v Praze', in *Umění doby posledních Přemyslovců*, exhibition catalogue (Prague 1983), 107–08.

23. J. Mocker, 'Archäologische Bilder aus dem südlichen Böhmen', *Mittheilungen der k. k. Central-Commission zur Erforschung und Erhaltung der Kunst- und Historischen Denkmale*, new series, 13 (1868), xcv–xcviii. See also F. B. [sic], 'Gotická klenba z doby Karlovy na Malém rynečku čp. 144', *Zprávy spolku architektů a inženýrů*, 22/4 (1887–88), 1. Another, unidentified building mentioned as designed by Mocker stood in Hybernská Street (Hybernská ulice).

24. F. Bock, 'Schloss Karlstein in Böhmen', *Mittheilungen der k. k. Central-Commission zur Erforschung und Erhaltung der Kunst- und Historischen Denkmale*, new series, 7 (1862), 69–78, 90–99.

25. 'Ein solcher Entwurf kann die Notwendigkeit in sich schließen, einzelne Gebäudetheile im Mauerwerk zu heben, andere auf ihre ursprüngliche Höhe zurückzuführen, wie dieß bei Burgen stets der Fall ist.' ('Such a proposal can include the possibility of removing individual building elements of the stone structure

and raising others to their original height, as is often the case with castles.'); *Friedrich von Schmidt (1825–1891): Ein gotischer Rationalist*, exhibition catalogue (Vienna 1991), 218.

26. P. Jakub, 'Dějiny památkové péče v českých zemích v 19. století', *Sborník archivních prací*, 25 (1975), 143–290; D. Menclová, 'Několik nových poznatků z dějin restaurace hradu Karlštejna', *Umění*, 16 (1968), 88–90; eadem, *České hrady*, 2 vols (Prague 1972), II, 47–63; Z. Chudárek, 'Příspěvck k poznání stavebních dějin věží na hradě Karlštejně v době Karla IV', *Průzkumy památek*, 13 (2006), 106–38.

27. On seals found at Karlstein, see *Mittheilungen der k. k. Central-Commission zur Erforschung und Erhaltung der Kunst- und Historischen Denkmale*, new series, 16 (1890), 200–01; 'Die Restaurierungen am Karlstein im Jahre 1890 und 1891', ibid., 18 (1892), 174–77.

28. Z. Chudárek, 'Velká věž hradu Karlštejna', *Zprávy památkové péče*, 54 (1994), 67–72; K. Benešovská, 'Architektura ve službách panovníka. Základní architektonická koncepce Karlštejna a její inspirační zdroje', *Průzkumy památek*, 13 (2006), 96–105.

29. J. L., 'Umělecká výstava', *Zprávy spolku architektů a inženýrů*, 25 (1891, 'Časopis výstavní'), pts 28–29 (233–35) and 34 (296–99); J. Fajt, J. Royt and L. Gottfried, *Posvátné prostory hradu Karlštejna* (Prague 1998).

Previous Volumes in the Series

Copies of these may be obtained from Maney Publishing,
Joseph's Well, Hanover Walk, Leeds LS3 1AB, UK
www.maney.co.uk